# Object-Oriented Analysis and Design Using UML

# Object-Oriented Analysis and Design Using UML

**K. Venugopal Reddy**

Associate Professor & Head,
Dept of Computer Science and Engineering,
Tudi Ram Reddy Institute of Technology and Sciences, Bibinagar,
Hyderabad, Telangana.

**Sampath Korra**

Associate Professor
Dept of Computer Science and Engineering,
Siddhartha Institute of Technology & Sciences,
Hyderabad, Telangana.

**BSP** **BS Publications**

A unit of **BSP Books Pvt., Ltd.**

4-4-309/316, Giriraj Lane,

Sultan Bazar, Hyderabad - 500 095.

**Object-Oriented Analysis and Design Using UML**
by *K. Venugopal Reddy* and *Sampath Korra*

**Published by:**

**BSP** **BS Publications**
A unit of **BSP Books Pvt., Ltd.**
4-4-309/316, Giriraj Lane,
Sultan Bazar, Hyderabad - 500 095.
Phone : 040 - 23445688, 23445600
e-mail : info@bspbooks.net
website: www.bspbooks.net

*Printed at*
**Aditya Offset Process (I) Pvt. Ltd.**
Hyderabad.

**Price: Rs. 395.00**
**ISBN: 978-93-87593-18-3 (Paperback)**

# Contents

## CHAPTER 1: Introduction to UML

## CHAPTER 2: Basic Structural Modeling

## CHAPTER 3: Advanced Structural Modeling Advanced Classes

## CHAPTER 4: Advanced Relationships

## CHAPTER 5: Interfaces, Types and Roles

## CHAPTER 6: Packages

## CHAPTER 7: Instances

## CHAPTER 8: Object Diagrams

## CHAPTER 9: Basic Behavioral Modeling Interactions

## CHAPTER 10: Interaction Diagrams

## CHAPTER 11: Activity Diagrams

## CHAPTER 12: Events and Signals

## CHAPTER 13: State Machine

## CHAPTER 14: Processes and Threads

## CHAPTER 15: Time and Space

## CHAPTER 16: Statechart Diagrams

## CHAPTER 17: Architectural Modeling Components

## CHAPTER 18: Architectural Modeling Deployment

## CHAPTER 19: Architectural Modeling Component Diagrams

## CHAPTER 20: Architectural Modeling Deployment Diagrams

# Preface

As Object-Oriented technologies emerged for the purpose of implementing robust and reusable software, UML (Unified Modeling Language) as pictorial language for developing software intensive systems became important. This book is about know how Object-Oriented Analysis and Design by using UML. This book assumes the reader to be reasonably proficient in any object oriented programming language and should have some exposure to database and Object-Oriented Design.

This book can be used by the people who wants to understand UML and apply it for developing system models. This book is written to be part of Computer Science and Engineering curricular, named as "OOAD by UML", for graduate and post graduate courses. The study of this book is part of the Computer Science and Computer Engineering discipline. This book discusses Object Oriented System Analysis and Design by developing models using UML. UML is used to develop software blueprints using which software systems can be developed. This book is primarily focused on developing system models applying UML.

We, as authors of this book backed by rich experience of teaching this subject for CSE (Computer Science and Engineering) discipline. We are grateful to our colleagues and family members for their continuous support and encouragement in writing this book. Every chapter of this book is lucidly explained and is associated with certain Essay type and Objective type questions, for better knowhow and understanding.

This book is organized into 22 chapters out of which the last 2 chapters are dedicated to Case Studies. The chapters 21 and 22 depicts the task of system analysis and design for unified library system and ATM system. The rest of the book is organized as follows:-

Chapter 1 deals with the history of UML, principles and importance of modeling understanding UML building blocks.

Chapter 2 deals with Modeling System, Primitive types and Non-software things. This chapter explains how to model common and extensibility mechanisms. It also gives insight into modeling views, modeling simple collaborations and modeling database schema.

Chapter 3 deals with the concepts of classifiers and Advanced classes, Advanced attributes and Operations. This chapter also explains about template classes and modeling the semantics of a class.

Chapter 4 deals with modeling advanced relationships, qualification interfaces and association classes. It also describes how to model composition, constraints and realization.

Chapter 5 deals with modeling roles, static and dynamic types it also specifies how to model the seams.

Chapter 6 deals with applications of packages and importing and exporting. This chapter explains how to model groups in the architectural views.

Chapter 7 deals with concepts of states and operations. This chapter also mentions how to model concrete instances and prototypical instances.

Chapter 8 deals with the uses of Objected diagrams and modeling object structures. It also mentions how to carry on forward and reverse engineering.

Chapter 9 gives the familiarity of modeling flow of control and modeling use cases and collaborations. It also deals with modeling the context of a system and modeling the requirements of a system. It also deals with forward and reverse engineering.

Chapter 10 describes how to model interaction diagrams such as sequence diagrams (Time ordering of messages) and collaboration diagrams (structural organization of the objects).

Chapter 11 gives insight into action and activity states, transitions, branching, forking and joining, swim lanes and object flow and how to model work flow.

Chapter 12 deals with events and kinds of events and sending and receiving events. It also depicts how to model signals and exceptions.

Chapter 13 deals with states and transitions, advanced states and advanced transitions. This chapter helps in modeling advanced state diagrams with nested and history states.

Chapter 14 deals with active classes, extensibility mechanisms and communication and synchronization. It also induces the modeling of multiple flows of control and inter process communication.

Chapter 15 deals with the modeling of real time and distributed systems. It also describes how to model timing constraints.

Chapter 16 deals with implementing state charts and modeling reactive objects.

Chapter 17 deals with components, classes and interfaces and it also gives know how in modeling executable tables files documents and libraries. It also deals modeling an API.

Chapter 18 deals with notes and components, modeling processors and devices, distribution of components.

Chapter 19 deals with modeling of source code and executable release. It helps in modeling physical databases and adoptable systems.

Chapter 20 deals with in modeling of embedded systems, client/server systems and distributed systems.

*- Authors*

# CHAPTER 1

# Introduction to UML

UML is an acronym for Unified Modeling Language. As its name indicates, it is a graphical language, used to create visual models of software intensive systems. The UML is an industry standard for object oriented design notation, supported by the Object Management Group (OMG). The UML represents a collection of best engineering practices for modeling large and complex systems. The UML uses graphical notations to design software projects. It is a visual language with graphical symbols used for visualizing, specifying, constructing and documenting various artifacts of a software system.

**LEARNING OBJECTIVES**

*After studying the chapter the students familiarize themselves with the following concepts:*

♦ History of UML
♦ Principles and Importance of Modeling
♦ Understanding UML with its Rules and Building Blocks

## Visualizing

The UML is the language used by every stakeholder involved in the software intensive system, to better understand the conceptual models of the system. UML can build models of the complex systems which are difficult to comprehend mentally. The UML models the software systems for better communication among all parties involved for good team work resulting into successful software projects. UML helps the project teams to communicate, explore potential designs and validate architectural design of the software systems.

## Specifying

The UML builds models which are precise, simple, complete and unambiguous. The

UML addresses the tasks of design, analysis and implementation to develop and deploy software intensive systems. By using UML we can model application's structure, behavior, architecture and data.

## Constructing

The UML is used for forward and reverse engineering. UML models can be mapped to any object-oriented programming languages such as Java, C++ and Visual basic. We can carry forward engineering, where source code can be generated by using system models. UML can also be applied for reverse engineering, where system models are generated from the source code.

## Documenting

The UML can be used for documenting various features and characteristics of any software-intensive system. UML can document system's requirements, system's architecture, test cases, project plan and release specifications of any software development project.

## 1.1  History of UML

In the late 1980s and early 1990s, people used a variety of object-oriented design techniques and notations. Different software development companies were using different notations to analyze, design and document their object-oriented systems. These diverse notations used, lead to confusion and ambiguity.

UML was developed to standardize the large number of object-oriented modeling notations that existed and used extensively in the early 1990s. The major ones used were, Object Management Technology notations developed by Rumbaugh in 1991, Booch's methodology notations developed by Grady Booch in 1991, Object-Oriented Software Engineering notations developed by Jacobson in 1992, Odell's methodology notations developed by Odell in 1992, and Shaler and Mellor methodology notations developed by Shaler in 1992. The UML adopted many concepts from all these techniques and notations.  Later, UML was adopted by Object Management Group (OMG) as a de facto standard in 1997.

## 1.2  Importance of Modeling

### What is a Model ?

A model is a simplification of reality. A model can be considered as a blue print. A blueprint describes an idea, a feature and a process involved. A blueprint can be defined as a paper based technical drawing, an architecture of a system or an engineering design. More generally, the term blueprint refers any detailed plan.

A potter, who makes a pot, has a model of the pot he is making, in his mind. The model could be conceptual and visual image of the pot, describing its size, shape and appearance. A pot model is simple, so the potter can easily comprehend it in his mind. The same potter, can make different varieties of pots based on different visual models of them, he has in his mind.

The following diagrams specify making of different pots based on the model the potter has in his mind.

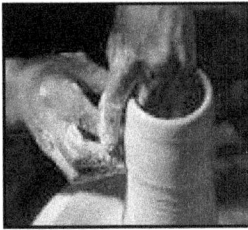

**Fig. 1.1(a)** Pot Model 1    **Fig. 1.1(b)** Pot Model 2    **Fig. 1.1(c)** Pot Model 3

Some of the models could be little complex to have them in mind. In such cases we have paper representation describing the model. The model can be a descriptive text or a collection of graphical figures. A tailor who is stitching a dress has the model of the dress in the form of specifications, requirements and measures given by the client.

The following diagrams indicate the model for stitching a suit.

**Fig. 1.2(a)** Taking the    **Fig. 1.2(b)** Construction    **Fig. 1.2(c)** Deployment
Model

The above models are quite easy to comprehend mentally. In cases of handling complex situations visual models can play a major role in understanding the system. Imagine how difficult it would be to understand the layout of a building without a set of visual plans or models.

**Fig. 1.3(a)** Model of a Construct        **Fig.1.3(b)** The actual Construct

A model is the simplified conceptual picture of the thing that is getting developed into a physical reality. A model is a complete description of the system specified textually or graphically, representing different aspects of it. Suppose, any aeronautical industry, developing a new fighter aircraft, the process starts with the design containing visual models representing different aspects of the new fighter aircraft. We cannot build a running prototype of the physical aircraft without having a model of it on a paper or on a computer, specifying all the features and details of it. The following gives the model of it representing different aspects and its physical reality when it is built.

Models representing Different aspects of Aircraft

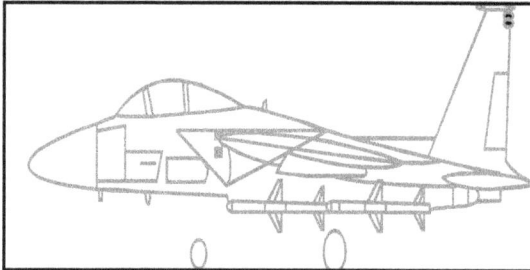

**Fig. 1.4(a)** Side View        The Physical reality

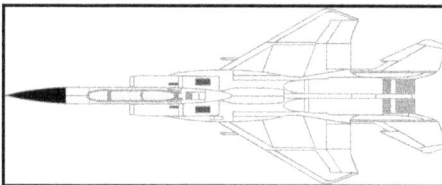

**Fig. 1.4(b)** Top View        **Fig. 1.4(c)** The Real Aircraft when developed

Hope you have understood what a model is. The same visual models are applicable even in the software engineering domain. Any software project must start with analysis and design using visual models of the system. Hence a model is the simplification of reality to start with. The following section answers why we need models.

## Why we need Models ?

Modeling plays a significant role in large projects belonging to the various engineering desciplines. Models are essential parts of any software engineering projects. A model plays a major roll in software development as blueprints and other plans such as site maps, elevation photos,and physical models play in the building of a skycraper construct. Modeling achieves the following objectives:

❖ Helps us to visualize a system as we want it to be.
❖ Permits us to specify the structure or behavior of a system.
❖ Gives us a template that guides us in constructing a system.
❖ Documents the decisions we have made.

We build models of complex systems because we cannot comprehend such a system in its entirety. We build models to better understand the system we are developing. Any software application is built without building models of it, is bound to fail. Software Modeling is an important aspect as it ensures software quality. Software source code and models are mutually related. We can generate source code from models, and models could be automatically created using source code. Models enhance communication among team members belonging to a project. Models ensure better planning, risk reduction, and reduced costs etc. There are many elements that contribute to a successful software organization; one common basis   is the use of modeling. Modeling is a proven and well-accepted engineering technique.

The model would provide a way to understand the business, a basis for the physical structure needed to support the business. The model also helps us to understand the project, and to comprehend the business in general. The model not only reflects the modeler's interpretation of the project scope and business needs, but it also provides a means to communicate with the client's business community. Another important aspect is that the model helps us understand our project within the context of the overall enterprise.

You can develop visual, system analysis models for any software systems using UML. UML helps in building a data model, using class and object diagrams. It helps in building visual models, depicting the system's functionality, using use case and activity diagrams. Visual models can be created, for specifying the entire system's behavior, using state chart diagram and interaction diagrams. UML will be discussed extensively in later chapters.

## 1.3 Principles of Modeling

A model is a descriptive, functional, or physical representation of a system. Modeling is a way of thinking and reasoning about systems. The goal of modeling is to come up with a representation that is easy to use in describing systems in a mathematically consistent manner.

*The four basic principles of modeling are as follows*:

- ❖ **Principle one:** The choice of what models to create has a profound influence on how a problem is attacked and how a solution is shaped.
- ❖ **Principle two:** Every model may be expressed at different levels of precision.
- ❖ **Principle three:** The best models are connected to reality.
- ❖ **Principle four:** No single model is sufficient. Every nontrivial system is best approached through a small set of nearly independent models.

## Principle One

The Choice of Model Is Important. In software, the models you choose greatly affect your world view. Each world view leads to a different kind of system, with different costs and benefits. If you build a system through the eyes of a database developer, you will likely end up with entity-relationship models that push behavior into stored procedures and triggers. If you build a system through the eyes of an object-oriented developer, you will end up with a system that has its architecture centered around many classes and patterns of interaction that direct how those classes work together.

## Principle Two

While you are building models, the levels of precision may differ based on what context you are in. While you are building a big apartments complex, sometimes the buyer is interested to see the front elevation, and yet other times he is interested in the internal architecture of an apartment. The best kinds of models are those that let you choose your degree of detail, depending on who is doing the viewing and why they need to view it. For example, when you are developing a GUI system, a quick executable model of the user interface without bothering about other details or quality constraints could be your intention. Other times, when you are dealing with cross-system interfaces of network bottlenecks, you need to model down to the bit level.

## Principle Three

Suppose, you have a mathematical model of the house that exists only in ideal environment, that is it cannot withstand, sun light and rains. Such model is the one which is away from the physical reality. When you have a model of the car, the model has to be connected to reality. The car when physically manufactured it should with stand all natural conditions such as it should run in sun light, rains and it should withstand snow fall etc. Even in case of software development, the models of it have to be build in a way, when software is ready, it should work in a realistic environment. It can happen, only when you develop models connected to reality. We know that, there can be several independent views of a system represented by different models. All these models are assembled into one semantic whole model of the system.

## Principle Four

Suppose you are constructing a shopping complex, there may not be single set of blueprints that reveal all its details. You have separate models for floor plans, elevations, electrical plans, and plumbing plans. Although these models are nearly independent, still they are interrelated. The model representing electrical plans can be studied in isolation, but you understand their mapping to the models of the floor plan and the plumbing plan. This is also applicable for object-oriented software systems. To understand the architecture of such a system, you need nearly independent but interrelated views such as use case view, a design view, a process view, an implementation view, and a deployment view. These views, together represent the system, which is under development. The following diagram indicates how all these views which are nearly independent but are interrelated.

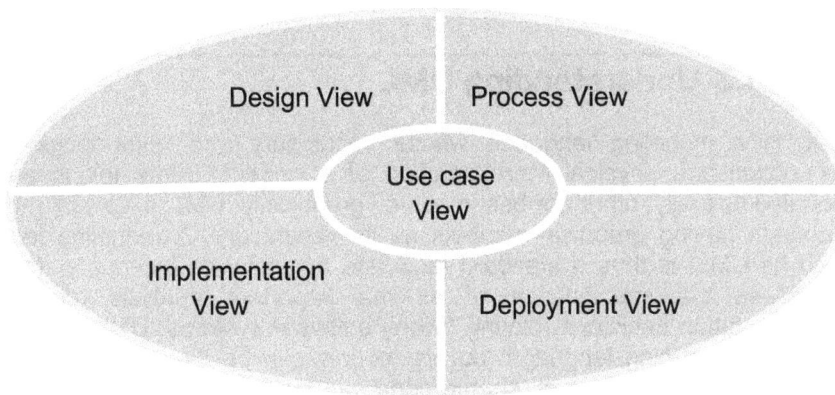

**Fig.1.5** Views of an Object Oriented system

## 1.4 Object-Oriented Modeling

Architects build many kinds of models. These models could be structural models that make people visualize and specify parts of systems and how they relate to one another. They may also build dynamic models to understand the behavior of the structure during cyclones and earthquakes.

In software, there are two most common ways to approach a model. You can build a model from an algorithmic approach and an object-oriented approach. In algorithmic approach, the basic building blocks of software are procedures or functions. A procedure or a function contains a set of instructions to accomplish a task or a purpose. In this approach, larger algorithms are decomposed into smaller ones and developed independently and later integrated. The systems built with this approach have problems in maintaining the software as requirements change or when the system grows.

In object-oriented approach, the major building blocks are objects or classes. A class is a category for a set of common objects. Every object has its own name to distinguish it from others. An object has state, in the form of attributes or data associated with it. It has behavior specified in the form of operations. The whole behavior of an object-oriented system can be expressed in the form of interactions among objects that constitute the system. The major advantage of an object-oriented approach is reusability. We can build a new system based on already available and fully tested objects by assembling them as we build a vehicle by assembling the various parts of it which are independently manufactured by independent vendors. New object-oriented systems can be built by assembling already existing components in the software market, such as Java beans or COM, DCOM.

Visualizing, specifying, constructing, and documenting systems which are built based on object-oriented approach is the primary purpose of UML.

## 1.5 Understanding UML

UML is a modeling language whose vocabulary and rules focus on the conceptual and physical representation of a system. Some things are best modeled textually; other are best modeled graphically. UML is a visual modeling language having graphical symbols as its vocabulary. A modeling language such as UML, is thus a standard language for software blueprints. The UML addresses the specification of all the important analysis, design and implementation decisions relating to any software systems. UML is not only a visual programming language, but its models can be directly connected to a variety of programs, in fact, source code can be generated directly from UML models. UML models can be used for analyzing the problem-domain which includes simplifying the reality, capturing requirements, visualizing the system in its entirety, and specifying the structure and/or behavior of the system. UML models can be applied for designing the solution which includes documenting the solution in terms of its structure and/or behavior. UML provides the notations for documenting some of the artifacts such as requirements, system design and test cases and test procedures.

The UML is largely process independent. However, to get the most benefit from the UML, you should consider a process that is:

❖ Use-case driven.
❖ Architecture-centric.
❖ Iterative and incremental.

The UML is not limited to only modeling softwares. You can also model non software systems such as:

❖ Work Flow in the legal system.
❖ The Patient Healthcare system.
❖ The Design of hardware.

## 1.6 Building Blocks of the UML

The vocabulary of UML include three kinds of building blocks:

❖ Things.
❖ Relationships.
❖ Diagrams.

*The Things are*:

❖ Structural Things.
   Classes, Interfaces, Collaborations, Use cases, Active classes, Components, Nodes.
❖ Behavioral Things.
   Interactions, State Machines.
❖ Grouping Things.
   Packages.
❖ Annotational Things.
   Notes

The Relationships are:

❖ Dependency.
❖ Association.
❖ Realization.
❖ Generalization.

**The Diagrams are:**

❖ Class Diagram.
❖ Object Diagram.
❖ Use case Diagram.
❖ Sequence Diagram.
❖ Collaboration Diagram.
❖ State chart Diagram.
❖ Activity Diagram.
❖ Component Diagram.
❖ Deployment Diagram.

## Structural Things

Structural things are nouns of the UML models. These are mostly static parts of the model, representing elements which are conceptual or physical. There are seven structural things supported by UML.

❖ Class
❖ Interface

❖ Collaboration
❖ Use case
❖ Active Class
❖ Component
❖ Node

## Class

A class is a category of set of objects that share common attributes, operations, relationships and semantics. Attributes are the named properties of a class depicting its state, whereas operations are the services offered by a class depicting its behavior. A class is graphically represented as a rectangle containing three components, indicating name, attributes and operations.

**Example:**

| Door |
| --- |
| height |
| width |
| movingDirection |
| open() |
| close() |
| lock() |
| unlock() |

Class Name

Properties/Attributes

Operations/Services

| Student |
| --- |
| rollNumber |
| name |
| branch |
| yearOfStudy |
| admitStudent() |
| removeStudent() |
| appearforExam() |

**Fig. 1.6 (a)** Class Definition (Door)    **Fig. 1.6(b)** Class Definition (Student)

## Interface

It is a collection of operations, which specify a service of a class or a component. Interface contains operations, but not their implementations. A TV Remote is an interface for the service of a class named TV Set. An interface is attached to the class or component that realizes an interface. An interface shares the same features as a class; in other words, it contains attributes and methods. The only difference is that the methods are only declared in the interface and will be implemented by the class implementing the interface. An interface is graphically represented as a circle with its name in UML.

**Example:**

TV Remote

| <<interface>> TVRemote |
| --- |
| tvOn() |
| tvOff() |
| changeChannel() |
| volumeControl() |

**Fig. 1.7(a)** Defining Interface    **Fig. 1.7(b)** Another way of defining Interface

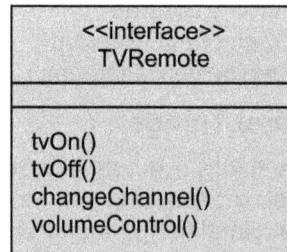

## Collaboration

It defines an interaction among different elements of UML to provide some cooperative behavior. Collaborations specify structure as well as behavior. These are implementations of patterns that make up the system. A collaboration is graphically represented as a dashed ellipse.

**Example:**

Fig 1.8(a)  Collaboration                Fig 1.8(b)  Collaboration

## Use case

It specifies the behavior of a system as a whole or a part of it in the form of set of functions. It is realized by a collaboration. A use case is graphically represented as a full ellipse.

**Example:**

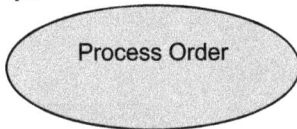

Fig 1.9(a)  Use case Definition          Fig 1.9(b)  Use case Definition

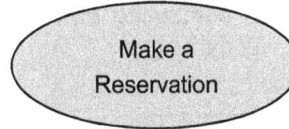

## Active Class

It is a class whose instance is an active object. An active object is an object that owns a process or thread. It can initiate control activity. An active class is graphically represented as an ordinary class but with thick boundary.

**Example:**

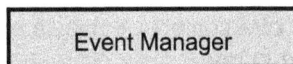

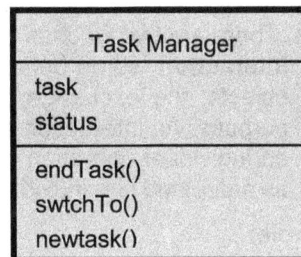

Fig. 1.10  Defining Active Class

## Component

It is a physical and replaceable part of the sytem. A component typically manifests itself as a piece of software. Graphically, a component is represented as a rectangle with tabs, usually including only its name.

**Example:**

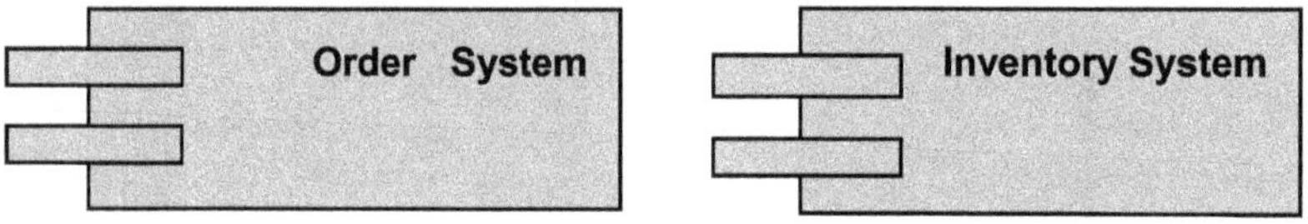

**Fig. 1.11**  Component Definition

## Node

It is a physical element that exists at run-time and represents a computational resource. It is typically, a hardware resource of the system. It has at least some memory and processing capability. A node can be a personal computer, a workstation, mini or main frame computer or an electronic device with some memory and computing power. A node is graphically represented as a cube containing its name.

**Example:**

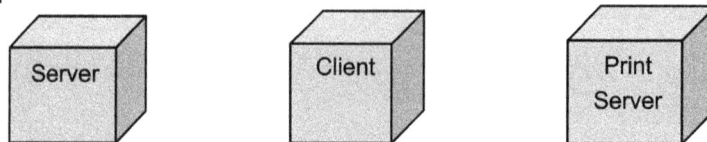

**Fig. 1.12**  Defining Nodes

## Behavioral Things

These are the the verbs of UML models; usually the dynamic parts of the system in question. They represent the behavior of the system over time and space. There are two kinds of behavioral things:

❖ **Interaction:** some behavior constituted by messages exchanged among objects; the exchange of messages is with a view to achieving some purpose. An interaction specifies the behavior of a society of objects or of an individual operation of a class. A message is graphically represented as a directed line including the name of its operation.

**Example:**

issue Book

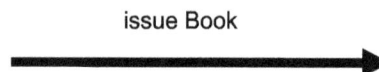

❖ **State Machine:** A behavior that specifies the sequence of "states" an object goes through, during its lifetime. A "state" is a condition or situation during the lifetime of an object during which it exhibits certain characteristics and/or performs some function. A state machine can be used to indicate the behavior of a class or a collaboration of classes. A state machine involves state (the current status), transition (flow from one state to the other state), event (that causes transition), and activities (response to a transition). A state machine is graphically represented as a rounded rectangle indicating the name of its current status and its sub states, if any.

**Example:**

**Fig. 1.13** Defining State

## Grouping Things

These are the organizational parts of the UML models. They provide higher level of abstraction. These are the containers into which a model can be placed. There is only one kind of grouping thing, named package.

## Package

It is a general-purpose element that comprises UML elements - structural, behavioral or even grouping things. Packages are conceptual groupings of the system and need not necessarily be implemented as cohesive software modules. A package is graphically represented as a tabbed folder including its name.

**Example:**

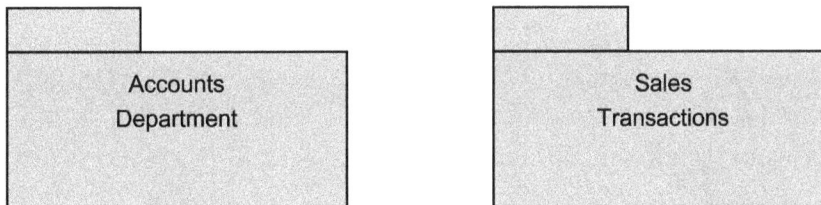

**Fig.1.14** Defining Packages

## Annotational Things

These are the explanatory part of the UML model; adds information/meaning to the model elements. There is only one kind of annotational thing, named Note.

**Note**

It is a graphical notation for attaching constraints and/or comments to elements of the model. Using notes you can attach explanatory comments to an element or a collection of elements. It is graphically represented as a rectangle with a dog-eared corner containing a textual or graphical comment.

**Example:**

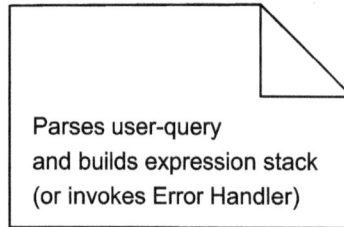

Parses user-query
and builds expression stack
(or invokes Error Handler)

**Fig.1.15** Defining Note

## Relationships

There are four relationships supported by UML models.

## Dependency

A dependency is a using relationship that states that a change in specification of one thing may affect another thing that uses it, but not necessarily the reverse. Usually a class may depend on another class or on interface. Typically, dependency relationships do not have names. As the following figure illustrates, a dependency is displayed in the diagram editor as a dashed line with an open arrow that points from the client to the supplier.

**Notation:**

(arrow-head points to the independent thing)

**Example:**

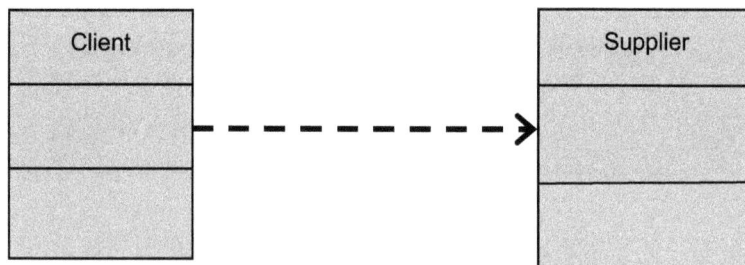

**Note:**  Client class depends on the Supplier class.

**Fig 1.16**  Defining Dependency

## Association

An association represents a structural relationship that connects two classifiers, such as classes or use cases, that describes the reasons for the relationship and the rules that govern the relationship. Like attributes, associations record the properties of classifiers. An association appears as a solid line between two classifiers, and association ends indicate the roles played by them including properties such as multiplicity and constraints.

**Notation** ─────────────────────────────

**Example:**

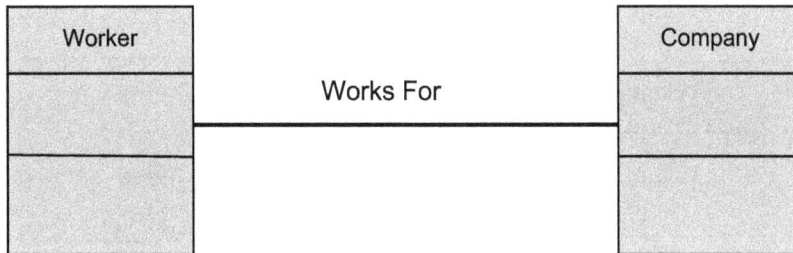

**Fig.1.17** Defining Association

**Note**: Worker works for a Company. Worker and Company play roles in association. More than one worker can work in a single Company indicating multiplicity at association ends.

## Generalization

It is a relationship in which one model element (the child) is based on another model element (the parent). The parent element is the generalized one and the child element is considered as the specialized one. This relationship is applicable to class, component, deployment, and use-case diagrams to indicate that the child receives all of the attributes, operations, and relationships that are defined in the parent. The model elements in a generalization relationship must be the same type. For example, a generalization relationship can be used between actors or between use cases; however, it cannot be used between an actor and a use case. The child model elements in generalizations inherit the attributes, operations, and relationships of the parent, you must only define for the child the attributes, operations, or relationships that are distinct from the parent. Graphically, a generalization relationship is displayed in the diagram editor as a solid line with a hollow arrowhead that points from the child model element to the parent model element.

**Notation**

**Example:**

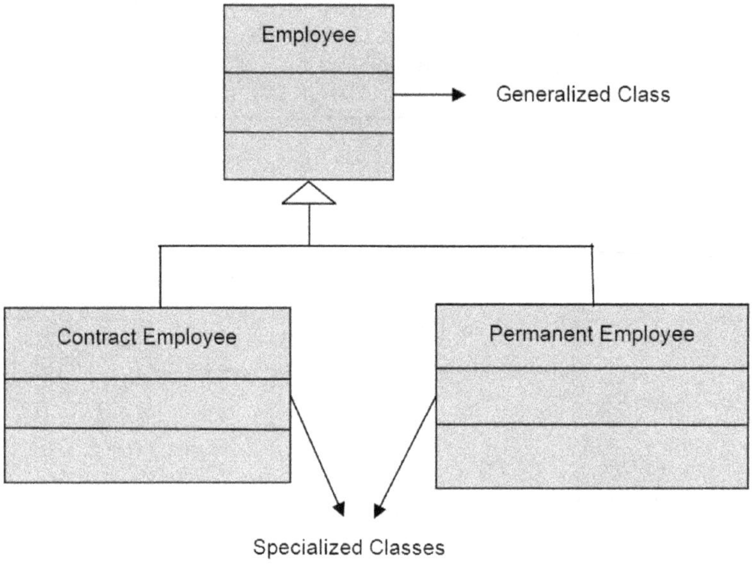

```
                    ┌─────────────────┐
                    │    Employee     │
                    ├─────────────────┤
                    │                 │ ─────────▶  Generalized Class
                    ├─────────────────┤
                    │                 │
                    └─────────────────┘
```

Fig 1.18  Defining Inheritance

## Realization

In UML modeling, a realization relationship is a relationship between two model elements, in which one model element, implements or executes the behavior that the other model element, specifies. This relationship is available between interfaces and the classes or the components that realize them and also between use cases and the collaborations that realize them. A realization is indicated by a dashed line with an unfilled arrowhead towards the supplier. Realizations can only be shown on class or component diagrams.

**Notation**

**Example:**

1. This relationship between a class and an interface indicates that the interface specifies the behavior to be carried out in the form of its operations, and the class implements that behavior.

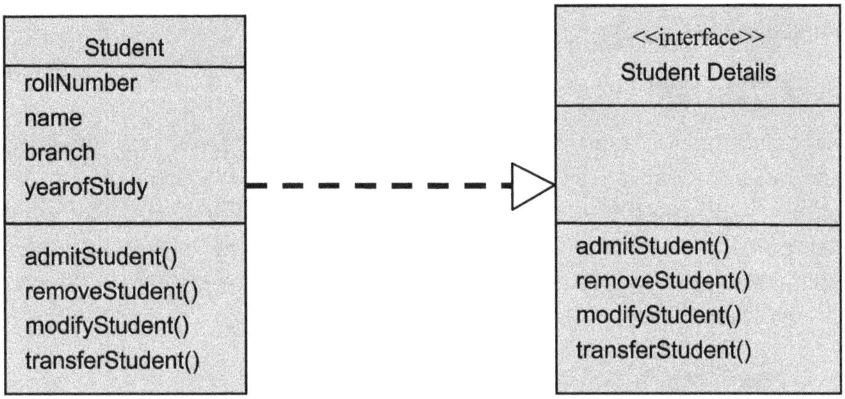

**Fig.1.19** Defining Realization

2. This relationship between a use case and the collaboration indicates that the use case specifies the behavior to be carried out and the collaboration implements it.

**Fig.1.20** Defining Realization among use cases

## Diagrams in the UML

A UML diagram is a graphical presentation of the UML model. It is represented as a connected graph containing vertices (things) connected by arcs (relationships). The UML diagrams help us to visualize a system from different perspectives. UML diagrams let developers and customers view a software system from different perspectives and in varying degrees of abstraction. UML includes nine diagrams - each capturing a different dimension of a software system architecture.

## Class Diagram

Class diagrams are widely used to describe the types of objects in a system and their relationships. It includes elements of a model, such as classes, interfaces and collaborations and how they are interrelated. Class diagrams indicate the structural or static part of the system. Class diagrams address static design view of the system. Class diagrams may also include design elements such as classes, packages and objects. Class diagrams describe three different perspectives when designing a system, conceptual, specification, and implementation. These perspectives become evident as the diagram is created and help improve the design.

## Object Diagram

Class diagrams are conceptual ones, but object diagrams are physical. An object diagram contains set of objects and how they are connected or linked together. It indicates the snapshot of an instance of a class diagram at a particular instance of time. Object diagrams address the real and prototypical perspectives of any software intensive system. Objects are nothing but instances of classes.

## Use Case Diagram

It is a graphical representation consisting of use cases and actors and how they are related. Use case diagrams address the dynamic part of the system. They are helpful in modeling the behavior of the system. A use case is a set of scenarios that describe an interaction between a user and a system. The two main components of a use case diagram are use cases and actors. An actor represents a user or another system that will interact with the system you are modeling. A use case is an external view of the system that represents some action the user might perform in order to accomplish a task.

## Interaction Diagrams

Interaction diagrams model the behavior of a use case by depicting the way a set of objects interact in order to complete a task. There are two kinds of interaction diagrams, namely sequence and collaboration diagrams. Both of these diagrams are isomorphic, i.e., they are semantically equivalent and one can be generated from the other without the loss of any information. Interaction diagrams address the dynamic view of the system.

**Sequence diagrams** demonstrate the behavior of objects in a use case by describing the objects and the messages they pass among themselves. Sequence diagrams emphasize the time ordering of messages. Sequence diagrams contain objects with their life lines coming from top to bottom. The interactions among objects is specified with the messages passed among them.

**Collaboration diagrams** demonstrate the structural organization of the objects that interact, it shows how objects are statically connected. If you have a sequence diagram, you can transform it into a collaboration diagram and vice versa. They show the relationship between objects and the order of messages passed between them. The objects are listed as icons and arrows indicate the messages being passed between them. The numbers next to the messages are called sequence numbers.  As the name suggests, they show the sequence of the messages as they are passed between the objects.

## State chart Diagram

It is a graphical representation consisting of sates, transitions, events and activities. A state machine displays the sequences of states that an object goes through during its life time in response to received external or internal events, together with its responses and actions. State diagrams are used to describe the behavior of a system.  State diagrams, describe all of the possible states of an object goes through as events occur. Each diagram usually represents objects of a single class and track the different states of its objects through the system.

## Activity Diagram

It is a special kind of state chart diagram where most of the states are action states and most of the transitions are triggered by completion of the actions in the source states. This diagram focuses on flows driven by internal processing. Activity diagrams describe the workflow behavior of a system. Activity diagrams can show activities that are conditional or parallel. Activity diagrams emphasize the flow of control among objects as activities are carried out by the system.

## Component Diagram

A component diagram shows how the various components that constitute a system are organized and physically related to each other. It displays the high level packaged structure of the code itself. Component diagrams show the software components of a system and how they are related to each other. Dependencies among components are shown, including source code components, binary code components, and executable components.  Some components exist at compile time, at link time, at run time as well as at more than one time. Component diagram addresses the static implementation view of the system.

## Deployment Diagram

A deployment diagram shows the configuration of nodes (processing elements) and the components that live on them. It gives the static deployment view of the system's architecture. This diagram displays the configuration of run-time processing elements and the software components, processes, and objects that live on them.  Software component instances represent run-time manifestations of code units.

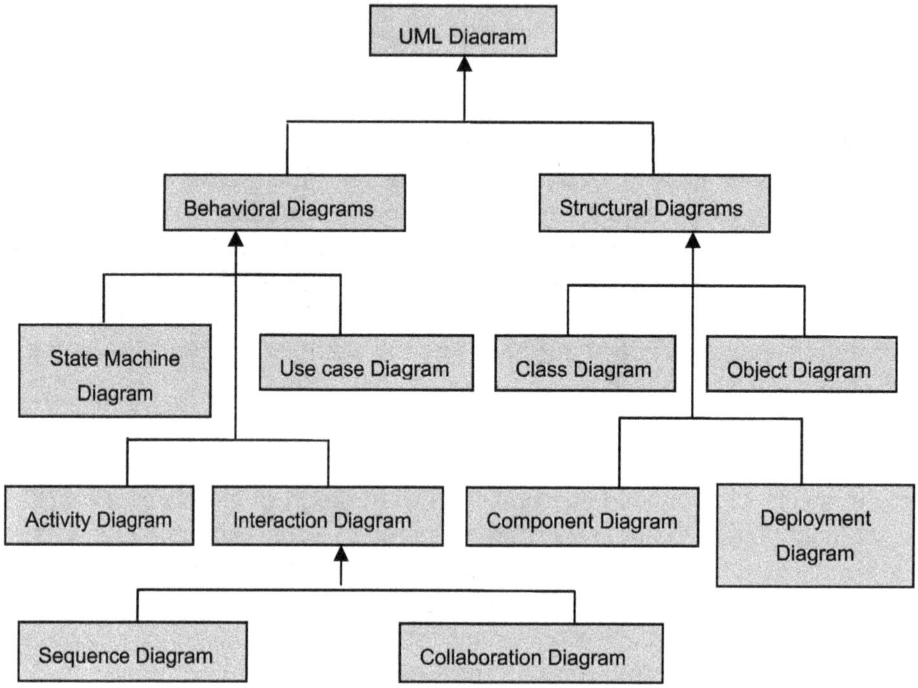

**Fig.1.21** Classification of UML Diagrams

## 1.7 Rules of the UML

UML being a visual modeling language, has number of rules indicating how UML's building blocks can be combined together to build various system models. These UML rules specify what a well-formed model should look like. Well-formed means that a model or model fragment adheres to all semantic and syntactic rules that apply to it.

**Example of a semantic rule**: If the class is concrete, there should be methods to realize all its operations.

**Example of a syntactic rule**: A class is drawn as a solid-outline rectangle with three compartments separated by horizontal lines. The first compartment contain the name of the class. The second and third compartments contain attributes and operations belonging to the class.UML has semantic rules for:
- ❖ Names
- ❖ Scope
- ❖ Visibility
- ❖ Integrity
- ❖ Execution

**Name:** The names you can call for things, relationships, and diagrams. There should be identifiable and distinguished names, to identify elements such as class, object, association, state, process, inheritance, and final state etc.

**Scope:** It is the context that gives specific meaning to the element named. For example, the scope could be instance scope meaning the named element appears in every instance of the class with different values. If the scope is classifier scope, the element will have only one value across the class, i.e., for all instances.

**Visibility:** This specify how an element can be seen and used by others. For example, the visibility could be public, meaning the element is accessible by everyone, private, meaning no outsider can access this element, protected, only the class and inherited classes can access.

**Integrity:** This identify how the things are properly defined and how they are related to each other. Here the relationships among the things has to be consistent. The data they contain should be relevant and accurate.

**Execution:** What it means if the model is built and run. What it will convey if the dynamic model of the system is executed or simulated.

However, during iterative, incremental development it is expected that models will be incomplete and inconsistent. Because, models build during the development of any software intensive system, tend to evolve as requirements are gathered and understood. These models are understood by different participants (stake holders) in different ways at different times.

## 1.8 Common Mechanisms in the UML

Building an apartment complex is made simpler if it confirms to certain patterns of common features. For example, the model of front room, the kitchen room pattern, and the bathroom pattern or its look and feel are some common patterns with their features are to be considered when building a flat. Similarly, building models of software systems becomes simpler in UML by using some common mechanisms that apply consistently throughout the UML, a visual modeling language.

There are four types of common mechanisms supported by UML. They are as follows:
- ❖ Specifications.
- ❖ Adornments.
- ❖ Common Divisions.
- ❖ Extensibility Mechanisms.

## Specifications

As we know that UML is a graphical language used to model software intensive systems. UML not only have the facility of creating the building blocks graphically, it also has provision for textual statements describing the syntax and semantics of those visual building blocks. UML graphical notation helps us in visualizing the system, whereas the specification state the system's details.

By using a specification, we are basically specifying something in detail so that the role and meaning of the thing being specified is more clear and concise. For example, we can give a class a detailed specification by defining a full set of attributes, operations, full signatures of operations, and behaviors. Then we will have a clear picture of the capabilities, responsibilities and limitations of that class. Specifications can be included in the class, or specified separately.

**Example:**

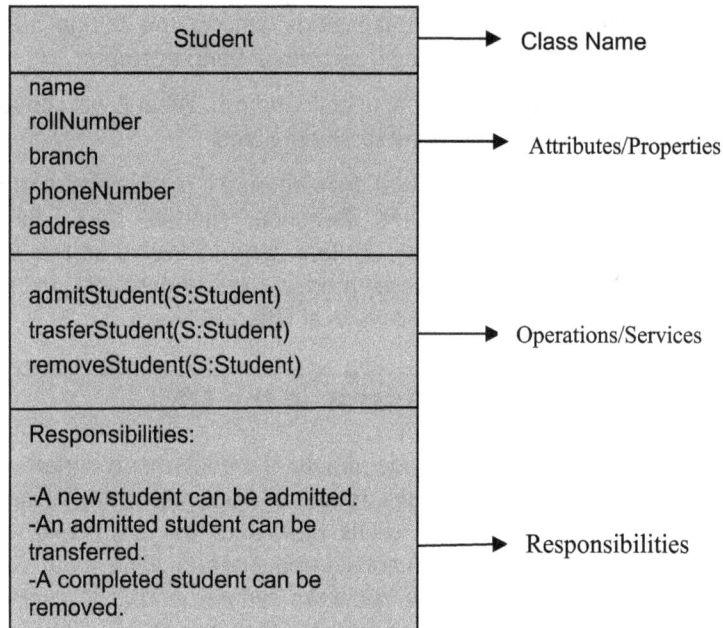

**Fig.1.22** Specifying a Class

## Adornments

Adornments are textual or graphical items, which can be added to the basic notation of a UML building block in order to visualize some details from its specification. For example, let us consider association, which in its most simple notation consists of one single line. Now, this can be adorned with some additional details, such as the role and the multiplicity of each end.

**Example:**

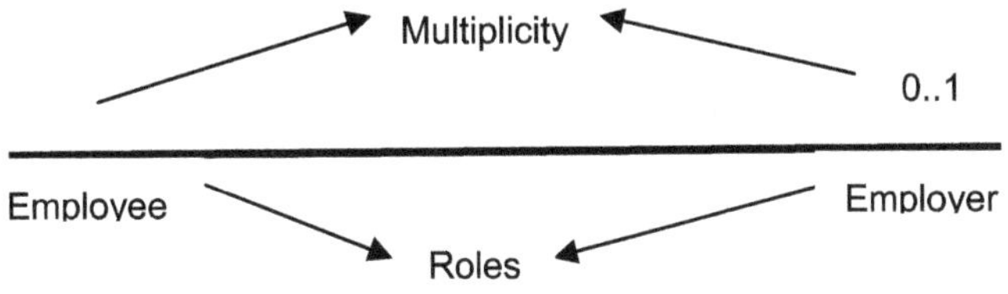

**Fig 1.23** Specifying Adornments

**Note:** In the above association, there are two roles, one Employee and another Employer. An Employer can have more than one Employee working for him. An Employee either can work for an Employer or cannot work.

A class's specification may include details other than general information, such as whether it is abstract (A class cannot have instances) or the visibility of its attributes and operations. These details can be specified as graphical or textual adornments. The following example specify a class adorned to indicate that it is an abstract class with two public, one protected, and one private attributes.

**Example:**

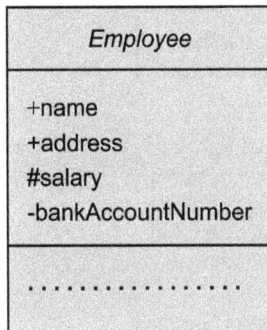

The attributes 'name' and 'address' are public, means known to everyone.

The attribute 'salary' is protected, means known to only him and his children.

The 'bankAccountNumber' attribute is private, means only known to him.

**Fig. 1.24** Specifying Adornments in a Class

The most important kind of adornments is a Note. A Note is a graphical symbol used for adding constraints or comments to an element/group of elements. By using Notes, we can attach additional information to a model such as observations, requirements, and explanations. The contents specified in Notes do not change the meaning of the model to which it is attached.

**Example:**

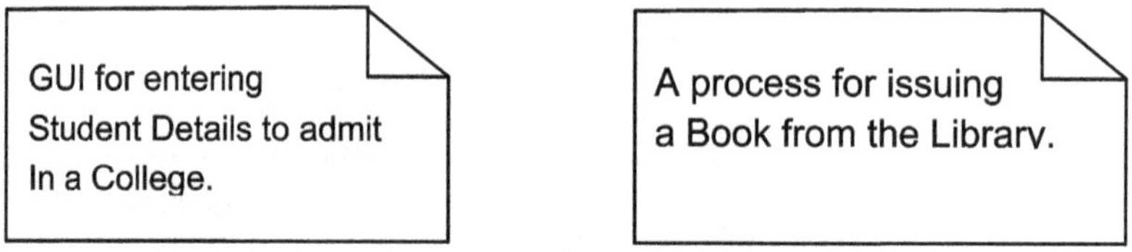

**Fig.1.25** Adornments in the form of Notes

## Common Divisions

These are used to distinguish between two things that might appear to be quite similar, or closely related to one another. There exist two main common divisions:

- ❖ Abstraction verses Manifestation.
- ❖ Interface verses Implementation.

In the former case, we mainly distinguish a class and an object. A class is an abstraction; and the object is the concrete manifestation of that class. Most UML building blocks have this kind of class/object distinction. For example, we have use cases and use case instances, components and component instances, and nodes and node instances.

**Example:**

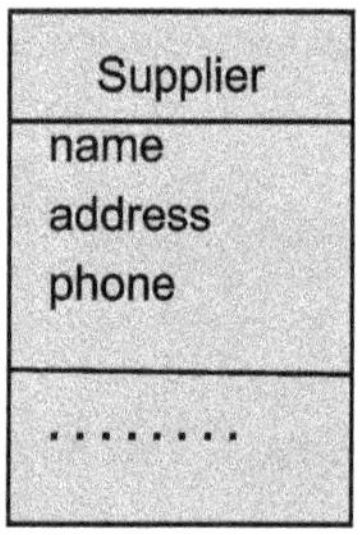

**Fig.1.26(a)** Supplier Class. 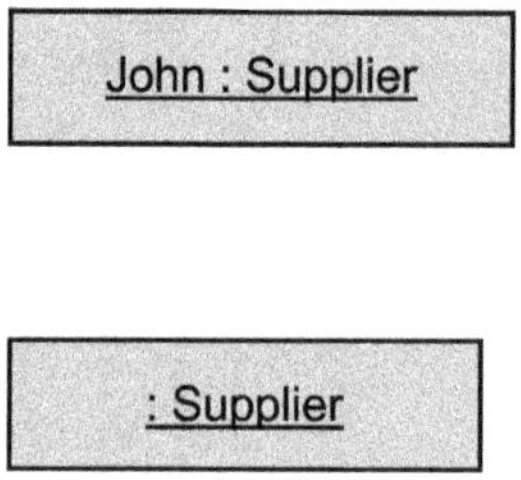    **Fig.1.26(b)** Objects of Supplier.

**Note:** The top most object represents a supplier named John. In our subject terminology, John is an instance of the class, named Supplier. The second object represents a Supplier without knowing him. Such an object is called anonymous object. We use it only when we refer just an instance of the class without bothering about the details of that instance.

In the later case, we distinguish Interface and Implementation and how they are related. In this case, we address that an Interface declares some kind of contract or agreement, where as an implementation is a concrete realization of that contract. The Implementation is responsible for carrying out the interface.

**Example:**

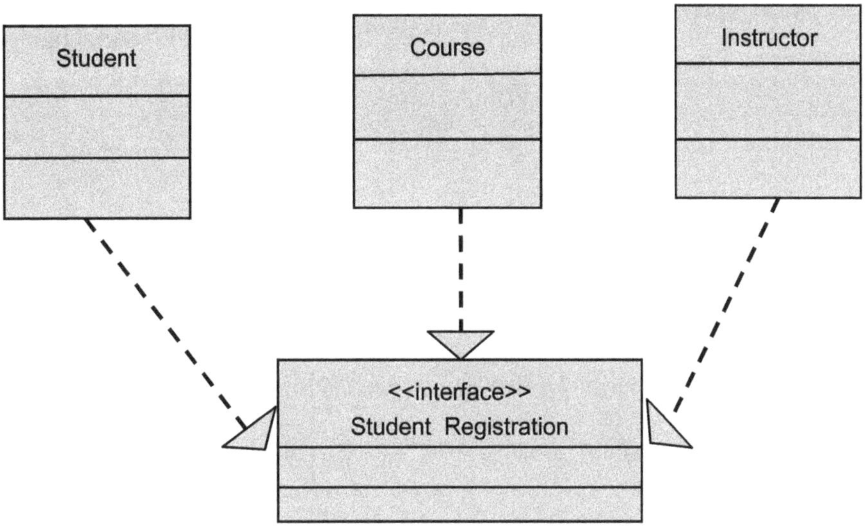

**Fig.1.27** Implementing Interface

## Extensibility Mechanisms

UML provides a standard graphical language for creating software blue prints, but not sufficient to express all possible things that happen across all models across all domains. Because of this constraint, UML is made open-ended, making you to extend the language capabilities. Extensibility mechanisms allow you to extend the UML by adding new building blocks, creating new properties and specifying new semantics in order to make the language suitable for modeling your specific problem domain. The UML's extensibility mechanisms include the following:

❖ Stereotypes
❖ Tagged Values
❖ Constraints

## Stereotypes

They extend the vocabulary of the UML by creating new model elements derived from existing ones but that have specific properties suitable for your domain/problem. Each stereotype defines a set of properties that are received by elements of that stereotype. For Example:

1. If you are modeling a network oriented system, you definitely need symbols for routers and hubs. The standard UML is not having model elements to represent them. You can use stereotypes to model hubs and routers. We can make use of stereotyped nodes to model them so that they appear as primitive building blocks. The hub and router can be

graphically represented as follows. Graphically, a stereotype is rendered as a name enclosed by guillemets (« » or, if guillemets proper are unavailable, << >>) and placed above the name of another element.

**Fig. 1.28(a)** Stereotype for Hub   **Fig.1.28(b)** Stereotype for Router

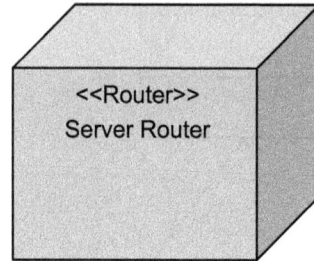

2. Another example, in java or in C++, you sometimes have to model exceptions as classes. You only want them to be thrown and caught. You can model them like basic building blocks, by marking them with a suitable stereotype.

**Example:**

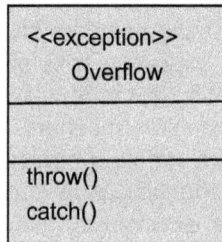

**Fig. 1.29(a)** Stereotype for exception   **Fig. 1.29(b)** Stereotypes for Component and Servlet

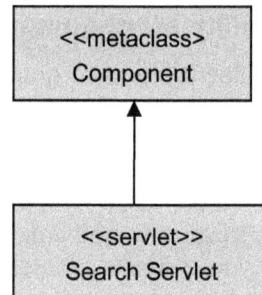

## Tagged values

Tagged values are properties for specifying keyword-value pairs of model elements, where the keywords are attributes. They allow you to extend the properties of a UML building block so that you create new information in the specification of that element. Tagged values can be defined for existing model elements, or for individual stereotypes, so that everything with that stereotype has that tagged value. It is important to mention that a tagged value is not equal to a class attribute. Instead, you can regard a tagged value as being a metadata, since its value applies to the element itself and not to its instances. For example:

1. One of the most common uses of a tagged value is to specify properties that are relevant to code generation or configuration management. So, for example, you can make use of a tagged value in order to specify the programming language to which you map a particular class, or you can use it to denote the author and the version of a component. Graphically, a tagged value is rendered as a string enclosed by brackets and placed below the name of another element. The string consists of a name (the tag), a separator (the symbol =), and a value (of the tag).

**Example:**

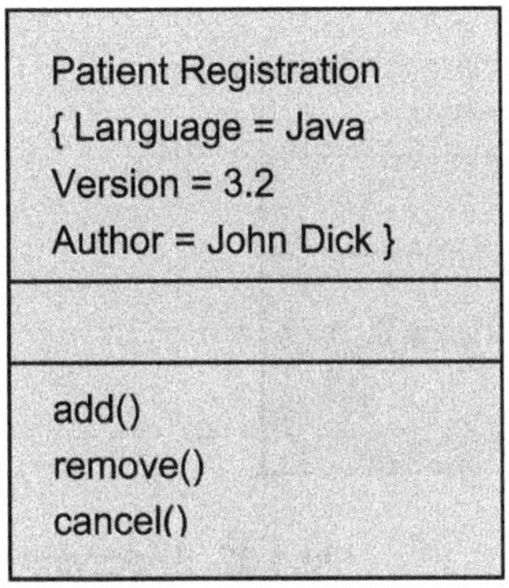

**Fig.1.30** Using Tagged Values

2. As another example, where tagged values can be useful, consider the release team of a project, which is responsible for assembling, testing, and deploying releases. In such a case it might be feasible to keep track of the version number and test results for each main subsystem, and so one way of adding this information to the models is to use tagged values.

**Example:**

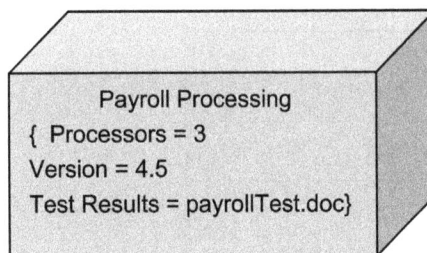

**Fig.1.31** Using Tagged Values

## Constraints

Constraints are properties for specifying semantics and/or conditions that must be held true at all times for the elements of a model. They allow you to extend the semantics of a UML building block by adding new rules, or modifying existing ones. For example, when modeling hard real time systems it could be useful to adorn the models with some additional information, such as time budgets and deadlines. By making use of constraints these timing requirements can easily be captured. Graphically, a constraint is rendered as a string enclosed by brackets, which is placed near the associated element(s), or connected to the element(s) by dotted lines. This notation can also be used to adorn a model element's basic notation, in order to visualize parts of an element's specification that have no graphical cue.

**Example:**

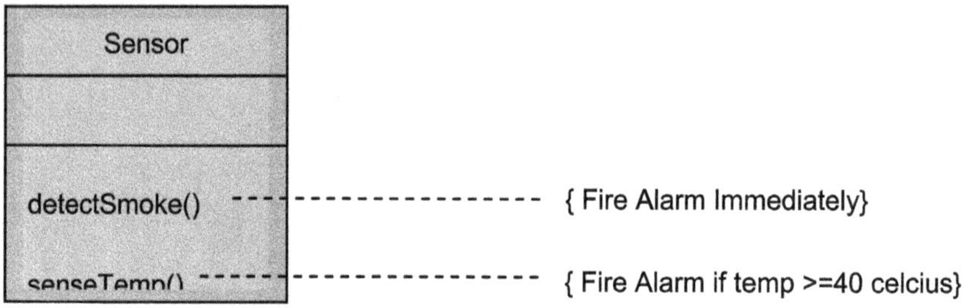

**Fig.1.32** Specifying Constraints for Sensor

**Note**: In the above diagram specifies the details of a sensor class. Whenever sensor detects smoke, it immediately raises the fire alarm. If the sensor senses the temperature above 40 celcius, it raises the fire alarm.

In the following example, an engineering college takes admissions based on the ranks in the engineering entrance test.

**Example:**

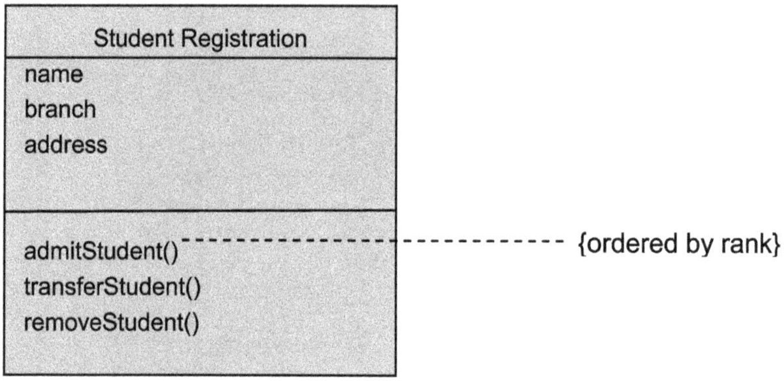

**Fig.1.33** Student Admissions are in the order of the rank obtained

## 1.9 System Architecture

Any system models developed by UML demands that the system be viewed from different perspectives based on different stakeholders. The different stakeholders are end users, system analysts, developers, testers, system integrators, technical writers, project leaders and project managers and others who are directly or indirectly connected with the system. Each of these stakeholders look at the system in different ways at different situations.

Here, the system's architecture is the main way of realizing these different views and to control system development life cycle. The software architecture of a system is the set of static structures of the system needed to reason about the system, which comprise software elements, relations among them, and properties of both. The term system architecture also refers to documentation of a system's software architecture. Documenting software architecture facilitates understanding and communication between various stake holders of the software intensive system. An architecture documents early decisions about high-level design, and allows reuse of design components and design patterns between different software projects.

Technically, system architecture can be defined as understanding the components that make the system, how they work together and how they interact with each other, and the world around them. The exact definition of system architecture according to SEI (Software Engineering Institute) can be as follows:

"The architecture of a software-intensive system is the structure or structures of the system, which comprise software elements, the externally visible properties of those elements, and the relationships among them."

Architecture specification includes the decisions about the following:

* ❖ The organization of the system.
* ❖ The structural elements and their interfaces that the system is composed off.
* ❖ The behavior specified by behavioral elements.
* ❖ The composition of these structural and behavioral elements.

Software architecture is not only concerned with structure and behavior, but also with usage, functionality, performance, and economic and technology constraints. The architecture of a software intensive system, can be best depicted by five related views as follows:

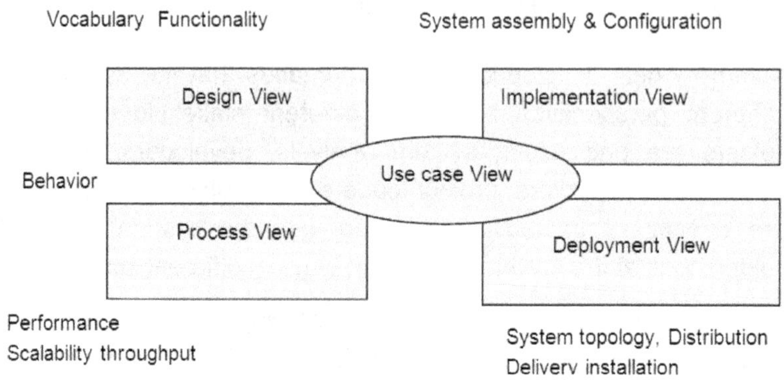

Vocabulary  Functionality                    System assembly & Configuration

| | |
|---|---|
| Design View | Implementation View |

Behavior                          Use case View

| | |
|---|---|
| Process View | Deployment View |

Performance
Scalability  throughput

System topology, Distribution
Delivery installation

**Fig.1.34** Five State View of a System

## 1.10 The Problem of Architectural Description

When you start the task of designing the architecture of a system, you will find that you have some questions to answer about the architecture. These could be as follows:

❖ What are the main functional elements of your system architecture?
❖ How will these elements interact with one another and with the outside world?
❖ What information will be managed, stored, and presented?
❖ What physical hardware and software elements will be required to support these functional and information elements?
❖ What operational features and capabilities will be provided?
❖ What development, test, support, and training environments will be provided?

A major role of an architect is to provide answers to these questions in a form that is understandable to the people who are concerned with the system. Most probably this can be achieved by creating an architectural description.

**Definition**: An architectural description (AD) is a set of artifacts that documents an architecture in a way its stakeholders can understand and demonstrates that the architecture has met their concerns.

### Use case View

The purpose of this view is to see the system as a set of activities or transactions. It is a technique to capture business processes from end user's perspective. It expresses the system's behavior as seen by users, system analysts and testers. It gives the elements and various other sources that shape the architecture of the system. Use case diagrams are the ways and means of expressing system requirements according to the client's perspective, and system functionalities according to the developers and testers perspective. The static aspect of this use case view is indicated by Use case Diagrams. The dynamic or the behavioral aspect of the system is expressed by interaction diagrams (state chart and activity diagrams).

## Design View

This is the structural view of the system which gives an idea of what a given system is made of. This view encompasses classes, interfaces, and collaborations that define the vocabulary of a system. This view expresses functional requirements of the system. The static aspect of this view is captured in class and object diagrams. The dynamic aspect of this view is captured through interaction diagrams. This view extensively expresses the problem definition and the way the solution is built for the problem.

## Process View

Through this view you can understand the behavior of a system. This view encompasses the threads and processes defining concurrency and synchronization mechanisms involved in the system. It not only addresses the processes that constitute your system, it also gives information about performance, scalability, and throughput of the system under consideration. This view includes various diagrams such as, the state diagram, activity diagram, sequence diagram, and collaboration diagram.

## Implementation View

This view includes various components and files used to assemble and release the system for customer base. This view is the procedure depicting how the system is assembled from its components and files that establish a running system. It addresses the configuration management of the system's release. It gives the picture of grouped modules that constitute your system. The static aspects of this view are captured in component diagrams, and the dynamic aspects of it are captured through interaction diagrams, state chart diagrams and activity diagrams.

## Deployment View

This is used to identify the deployment modules for a given system. This view encompasses the nodes that form the hardware topology on which the system executes. This view addresses the distribution, delivery, and installation of the parts that make up the physical system. You find the static aspects of this view , in deployment diagrams and dynamic aspects in interaction diagrams, state chart diagrams, and activity diagrams.

## 1.11 Software Development Life Cycle

The models developed by UML are process-independent, means that they do not depend on any particular software development methodology. To utilize UML for a greater extent, it is better to have processes that are use case driven, architecture centric, and iterative and incremental.

### Use Case Driven

The desired behavior of the system is established by use cases. Use cases are used as primary source for verifying, and validating the system's architecture. Use cases are used as the major resources for establishing testing, and communication among various stakeholders of the system.

### Architecture-Centric

The system's architecture is considered as the primary artifact. The system's architecture is taken as the basis for conceptualizing, managing, constructing and evolving the system under consideration.

### Iterative and Incremental

Here, the iterative process refers to the management of the stream of executable releases. Incremental process refers to the continuous integration of system's architecture for the releases. Each new release will be the improvement of the previous release in terms of end user's perspective of the system in its functionality.

Any process with the above mentioned characteristics can be broken into phases. A phase is the span of time between two major milestones of the process. There are four phases in the software development life cycle, and they are Inception, Elaboration, Construction, and Transition.

### Inception

This is the first phase in the software development process. It involves the basic idea of what to implement. The end of this phase begins the next phase, that is Elaboration.

### Elaboration

It is the second phase of the software development process, which include the definition of the product vision and its architecture. In this phase, system's requirements are considered and formulated. This phase also specify functional or non functional behavior of the system. This phase also forms the basis for testing the system.

## Construction

In this phase the system is made ready to be transferred to the user community. In this phase, the system's requirements, and its evaluation criteria are constantly examined against the business needs of the system.

## Transition

In this phase, the system is fully tested and it is delivered to the end user. But this phase is not the end of the development process. In this phase still requirements are gathered, bugs are fixed, and new enhancements are taken from the user and they are implemented in the new incremental release of the system.

## Essay Questions

1. What is UML? Explain it briefly.
2. Give importance of modeling.
3. Explain principles of modeling.
4. What is object oriented modeling?
5. Briefly explain the following
   (a) Things        (b) Relationships
6. Briefly explain the following
   (a) Relationships  (b) Diagrams
7. Explain common mechanisms in UML
8. Explain extensibility mechanisms in UML.

## Objective Type Questions

1. What is a model?
   (a) Simplification of reality        (b) It is a blue print
   (c) Both a & b                       (d) None
2. A model is needed for
   (a) Visualizing the system
   (b) Specifying structure & behavior of a system
   (c) Documenting the decisions we make
   (d) All the above.
3. UML builds data model by using
   (a) Class diagrams                   (b) Object diagrams
   (c) Both a & b                       (d) None

4. The system's functionality can be specified by using
   (a) Use case diagrams
   (b) Activity diagrams
   (c) Both a & b
   (d) component diagrams

5. The best models are connected to reality is what principle of modeling
   (a) Principle One
   (b) Principle Two
   (c) Principle Three
   (d) Principle Four

6. The building blocks of UML are
   (a) Things
   (b) Relationships
   (c) Diagrams
   (d) All the above

7. Classes and interfaces come under the category of
   (a) Behavioral things
   (b) Structural things
   (c) Annotational things
   (d) Grouping things

8. Packages come under the category of
   (a) Structural things
   (b) Behavioral things
   (c) Annotational things
   (d) Grouping things

9. The set of objects that share common attributes, operations, relationships and semantics is called
   (a) Interface
   (b) Class
   (c) Component
   (d) Node

10. A collection of operations, which specify a service of a class or a component is
    (a) Interface
    (b) Class
    (c) Node
    (d) Component

11. A collaboration is graphically rendered as
    (a) Solid ellipse
    (b) Dotted ellipse
    (c) Rectangle
    (d) A tagged rectangle.

12. A physical and replaceable part of the system is called
    (a) Class
    (b) Object
    (c) Component
    (d) Use case

13. ----------------- represents a computational resource of a system
    (a) class
    (b) Object
    (c) Component
    (d) Node

14. The behavioural things are
    (a) Interactions
    (b) State machine
    (c) Both
    (d) None

15. A Note comes under the category of
    (a) Grouping Things              (b) Structural Things
    (c) Behavioral things            (d) Annotational Things

16. ─────────────────▷ Is a graphical symbol for
    (a) Realization Relationship
    (b) Generalization Relationship
    (c) Dependency Relationship
    (d) Association Relationship

17. ‒ ‒ ‒ ‒ ‒ ‒ ‒ ‒ ‒ ‒▷ is a graphical symbol for ‒‒‒‒‒‒‒‒‒
    relationship
    (a) Association                  (b) Dependency
    (c) Composition                  (d) Realization

18. ------------------------------ diagrams represent static design view of the
    system
    (a) Class Diagrams               (b) Object Diagrams
    (c) Both a and b                 (d) None

19. The diagram which emphasizes the time ordering of messages is
    (a) Collaboration diagram        (b) State chart
    (c) Activity diagram             (d) Sequence diagram

20. State chart diagram contain
    (a) States                       (b) Transitions
    (c) Events and activities        (d) All the above

21. The diagram which indicate static implementation view of the system is
    (a) Activity diagram             (b) Deployment Diagram
    (c) Component diagram            (d) Object diagram

22. These are the common mechanisms supported by UML
    (a) Specifications               (b) Adornments
    (c) Common divisions             (d) All the above

23. The Extensibility mechanisms supported by UML are
    (a) Stereotypes                  (b) tagged values
    (c) constraints                  (d) All the above

24. The view which encompasses the threads and processes is
    (a) design view                  (b) process view
    (c) use case view                (d) implementation view

25. It is the phase in which the system is fully tested
    (a) inception                    (b) construction
    (c) transition                   (d) elaboration

---

> **Answers**

| | | | | | |
|---|---|---|---|---|---|
| 1. (c) | 2. (d) | 3. (c) | 4. (c) | 5. (c) | 6. (d) |
| 7. (b) | 8. (d) | 9. (b) | 10. (a) | 11. (b) | 12. (c) |
| 13. (d) | 14. (c) | 15. (d) | 16. (b) | 17. (d) | 18. (c) |
| 19. (d) | 20. (d) | 21. (c) | 22. (d) | 23. (d) | 24. (b) |
| 25. (c) | | | | | |

# CHAPTER 2

# Basic Structural Modeling

A UML class diagram is the visual specification of types of objects that exist in a system and the relationships that exist among them. A class diagram include classes, interfaces, and collaborations. It expresses the static structure of the system. Class diagrams may specify both the conceptual and implementation details of the system. Class diagrams represent structural and not behavioral relationships that exist among system elements. Class diagrams form the basis to develop other UML diagrams, such as sequence and collaboration diagrams.

## 2.1 Classes

A UML class describes a set of objects that share the same attributes, operations, relationships, and semantics. A class can be considered as a blue print for a set of objects. A class can be a template that is useful to create a set of objects, which are having similarities.

**Example:** A Car is a class or a blueprint or a model based on which several Car objects could be created (manufactured).

**LEARNING OBJECTIVES**

*After studying the chapter the students familiarize themselves with the following concepts:*

- Modeling the System
- Modeling Primitive Types and Non-Software Things
- Modeling Relationships
- Modeling Common and Extensibility Mechanisms
- Modeling Diagrams
- Modeling Views and different levels of Abstraction
- Modeling Simple Collaborations
- Modeling Database Schema

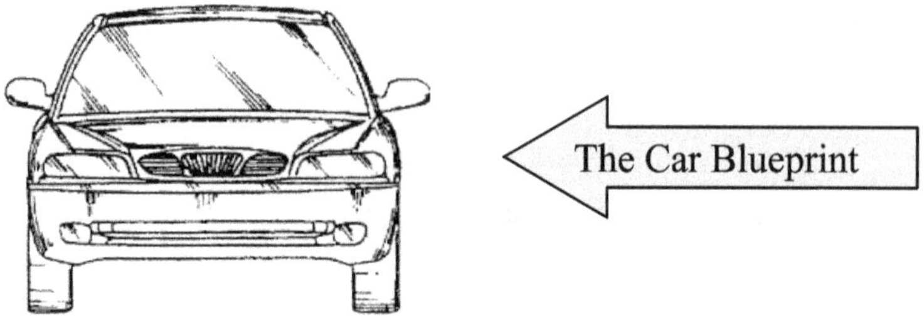

**Fig. 2.1**  Car Model or Class

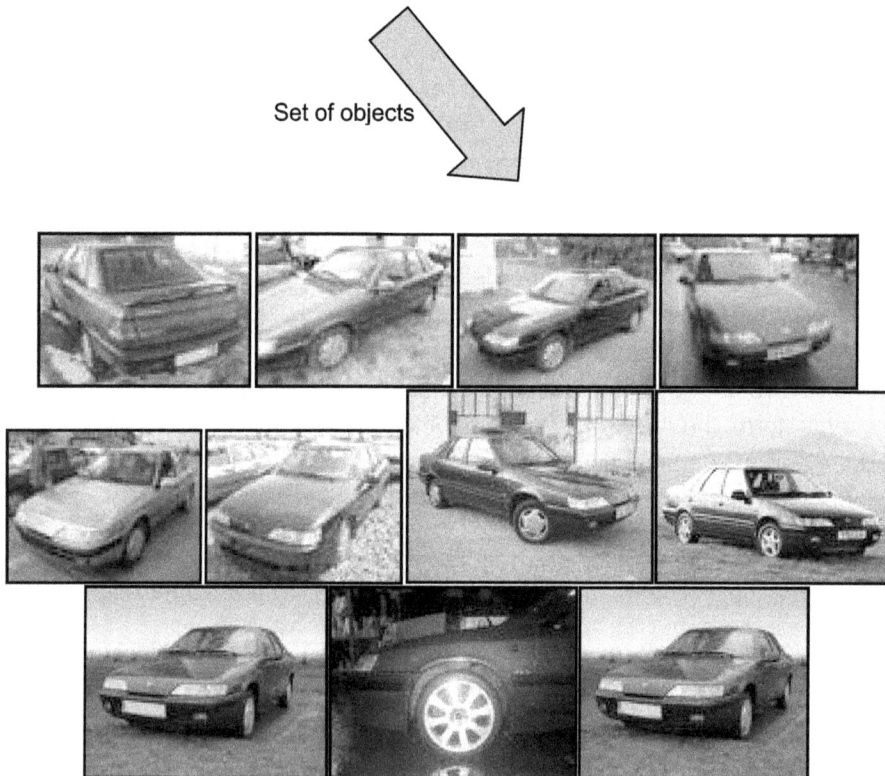

**Fig 2.2**  Car Objects

A class is depicted in UML as a rectangle having compartments. The first compartment includes the name of the class to distinguish it from other classes. The second compartment contains attributes of the named class. The third compartment contains operations or services that the named class offers to the external world. A class may also have a fourth compartment, used to describe the responsibilities of the class in a textual form. When designing classes consider what attributes and operations it will have.  Then try to determine how instances of the classes will interact with each other. A class can be represented graphically by UML as follows:

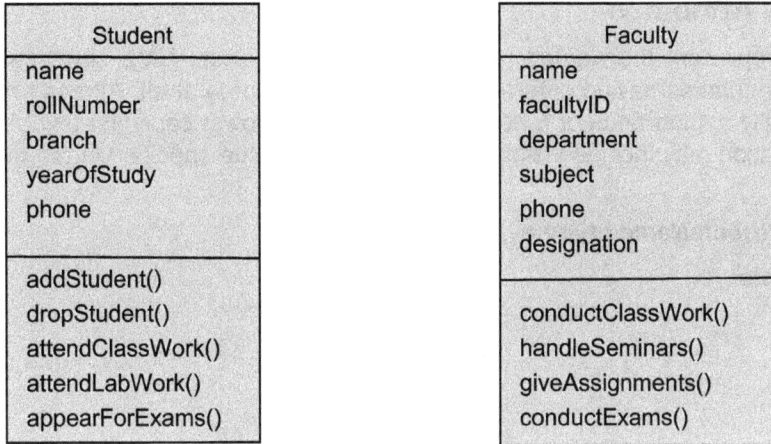

| Student |
| --- |
| name<br>rollNumber<br>branch<br>yearOfStudy<br>phone |
| addStudent()<br>dropStudent()<br>attendClassWork()<br>attendLabWork()<br>appearForExams() |

| Faculty |
| --- |
| name<br>facultyID<br>department<br>subject<br>phone<br>designation |
| conductClassWork()<br>handleSeminars()<br>giveAssignments()<br>conductExams() |

**Fig.2.3** UML Class Specification

## Class Names

Every class must have a name that uniquely identifies it. A class name is a textual string. A class name can be a simple name, or a path name where the class name is prefixed with the name of the package to which the class belongs.

### Simple Names

| Customer | | Window | | Bank Account | | Smoke Detector |
| --- | --- | --- | --- | --- | --- | --- |

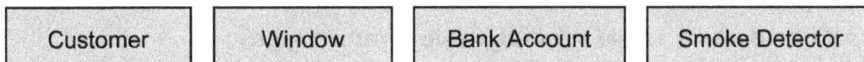

**Fig.2.4** Simple Class Names

### Path Names:

| Admin::Clerk | | Purchase::Purchase Order | | java::awt::Rectangle |
| --- | --- | --- | --- | --- |

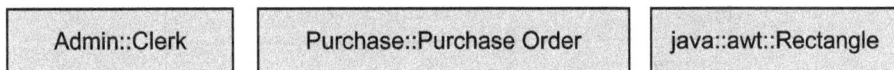

**Fig.2.5** Class Path Names

**Note:** In the above figure, the class 'Clerk' is included in the package named 'Admin'. The 'Admin' package may group up all elements belonging to Admin department. Similarly, 'PurchasOrder' is the class embedded in the package named 'Purchase'. Here, the 'Purchase' package groups all elements belonging to 'Purchase' department. The 'Rectangle' class is included in 'awt' package, which is packed in another package named 'java'.

## Class Attributes

They represent the named properties of a UML class. UML class can have many attributes having different names or no attributes at all. Attribute name is generally a short noun or a noun phrase written in lower case first text. Attribute declaration may include visibility, type and initial value specified in the following form:

**+attributeName : type = initial value**

**Example:**

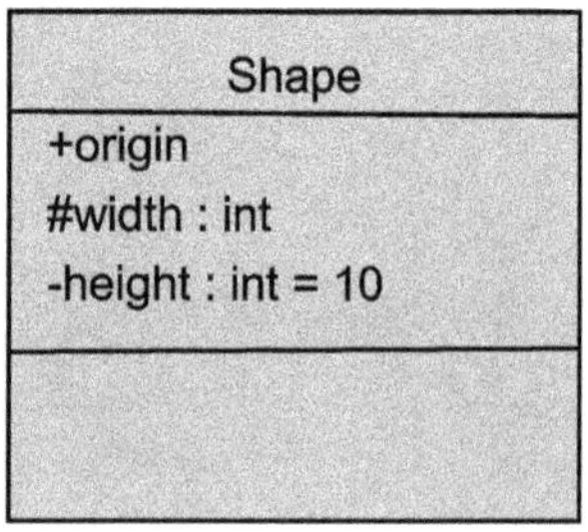

| Shape |
|---|
| +origin<br>#width : int<br>-height : int = 10 |
|  |

**Fig.2.6** Attributes Specification

## Class Operations

They represent named services provided by a UML class. UML class can have many operations having different names or no operations at all. Operation name is generally a short verb or a verb phrase written in lower case first text. Operation may include visibility, parameters, and return type specified in the following form:

**+opName(param1 : type = initial_value) : return-type**

**Example:**

| Shape |
|---|
|  |
| +move()<br>#resize() : Boolean<br>-display(always : Boolean = true ) : Boolean |

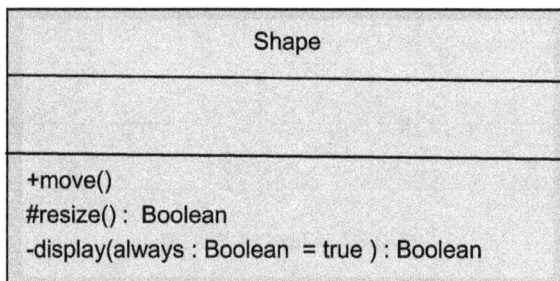

**Fig.2.7** Operations Specification

## Class Visibility

There are three levels of visibility constraints that are specified while you are defining a class, attribute and operation. If any attribute or an operation specification precedes with the following symbols, it specifies visibility. The three visibility constraints are as follows:

❖ If the symbol is '−', it means private visibility. Any attribute or an operation with private visibility is available only to the current class in which they are defined.

❖ If the symbol is '#', it means protected visibility. Any attribute or an operation defined with protected visibility is available only to the current class and its inherited classes.

❖ If the symbol is '+', it means public visibility. Any attribute or an operation defined with public visibility is available to the current and other classes.

**Example:**

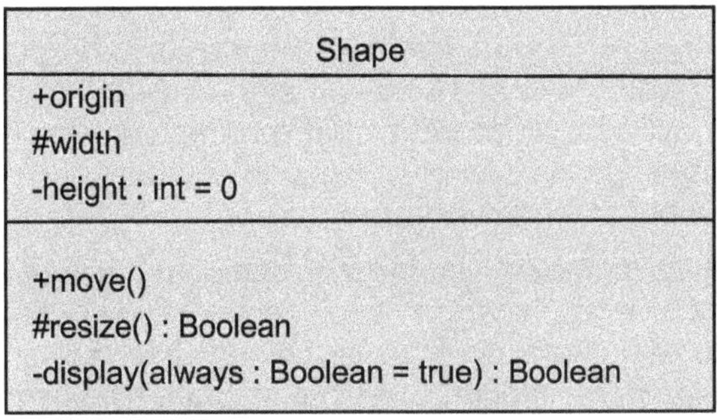

```
┌─────────────────────────────────────────────────┐
│                      Shape                        │
├─────────────────────────────────────────────────┤
│ +origin                                           │
│ #width                                            │
│ -height : int = 0                                 │
├─────────────────────────────────────────────────┤
│ +move()                                           │
│ #resize() : Boolean                               │
│ -display(always : Boolean = true) : Boolean       │
└─────────────────────────────────────────────────┘
```

**Fig.2.8** Class with Visibility

**Note:**

The above diagram is the graphical representation of the class named 'Shape'. It has three attributes and three operations. The attribute 'origin' and the operation 'move' have public visibility. The attribute 'width' and the operation 'resize' have protected visibility. The attribute 'height' and the operation 'display' have private visibility.

**Another Example**

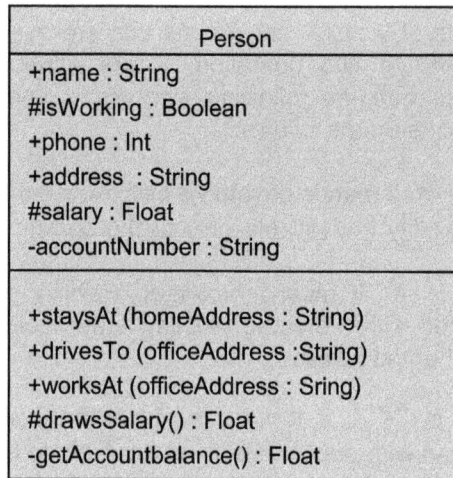

| Person |
|---|
| +name : String |
| #isWorking : Boolean |
| +phone : Int |
| +address  : String |
| #salary : Float |
| -accountNumber : String |
|   |
| +staysAt (homeAddress : String) |
| +drivesTo (officeAddress :String) |
| +worksAt (officeAddress : Sring) |
| #drawsSalary() : Float |
| -getAccountbalance() : Float |

**Fig.2.9** Class with Visibility Constraints

**Note:** The above figure shows the graphical specification of the class named 'Person'. The attributes 'name', 'phone' and 'address' have public visibility, meaning this information is available to everybody. Similarly the attributes 'isWorking' and 'salary' have protected visibility, meaning this information is available to the person himself as well as to the children of the person. On the same lines, the attribute 'accountNumber' has private visibility, meaning only the person himself knows his bank account number, no one including his children are unaware of this information.

The above class definition also includes the data types of its attributes, such as the attributes 'name', 'address' and 'accountNumber' are of type String, meaning they contain character or alpha numeric information. The data type of the attribute 'phone' is an integer. Similarly, the data type of the attribute 'salary' is a real number with decimals. Based on the above class definition, we can understand that the person's house address and his office location as well as the information that daily he goes to the office by driving a car is available to everyone. Himself or his children can only collect his salary. He alone can know his bank balance.

## Responsibilities

A responsibility is a contract or obligation of a class to perform a particular service.  When you create a class, it means that you are specifying all objects belonging to the class have similar state and similar kind of behavior. The attributes and operations you define for a class are the features by means of which you carry   the responsibilities of the class. A **Door** class is responsible for knowing its width, height, and thickness and for opening and closing  and for locking and unlocking. A **TemperatureSensor** class is responsible for measuring temperature, and raising an alarm if the temperature reaches a certain point. A **TeachingFaculty** class is responsible for conducting class work, for conducting seminars, for maintaining attendance and for carrying out examinations.

When you are modeling a class from the vocabulary of your system, it is good practice to specify the responsibilities to start with. Later you translate these responsibilities into a set of attributes and operations of a class. A class may also include its responsibilities in a class diagram. Responsibilities are provided in a separate compartment at the bottom of the graphic symbol for the class. Responsibilities are written as free form text in the form of a phrase, a sentence, or in the form of a short paragraph.

**Example:**

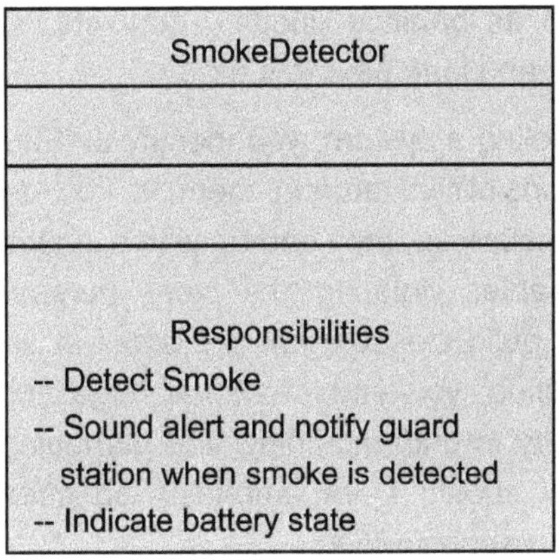

**Fig.2.10**  Class with Responsibilities

# 2.2 Modeling the Vocabulary of a System

Classes represent an abstraction of entities with common characteristics. These abstractions are drawn from the problem statement of your system. When you develop a solution, you identify classes. The solution you implement using object-oriented analysis involve the process of identifying classes, responsibilities, attributes, and operations.

**To model a system:**

❖ Identify the things that are used to describe the problem or a solution.

❖ For each abstraction, identify a set of responsibilities, such that there is a balance of responsibilities among classes.

❖ Identify attributes and operations that are needed to fulfill these responsibilities for each class.

**For Example**:

- ❖ Nouns and/or objects that share common properties and enable system functionality become classes.
- ❖ Other nouns related to class nouns become class attributes.
- ❖ Verbs related to class nouns become class operations.

The following Fig.(2.11) shows a set of classes drawn from a banking system, including Customer, Bank, ATM System. This figure also includes other abstractions drawn from the vocabulary of the problem, such as Bank Account (Record showing that the customer is a valid account holder), Transaction (contains actions such as balance enquiry, deposits, withdrawals, inter bank transfer, loan receiving and loan payment etc.).

When you are modeling a system, you identify and built classes considering balanced set of responsibilities among them. If you develop classes having more number of responsibilities, they end up with a system model that is difficult to change and reusable, violating the very purpose of object oriented methodologies. If you build classes that are small in size, meaning with little number of responsibilities, you end of with a huge number of classes for a system causing difficulty in understanding and managing them. While you are building a model, you should have emphasis on specifying classes with a reasonable balance of responsibilities.

To model distribution of responsibilities, the following steps are followed:

- ❖ Identify a group of classes that work together to carry out some cooperative behavior.
- ❖ Identify a set of responsibilities for each of the classes defined.
- ❖ Split larger classes into smaller ones, collapse smaller classes into bigger ones, so that the identified classes implement a balanced set of responsibilities.
- ❖ Understand how these classes collaborate with each other, and redistribute responsibilities in such a way that no class is over loaded or under loaded with responsibilities.

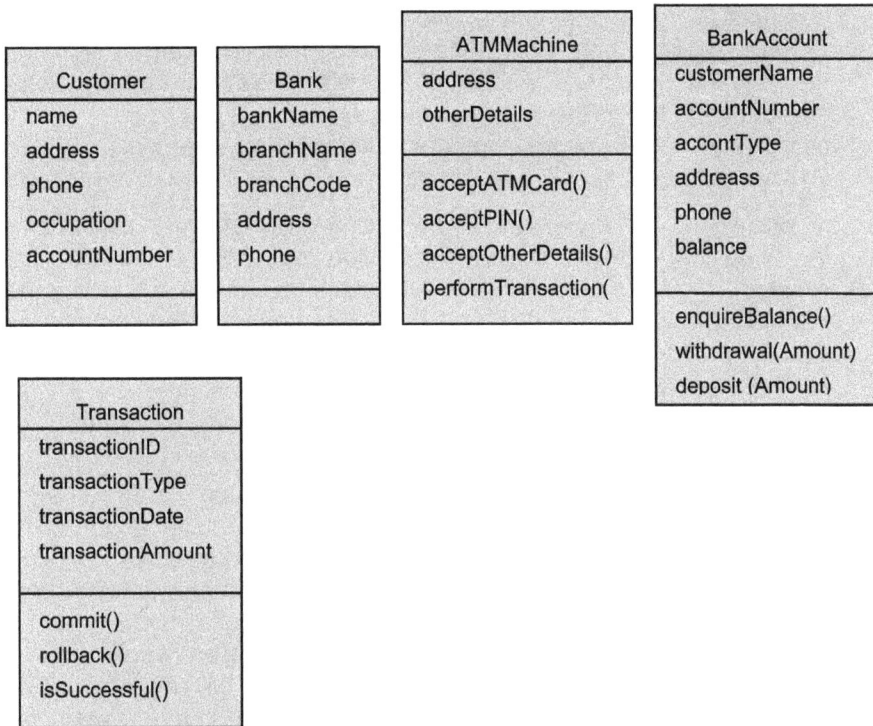

**Fig.2.11** Modeling the Vocabulary of a Banking System

The following figure represents the modeling of how to distribute responsibilities in a retail system.

**Fig.2.12** Modeling the Distribution of Responsibilities in a System

## 2.3 Modeling Non-Software Things

Although UML is becoming a de facto standard for developing models in Object Oriented Analysis and Design because of its fundamental Object Orientation concepts (like class, attributes, and operations), it can be used in non Object Oriented environments, it can also be used in non-software systems too. There are several incidents where UML being used in totally non-software environments like military, engineering, finance. I have seen it being used in conjunction with BPM and process reengineering scenarios, where you use UML for business modeling and analysis.

Sometimes, what you model may not have analog in software. For example, the people who collect course registration fees, the people who arrange for seminars in class rooms, and the mechanism involved in conducting exams and evaluating students' performance might not have software analog when you built a model for university system. Your university education system might not have any piece of software that represents them, still the system will probably want to maintain this information. So, modeling non software things may become an essential part of modeling various systems using UML.

The UML can be quite expressive for modeling hardware systems. Of course, any process (regardless of being subject to automation or not) can be modeled (in general) by UML. UML was used many times for non-software related activities. UML is applicable not only in system modeling, but also for documenting and analyzing other things. As we are aware that, UML notation is one possible approach, for documenting software architecture . In the case of hardware/software systems it could definitely be used to document the overall system architecture (hardware + software) and the interaction between hardware and software.

The method adopted for modeling non software things involve the following steps:
❖ Model your abstraction from the non software system as a class.
❖ If you want to distinguish these building blocks from UML's standard things, you can use stereotypes to specify these new semantics.
❖ If the modeling element is a piece of hardware that contains software, model it as a kind of Node, you can further associate additional information to its structure.

**Examples**:

1. Look at your surroundings, what is happening around you can be modeled using UML. Suppose, you are in a Room and wants to put on a Ceiling Fan in the Room. You being an object belonging to the class named Person, go to the Switch Board, which is an object of Switch Board class, puts on the Fan. Then you use the Regulator to adjust the rotating speed of the Fan for your required comfort . This entire activity or the whole process can be easily modeled using UML, though it is a non software system. Your Fan operating system has classes, such as Person, Fan, SwitchBoard, and Regulator.

The class diagram for the above system can be represented as follows:

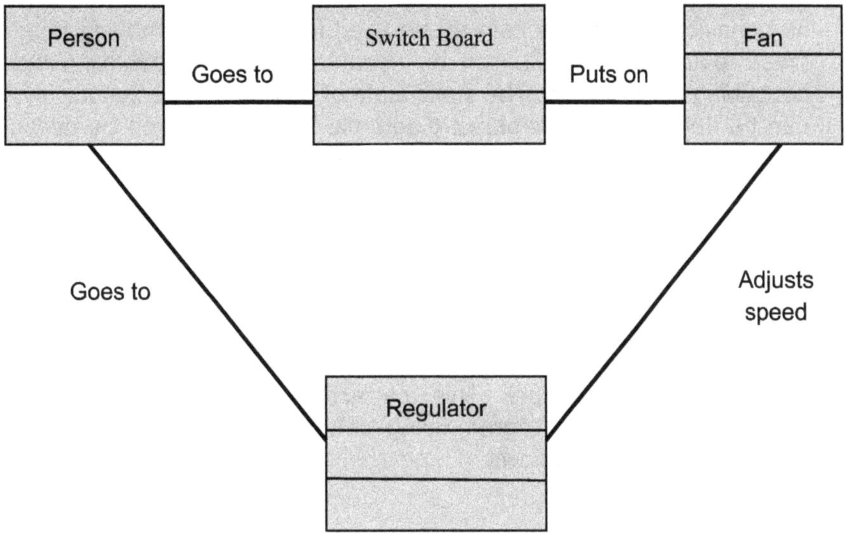

**Fig. 2.13**  Class Diagram

The instance of the above class diagram can be represented in the form of an object diagram with links between them. The dynamic behavior of the above system could be expressed in the form of a sequence diagram or in the form of a collaboration diagram indicating interactions among the objects by means of exchanging messages or by executing each other's operations.

2. In the below university course registration system, the accounts department clerk (Course Registrar) who collects course registration fee and the TechnicalAssistant who arranges seminars can be expressed as below:

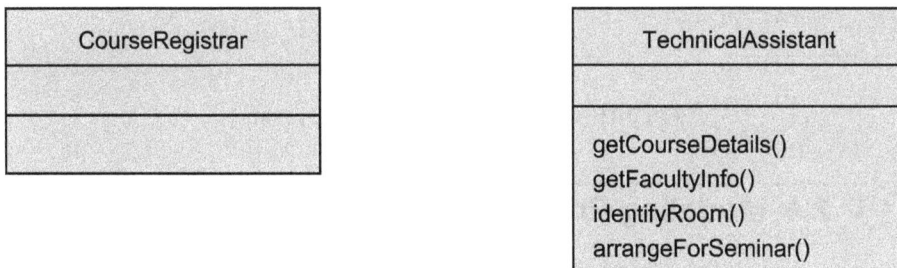

**Fig.2.14**  Modeling Non-software Systems

3. A car is a mechanical device, which is a non-software thing. When Car is parked, it is in static state which can be represented by an object diagram, indicating how various components (can be objects) are linked

together to form a Car which itself is an object. A car can be described as an object containing other objects linked together in a fashion which suits its behavior, meaning a car can be used for physically moving from one place to the other. UML can be used to model the car as a system containing components. The static state of a Car as a mechanical system can be defined by class/object diagrams. Its behavior can be described as an interaction among other objects that form the car system.

A car has objects, such as body, doors, windows, seats, engine, steering, brakes, accelerator, wheels, and gears. When a car is parked, its static structure can be expressed as an object diagram depicting how various objects are physically inter linked together to form a car, which is a physical system. The behavior of the car happens when you are driving it. When you are driving a Car, the behavior of it can be depicted as an interaction among objects that form the car physical structure. This interaction can be represented as a sequence or a collaboration diagram using UML. The object diagram depicting stationary Car system is as follows:

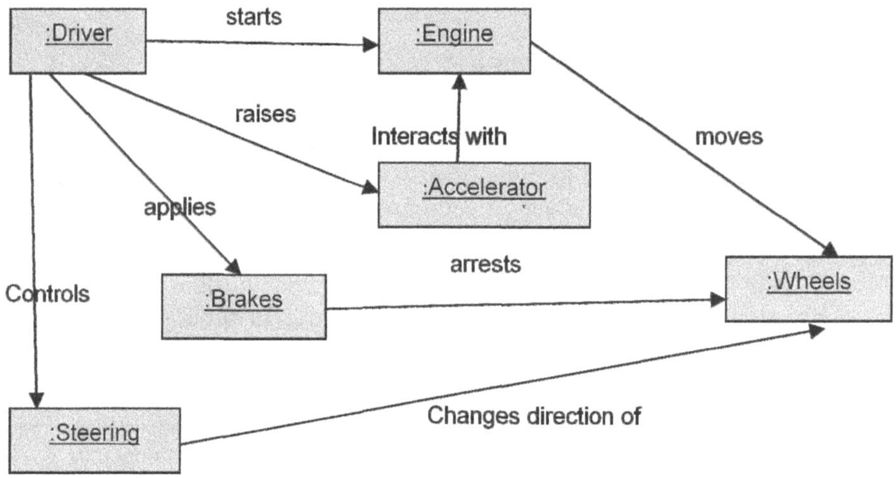

**Fig.2.15**  Object Diagram of a Car System

## 2.4 Modeling Primitive Types

When you are developing a model for a solution, the things you model may be directly drawn from the programming language you are using for implementing a solution. Usually, these could be primitive types, such as integers, characters, strings, and enumeration data types. You might create models to represent these types.

To model primitive types:

❖ Model the things you consider as types or enumerations, which are graphically represented using class notations, using appropriate stereotypes.

❖ The range of values for this type can be expressed using constraints.

The following figure gives the details of modeling primitive types and their applicability.

**Example:**

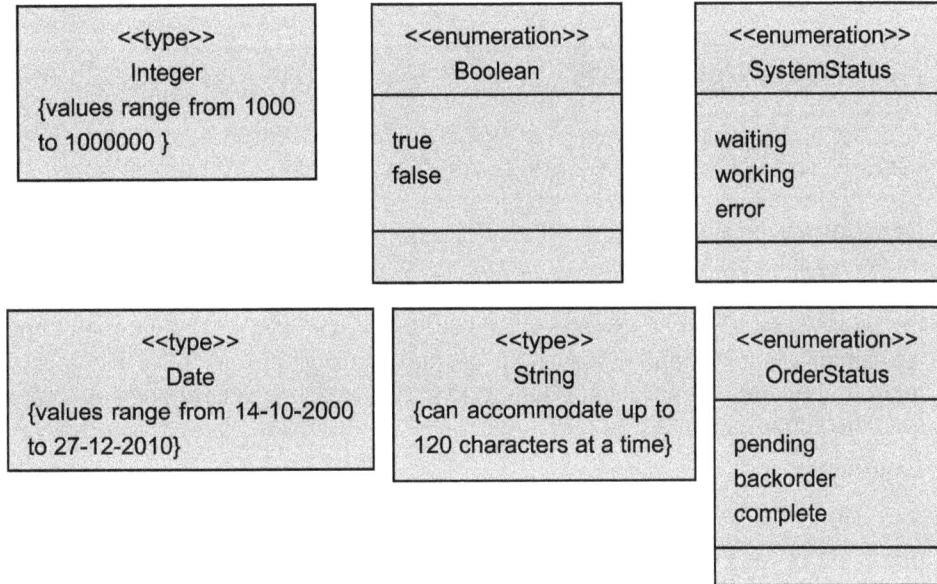

**Fig.2.16**  Modeling Primitive Types

**Note:** The above models can be used while modeling certain things as follows:

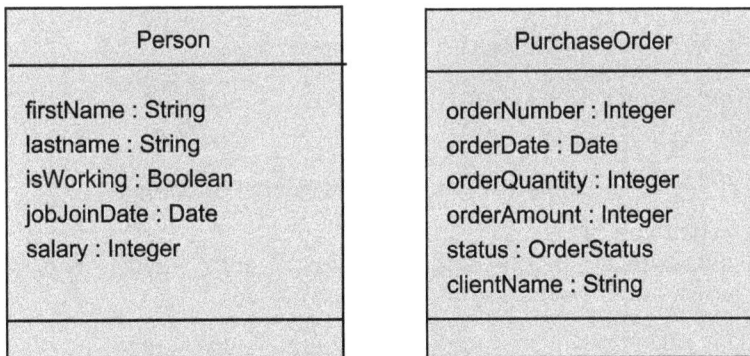

**Fig.2.17**  Classes using Primitive Types

## 2.5 Relationships

When you are building models for solving object oriented problems, using UML, you find that not many things are independent. You observe that, the things you model, tend to relate with each other. UML has facilities to express these relationships among things which you identify. So, when you model, you not only identify the things, but you also need to identify how they are related or connected. There are three kinds of relationships that are important in UML are dependencies, generalizations, and associations. All these relationships have graphical notations to express them.

## 2.6 Dependency

A dependency exists between two defined things in UML model, if change to the definition of one may have impact on the other things. Dependency can be considered as a model-level relationship and not a run-time relationship. Dependency is a semantic relationship where a change to the independent modeling thing may affect the semantics of the dependent modeling thing. Dependency relationship identifies a set of model things that requires other model things for their specification or implementation. The dependency relationship in UML is indicated by a dashed line pointing from the dependent thing to the independent thing. The arrow that represents dependency specifies the direction of a relationship, not the direction of process.

**Examples:**

1. In this example, we have two classes named 'Shape' and 'DrawingContext', where 'Shape' is a dependent class and the other is the independent class. The 'draw' function of the 'Shape' class takes an argument of type 'DrawingContext'.

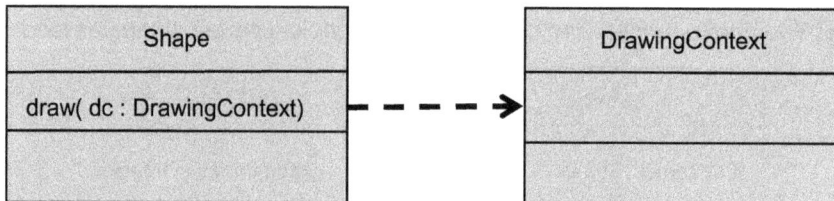

**Fig.2.18** Modeling Dependency Relationship

2. When you are working with a DVD player, the DVD program which you see depends on the DVD you are currently playing. The dependency relationship can be expressed as follows:-

DVD Player DVD

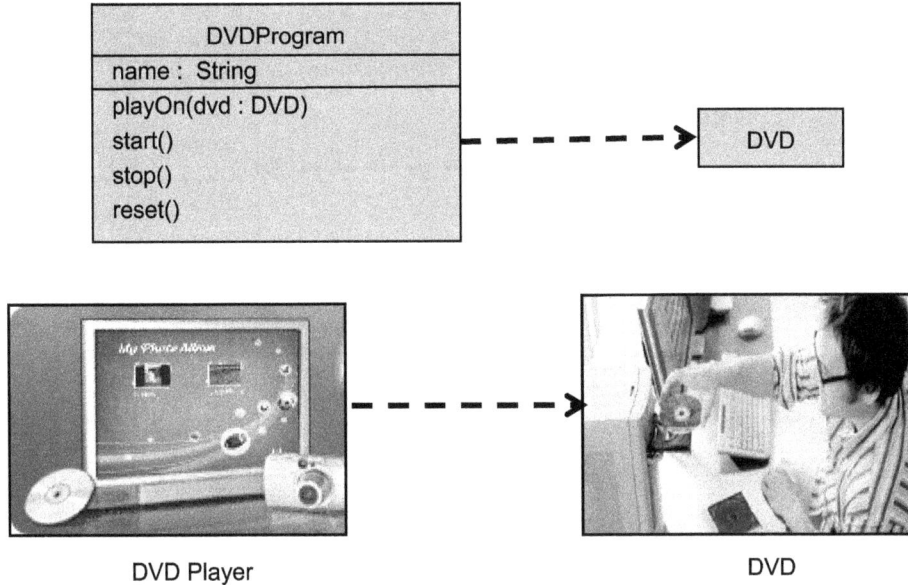

**Fig.2.19** Modeling Dependency Relationship

3. In a university course registration system, the course you register for (subject) depends on the syllabus of that course. The following diagram represents a segment of the model for course registration system in universities.

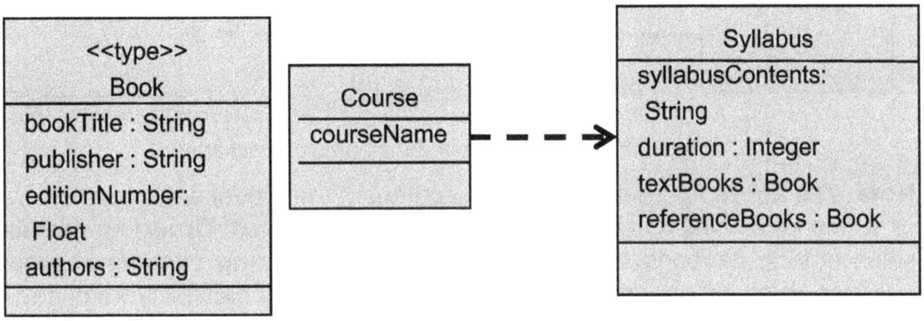

**Fig.2.20** Modeling Dependency Relationship

4. When a customer pays the bill using credit card, it is verified for its validity during payment. The verification process can be represented as dependency relationship between 'CreditcardVerifier' and the 'Customer' as follows:

Credit Card Verifier　　Customer with Credit Card

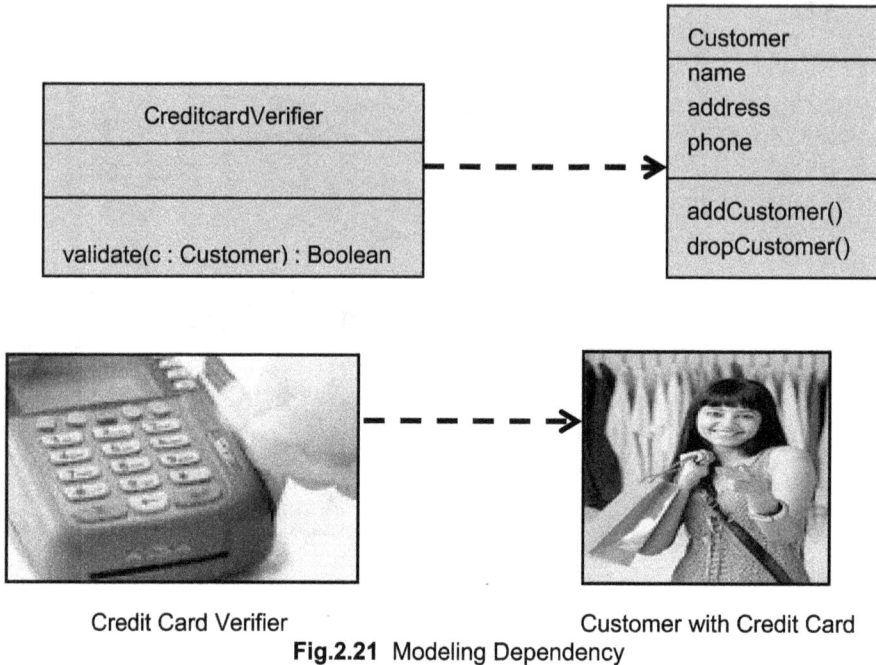

**Fig.2.21** Modeling Dependency

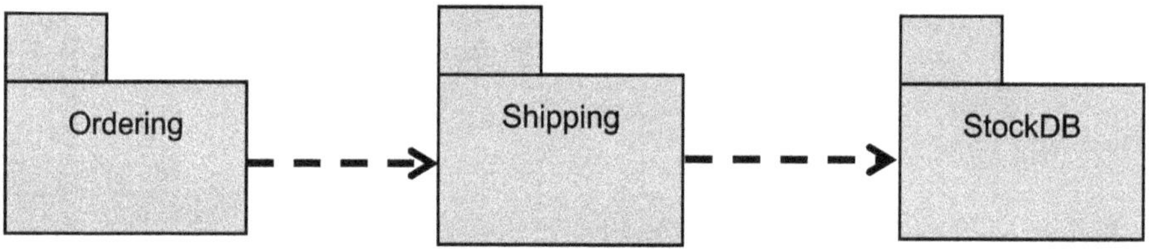

**Fig.2.22** Modeling Dependency among Packages

**Note:** The above figure expresses a fragment of the model developed for Sales or a Manufacturing Organization. The package named **Ordering** containing sales orders, depends on the package named **Shipping** carrying shipments, because sales orders are accepted based on shipping capability. Similarly, the package named **Shipping** depends on the package named **StockDB** containing the stock of goods in the company warehouses, because we cannot ship the things that are not available in the Company's stock of goods.

A dependency is a catch-all relationship that signifies that a model element is dependent or relies on another element or group of elements in some way. The dependency does however have a number of predefined stereotypes that increase the precision of the relationship. A name can also be applied to indicate the nature of the dependency. A dependency can be drawn between any two model elements or sets of elements so that the model is precise. In practice it is most commonly used between elements like packages that contain other elements.

The dependency relationship can be used with the addition of stereotypes which gives more precise meaning to the relationship. The dependency relationship is the least specific of the other relationships supported by UML. Because of this, the dependency relationship can be used in a variety of circumstances with greater flexibility. The UML dependency relationship can be made more specific by using three predefined types of dependencies, which are abstraction, permission, and usage relationships. Each of these has a number of stereotypes that denote various types and aspects of them.

## Abstraction

An abstraction is a type of dependency relationship. It specializes the more general dependency relationship. It conveys the model evolution and gives different viewpoints or perspectives of UML model. There are a number of standard stereotypes that may further qualify the standard abstraction relationship.

**Example:**

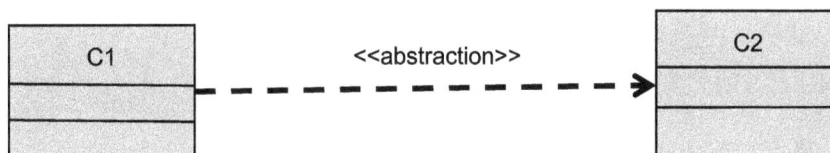

**Fig.2.23** Modeling Abstraction Dependency

## Usage

A usage is a type of dependency relationship. It conveys that one element requires the other element in some way. You can attach a number of stereotypes to usage relationship to further qualify its meaning and add more precision.

**Example:**

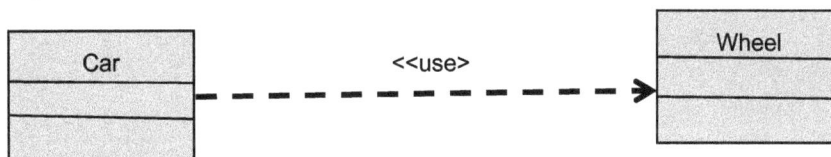

**Fig.2.24** Modeling Usage Dependency

## Permission

A permission is a type of dependency relationship. The permission relationship conveys that one element is granted rights to view the other element in some way. There are no standard stereotypes defined for permission dependency relationship.

**Example:**

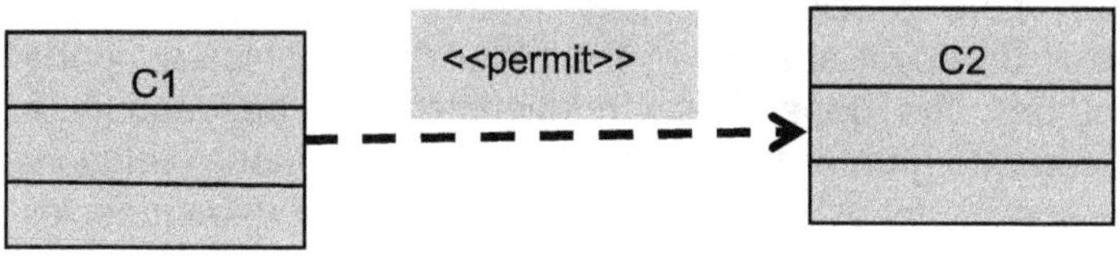

**Fig.2.25** Modeling Permission Dependency

**extend Relationship**

An extend relationship is a type of dependency. It has the same graphical notation as dependency with the addition of the stereotype on the relationship. This relationship means that the base use case depends on the addition use case.

**Example:**

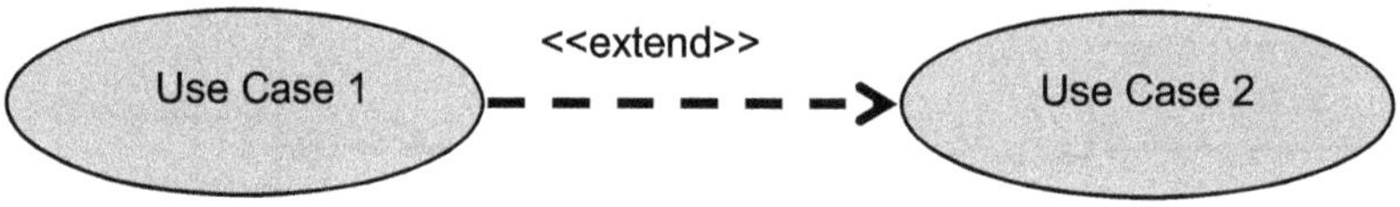

**Include Relationship**

An include relationship is a type of dependency. It has the same graphical notation as the dependency with the addition of the stereotype on the relationship. This relationship means that the base use case depends on the included use case.

**Example:**

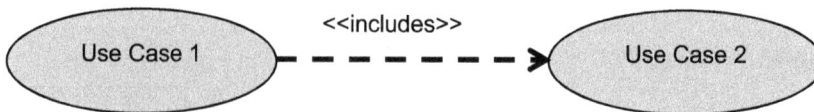

**Fig.2.26** Modeling Include Dependency

## 2.7 Generalization

This is a kind of relationship between a general category (called super class or parent class) and a more specific category (called the subclass or child or a derived class). Generalization is called an is-a-kind–of relationship. In generalization, the child is substitutable for the parent, meaning the objects of the child can be used wherever the parent objects appear, but not the reverse. In UML model, the child element is based on the parent element. Generalization relationships are applicable in class, component, deployment, and use case diagrams. As per the UML semantics, the generalization relationship is allowed between the model elements of same type. It means that, you can have generalization relationship among actors, and among use cases, but not between actors and use cases.

The major application of generalization relationship is, the reusability of model elements. In this relationship, child inherits the properties, services, and responsibilities of the parent, and apart from this, it can contain its own attributes and operations facilitating reusability of existing elements. A child can have more than one parent, and a parent can have any number of children. A class that has no parents and one or more children is called a root class or a base class. A class that has no children is called a leaf class. Generalization relationships do not have names.

This relationship can also be called as inheritance or "is a" relationship. Model element A is a type of another element B.

Examples; an automobile is a type of vehicle. A tiger is a kind of cat.

It is natural that you classify elements into categories, and categories into sub categories when you model a system. If the parent and child has the same operation, the child's operation overrides the operation of the parent; this is known as polymorphism, one of the major applications of object-oriented systems.

The process of identifying generalization/specialization relationship among classes is as follows:

- ❖ **Identify Sub Classes:** Identify classes that have the same attributes and/or operations. They tend to become subclasses in the Generalization/Specialization hierarchy.
- ❖ **Create Super Classes:** Provide a super class for a set of subclasses that hold common attributes/operations belonging to the subclasses.
- ❖ **Add Common Features to the Super Class:** Add common features to the super class and remove them from the corresponding subclasses, so that subclasses contain only their own specific features.
- ❖ **Establish Generalization Hierarchy:** Move super classes up and subclasses down. Establish inheritance hierarchy by using generalization/specialization relationship extending from subclasses into super classes.

The Generalization/Specialization relationship is graphically rendered as a solid line with a hollow arrow head that points from the child model element to the parent model element.

**Examples:**

1. In the following figure, we have a general class named Shape, and the specialized ones named Rectangle, Circle, Triangle, and Square.

   **Note:** In the below figure, we can say that a Rectangle is a Shape, and a Square is a Rectangle.

2. A parrot is a bird belongs to the flying birds category, which is a specific category of the more general category named birds.

3. Any Customer in a banking system is a generalized one, we have PersonalCustomer and CorporateCustomer as specialized ones depicted as follows:

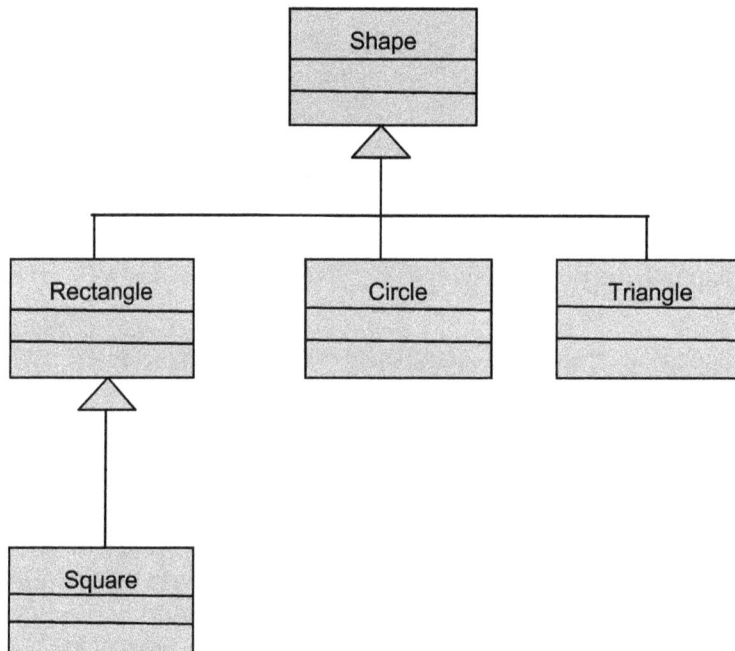

**Fig.2.27** Generalization/Specialization

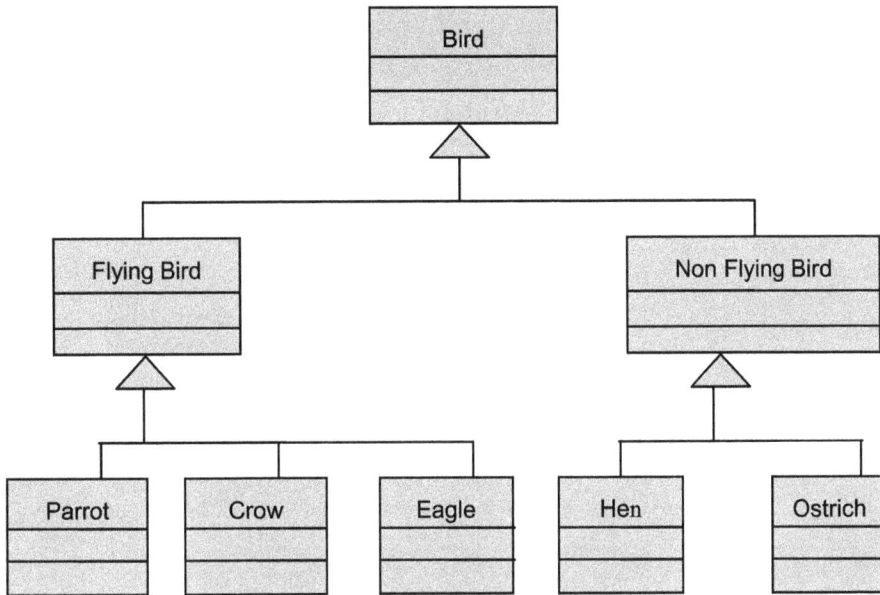

**Fig.2.28** Generalization/Specialization

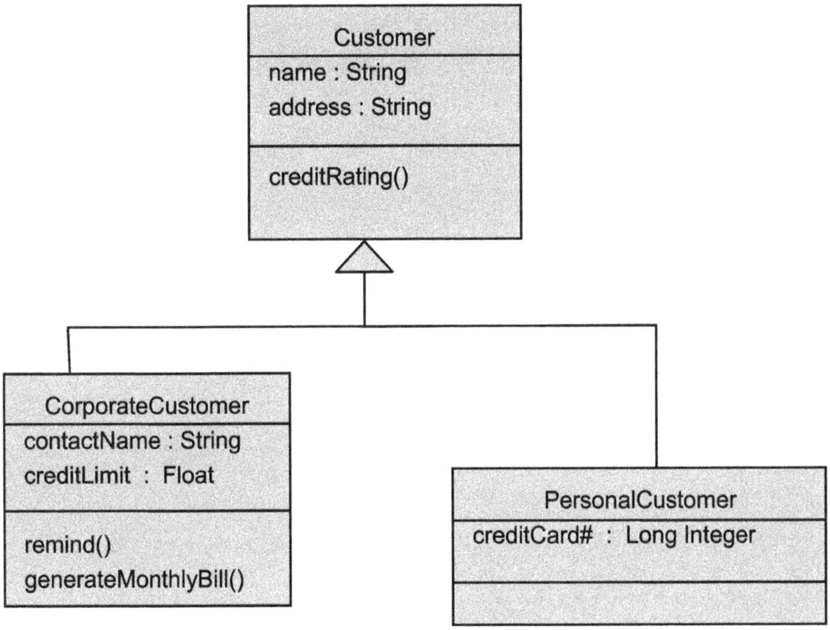

**Fig.2.29** Generalization/Specialization

4. The following figure gives the inheritance relationship that can exist in any university registration system.

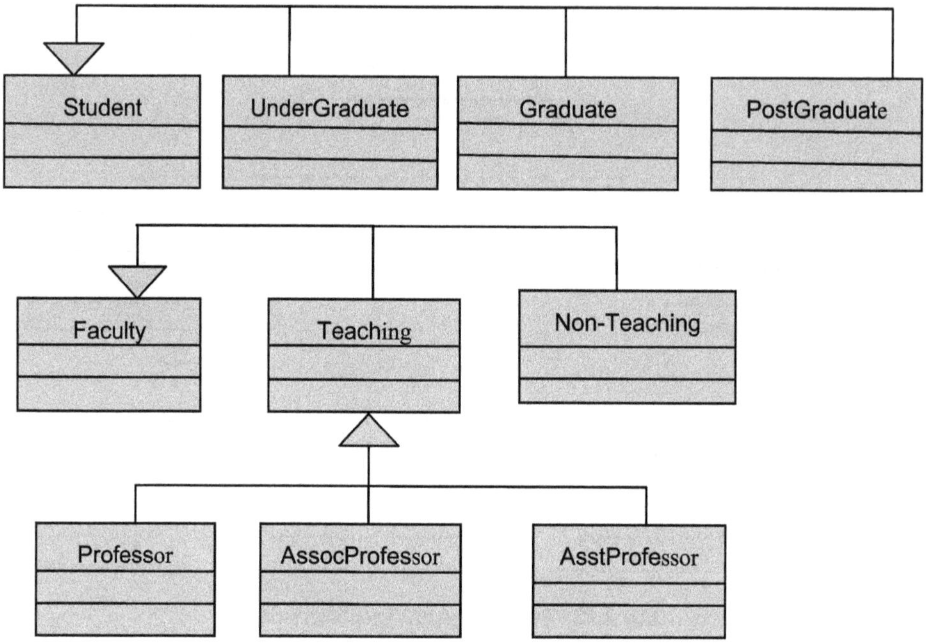

**Fig.2.30** Inheritance Hierarchy

5. The following figure shows the inheritance hierarchy among actors. An actor can be a human user or another system. The figure gives a fragment of a model of Library System.

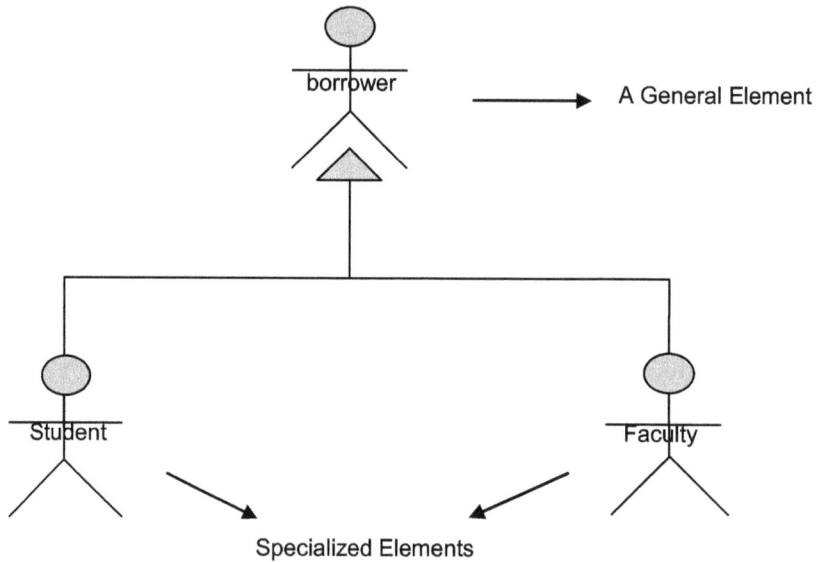

**Fig.2.31** Generalization among Actors

# 2.8 Association

An association is a structural relationship that specifies the links between objects of things in a model. An association represents a family of links among objects of classes that form part of your model. This relationship happens among classes and use cases. It describes the association among classifiers and the rules that govern the relationship. When there is an association among two classes, you can navigate from an object of one class to an object of the other class and vice versa. There can be associations among objects of the same class. This relationship circles back to the same class indicating self association.

While modeling association between classes, you can specify its name and its direction. An association can be adorned with role names, ownership indicators, multiplicity, visibility, and other properties. Out of the several different types of associations, uni-directional and bi-directional associations are the most common ones. Association represents the static relationship shared among the objects of two classes which are in association with each other. We can say that: "College Offers Degrees", is an association relation.

Binary associations (with two ends) are normally represented as a sold line with adornments, with each end connected to a class symbol in the model. Higher order associations can be drawn with more than two ends. In such cases, the ends are connected to a central diamond. The name of an association describes the nature of the relationship between two classifiers and should be a verb or phrase. A typical association between two classes with adornments can be graphically represented as:

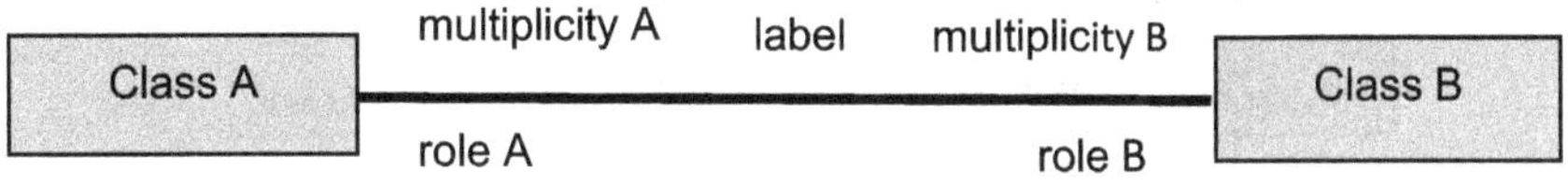

**Fig.2.32** A Binary Association

**Explanation:** The above figure specifies the association between two classes class A and class B. The roles role A and role B are the roles played by the respective classes in the association relationship. In the above figure, label indicate the association name, and multiplicity specifies the respective multiplicities at both ends. You can also specify the direction of association, in any association relationship.

The various adornments you specify in any association are described below:

**Name**

An association relationship can be adorned with a name, this name describes the nature of the relationship without any ambiguity. You can also specify the direction of association by using a direction triangle. The following figure shows the explanation.

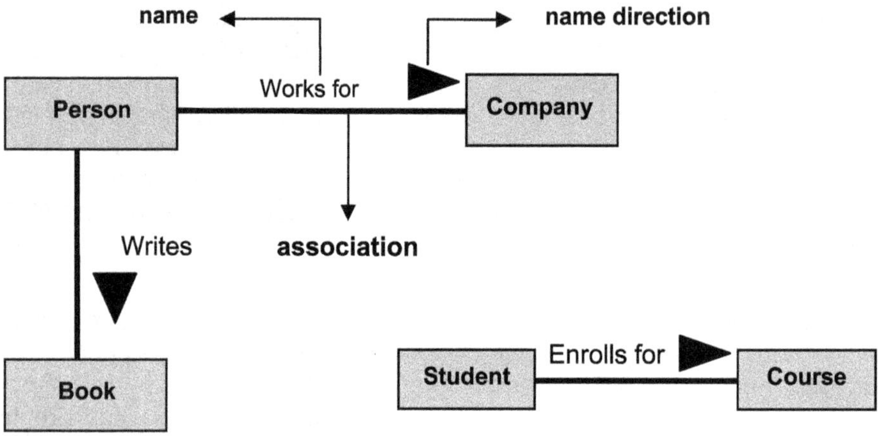

**Fig.2.33** Association Names

## Role

Every class participating in an association relationship has a specific role to play in that relationship. The role is specified with a name near to the participating class at the ends of association. In the following figures, Person class plays the role of Employee, and Company class plays the role of Employer. In the next association between Person class and Book class, Person plays the role of an Author, and Book plays the role of Text Book. The same class may play a different role in other associations.

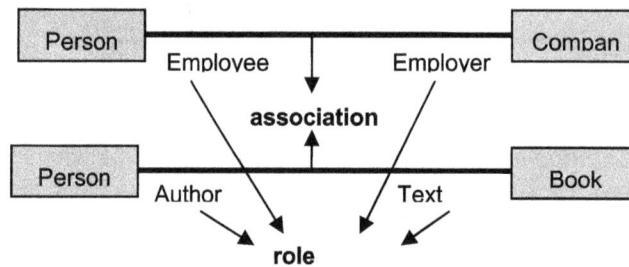

**Fig.2.34** Association Roles

## Multiplicity

An association is a structural relationship among objects. When you are modeling, you may specify the number of objects at both ends of association, indicating how many objects are involved in an instance of an association relationship. This is called multiplicity, it can be an explicit value or an expression that evaluates to a range of values. When you specify multiplicity at one end of an association, you are indicating that, there are these many objects for each object at the other end of an association.

*The multiplicity value and its meaning is given as follows:-*

| S. No. | Multiplicity Value | Meaning |
|--------|--------------------|---------|
| 1. | 0..1 | Zero or One |
| 2. | 1 | One Only |
| 3. | 0..* | Zero or More |
| 4. | 1..* | One or More |
| 5. | n | Only n , where n > 1 |
| 6. | 0..n | Zero to n, where n > 1 |
| 7. | 1..n | One to n, where n > 1 |

**Note:** You can specify more complex multiplicities by using a list of multiplicities, such as 1..3 , 5 , 8..* , which means, any number of objects other than 4 , 6 and 7.

**Examples:**

1. The following figure indicate a fragment of University Course Registration System model. Any student can enroll up to six courses, and a course can be enrolled by any number of students including none.

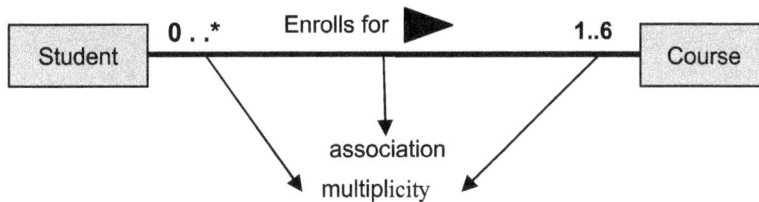

2. The following figure indicate a fragment of Publishing System Model. Any author can write any number of books and a book can be written by any number of authors. Such an association with multiplicities are shown as follows:

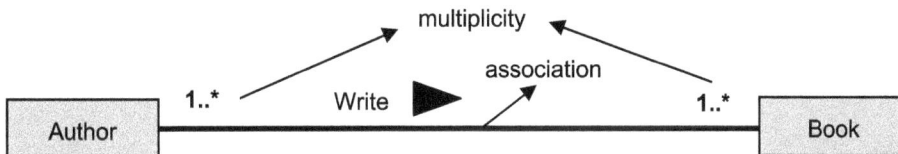

**Fig.2.35** Association Multiplicity

**Examples For Associations:**

1. In this figure, an Account can belong to only one Customer, and a Customer can have only one Account. But an Account can generate any number of bills including none.

**Fig 2.36** Association among Classes

2. In the following figure, it gives a portion of Sales Order Processing System model. In this fragment, A Customer can place 'n' number of orders.

**Fig.2.37** Binary Association

3.

**Fig.2.38** N-ary Association

4.

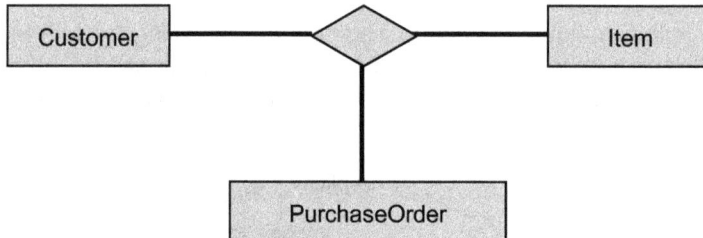

**Fig.2.39** N-ary Association

## 2.9 Aggregation

The classes which participate in any plain association relationship, are conceptually at the same level, meaning all of them are equally important. Sometimes, you may have to model a whole and part relationship, in which one class is larger called whole, and the other are smaller which may become the parts of the larger class. This kind of relationship, which is a variant of association, is called aggregation. Aggregation is more specific than association. This relationship is also called "has-a" relationship, because the whole Object has objects of the parts. Aggregation relationship can occur when a class is a collection or container of other classes. The classes that form parts may not be destroyed even if the whole class, that is the container class is destroyed.

**Examples:** A car can be represented as an aggregation between it, and various parts it contains.  Even if the whole class, here the car is destroyed, it does not mean that every part of the car is damaged or useless. They can well be removed from the damaged car and can be used for another car. It means that the life of parts may not depend on the whole, even if the whole is destroyed, its parts can very well be used for other wholes. Based on this we my conclude that in aggregation relationship, the objects which form parts of the relationship can be physically replaceable and reusable. In UML, an aggregation relationship is represented as an association with a hollow diamond at the whole end.

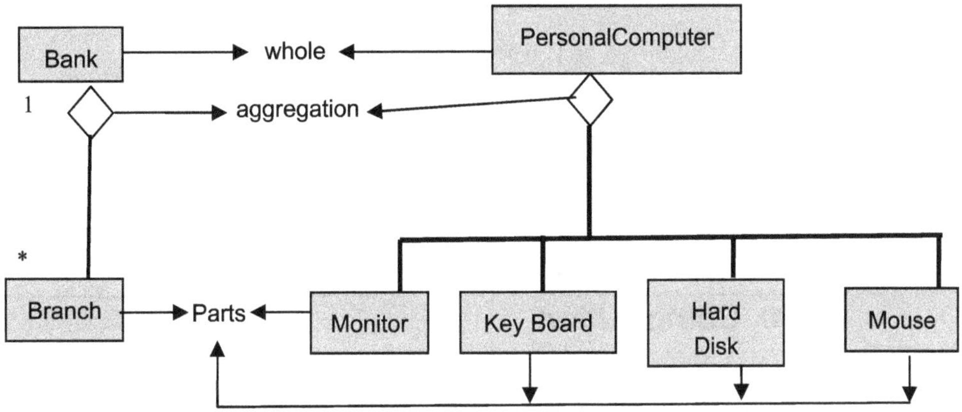

**Fig.2.40** An Aggregation Relationship

An aggregation is a more specific type of association, where objects are assembled together to generate objects that are more complex. An aggregation describes a group of objects and how you interact with them. Aggregation protects the integrity of an assembly of objects by defining them in the object that represents the assembly. A car is an engineered assembly of various components (objects or parts). As we are aware, an aggregation is the relationship between whole (a classifier) and parts (other classifiers) who constitute the whole. A part classifier can be a part, for more than one whole classifier. Even the part classifier can exist independently of the whole classifier.

For example, a Department class can have an aggregation relationship with a Company class, which specifies that the department is part of the company. All parts or components of a car can have aggregation relationship with the car.

A car is the whole and the parts are engine, steering, brakes, wheels, and body etc. The following diagrams describe the aggregations.

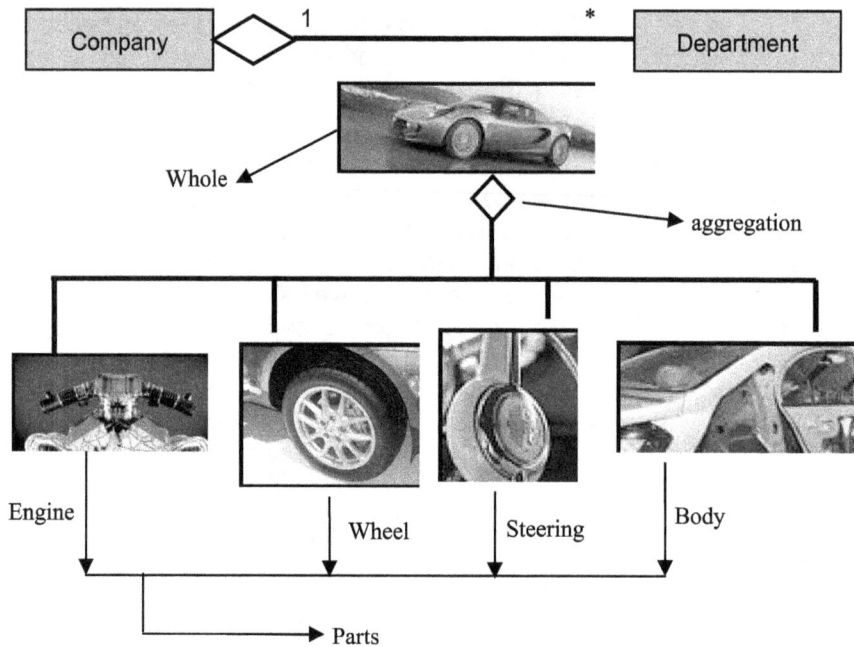

**Fig.2.41** Aggregation

## 2.10 Composition

A composition is a form of aggregation with strong ownership, meaning whole and parts have coincident lifetimes. Parts may be created after the whole itself, but once created they live and die together (they share life times). Once the composite whole dies, all its parts also die becoming useless.

A composition relationship is graphically rendered as similar to aggregation, but with the filled diamond. Examples of composition could be human body and its various organs, Similarly, a stadium and its pitch and seats, a wall and the bricks from which it is built, a coffee table with its legs, and so on. In each of these cases, the composite is composed of its parts. You could consider writing a class diagram for the composite showing the parts as attributes. The attribute notation denotes composition, and so this would seem to make sense.

**Example:**

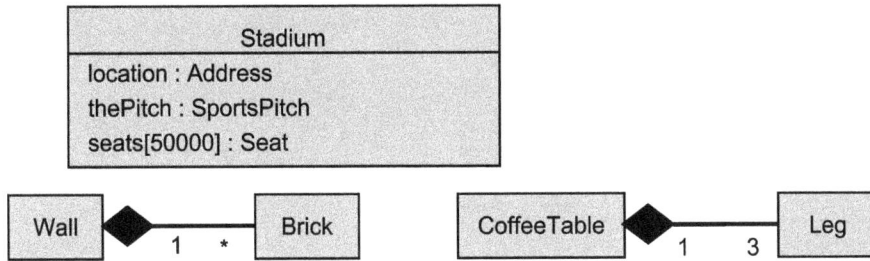

Fig.2.42 Composition

The following discussion gives various examples for classes and their relationships.

**Examples:**

1. The figure below contains a small portion of the model built for Evolution of Species on Planet Earth.

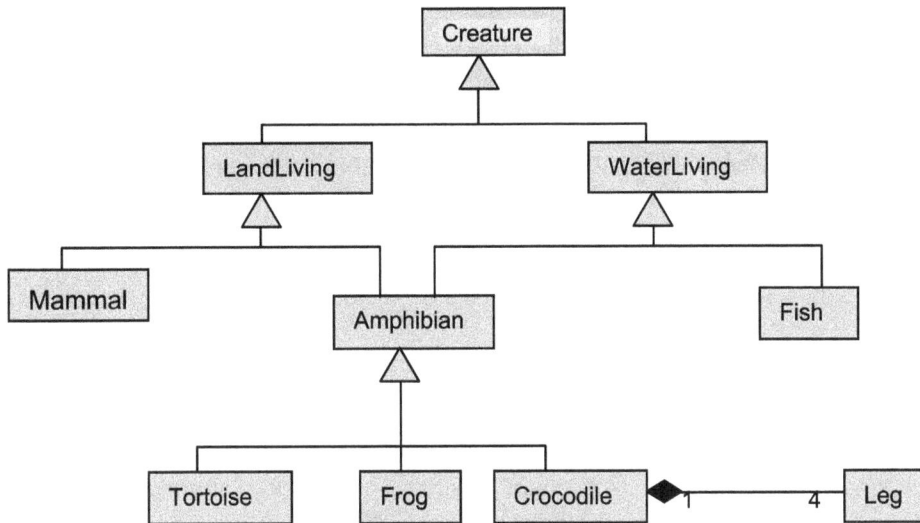

Fig.2.43 Class Diagram

**Explanation:** The above figure contains classes with generalization and composition relationships. LandLiving and WaterLiving things are a kind of creatures. A Mammal is a land living creature and a Fish is a water living creature. But an Amphibian is the derived class of both water living and land living creatures. A crocodile is a kind of amphibian which has four legs. If the crocodile dies, its legs die or have no significance, that is why the relationship between Crocodile class and Leg class is composition.

**2.** The figure below gives you a fragment of a model developed for playing any game.

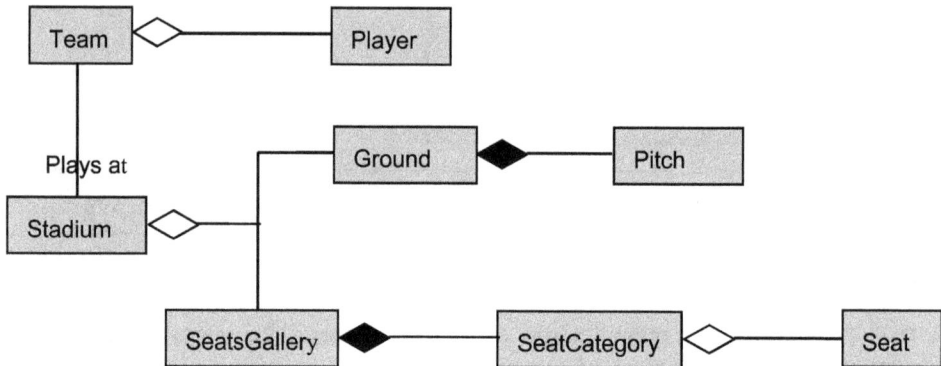

**Fig.2.44** Class Diagram

**Explanation:** In the above diagram, a Player is a part of the Team, that is why there is an aggregation relationship between classes Team and Player. Team is a whole, where as Player is a part of team. Team plays in a Stadium, indicating an association between Team and Stadium. The Stadium is an aggregation of Ground and SeatsGallery. Whereas Pitch is strongly dependent on Ground, meaning if Ground is destroyed, the Pitch is also destroyed. That is why composition relationship among Ground and Pitch, as well as SeatsGallery and SeatCategory. Here, SeatCategory means individual compartments having different comfort levels for the spectators.

**3.** The following figure indicates a part of the model built for a banking system.

**Explanation:** The below figure depicts various kinds of relationships among classes. There is an aggregation relationship between a Bank (whole) and its Branches (parts). BankAccount depends on the Bank, hence dependency between Bank and BankAccount classes. A branch manager has no significance when there is no branch, hence composition relationship between Branch and BranchManager classes. Similarly composition relationship among Bank and BankManager classes. Bank Account can be of two types, either it can be PersonalAccount, where an account holder is an individual, or it can be CorporateAccount, where the account holder is a corporation.

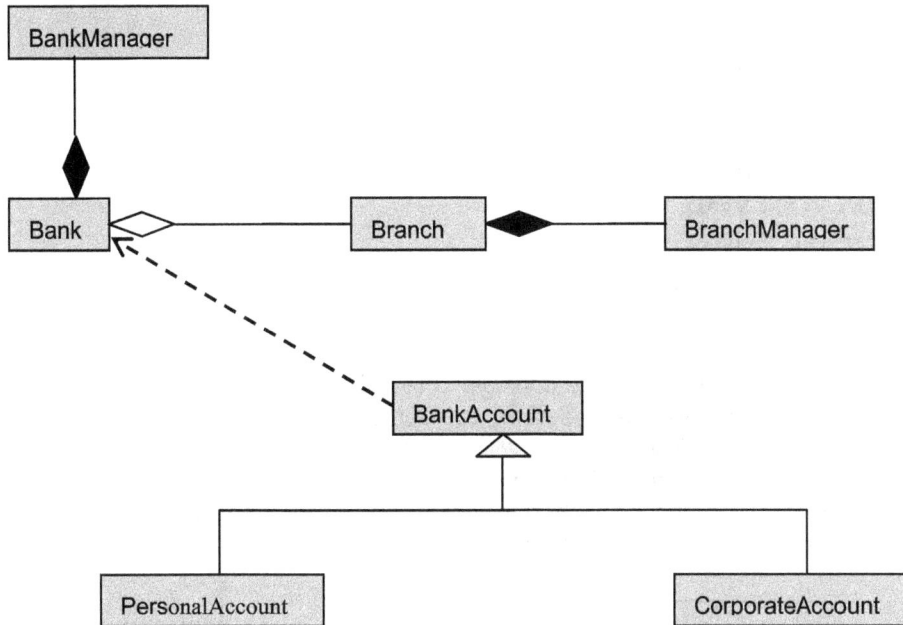

**Fig.2.45** Class Diagram

Hope, you have sufficient understanding of relationships among structural elements, such as classes.

## 2.11 Modeling Simple Dependencies

The more general kind of dependency relationship is the connection between a class and another class which is used as a parameter in the formal class's operation. This is also called using relationship. In order to model this relationship, create a connection pointing from the class with the operation to the class used as a parameter in the operation. The following example indicates how dependency can be established. Let us consider a system where courses and various other schedules are drawn based on registrations of students in a university.

In the following figure, there is dependency between the classes CourseSchedule and the class Course, because Course class is used as a parameter for operations add and remove belonging to the CourseSchedule class.

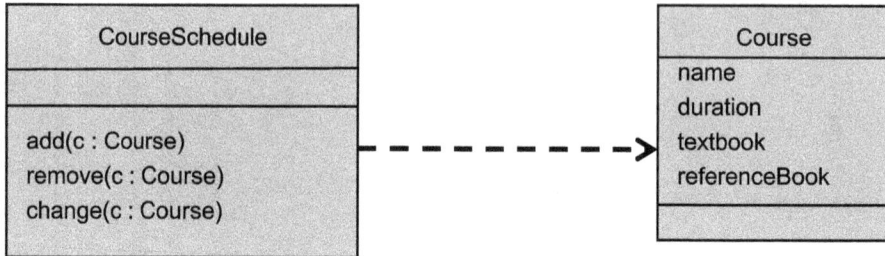

**Fig.2.46** Dependency (example)

As another example, let us consider a real life situation where you go to a shopping mall and add various items to your Shopping Cart. If you model this context using UML, ShoppingCart will be a class dependent on the Item class, because you go on adding items which you want to purchase into a shopping cart. You may remove or exchange items you do not want to purchase. This whole scenario can be described by the dependency relationship as follows:

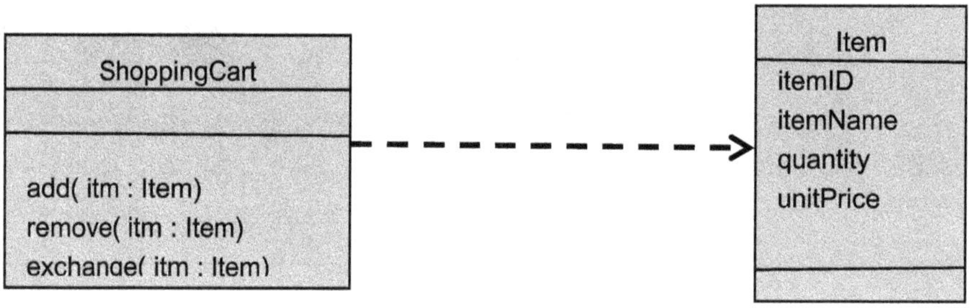

**Fig.2.47** Dependency (example)

As another example, consider diagnosis of a patient in any diagnostic centre. The patient might be asked to undergo some sample tests such as blood or urine examination. The doctor diagnose patient based on the results of the sample examinations. A model describing the diagnosis of a doctor can be given as dependency between two classes, one depicting the diagnosis and another depicting samples' test results. It can be graphically represented as follows:-

**Fig.2.48** Dependency (example)

## 2.12   Modeling Single Inheritance

In UML inheritance is the relationship between the general and more specific classes. That is why this relation is also called generalization/specialization relationship. The major purpose of inheritance in object oriented concepts is to facilitate reusability. The class from which inheritance happens is called parent class or base class, and the class which inherits is called child class or derived class. If there is only one base class and one or more derived classes, that type of inheritance is called single inheritance.

While you are modeling abstractions from your problem domain, you find many classes that cluster together based on their structural, behavioral and semantic similarities. These classes having common structural and behavioral features can be included in inheritance relationship. It can happen by extracting common features and associating them with general classes, from which specialized classes can be inherited.

The various steps involved to model inheritance relationship are as follows:

❖ Based on the set of classes that are abstracted from the problem domain, look for responsibilities, attributes and operations that are common among two or more classes.

❖ Associate these common responsibilities, attributes and operations to a more general class. You can also assign these elements to a new class if it is needed, but be careful about introducing too many levels of inheritance, which makes the implementation tougher.

❖ Identify specialized features and create more specific classes containing common information in generalized ones. Push up generalized classes as parent classes, pull down specialized classes as child classes which inherit from the parent classes.

❖ Establish generalization relationship that is drawn from specialized child classes to its more general parent.

Let us consider a university application, where inheritance happens among classes. A Person class is a more general class containing common information general to all persons who are directly or indirectly connected to the university. We also know that inheritance is "is a kind of" relation. In the following figure, we have person as a general class, Student and Faculty as more specialized ones. There are additional inherited classes even from Student class, as well as from Faculty class. The figure is very much self explanatory of inheritance relationship.

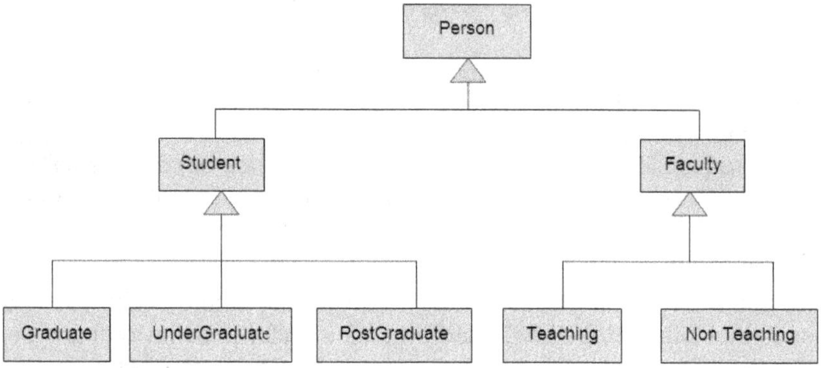

**Fig.2.49** Single Inheritance

## 2.13 Modeling Structural Relationships

In UML class diagrams, an association is a structural relationship in which objects of one classifier (class or interface) are connected and can navigate to objects of another classifier. Associations help you make decisions about the structure of the data. Association supports data sharing between classes. In the case of a self association, data is shared between the objects of the same class.

When you are modeling dependencies or generalizations, you model classes that represent different level of abstractions. If a class depends on the another class, that means, classes are in dependency relationship, the independent class has no idea of its dependent class. Similarly, in inheritance relationship, the children are derived from the definition of a parent, but the parent has no knowledge of its children. This indicates that these kind of relationships are unidirectional or one sided.

When you have association between two classes, it means that, both the classes relay on each other in some way and both the classes are at the same level of importance (peers). In association, you can navigate from one classifier to another in both directions. As we are aware that dependency is a using relationship, and generalization is "is a kind of" relationship, an association is a structural connection across which the objects of the classes interact.

The various steps involved in modeling structural relationships are discussed below:

❖ For a pair of classes, if you need to navigate from objects of one to objects of another, establish an association between the two.

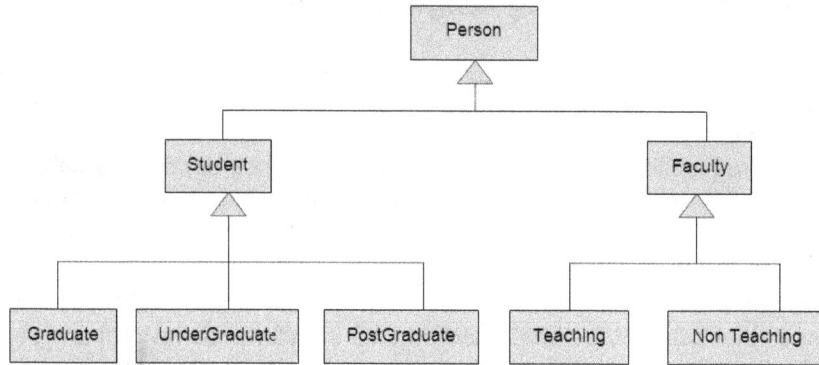

❖ For a pair of classes, if objects of one class need to interact with the objects of the other class other than as parameters to an operation, establish an association between the two.

❖ For each of identified associations, specify multiplicity as well as role names at association ends to adorn the relationship.

❖ If the association between the classes is such that one class is a whole containing other classes as its parts, then transform the association to be an aggregation relationship.

The following figure is a small part of the model built for any organization or any enterprise.

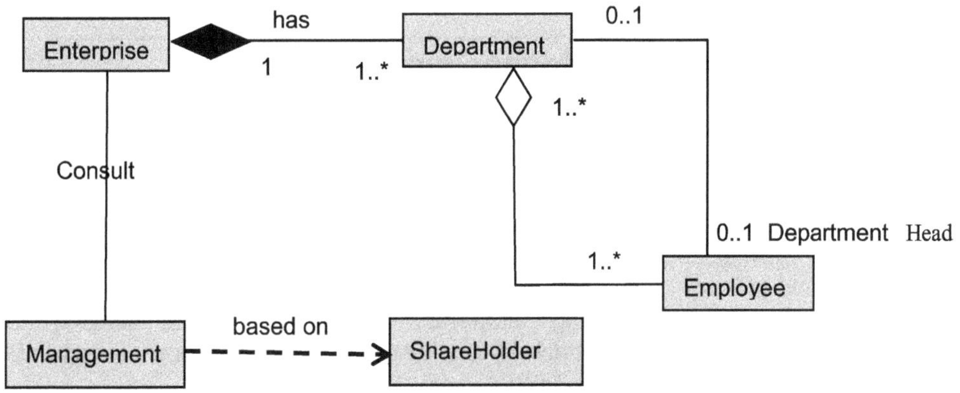

**Fig.2.50** Structural Relationships

## Explanation

The above figure represents dependency, association, and the two variants of association, such as aggregation and composition relationships. An enterprise will have departments. A department cannot exist without an associated enterprise, meaning an enterprise and its departments are very closely related having similar life spans. So, the relationship between an enterprise and its departments is a composition. The multiplicity of this composition specifies that an enterprise can have one or more departments.

Similarly, a department contains employees working for it. One of the employees in the department becomes the department head. Because of this, there are two kinds of relationships are possible between the classes, department and employee. The relationship between department and employee is an aggregation, as employees working for a company can form parts of the department, establishing whole/part relationship between Department and Employee classes. An employee may belong to more than one department, a department may have more than one employee, hence the multiplicity specification.

Similarly we have an association relationship between department and department head. Department head is an employee belonging to the department. So, there is also association between Department and Employee classes with multiplicity specifying a department can have only one head or no head at all, and an employee can become a head for only one department, or he may not be a head at all.

An enterprise always works by consulting the management. So, there is a plain association relationship between the classes Enterprise and Management. Whatever business decisions the management makes depends on the views expressed by the share holders of the company .Hence dependency relationship between classes Management and ShareHolder, pointing towards the class named ShareHolder.

## 2.14 Common Mechanisms

We have already discussed about common mechanisms; specifications, adornments, common divisions, and extensibility mechanisms. Here, we discuss extensively adornments and extensibility mechanisms. The most important of all adornments is a Note. A note is graphically rendered as a rectangle with a dog eared corner. A note contains textual or graphical explanations of model elements. In fact, these are the comments explaining the purpose of various modeling elements, making the model simpler to understand. A note can be attached to a single element or group of elements based on the context of the model.

Extensibility mechanisms in UML, permit you to extend the language in controlled ways. By using these extensibility mechanisms, you can tailor UML to the specific needs of your application domain. These mechanisms include stereotypes, tagged values, and constraints. A stereotype is used to create new kinds of building blocks specific to your problem scope. We use stereotypes when there is no standard building block is available in UML to represent elements. A tagged value extends the properties and provides additional information about the UML building blocks. Here, the building block can be a standard one available in UML or a new one created by applying stereotypes. A constraint extends the specification of a UML building block by adding new rules or extending the existing rules. A rule can be a condition which should be met by an element of a UML model.

A note typically contains comments attached to an element or a group of elements. A note is adorned with a textual or a graphical information. During a note specification, you can attach simple text, an embedded URL, and also link to an another document. The graphical representations are as follows:

**Simple Text**

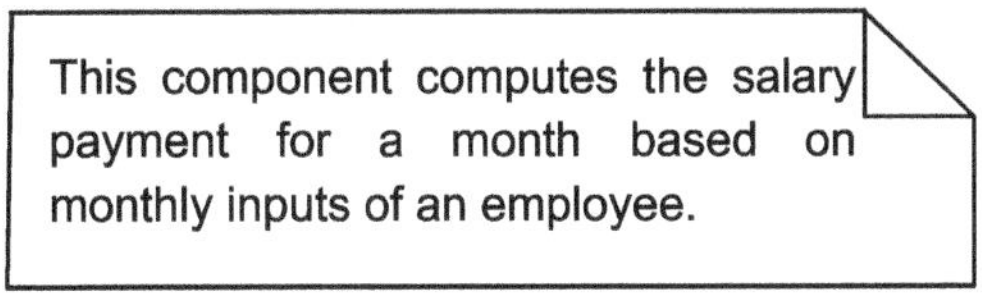

This component computes the salary payment for a month based on monthly inputs of an employee.

**Link to a Document**

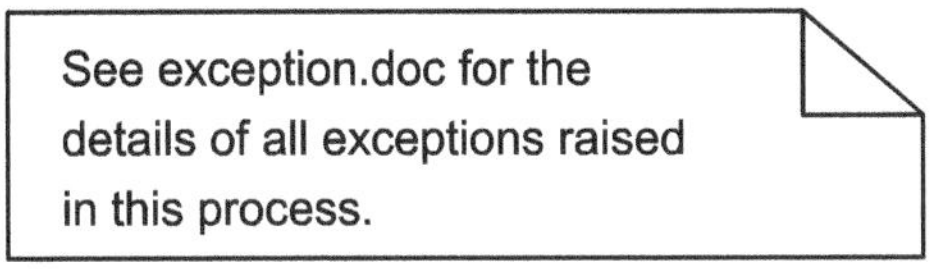

See exception.doc for the details of all exceptions raised in this process.

**Embedded URL**

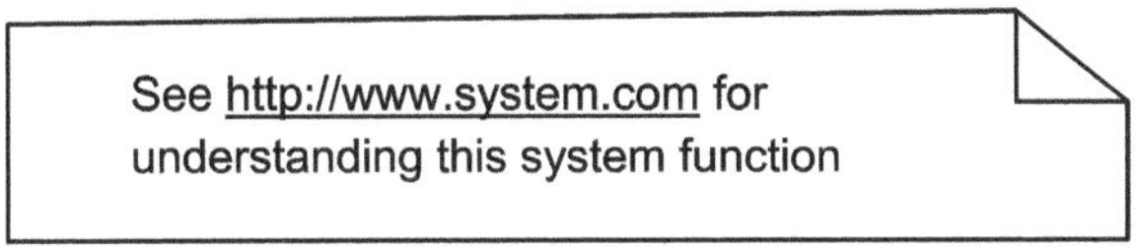

See http://www.system.com for understanding this system function

**Fig.2.51** Specifying Notes

We use notes to attach additional information to a model. Notes are the mechanism provided by the UML to let you capture arbitrary comments and constraints to help illuminate the models you've created. Notes may represent artifacts that play an important role in the software development life cycle, such as requirements, or they may simply represent free-form observations, reviews, or explanations. A note that renders a comment has no semantic impact, meaning that its contents do not alter the meaning of the model to which it is attached. Notes may be attached to more than one element by using dependencies. A note may contain any combination of text or graphics. Most adornments are rendered by placing text near the element of interest or by adding a graphic symbol to the basic notation.

## Other Adornments

Adornments are additional textual or graphical information included in the element's specification to better understand the element. Adornments are graphically rendered by placing text or a graphical notation to the basic notation of an element. Sometimes you can also attach extra compartment to describe the very purpose of classes, components, and nodes. The following figure gives some examples.

## Stereotypes

A stereotype extends the vocabulary of the UML, allowing you to create new kinds of building blocks that are derived from existing ones .When you stereotype an element such as a node or a class, you are in effect extending the UML by creating a new building block just like an existing one but with its own special properties (each stereotype may provide its own set of tagged values), semantics (each stereotype may provide its own constraints), and notation (each stereotype may provide its own icon).

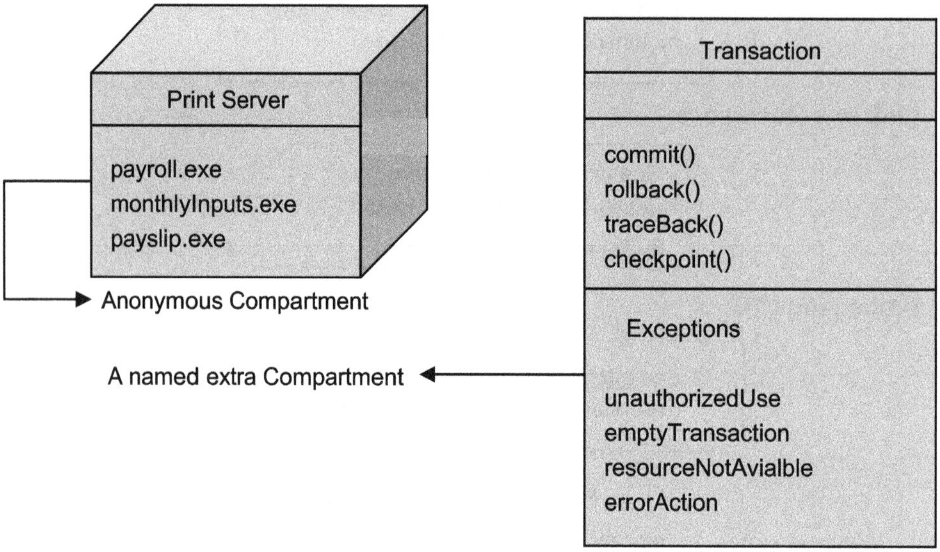

**Fig.2.52** Extra Compartments

In its simplest form, a stereotype is rendered as a name enclosed by guillemets and placed above the name of another element. As a visual cue, you may define an icon for the stereotype and render that icon to the right of the name (if you are using the basic notation for the element) or use that icon as the basic symbol for the stereotyped item.

Stereotype servlet applied to the model element SearchServlet can be as follows:-

**Fig.2.53** Applying Stereotypes

When a stereotype includes the definition of an icon, this icon can be graphically attached to the model elements extended by the stereotype. Every model element that has a graphical presentation can have an attached icon. When a model element is extended by one single stereotype the icon can be presented in a reduced shape, inside and on top of the box representing the model element. The above second figure with an icon is an example for this.

When stereotype is applied, the whole classifier box can be replaced by enlarged icon of the stereotype. The above third figure is example for this.

If multiple stereotypes are applied to the same element, the names of the applied stereotypes are shown as a comma-separated list within a pair of guillemets. When the extended model element has a keyword, then the stereotype name could be displayed close to the keyword, within separate guillemets.

**Example:**

**Fig.2.54** Extended Stereotypes

## Tagged Values

Every element in the UML has its own set of properties. With stereotypes , you can add new things to the UML, with tagged values, you can attach new properties. Typically a tagged value extends the properties of a UML building block, allowing you to create new information in that element's specification. If you are part of your project's release team, responsible for assembling, testing, and then deploying releases, you might want to keep track of the version number and test results for each major subsystem. You can use tagged values to add this information to your models.

**Example:**

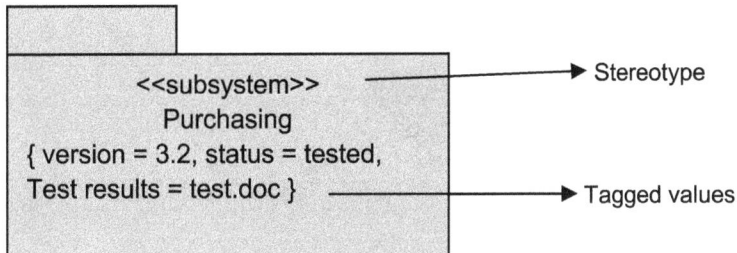

**Fig.2.55** Tagged Values

You can define tags for existing elements of the UML, or you can define tags that apply to individual stereotypes so that everything with that stereotype has that tagged value. A tagged value is not the same as a class attribute. Rather, you can think of a tagged value as metadata because its value applies to the element itself, but not to its instances.

One of the most common uses of tagged values is to specify properties that are relevant to code generation or configuration management. For example, you can use tagged values to specify the programming language to which you map a particular class. Similarly, you can use tagged values to specify the author and version of a component.

**Examples:**

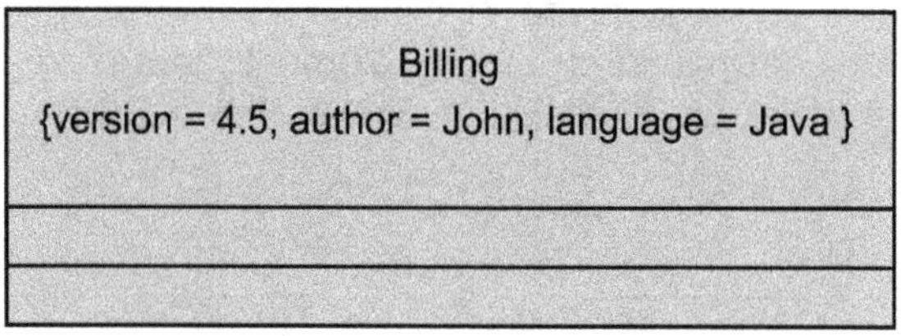

**Fig.2.56** Billing Class with Tagged Values

**Examples:**

1. You might want to specify the number of processors installed on each kind of node in a deployment diagram.

2. You might want to require that every component be stereotyped as a library if it is intended to be deployed on a client or a server.

The above examples can be graphically represented as follows:

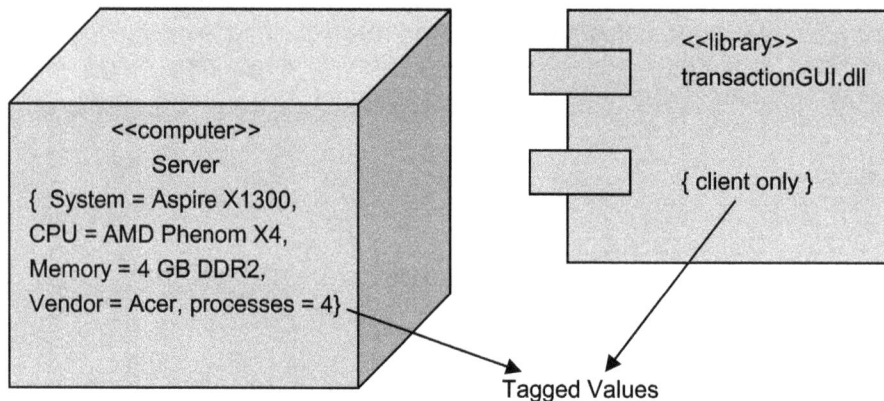

**Fig.2.57** Tagged Values for a Node and Component

## Constraints

A constraint extends the semantics of a UML building block, allowing you to add new rules or modify existing ones. A constraint specifies conditions that must be held true for the model to be well-formed. If you are modeling hard real time systems, you might want to adorn your models with information about time budgets and deadlines; you can use constraints to capture these timing requirements.

A constraint specifies conditions and propositions that must be maintained as true. A constraint is placed directly after the element it applies to (e.g., attribute), with a dashed arrow connecting elements concerned, or in a comment box. A constraint is placed always in {} (opening and closing braces).

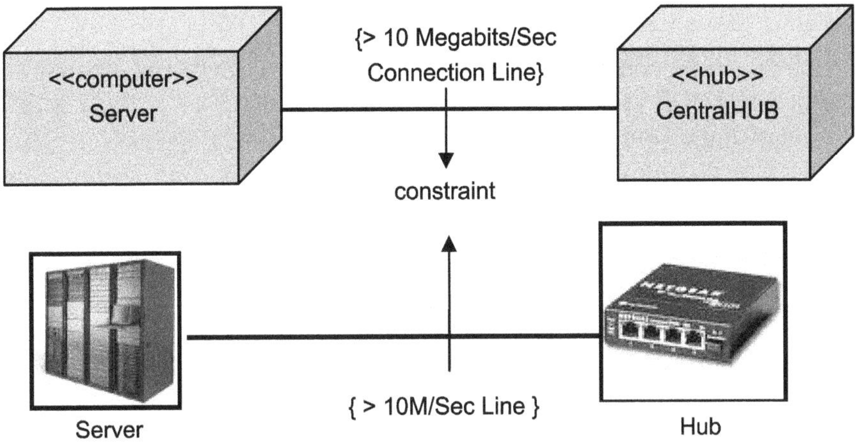

**Fig.2.58** Constraints

**Note :** The transmission speed of the network cable connecting server and central hub is shown.

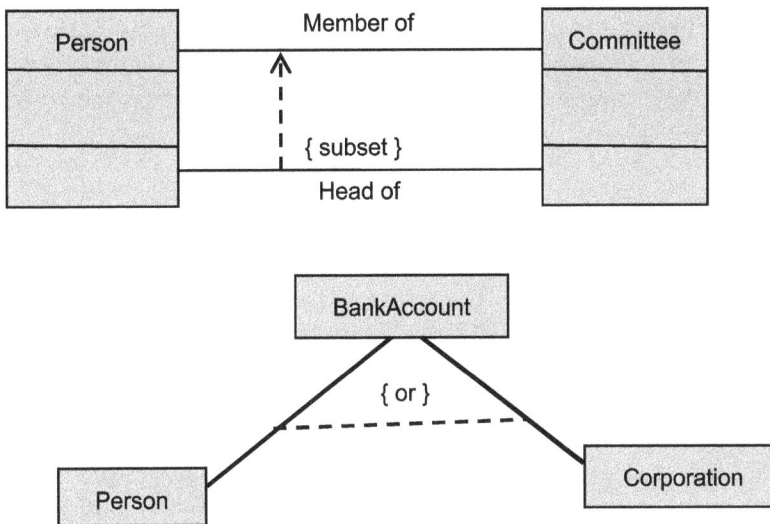

**Fig.2.59** Constraints across Relationships

**Explanation**

In the above first figure, two associations are shown between Person and Committee classes. The association, Person is a member of Committee with respective multiplicity is shown. Similarly, the association, one person among the members of the committee becoming head of the committee is between Person and Committee classes. The constraint {subset} indicates that the association head of is a subset of the association member of, as shown by the direction of dependency.

In the above second figure, there are two kinds of associations, one between BankAccount and Person and another between BankAccount and Corporation. The constraint {or} indicates that only one of the associations exist at a time.

## ⟫ 2.15 Modeling Comments

The major application of notes in any UML model is to write down free form observations, reviews, or explanations. Including comments in a model improves the understanding of it. The notes can be used to visualize requirements. By using notes you can tie system requirements to the parts of the model which improves the quality of the model. The following discussion describes various steps involved in modeling comments in any UML model.

❖ Create a note, and place plain text in it describing the corresponding element of the model. Attach this note to its referring element by placing it adjacent to the element. You can graphically show this relationship, by connecting a note to its elements using dependency relationship.

❖ In an UML model, you can hide or make visible the elements of your model. Similarly, you need not make your comments always visible whenever you make your elements visible. Rather, you can only make visible the relevant comments of your elements that suits the context you are referring.

❖ If you include lengthy text as a comment, it is better to include that text in a separate file, and establish link to that file from your note or indicate where the file is available.

As your system development process is iterative and incremental, your model also evolves with time. Use comments to record significant decisions you make, because they cannot be directly inferred from the model itself.

**Explanation:** The below figure is a fragment of the model for course registration system in a university. A student registers for courses. A student can register a minimum of four courses and a maximum of six courses. The university registrar records student registrations after collecting fee from them. Here, the class named CourseRegistration is the result of the association between Student and Course classes. The technical assistant collects information about courses and their respective instructors and physically arranges the seminars for the courses. Students attend their registered course seminars.

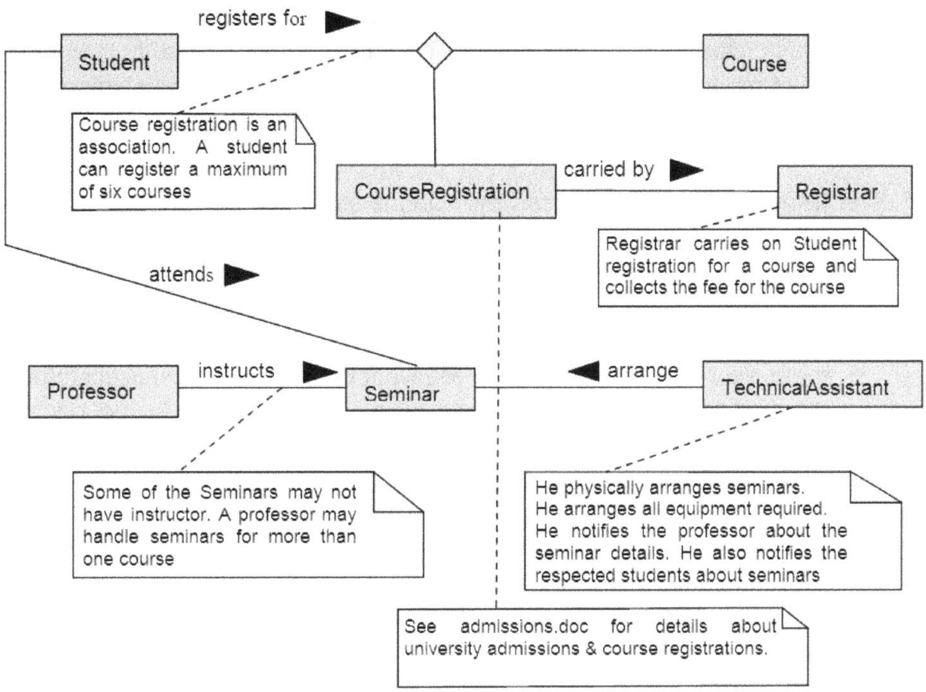

**Fig.2.60** Modeling Comments

## 2.16 Modeling New Building Blocks

The standard building blocks of UML, such as classes, interfaces, collaborations, components, nodes, associations and others are sufficient enough to build models. Whenever you want to extend your modeling elements, or creating new building blocks, we require a special mechanism named stereotypes. We use stereotypes to represent new visual cues to the elements which cannot be represented by standard UML building blocks.

A stereotype denotes a variation on an existing modeling element with the same form but with a modified intent. Stereotypes are effectively used to extend the UML in a consistent manner. UML Stereotype is a mechanism to categorize an element in some way. A stereotype name is surrounded by Gulliments <<>>.

You might have defined a standard UML element such as a class, interface, an association etc. but still you are not able to provide full information like the type of the class (<<entity>> , <<processclass>> ) or you have applied certain patterns to the class, or the class denoted is an interface. In such cases, you can specify stereotypes which explain these functionalities.

Stereotypes are used to classify and extend associations, inheritance relationships, classes and components. They provide the capability to create a new kind of modeling element. Stereotypes must be   based on elements that are part of the UML meta model. Some common stereotypes for a class are entity, boundary, control, utility and exception etc.

The following section discusses the various steps involved in modeling new building blocks:

- ❖ If you find that there is no standard way of representing certain elements which you find in your problem domain, try to find out ways to represent them using standard stereotypes.
- ❖ If you are sure that the element you want to model is not possible through standard UML, create a new stereotype and attach it to the primitive things in UML, such as  class, interface, component, node, association, and so on. You can also define hierarchies of stereotypes, so that there are general kind of stereotypes along with their special types.
- ❖ If the element being stereotyped has additional properties and semantics, define them using tagged values and constraints for that element.
- ❖ If you want your stereotyped element to have a distinct visual cue, define a new icon for it.

Stereotypes signify a special use or intent and can be applied to almost any element of UML notation. They modify the meaning of an element and describe the element's role within your model.

**Examples:**

1. Stereotype applied to a class:

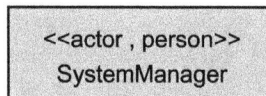

&lt;&lt;actor , person&gt;&gt;<br>
SystemManager

**Fig.2.61 (a)**  A class Stereotype

2. Stereotypes applied to a class:

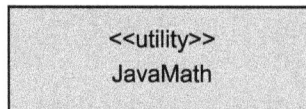

&lt;&lt;utility&gt;&gt;<br>
JavaMath

**Fig.2.61 (b)**  A Class Stereotype

**Note:** Represents a class that provides utility services through static method.

3. Stereotypes applied to a component:

**Fig.2.61 (c)**  A Component Stereotype

**Note:** A stateless, functional component that computes a value; could be used to represent a web service.

4. Stereotypes applied to a component:

**Fig.2.61 (d)**  A Component Stereotype

**Note:** A large component that is actually a subordinate system of larger system.

5.  Stereotypes applied to artifacts:

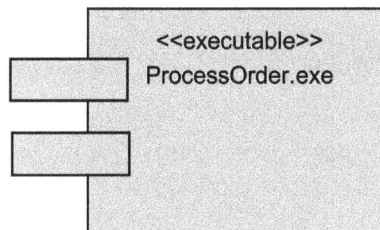

**Fig.2.61 (e)**  An Executable Component

**Note:** ProcessOrder is an executable file.

6.  Stereotypes applied to artifacts:

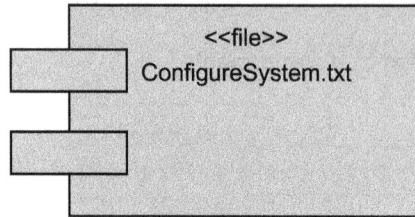

**Fig. 2.61 (f)** A File Stereotype

**Note:** A physical file used by your system; this could be a configuration file or a help file such as a .txt file.

7. Stereotypes applied to artifacts:-

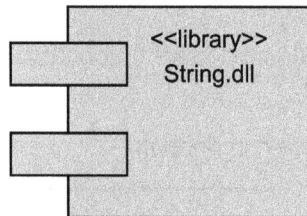

**Fig.2.61 (g)** A Library File Stereotype

**Note:** A static or dynamic library file; you could use this to model .dll or .jar library files.

8. Stereotypes applied to artifacts:

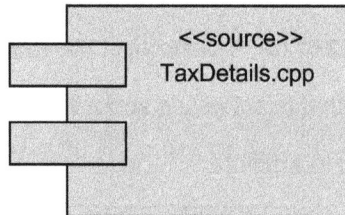

**Fig.2.61 (h)** A Source Code File Stereotype

**Note:** A source file containing code, such a .java or .cpp file.

Stereotypes can contain extra information that relates to the element to which they are applied. This extra information is specified using tagged values. UML has certain standard model element stereotypes which we discuss extensively in the coming chapters. You can also associate stereotypes with relationships as well as with attributes and operations of a class. Stereotypes are applicable to organizing attributes and operations in a class. The following examples illustrate the use of stereotypes.

**Example:**

```
                   <<business domain>>
                        Customer
─────────────────────────────────────────────────
<<unique ID>>  #customerNumber : Integer
-homeAddress : Address
-name : String
─────────────────────────────────────────────────
<<constructor>>  +Customer() : Customer
<<search>>  +findAllInstances() : Vector
<<search>>  +findForID(customerNumber) : Vector
<<search>>  +findForOrder(order) : Vector
<<getter>>  +getTotalBusiness(sinceDate) : Currency  { default = 0 }
+scheduleShipment(forDate) : Shipment
```

**Fig.2.62** Indicating Stereotypes

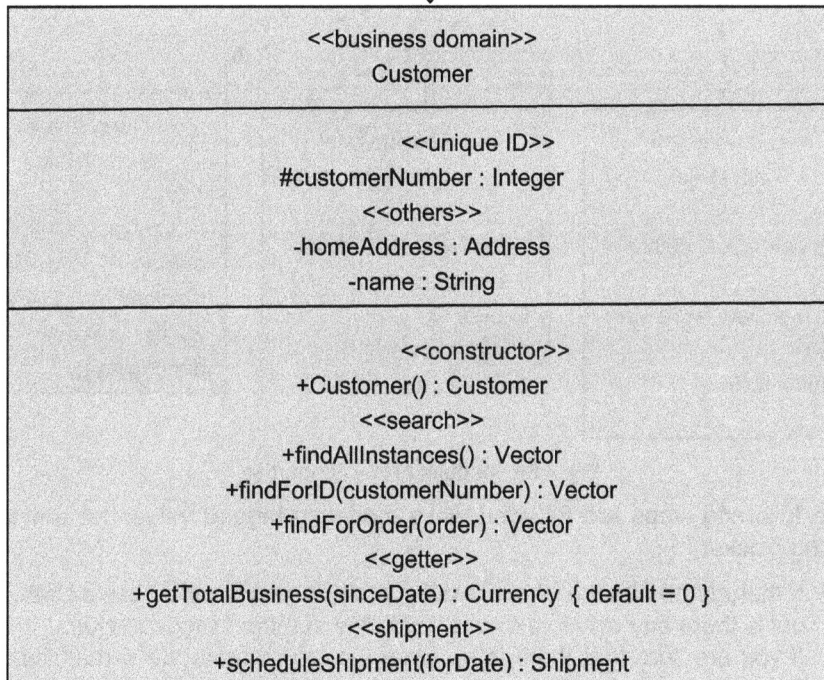

```
                   <<business domain>>
                        Customer
─────────────────────────────────────────────────
                    <<unique ID>>
                #customerNumber : Integer
                      <<others>>
                 -homeAddress : Address
                    -name : String
─────────────────────────────────────────────────
                   <<constructor>>
                +Customer() : Customer
                     <<search>>
                +findAllInstances() : Vector
           +findForID(customerNumber) : Vector
              +findForOrder(order) : Vector
                     <<getter>>
     +getTotalBusiness(sinceDate) : Currency  { default = 0 }
                    <<shipment>>
           +scheduleShipment(forDate) : Shipment
```

**Fig.2.63** Organizing Attributes and Operations

## 2.17 Modeling New Properties

The basic properties of the UML's building blocks are very much enough to address most of the things of your model. If you want to extend these properties of the basic building blocks or the new building blocks created by using stereotypes, you need to use tagged values. The very purpose of tagged values is to model new properties for the UML elements.

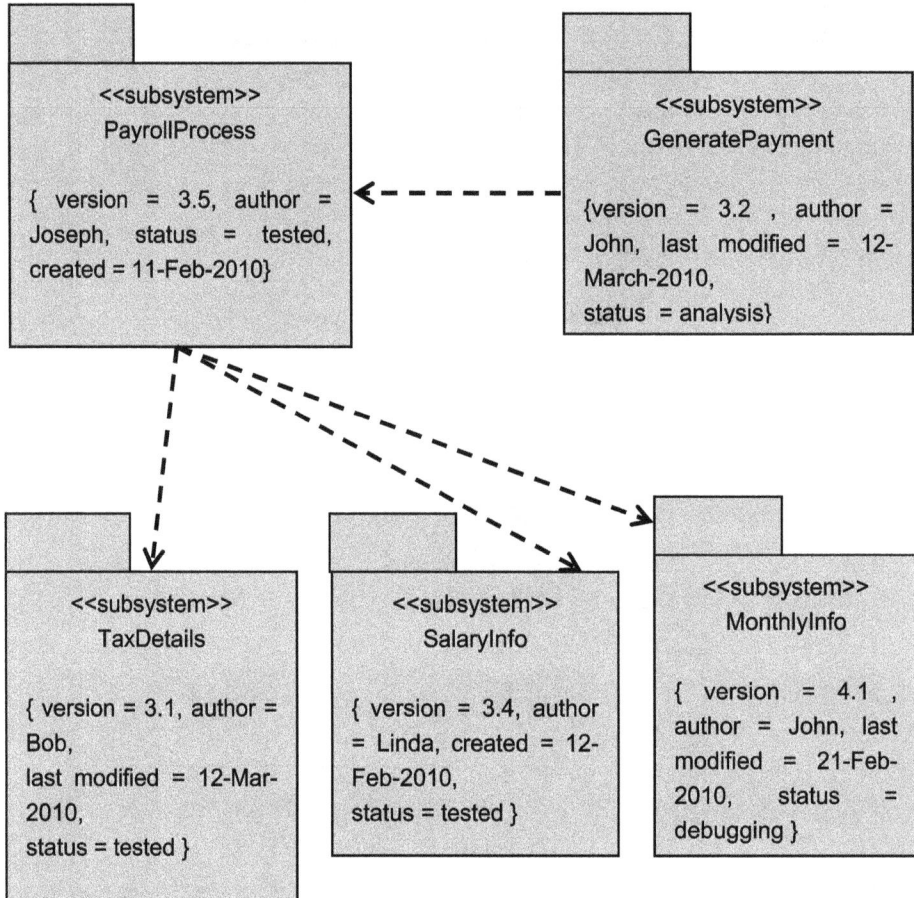

**Fig.2.64** Modeling New Properties

The following steps are followed while modeling tagged values for any UML building blocks:

❖ If there is no chance of expressing what do you want by basic UML, find out is there any way to express it with the standard tagged values.

❖ If you are sure that there is no other way to express the semantics, add this new property as a tagged value to a basic UML building block or newly created building blocks using stereotypes.

**Example:** Suppose you want to attach your model to your project's configuration management system. As the software development process is iterative and incremental, it is mandatory to maintain additional information for each sub system that are contained in a system. The following diagram is a fragment of the model developed for any payroll system of any enterprise. This model contains subsystems such as PayrollProcess, MonthlyInfo, SalaryInfo, TaxDetails, GeneratePayment etc.

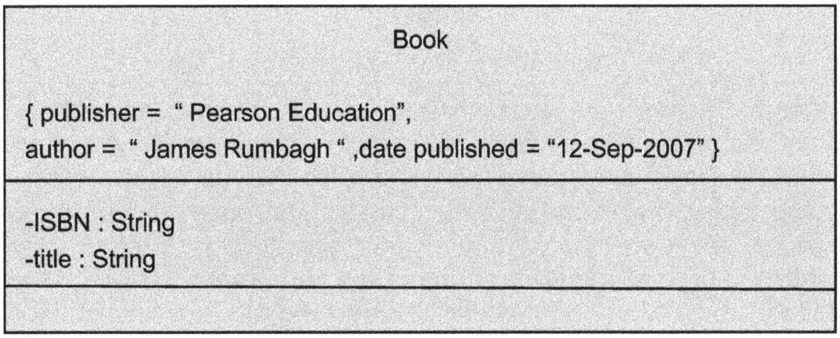

```
                              Book

{ publisher = " Pearson Education",
  author = " James Rumbagh " ,date published = "12-Sep-2007" }

-ISBN : String
-title : String


```

**Fig.2.65** Modeling New Properties

## 2.18  Modeling New Semantics

Whenever you build a model using UML, you always work within the rules of UML. These rules help others who are linked with the model, to better understand the intent of the model. Suppose you want to attach new semantics, new rules, or modifying the existing rules, then you need to define constraints. Constraints is the way of modelling new semantics that are not supported by standard UML. The following topic discusses the step by step procedure of modeling new semantics:

❖ Make sure that there is no standard mechanism available in UML to model your intended purpose. Find out, are there any ways to use standard constraints to express your intensions.

❖ If you are sure that there is no way to express your intension by using any of your standard UML elements, write your new semantics as text in a constraint and place it adjacent to the element to which it refers. You can specify a constraint more explicitly by attaching it with its respective element by using dependency relationship.

If you want to model new semantics more formally, then you can use OCL (Object Constraint Language).

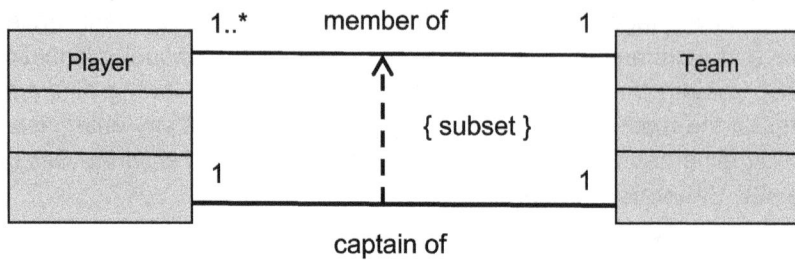

**Fig.2.66** Modeling New Semantics

**Explanation:** The above diagram shows that each Player is a member of only one team, and each Team contains one or more Players. A Player is a member of Team. One Player among the Team members will become a captain. There is only one captain for a team, a captain can lead only one team. There are two associations, one is member of and another is captain of. In order to express the fact that captain of the team is one of the players of the team, we are not provided with any UML standard definitions. So, we use a constraint { subset } , indicating that a captain is the subset of members of the team.

## 2.19 Diagrams

When you model a system, you simplify reality so that you can better understand the system. We generally build our models using basic UML building blocks, such as classes, interfaces, collaborations, components, nodes, dependencies, generalizations, and associations. Diagrams typically include all these building blocks representing the model of the system under development. These diagrams are helpful in understanding the system from different perspectives. Because we cannot understand the system in its entirety without having multiple views of it. UML supports number of diagrams, so that you can focus on different aspects of the system independently.

Good diagrams comfort you in understanding and approaching the system you are developing. In any software system, there are five complementary views which are helpful in visualizing, specifying, constructing and documenting. The five views are; the use case view, the design view, the process view, the implementation view, and the deployment view. Each of these views involve structural as well as behavioral elements.

Diagrams make us to organize the various system elements so as to understand the system from different aspects. As an example, the static aspects of implementation view, can be known from component diagrams, and its dynamic aspects can be known from interaction diagrams. The major application of these UML diagrams is to construct executable systems from models (forward engineering), or to build models from the executable system (reverse engineering). However, these diagrams creation is not a single step process, but an iterative and incremental one.

A system is a collection of subsystems arranged in a fashion to accomplish a particular purpose. You can describe the system, by means of a set of models, where each model expressing a different view point or a different aspect of the system. A model is a semantically closed abstraction of a system, meaning, it represents the simplification of reality for better understanding of the system. A diagram is a graph representing the elements that constitute your system, and how they are connected.

The static part of the system can be viewed from the following four diagrams.

- ❖ Class Diagram
- ❖ Object Diagram
- ❖ Component Diagram
- ❖ Deployment Diagram

To view the dynamic aspect of the system, we use these five diagrams.

- ❖ Use case Diagram
- ❖ Sequence Diagram
- ❖ Collaboration Diagram
- ❖ State chart Diagram
- ❖ Activity Diagram

## 2.20  Structural Diagrams

The UML's structural diagrams are used to visualize, specify, construct, and document the static aspects of a system. These diagrams include the elements such as, classes, interfaces, collaborations, components, and nodes. Structure diagrams emphasize the things that must be present in the system being modeled. Since structure diagrams represent the structure, they are used extensively in documenting the architecture of software systems. The UML's structural diagrams are organized around the things when you build a model for a system.

- ❖ Class Diagram include classes, interfaces, and collaborations.
- ❖ Object Diagram include objects.
- ❖ Component Diagram include components.
- ❖ Deployment Diagram include nodes.

### Class Diagram

A class diagram depicts a set of classes, interfaces, and collaborations and their relationships. You build class diagram to understand the static design view of a system. A class diagram with active classes represent the static process view of a system. A class diagram may contain objects and packages and their interrelationships. Class diagrams also display relationships such as containment, inheritance, associations and others.

**Example:**

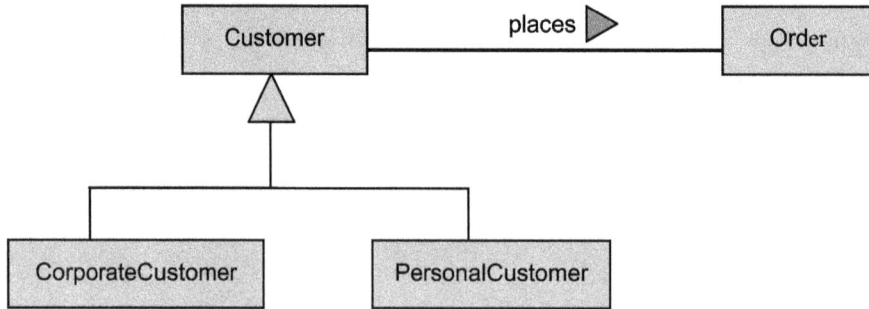

## Object Diagram

Depicts objects and their relationships at a point in time, typically a special case of either a class diagram or a communication diagram. This diagram shows a set of objects and their inter links. It gives a static snapshot of the instance of the class diagram. It addresses static design view or static process view of the system.

**Explanation:** The below figure gives an object diagram of using an ATM machine. It gives a snapshot of object interactions of using ATM machine by a customer at a particular instant of time.

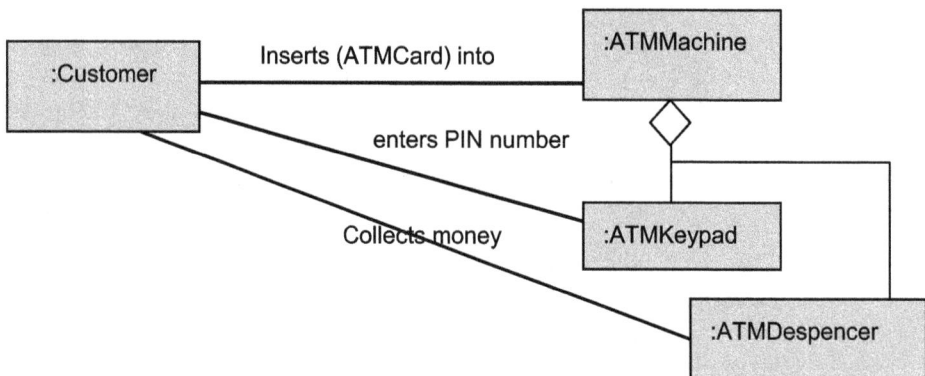

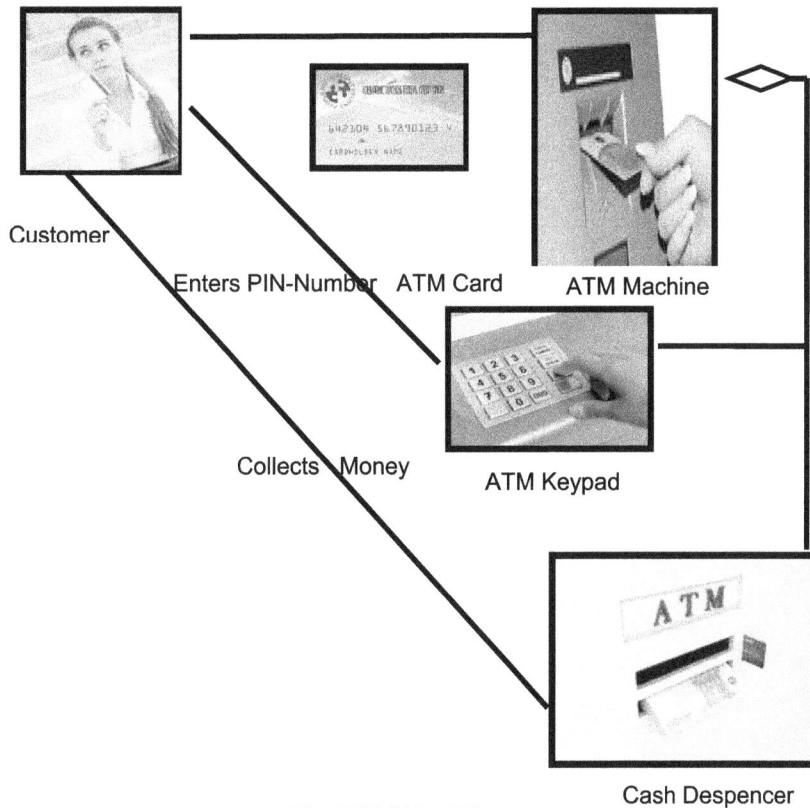

**Fig.2.67** Object Diagram

**Note :** The above figure is a snapshot of an ATM transaction at a given point of time. It is an object diagram.

## Component Diagram

This diagram shows a set of components and their relationships. Component diagram depicts the static implementation view of a  system. A component may map to one or more classes, interfaces, and collaborations. This diagram depicts the components that compose an application, system, or enterprise. This diagram describes the components, their interrelationships, interactions, and their public interfaces.

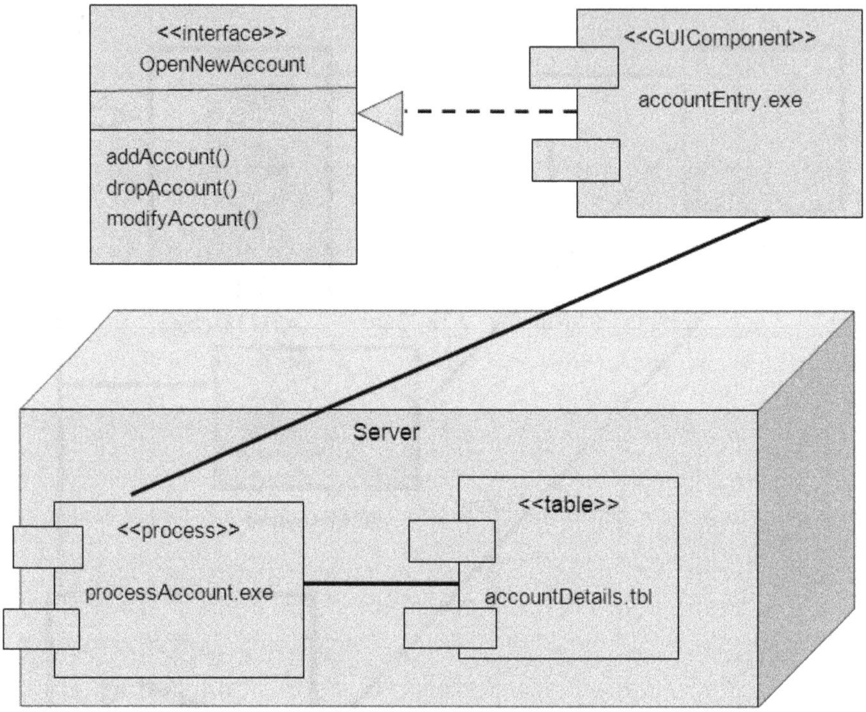

**Fig.2.68** Component Diagram

**Note:** The above diagram shows a small part of a model for a banking system. The OpenNewAccount interface is implemented by the component named accountEntry, which is an executable file. After accepting the account details the account information is processed for verification by the component named processAccount which is an executable file and resides on server machine. If the account information is valid, then a new account is opened and all the details of the new account are placed in a database table component named accountDetails which also resides on the server machine.

## Deployment Diagram

This diagram includes a set of nodes and their physical connections. The deployment diagram gives the static deployment view of the system. A node may contain one or more components that constitute your system. A deployment diagram shows the execution architecture of a system. This includes nodes, either hardware or software execution environments, as well as hardware topology such as client/server or multitier architectures on which your system runs.

**Example:**

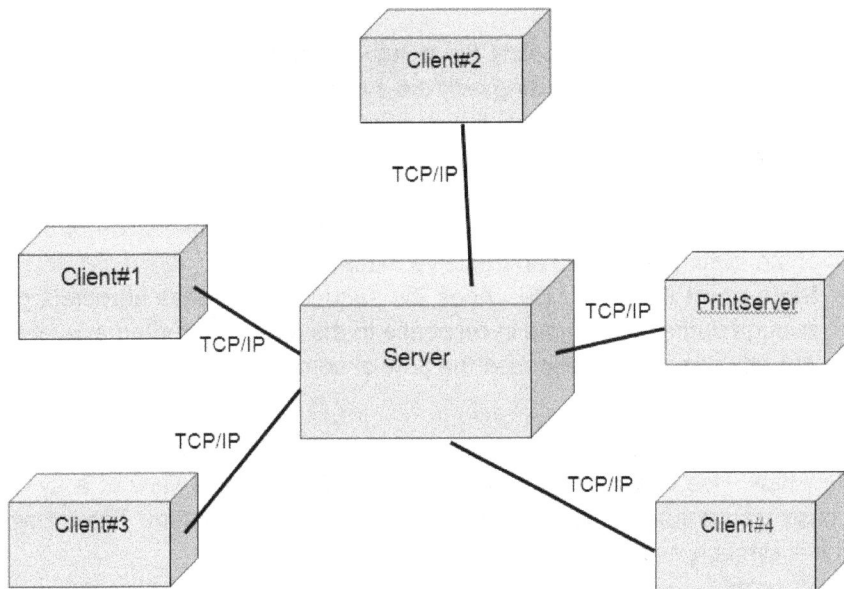

**Fig.2.69** Deployment Diagram

**Note:** The above figure is the deployment diagram for a typical Client/Server architecture or hardware topology. The GUI components of your system are installed on client machines, meaning your client nodes contain your system interfaces. The processing as well as database related components are placed on server machine. A server is a node with higher memory and higher processing power when compared with client nodes. Typically, the client nodes can be personal computers or workstations, whereas the server node can be mini or a mainframe computer. In the deployment diagram, the client machines are connected to the server using LAN network topology using TCP/IP network protocols. The deployment diagram specifies the static deployment view, that is the physical arrangement of nodes and their physical connections providing a hardware environment or the platform on which your system can be deployed for execution.

## Behavioral Diagrams

Behavioral diagrams express the dynamic aspects of a system. There are five types of behavioral diagrams. The dynamic aspects of a software system include the flow of messages over time and the movement of components across a network. Behavior diagrams emphasize what must happen in the system being modeled. Since behavior diagrams illustrate the behavior of a system, they are used extensively to describe the functionality of software systems. The following topics discuss how the behavioral diagrams are organized.

- ❖ **Use case Diagram:** Depicts the behaviors of the system as seen by the external end user interacting with the system.
- ❖ **Sequence Diagram:** Describes the time ordering of messages exchanged between objects to accomplish certain behavior or a purpose of a system.
- ❖ **Collaboration Diagram:** Describes the structural organization of objects of the system that send and receive messages.
- ❖ **State chart Diagram:** Describes the sequence of states an object goes through during its life time in response to the external or internal events.
- ❖ **Activity Diagram:** Describes the flow of control from activity to activity in the system.

A use case diagram shows a set of use cases, actors and their inter relationships. Use case diagram depicts the static use case view of a system. Use case diagram helps us to model the behaviors of a system. The following graphical symbols are used in any use case diagram.

Actor

Borrow Book

Use case

An actor is represents a user or another system that will interact with the system you are modeling. A use case is an external view of the system that represents some action the user might perform in order to complete a task. Use cases are helpful in exposing requirements of a system and planning the project.

## Interaction Diagrams

Interaction diagram is the collective name given to sequence diagrams and collaboration diagrams. As the name indicates they describe the interaction among objects to accomplish a behavior of a system which you are modeling. These two diagrams are semantically equivalent, meaning one can be generated from the other without loosing any information. A sequence diagram can be generated if you have a collaboration diagram, similarly, a collaboration diagram can be generated if we have a sequence diagram.

Interaction diagrams model the behavior of a use case by describing the way groups of objects interact to complete the task specified by a use case. Sequence diagrams generally show the sequence of events that occur. Collaboration diagrams demonstrate how objects are statically connected. Both diagrams are relatively simple to draw and contain similar elements. These two interaction diagrams are isomorphic, meaning one can be converted to the other without losing any information.

## Sequence Diagram

A sequence diagram   is an interaction diagram that expresses the time ordering of messages. A sequence diagram shows a set of objects and their interaction by means of sending and receiving messages among them. This diagram contains objects which are mostly named or anonymous instances of classes. This diagram may also include instances of collaborations, components, and nodes. Sequence diagram describes the dynamic view of a system.

## Collaboration Diagram

A collaboration diagram is an interaction diagram that typically focus on the structural organization of objects that send and receive messages. A collaboration diagram describes a set of objects, links among those objects, and messages sent and received by those objects. This diagram contains objects which are mostly named or anonymous instances of classes. This diagram may also include instances of collaborations, components, and nodes. Collaboration diagram describes the dynamic view of a system.

## State Chart Diagram

This diagram represents the sequences of states that an object of an interaction goes through during its life time in response to received stimuli, together with its responses and actions. State chart diagrams are used to describe the behavior of a system.  State chart diagrams describe all of the possible states an object goes through as events occur. Each diagram usually represents objects of a single class and track the different states of its objects through the system. You use state chart diagrams to model the behavior of an interface, class, or collaboration. A state chart diagram consists of states, transitions, events, and activities.

Use state chart diagrams to demonstrate the behavior of an object through many use cases of the system.  Only use state chart diagrams for classes where it is necessary to understand the behavior of the object through the entire system.  State chart diagram is also called state machine.

**Example:**

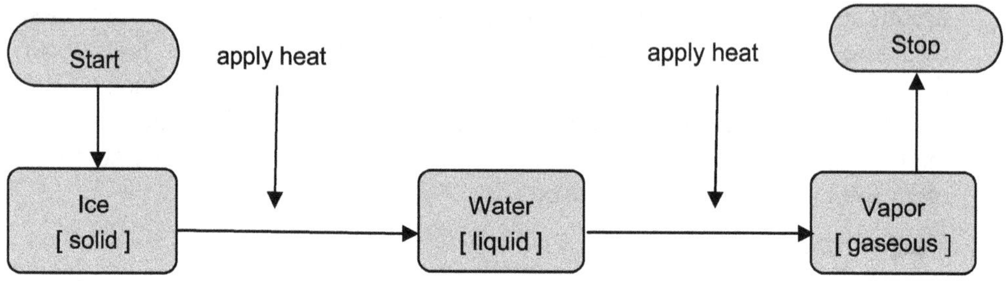

**Fig.2.70** State Chart Diagram

**Explanation:** The above figure represents the state machine for water. Initially it is in the solid state, when you apply heat (An external event), ice melts to become water. It means that there is state transition from solid state to liquid state due to the external event happening, meaning heating ice. When it is in liquid state, you apply heat again (an external event), water becomes vapor, changing its state from liquid to gaseous. Here, the state transitions are caused by an external event, applying heat.

## Activity Diagram

An activity diagram depicts the flow from activity to activity within a system. You apply activity diagrams to illustrate the dynamic view of a system. Activity diagrams are helpful in modeling the functionality of a system. It normally describes the business and operational workflows of components in a system. An activity diagram shows the overall flow of control in a system you are modeling.

An activity diagram displays a special state diagram where most of the states are action states and most of the transitions are triggered by completion of the actions in the source states. This diagram focuses on flows driven by internal processing. Activity diagrams are similar to state diagrams, because activities are the state of doing something. This diagram describes the state of activities by clearly showing the set of sequence of activities performed.

While you are modeling activity diagrams, they should be used with other modeling things such as interaction diagrams and state chart diagrams. The main use of activity diagrams is to model the workflow of the system being designed or modeled. By using activity diagrams you can analyze a use case by describing what actions need to take place and when they should take place. Activity diagrams do not give details about how objects behave or how objects collaborate.

Activity diagrams show the flow of activities through the system. Diagrams are read from top to bottom and have branches and forks to describe conditions and parallel activities. A fork is used when multiple activities are occurring at the same time. The branch describes what activities will take place based on a set of conditions.  All branches at some point are followed by a merge to indicate the end of the conditional behavior started by that branch.   After the merge, all of the parallel activities must be combined by a join before transitioning into the following activity state.

**Example:**

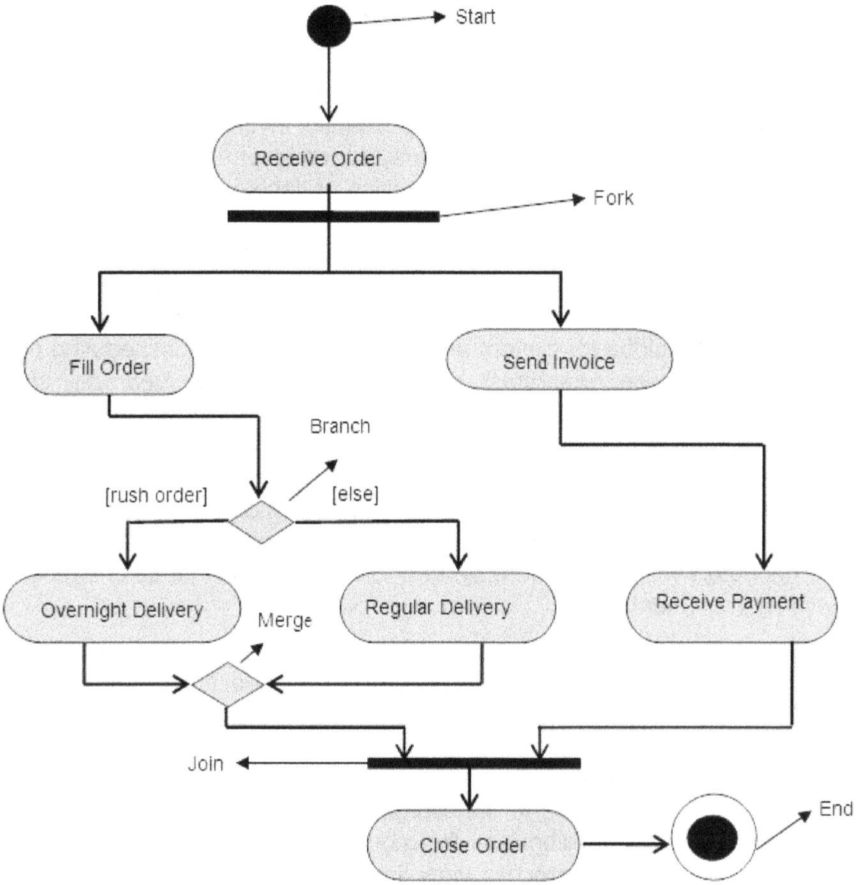

**Fig.2.71** Activity Diagram

**Explanation:** The above figure expresses some part of a model for order processing systems. It is an activity diagram depicting how the sales order is processed in the system. Fork is a location in the control flow where the flow splits into parallel flows and the Join is the location where parallel flows combine or join. The rest of the diagram is very much self explanatory.

## 2.21 Modeling Different Views of a System

When you model a system, you always consider different aspects of it. As we are aware that the system can be seen in five different perspectives. Choose the view of the system which suits your context, while you are developing models of a system. If you choose right set of views, you have a guarantee of successful system otherwise you end up with a failed system. Developing system models from different views is again a key task. The following section discusses various steps involved in modeling a system from different views:-

❖ While you model a system, explore which view can better express your system's architecture which will expose risks involved in your project. You can start from the 4+1 views that a system might have always.

❖ Once you choose a view, identify which artifacts you need to capture for the complete specification of that view. Mostly these artifacts could be various UML diagrams that describe your identified view of a system.

❖ Identify which of these diagrams are useful for planning various processes belonging to a system you are modeling. These diagrams are very much helpful for system analysis, project plan, for scheduling project reviews. These diagrams are very much preserved as starting documentation for the system you develop.

❖ Try to think of including diagrams that are not totally concerned with the views of the system. Such transitory artifacts help us a lot in understanding the impacts of our design decisions. These diagrams are also applicable for experimenting with changes to the system, as it is mandatory for any software system to undergo continuous changes even after implementation.

The diagrams or the artifacts required for a system, depends on what kind of system you are developing. If your system is a simple application such as a computer game that runs on a single machine, mostly on a personal computer, you only require few of your UML diagrams to represent only two of your system views, such as use case view, and design view. It means you only require use case diagrams for specifying its functionality, class diagrams for modeling its structure, and interaction diagrams for modeling its behavior. The rest of the diagrams used to express process view, implementation view, and deployment view are not required.

If you are developing a system which focuses on process flow, your system model may include activity and state chart diagrams to model your system's processes. Similarly if you are developing a two tier system such as client/server system, you may require component diagrams, as well as deployment diagrams to specify various components of a system, and the hardware structure on which your system works. If your system is a complex and full fledged distributed system that can function on a multi tier architecture, we may require almost all diagrams our UML supports to model such a system.

## 2.22  Modeling Different Levels of Abstraction

So far we have discussed the different views of the system. There are typically 4+1 views (5 different views) of the system, and each view could be expressed by different diagrams belonging to the same model. We need these different views for the efficient implementation of any software intensive system. As the software development process continues we need these different views at different contexts of your software development.

We not only need to view the system from different angles, we need different levels of abstractions of the same view as seen by various stakeholders of the system. This helps various people involved in the system to carry on their responsibilities efficiently to result in a better system.

For example, if you are a programmer concerned with the design view of a system. We are aware that the design view of a system includes classes, interfaces and collaborations and their relationships. A programmer will look for classes and their internal details, such as attributes, operations, and responsibilities etc. Whereas a system analyst looks for the services offered by a class. Whereas a tester looks for responsibilities of classes. A developer thinks of how to develop an interface and its associated class or a component, whereas a tester thinks of operations carried by interface, and whether they are carried on properly according to the problem specification.

Looking only for the responsibilities of a class is at a higher level of abstraction, whereas looking for its internal details such as attributes and operations is at a lower level of abstraction. So, different stake holders have different levels of understanding of the same view of your model. All the diagrams which you draw in UML for modeling a system, might be viewed differently with different levels of details by different people.

Basically, there are two ways by means of which you model a system at different levels of abstraction. They are:

❖ Develop a single model and specify different diagrams that describe different levels of detail.
❖ Develop different models, so that each model gives its own level of abstraction with diagrams that trace from one model to another.

The following topic discusses various steps involved in modeling a system at different levels of abstraction by showing diagrams with different levels of detail:

❖ Collect the needs of your stakeholders, and begin with a given model of your system.
❖ If your stakeholders want to construct an implementation, they need diagrams at a lower level of abstraction, meaning, they look for complete details of each abstraction. If your stakeholders are interested in developing a conceptual model of the system for end users, they require

diagrams at a higher level of abstraction, meaning hiding lot of internal details.

❖ Based on your model, create diagrams that reveal or hide the relevant details for your intended level of abstraction. Specifically, concentrate on the following four categories of things from your model.

➢ **Building blocks and relationships:** Hide the details that are not relevant for the context from the diagram, or that are not in the interest of your stakeholder.

➢ **Adornments:** Reveal only adornments that are related to the things and relationships of those elements that are only concerned with your intent. It means that hide the documentation for the things which are not of your current interest.

➢ **Flow:** Express only those messages or transitions in the context of your behavioral diagrams that are relevant to the intent of your stakeholder.

➢ **Stereotypes:** As we are aware that we use stereotypes for modeling new building blocks, and for arranging attributes and operations in a class. Reveal only those stereotyped details that are needed to understand your intent.

The major advantage of this approach is, you are always using the same common model for expressing different levels of abstractions. The major disadvantage of this approach is, diagrams at one level of abstraction may become obsolete at a different level of abstraction.

Let us discuss various steps involved for creating models of a system at different levels of abstraction. Here, we create different models of the system for different levels of abstraction. The sequence of steps for developing those models are as follows:

❖ Discuss the needs of your stakeholders, decide the level of abstraction that each of your stakeholder needs. Build a separate model for each of these abstractions.

❖ If your model represents a higher level of abstraction, include all simple abstractions in your model. If your model represents a lower level of abstraction, include all detailed abstractions in your model. Establish dependencies among the related elements belonging to different models.

❖ While you model a system at different levels of abstraction, if you follow only the five views of your system, there are four common situations you will face:

➢ **Use cases and their realization**: Use cases you define in use case model may have relationships with collaborations defined in the design model of your system.

> **Collaborations and their realization**: Collaborations may have relationships with a set of classes that work together to carry out the collaboration.
> **Components and their design:** Components belonging to an implementation model may have relationships with the elements in a design model.
> **Nodes and their Components:** Nodes in a deployment model may have relationships with components in an implementation model.

The major advantage of this approach is that the diagrams representing different levels of abstraction are loosely coupled, meaning the models are mostly independent and changes in one model will have the least impact on other models. The major disadvantage of this approach is, it will consume more resources to keep your models and their diagrams synchronized. Especially this happens when you are in the software development life cycle, where you want to maintain an analysis model different from a design model.

Let us discuss a fragment of a model developed for university admissions system. In this system we consider the interactions among various objects involved. The objects are, a student who submits all details of him to the university administration clerk who is another object. After submission by the student, the university administration clerk verifies all the documents; if the documents are valid, he gives a receipt to the student specifying his admission into a college. The following sequence diagram depicts this interaction at a higher level of abstraction.

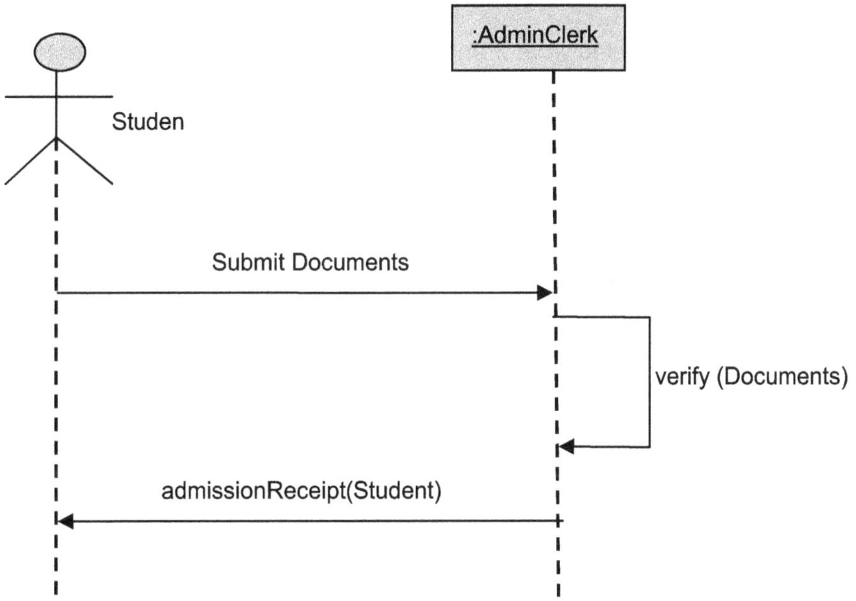

**Fig.2.72** A Sequence Diagram

**Explanation:** The above figure is a sequence diagram which describes the interaction between a student and a university Admin Clerk. During counseling the student submits all his relevant documents required for course admission with his rank card and reservation category details. The Admin Clerk verifies these documents, if they are valid, he admits the student and acknowledges the student with an admission receipt.

**Note**: The above diagram shows interactions at higher level of abstraction, which hide a lot of associated details. The dotted line indicates object's life line which starts from above and extends to below. The interactions in the above diagram happens as: when a student submits his documents, the verification process happens, after verification, the student admission takes place. The interactions are specified in the order they happen. The interaction specified above in the life line happens before the interaction specified below in the life line. For example; student admission happens after the documents are verified.

In order to have a detailed interaction required for a student admission into a university college, we require additional objects, such as college, which stores information about admitted student in a college. The admission process can be explained as follows:

❖ The student goes to the Admin Clerk's cabin and submits all his required documents along with his rank card and his reservation category information.

❖ The student indicates what branch (course curriculum) he is interested in.

❖ The Admin Clerk verifies the student's documents, if the documents are valid, he will search for seat availability in the student's required branch and college by using the details such as rank, reservation category and zonal area.

❖ If the seat is available, the student will be asked to pay the required fees.

❖ The Admin Clerk updates the database in the relevant college showing new student admission.

❖ The Admin Clerk gives a receipt to the student acknowledging his admission indicating his branch, his college etc.

The detailed interaction can be expressed by using the following sequence diagram. This interaction diagram gives the model at a lower level of abstraction, because of this, it is more detailed.

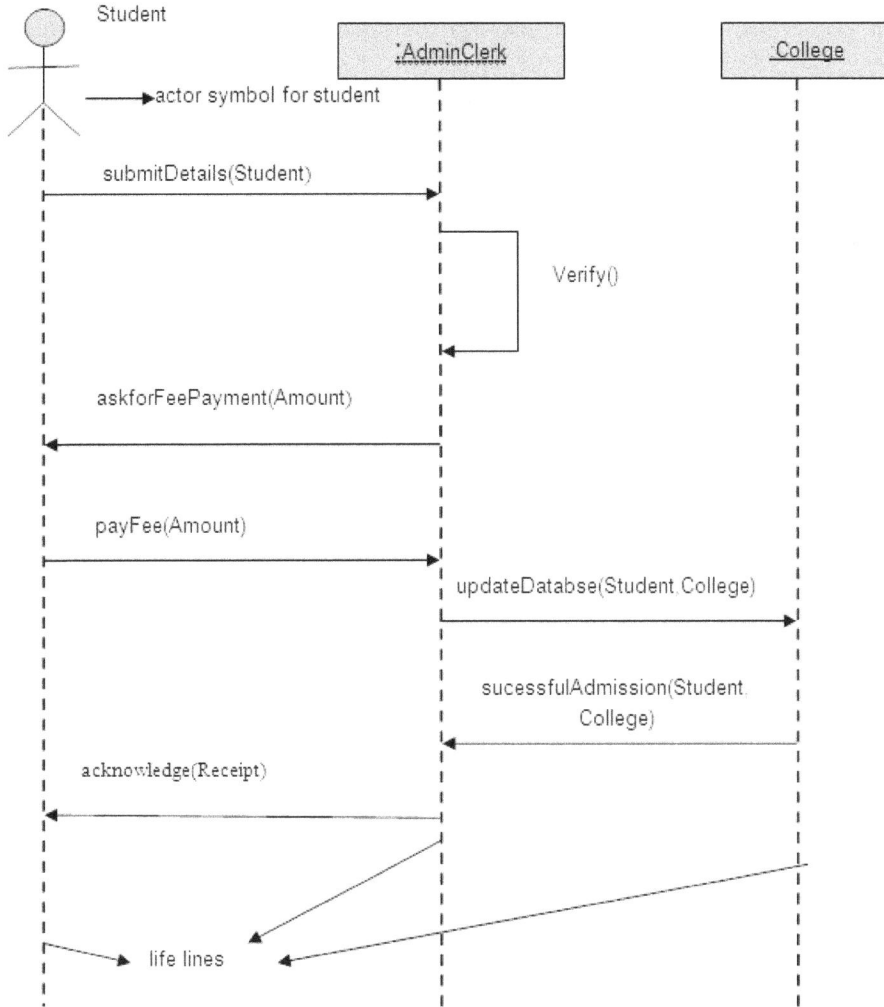

**Fig.2.73** A Sequence Diagram

**Note:** The above interaction expresses a lower level of abstraction, because of this, it is more detailed. The dotted lines indicate life lines of objects participating in the interaction.

Models help us by letting us work at a higher level of abstraction. A model may do this by hiding or masking details, bringing out the big picture, or by focusing on different aspects of the prototype. In UML 2.0, you can zoom out from a detailed view of an application to the environment where it executes, visualizing connections to other applications or, zoomed even further, to other sites. Alternatively, you can focus on different aspects of the application, such as the business process that it automates, or a business rules view. The new ability to nest model elements, added in UML 2.0, supports this concept directly.

## 2.23 Modeling Complex Views

To what extent you can simplify your models, there can be situations where you have to have large and complex diagrams. The diagrams you create for analyzing a database schema, for analyzing a real time system or for designing embedded systems could become large and complex. Even if you break up these complex diagrams, the complexity may still persist.

For example, you have created a class diagram for analyzing a database system, you study this diagram showing classes and their associations. You may identify some common patterns of collaboration (collaborations having common mechanisms). If you want to show this model to a reader who expects it to be at a higher level of abstraction, you may hide certain details and you may highlight certain details in the model on which the reader is interested in. While doing so, meaning eliding some details of your model may result in loosing the information about the common patterns.

While you are modeling complex views of your system, the following sequence of steps are followed.

❖ Explore all ways and means of presenting your model at a higher level of abstraction. Based on the context, you may elide some parts of your diagram or retain the same in other parts of your diagram. If you are convinced that whatever you do could not reduce complexity, follow the next step.

❖ Even though you have hidden as much information as you can and your diagram is still complex, think of grouping some elements in packages or in higher level collaborations. After this, expose only the higher level packages and collaborations in your diagram.

❖ Even after, your diagram is still complex, you can draw the attention of the reader to your intention by using sparingly notes and other visual queues. These adornments may help you to specify your intended purpose to the reader.

If your diagram is still complex, you better take the print out of it. By going through the printed diagram, you can trace back from the diagram and study it for common patterns. You can convey your intent of the diagram based on experience and expertise provided by the common patterns.

## 2.24 Class Diagrams

When you model a system, class diagrams are the most common diagrams you find. A class diagram contains classes, interfaces, and collaborations and their relationships. It may also contain notes and constraints. A class diagram may also include packages when you want to express the model at a higher level of abstraction. Class diagrams are the graphical representations of the static design view of the system you are modeling. Class diagrams are the richest notation in UML and a central modeling technique that runs through all object oriented methods. A class diagram describes the types of objects in the system and the various kinds of static relationships that exist among them.

Class diagrams are helpful in modeling the vocabulary of a system, modeling collaborations, or modeling schemas. Class diagrams act as foundation for component and deployment diagrams. The structural model of a system build by class diagrams is applicable to construct executable systems by using forward engineering techniques. A class diagram is a pictorial representation of the detailed system design. The structure of a system is represented using class diagrams. Class diagrams are referenced time and again by the developers while implementing the system.

Let us see how class diagrams are related with use cases. Use cases indicate the requirements of a system. The major purpose of designing classes is to realize these requirements. While analyzing use cases, they can be broken up into atomic components that form the basis for designing   classes. Class diagrams are used for a wide variety of purposes, including both conceptual/domain modeling and detailed design modeling.

## 2.25 Common Uses of Classes

1. By using classes you can model the vocabulary of a system. This includes identifying system scope and boundaries, and deciding what abstractions are part of the system and what are outside the system. You use class diagrams to specify these abstractions and responsibilities.

2. By using class diagrams you can model simple collaborations. A collaboration is a society of classes, interfaces, and other elements that work together to accomplish a function or a task of a system you are modeling. You use class diagrams to visualize and specify this cooperative behavior which involves a set of classes and their relationships. Collaborations imply the basic associations between classes. Collaborations are often used to:
   ❖ Provide a higher level understanding of collection of collaborating objects.
   ❖ Allocate functionality to classes by exploring the behavioral aspects of a system.

❖ Model the logic of the implementation of a complex operation, particularly one that interacts with a large number of other objects.
❖ Explore the roles that objects take within a system, as well as the different relationships they are involved with, when in those roles.

**Example:**

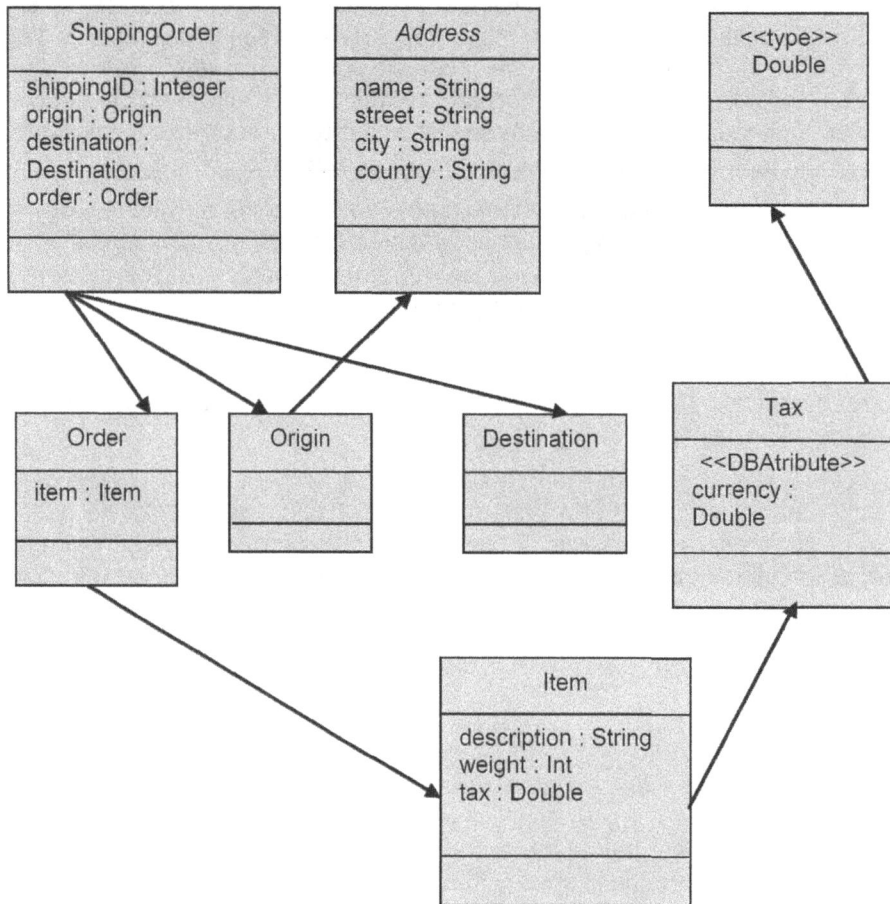

**Fig.2.74** Modeling Vocabulary

Collaboration diagrams represent a combination of information taken from class, sequence, and use case diagrams describing both the static structure and dynamic behavior of a system. A collaboration describes a behavior, the resources used to perform the behavior, and the roles the resources assume during the behavior. The following figure models a collaboration in which a venue manager secures the services of an agent.

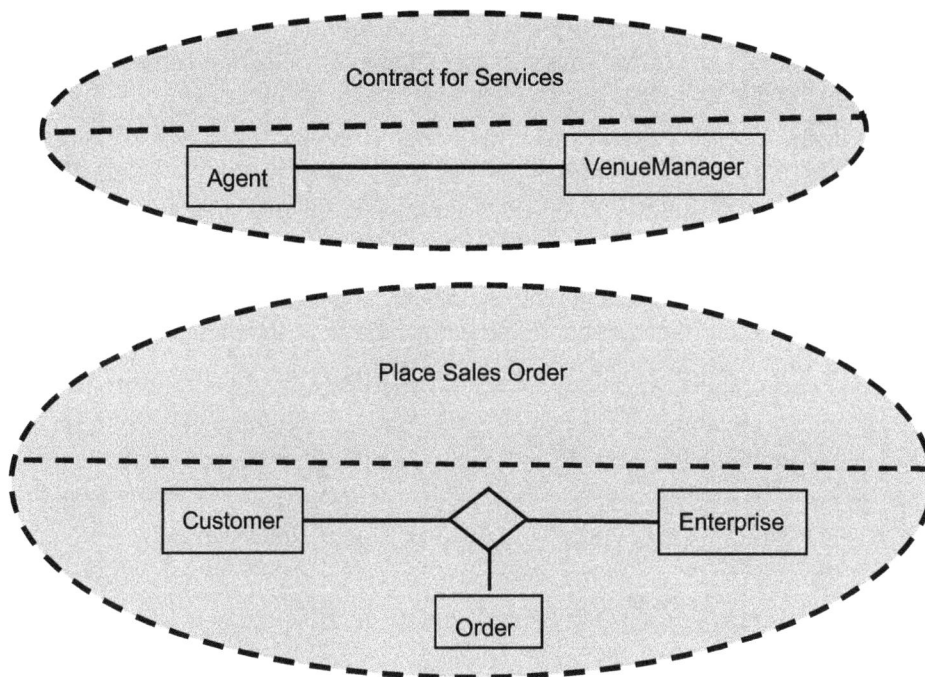

**Fig.2.75**  Modeling Collaborations

A collaboration may also model the implementation of an individual operation. The following figure shows how to associate a collaboration with the operation that it realizes/implements.

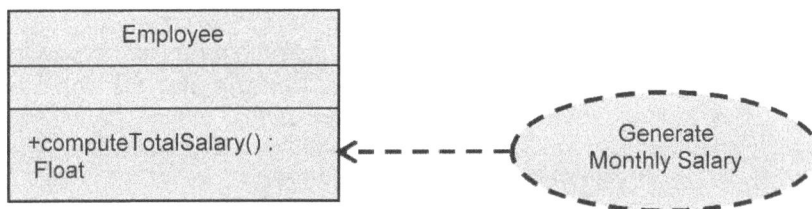

**Fig.2.76**  Modeling Collaboration that Realize an Operation

**Note:** Generate Monthly Salary is a collaboration of elements using which each employee's monthly total salary is computed as a cooperative behavior of these elements.

This representation is most valuable when the implementation is complex. The collaboration may include both structural and behavior diagrams to explain the collaboration. The benefit of using a collaboration to describe the requirements, is the separation of the implementation from the requirements. This separation permits the design, review, and maintenance of the implementation without altering or losing sight of the original requirement. The operation computeTotal Salary() is a kind of requirement for the Payroll System. This requirement is not lost even if you change its implementation, meaning changing the algorithm for Generate Monthly Salary collaboration.

3. Class diagrams are helpful to model a logical database schema. A schema can be a blueprint for the conceptual design of the database. The persistent classes you build in a class diagram can be stored in a relational or in an object oriented database. To represent schema within the database, use the «schema» stereotype on a package. A table may be placed in a «schema» to establish its scope and location within a database. The following diagrams describe how schemas and tables can be defined as a class diagram.

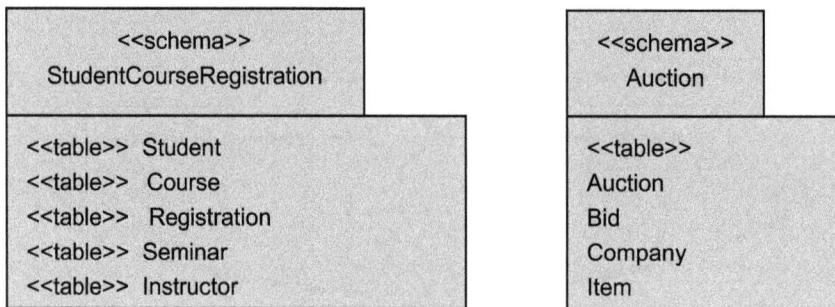

| <<schema>> StudentCourseRegistration | <<schema>> Auction |
|---|---|
| <<table>>  Student | <<table>> |
| <<table>>  Course | Auction |
| <<table>>  Registration | Bid |
| <<table>>  Seminar | Company |
| <<table>>  Instructor | Item |

**Fig.2.77** Modeling Schema

**Explanation:** In the above figures, the first diagram represents the schema for a university course registration system. The name of the schema is StudentCourseRegistration, and it contains persistent classes named Student, Course, Registration, Seminar and Instructor which become tables in the associated database. In the second diagram, a schema for auctioning an item is created. The name of the package is Auction, which is also the name of the schema. This auction schema contains four tables named, Auction, Bid, Company, and Item in the associated database. The associated database can be a relational database or an object oriented database.

## 2.26 Modeling Simple Collaborations

When you model, you capture the vocabulary of your system. All the elements and the things you capture become vocabulary of your system. These abstractions do not stand alone, but work together to accomplish a cooperative purpose. A collaboration is a way of visualizing, specifying, constructing, and documenting the ways and means these elements work together. You may require a set of class diagrams to represent a set of collaborations which form the design view of your system. To model a collaboration, the following steps are followed:

❖ Identify some function or behavior of a part of the system. Find out the mechanism which implements this function or behavior in the form of interactions among the set of classes, interfaces, and other elements. The mechanism describes the collaboration.

❖ Identify the classes, interfaces and other elements that involve in each mechanism. Establish the relationships among the things that participate in the collaboration to carry out each mechanism.

❖ Associate scenarios for each function or part of a behavior of the system which you are modeling. Use these scenarios to walk throuth the collaboration to identify what you are misssing and what is not needed.

❖ Once you identify elements in a collaboration, fill up these elements with their contents. For example, in cases of classes, identify the responsibilities and ensure that there is good balance of these responsibilities among the classes. As a next step, find out the required attributes and operations to carry on these responsibilities.

**Examples**:

1. The following figure expresses the scenario of activities of a librarian in any library application. This figure describes the mechanism discharging his duties as a librarian.

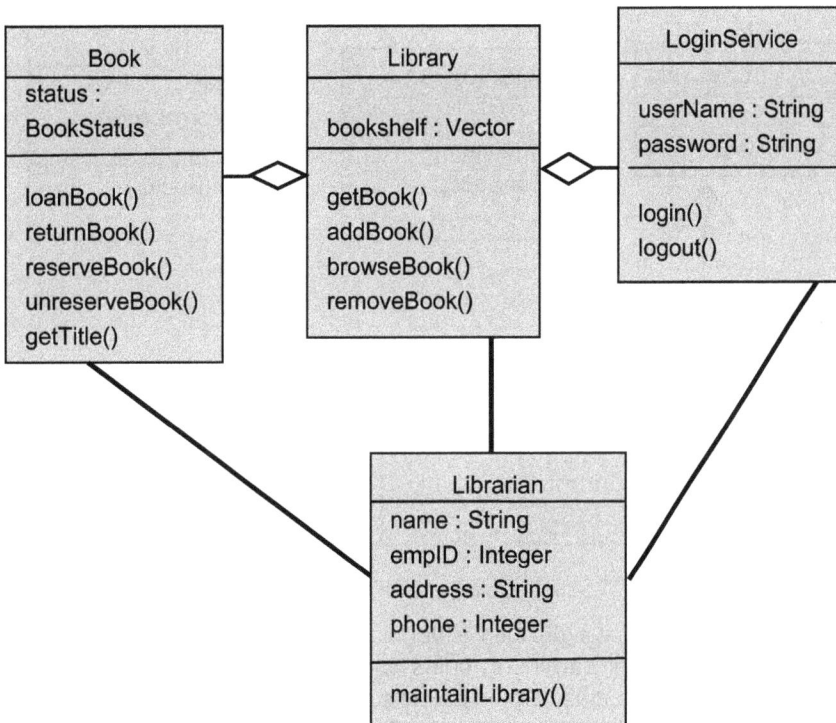

**Fig.2.78** A Simple Library Collaboration

**Explanation:** This is a collaboration which expresses the duties discharged by a librarian. The Librarian class is in association with Book, Library and LoginService classes. The classes Book and LoginService are in aggregation relationship with class named Library. The Librarian maintains Library, whose duties include ordering new books and removing outdated or old books from the Library. He can also browse through a selected book.

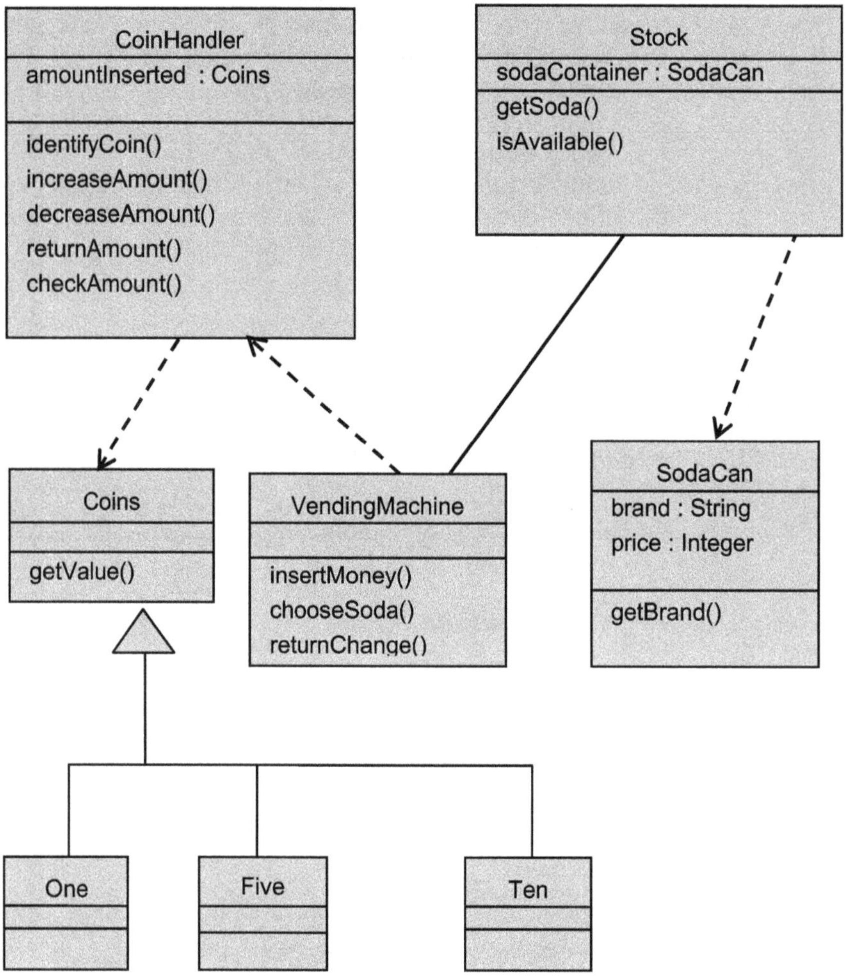

**Fig.2.79** A Simple Collaboration for a Vending Machine

2. In this example, we discuss a vending machine. A vending machine is one where a user can insert coins and get a brand of Soda Can he has selected for. The class Coins collects all the coins, such as one, five and ten valued coins and computes the total value of them. The CoinHandler takes the amount from the user by collecting user entered coins and works in association with the class named VendingMachine. The

VendingMachine accepts the money and the brand of soda the user wants, and it returns remaining change with soda can of his choice. The Stock class maintains Soda Cans. The SodaCan class contain information about the brand and price of the Soda Can. The above diagram gives the collaboration describing the function of a vending machine.

## 2.27  Modeling a Logical Database Schema

Many systems you model will have persistent objects, that they can be stored in a database for later retrieval and use. These persistent objects can be stored by using relational database, an object oriented database or a combination of relational/object oriented databases. The UML is very helpful in modeling logical database schemas, as well as physical databases. As we are aware that E-R (Entity Relationship) diagrams are the common modeling technique for modeling logical database design. The purpose of E-R diagrams is to model data and how the data is related. Whereas class diagrams not only represent data but also specify behavior that can be applied on that data in the form of operations. When you are changing from object oriented domain to the relational database domain, the data represented by persistent classes become the physical tables, and the operations defined for a class become triggers or stored procedures that can operate on physical tables in a physical database.

We can say that a class model for a system is the superset of the data model for that system. First we model   class diagrams and make them as a base for data modeling. That is to say that we engineer a new relational database schema from a class model we have created. This approach will make us to have control on our models and optimize them to our satisfaction. The relationships, such as association, inheritance, aggregation that exist among classes in a class model will get transformed into relations among database tables in the data model.

The process of building a relational database schema from a class model includes identifying persistent objects. We need to identify those classes whose objects are non persistent, meaning these objects get created and destroyed during the execution of various business processes that constitute your system. The next step is to identify   persistent objects, whose associated classes' data is stored in the database for future use. These persistent classes contribute to the design of the relational database schema. Here, we can assume that each persistent class maps to a relational table, either in whole or in part. Each instance of a persistent class  (persistent object)  maps to a single row of its associated relational table.

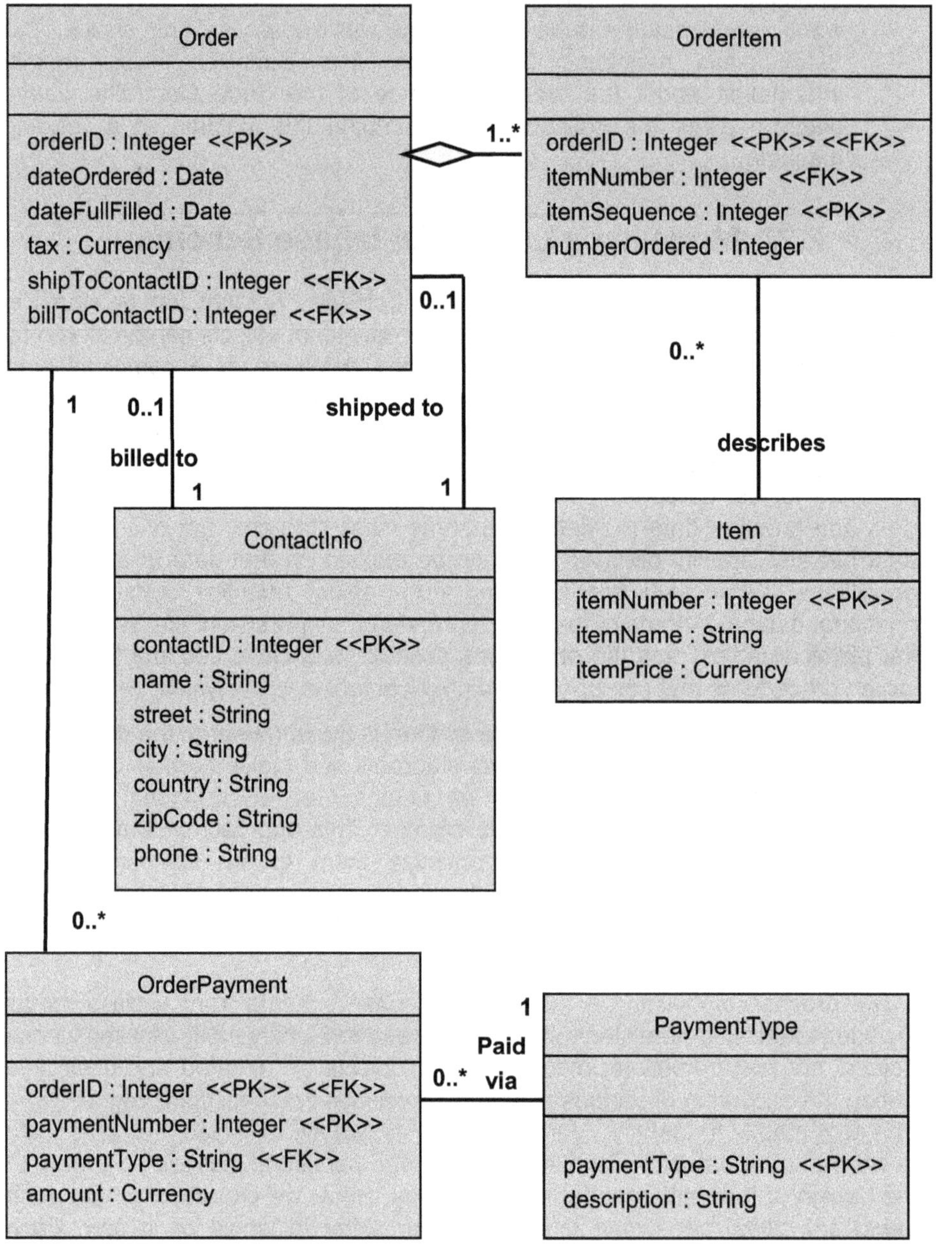

**Fig.2.80** Modeling Logical Database Schema

The following section discusses various sequence of steps required to model a logical database schema using UML:

❖ Identify those classes in your model whose data is not volatile but permanent. Identify those classes in your application, in which there  are models  that describe the activities in the application.

❖ Create a class diagram containing these classes and also identify attributes that become columns of the corresponding relational table. Identify these classes as persistent (a standard tagged value). You can also define several tagged values to express other database specific details such as primary keys and foreign keys.

❖ Expand the structural details of these classes, this means that the various adornments related to the attributes are exposed. These adornments could be the data types and visibility constraints of the attributes. Identify the associations and their cardinalities of the attributes that structure these classes.

❖ Watch for common patterns that formulate physical database design, such as cyclic associations, one-to-one associations, and n-ary associations. Wherever necessary, create intermediate abstractions to simplify your logical database design.

❖ Understand the behavior of these classes by expanding their operations which operate on the database. You should also ensure that the business rules concerned with your application are followed while you manipulate this database.

❖ Apply wherever possible, the tools which transform your logical design into a physical design.

The Fig.(2.76) illustrates the logical database design for an order processing application using UML.

**Note:** All the classes involved in the above class diagram are persistent, meaning they are stored as database tables in the database for further use. The stereotypes <<PK>> and <<FK>> associated with attributes are primary key and foreign key according to the definition of relational database tables. For example, the attribute named paymentType in the above class named PaymentType is the primary key for the associated database table named with the same name as the class. Whereas in OrderPayment class, the attribute paymentType acts as a foreign key. The attributes which are of type String can also be defined as char(50) or varchar(50) which are the standard database data types to represent a sequence of characters.

## 2.28  Forward and Reverse Engineering

Though UML models do not specify a particular mapping to any object oriented programming language, but UML was designed with such mapping in mind. Your UML models can be mapped to various industrial object oriented languages such as Java, C++, Smalltalk, Ada, ObjectPascal, and Forte etc. UML was also designed to map to a variety of commercial object based languages, such as visual basic, C#.

Forward engineering is the process of generating code from UML models by mapping to an implementation language. There is always a chance that forward engineering involves loss of information. This happens, because the models convey more information than the underlying object oriented programming language. We can easily, clearly, and effectively visualize structural features, such as collaborations, and behavioral features, such as interactions in the UML models than the corresponding code.

**To generate code from a class diagram in a UML model, we need to follow the steps discussed below:**

❖ Find out the various rules and regulations that are required to map your UML model to an implementation language. This may apply to the whole project.

❖ Based on the language you choose, you need to cut short your UML features. For example, your UML supports multiple inheritance, but the mapped language might not support it.

❖ In order to have clear understanding of your underlying language, you can use tagged values sparingly. You can associate these tagged values with classes, components and collaborations or packages of your UML model to specify your target language.

❖ Apply the forward engineering tools to generate raw code in the mapping language from your UML model.

Reverse engineering is the process of generating UML models from the mapping implementation language code. Because, the raw code contains a flood of information with lower level of details, which may create only modeling elements at a very lower level of abstraction. You need to re coup all these lower level abstractions for your higher level modeling elements or diagrams. Generally, it might not be possible to build UML models completely by using corresponding raw code written in your mapping language. This is because there is loss of information in this conversion or transformation, either from code to model or from model to code.

**In order to create models from the underlying code, you need to follow the steps described below:**

❖ Identify the rules needed to map from your implementation language to the UML. Choosing the implementation language may hold good for the entire project.

❖ Apply your reverse engineering tool to focus on the code segment. Your tool may generate a new model from the code, or it may modify the existing model which was created in the previous reverse engineering process.

❖ Your reverse engineering tool may create various classes that are implemented in the mapping language. Then this model might be modified to contain classes and their relationships based on the coding, as you expand your focus on it.

❖ Expose those details of your created models by hiding the details that are not required to express your intent.

## Essay Questions

1. What is visibility of operations and attributes.

2. How to model the vocabulary of a system. Explain various steps with examples.

3. Explain modeling of non-software things with an example.

4. Explain modeling primitive types with examples.

5. Define extend and include relationships in use cases.

6. Explain various steps involved in establishing generalization relationship.

7. Write short notes on the following:-

   (a) Association    (b) Aggregation    (c) Composition

8. How to model simple dependencies? Explain with examples.

9. Give various steps involved in modeling structural relationships with an example.

10. What are structural diagrams? Explain them with examples.

11. What are behavioral diagrams? Explain them with examples.

12. Give various steps in detail for modeling different views of a system.

13. Give steps involved in modeling simple collaborations with examples.

14. Write short notes on modeling a logical database schema.

15. Explain forward and reverse engineering in case of class diagrams.

## Objective Type Questions

1. Class path names indicate
   (a) class belonging to a package
   (b) class belonging to collaboration
   (c) class diagram
   (d) object model

2. These are the class visibility constraints
   - (a) public
   - (b) private
   - (c) Both a & b
   - (c) None

3. The attribute or operation that can be referred by inherited child only is
   - (a) public
   - (b) private
   - (c) protected
   - (d) All the above

4. '#' symbol indicate
   - (a) private visibility
   - (b) protected visibility
   - (c) public visibility
   - (d) All the above

5. '+' symbol indicate
   - (a) private visibility
   - (b) protected visibility
   - (c) public visibility
   - (d) All the above

6. Identifying abstractions and their responsibilities is part of
   - (a) class diagram
   - (b) Modeling the vocabulary of system
   - (c) Modeling primitive types
   - (d) Modeling the distribution of responsibilities.

7. The relationship that exists between two classes where one class is a parameter of an operation belonging to another class
   - (a) association
   - (b) generalization
   - (c) dependency
   - (d) composition

8. The usage dependency uses the stereotype
   - (a) abstraction
   - (b) permit
   - (c) include
   - (d) use

9. The relationship with inheritance hierarchy is
   - (a) association
   - (b) aggregation
   - (c) Generalization
   - (d) realization

10. The multiplicity 1..* means
    - (a) zero or more
    - (b) one only
    - (c) zero only
    - (d) one or more only

11. The association which is the result of association between two classes
    - (a) unary association
    - (b) binary association
    - (c) N-ary association
    - (d) All of the above

12. The whole and parts relationship is also called
    - (a) dependency
    - (b) composition
    - (c) generalization
    - (d) aggregation

13. ◆————————This graphical symbol represents
    (a) composition           (b) association
    (c) dependency            (d) generalization

14. This is single inheritance where there are
    (a) Three parents         (b) one parent
    (c) two parents           (d) None

15. Any generalization with more than one parent is
    (a) single inheritance    (b) multiple inheritance
    (c) both                  (d) none

16. For a pair of classes, if you need to navigate from objects of one to objects of another then it is
    (a) generalization        (b) realization
    (c) association           (d) dependency

17. A Note may include
    (a) simple text           (b) embedded URL
    (c) link to a document    (d) All the above

18. The additional textual or graphical information included in the element's specification is
    (a) adornments            (b) tagged values
    (c) stereotypes           (d) constraints

19. A tagged value is same as
    (a) class attribute       (b) not a class attribute
    (c) metadata              (d) both b & c

20. New properties in UML model can be specified as
    (a) tagged values         (b) constraints
    (c) stereotypes           (d) primitive types

21. Modeling additional semantics can happen with
    (a) stereotypes           (b) tagged values
    (c) both a & b            (d) constraints

22. The static part of the system can be viewed from
    (a) class diagram         (b) object diagram
    (c) component diagram     (d) All the above

23. To view the dynamic aspect of the system, we use
    (a) class diagram         (b) deployment diagram
    (c) use case diagram      (d) component diagram

24. The diagram which includes a set of nodes and their physical connections is

    (a) component diagram                    (b) deployment diagram
    (c) class diagram                         (d) object diagram

> **Answers**

| | | | | | |
|---|---|---|---|---|---|
| 1. (a) | 2. (c) | 3. (c) | 4. (b) | 5. (c) | 6. (d) |
| 7. (c) | 8. (d) | 9. (c) | 10. (d) | 11. (d) | 12. (d) |
| 13. (a) | 14. (b) | 15. (b) | 16. (c) | 17. (d) | 18. (a) |
| 19. (d) | 20. (a) | 21. (d) | 22. (d) | 23. (c) | 24. (b) |

# CHAPTER 3

# Advanced Structural Modeling
# Advanced Classes

We know that classes are the important building blocks of our UML models. We have a more general concept of our building blocks in UML, you name them as classifiers. A classifier can be defined as a mechanism that describes behavioral and structural features. A classifier can be a class, an interface, a data type, a signal, a component, a node, a use case, and a subsystem. All these classifiers have many advanced features rather than simply attributes and operations.

**LEARNING OBJECTIVES**

*After studying the chapter the students familiarize themselves with the following concepts:*

♦ Classifiers and Advanced Classes

♦ Advanced Attributes and Operations

♦ Template Classes

♦ Modeling the Semantics of a Class

## 3.1 Classifiers

When you are building a model for a software intensive system, you find abstractions that represent things in your solution. Some of the things which you identify may have instances. Some things, such as packages and generalization/specialization relationships in any UML model do not have instances. The modeling elements that have instances are called classifiers. A classifier describes a set of instances that have common structural and behavioural features (attributes and operations). The UML provides a number of classifiers to build your models. They are as follows:

117

**Interface:** It contains a collection of operations that specify a service offered by a class or a component. The purpose of interface definition in UML models is to separate interface and its implementation. The interface contains only operations but not their implementations. The implementation of operations happens in a class or in a component associated with the interface. The services of a class or a component can be offered through the interface with which it is associated.

**DataType:** In a broad sense, a data type defines a set of values, and the allowable operations on those values. A dataType classifier may include primitive built-in types (such as numbers and strings), as well as enumeration types (such as Boolean).

**Signal:** It specifies an asynchronous communication that happens between instances while they interact.

**Component:** It is mostly a software component that is physical and replaceable part of a system. Physical components include files, headers, link libraries, modules, executables, or packages. A component may confirm to a set of interfaces by providing realization of them. Components can be used to model and document any system's architecture. Components are generally types, but only executable components have instances.

**Node:** A node indicates a physical computational resource that exists at run time. A node is an electronic device that has some memory and some processing capability.

**Usecase:** A use case describes a system's behavior when it is interacted by actors that lie outside the system. An actor is a thing or a person that exists outside the system and interacts with the system to accomplish a task. An actor can be an end user, an another system or an electronic device that interacts with the system. The UML use cases are used to capture the functional requirements of a system. Use cases are generally created by end users or system analysts. They usually represent a higher level of abstraction of the system. Each use case may contain a set of scenarios depicting the system's behavior.

**Subsystem:** A system is an integrated whole of its elements and their relationships,   which has some purpose and some set of objectives. A system is a collection of interconnected parts that are arranged in a specific fashion. Every system has its own boundary within which it operates. A Subsystem is a set of elements, which is a system itself, or a part of a larger system. In a way it is a grouping of elements which specify certain intended behavior.

The following diagram describes the graphical symbols in UML for various classifiers.

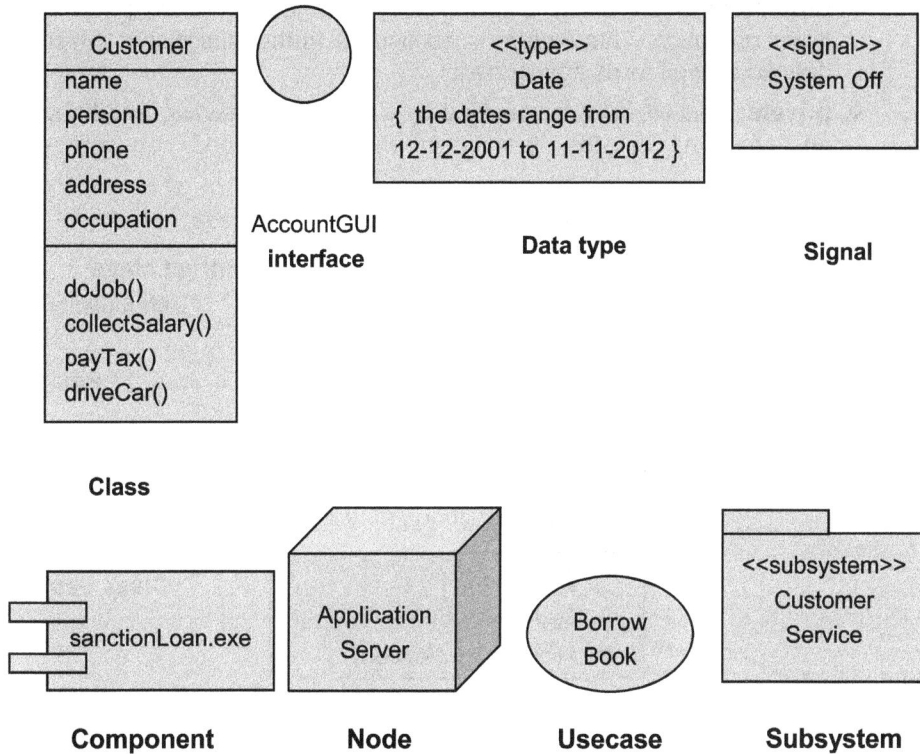

**Fig.3.1**  Classifiers

## Advanced Class

A class notation in UML provides a number of advanced features. These features help us to visualize, specify, construct and document a class to any level of detail which helps us in carrying forward and reverse engineering. UML supports a number of advanced modeling features for classes, they are:-

❖ Class and Attribute Properties
❖ Class Multiplicity and Attribute Multiplicity
❖ Class-Scope Attributes and Operations
❖ Visibility of Attributes and Operations

## Visibility

The visibility of an attribute or an operation of a classifier specifies whether it can be used by other classifiers. The default visibility is public visibility. The visibility can be classified into three types:-

❖ **public:** This visibility is specified by a '**+**' sign preceding an attribute or an operation. Any outside classifier can access this feature.

❖ **protected:** This visibility is specified by a **'#'** sign preceding an attribute or an operation. This feature is accessible to the classifier in which it is defined as well as its descendant.

❖ **private:** This visibility is specified by a **'-'** sign preceding an attribute or an operation. Only the classifier in which it is defined, can access this feature.

The following diagram gives an example of an advanced class:

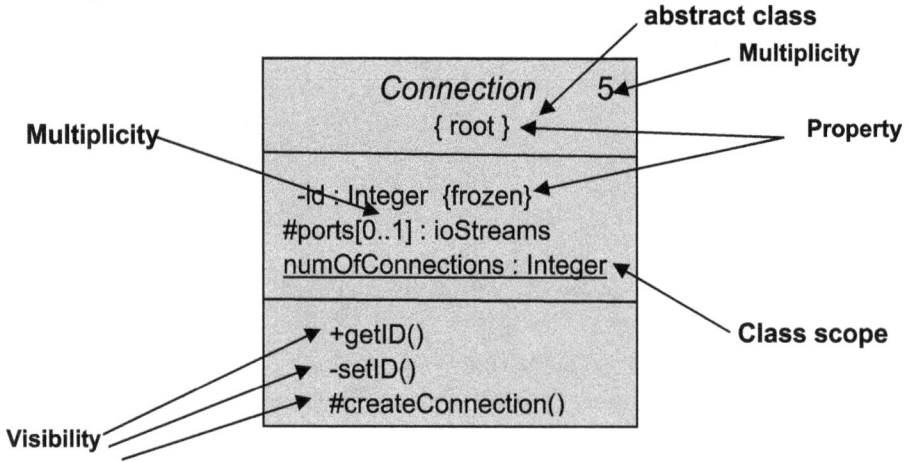

**Fig.3.2** Advanced Class

**Example:**

**Explanation:** The following class named Person has features with visibility constraints. The attributes named name and address and operation named getOccupation() have public visibility. The attribute named phone and operations named addPerson() and dropPerson() have protected visibility. The attribute named bankAccount and the operations named drawSalary() and enquireBalance() have private visibility.

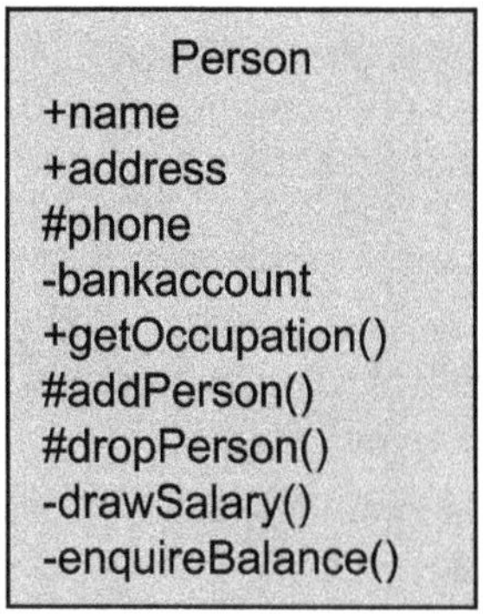

**Fig.3.3** Visibility

## 3.2 Scope

A feature (attribute or operation) in a classifier can be assigned a scope. If the scope of the feature is instance, then each instance of the classifier holds its own value for the feature. If the scope of the feature is classifier, then there is only one value of the feature for all instances of the classifier. Classifier scope is indicated by underlining the feature definition.

**Example:**

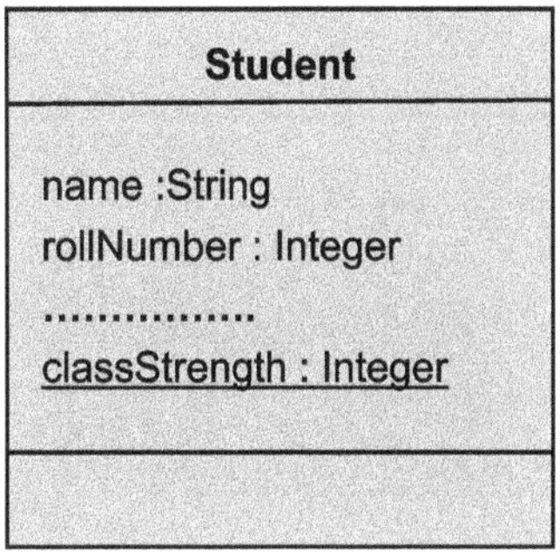

**Fig.3.4** Owner Scope

**Note:** In the above figure, the class named Student have attributes named name and rollNumber etc. have instance scope, meaning every object of Student will have its own values for these attributes. Every student has his own name and his own roll number. Whereas the attribute named classStrength has classifier scope, meaning its value holds good for the entire class. Obviously, class strength will have single value for all instances of the Student classifier.

## 3.3 Advanced Properties

A class can be assigned two properties in the form of standard tagged values. If you associate a tagged value 'root' with the class, then that class is the base class which do not have parent classes. If you associate a standard tagged value 'leaf' with the class, then that class do not have children. We include this advanced property by placing it below the class in flower brackets. For example, {root} or {leaf}.

The attributes and operations of a class can also have advanced properties, which we discuss in the coming section. A class can also be specified as abstract, which means that the specified class cannot have instances. An abstract class is indicated by writing its name in italics. Abstract class is defined when you want the root class to serve as a template for creating various subclasses. A class that can have instances is called concrete class.

**Example:**

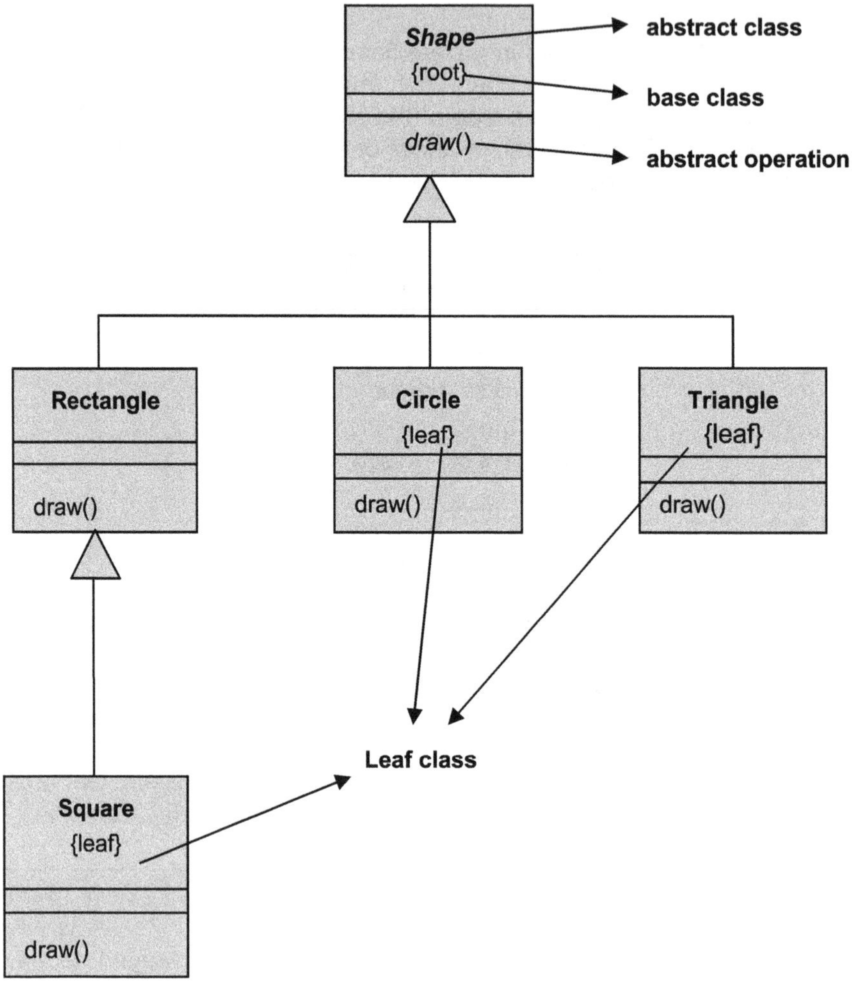

**Fig.3.5** Abstract and Concrete Classes

**Note:** Abstract operations map to what C++ calls pure virtual operations (functions).

## 3.4 Multiplicity

So far we have seen multiplicity used for association relationships. We have multiplicities associated with classes as well as with attributes. In case a class, multiplicity specifies the number of instances a class can have. The multiplicity for classes is indicated in the top right corner of the class. If you specify zero instances for a class, it means that the multiplicity is zero, then such a class is called utility class that exposes only class scoped attributes and operations. If a class has only one instance, then that class is called a singleton class.

In case of attributes, multiplicity constraints the number of values an attribute can have. This lets you specify attributes that can be modeled as arrays. We consider the same Student class which belongs to the university course registration system as an example. The following diagram illustrates the specification of multiplicities with respect to classes and attributes.

**Example:**

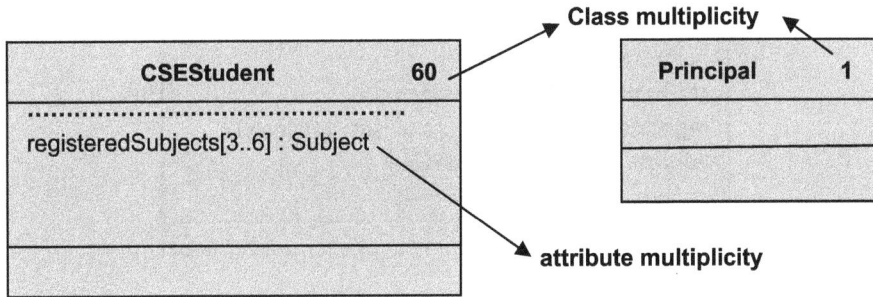

**Fig.3.6** Multiplicity for Classes and Attributes

**Explanation:** In the above diagram, the class CSEStudent represents a student belonging to the CSE branch. If the maximum available seats for CSE branch in your college is sixty. Then we can specify the multiplicity for the class CSEStudent as 60, because at most sixty students can be admitted in CSE branch. Suppose there is a rule that a student can register a minimum of 3 subjects and a maximum of 6 subjects for each semester, then the attribute named registeredSubjects has multiplicity in the range of 3 to 6. Another class named Principal is a singleton class, because there can be only one principal for a college. The remaining parts of the diagram are self explanatory.

## 3.5 Advanced Attributes

While you are modeling a class you simply write the names of attributes that determine the state of the class. This higher level of abstraction is quite sufficient to understand the intent of the model. As a developer you may want to have every detail at very lower level of abstraction. As we have already seen, we can associate additional details such as visibility, scope, and multiplicity for each attribute. You can also indicate the type, initial value, and changeability of each attribute.

There are three standard defined properties that you can apply to your attributes.

❖ **changeable:** If this property is specified for an attribute, it means that the attribute value can be changed.

❖ **addonly:** If this property is specified for an attribute which has multiplicity greater than one, you can add new values, but once added, the value cannot be removed or altered.

❖ **frozen:** If this property is specified for an attribute, it means that you cannot change the value of the attribute once it is initialized.

**Note:** We use frozen property when modeling a constant or write-once attribute. The frozen property maps to const definition in C++.

**Example:**

| Student |
|---|
| name : String   {frozen} |
| rollNumber : Integer   {frozen} |
| registeredSubjects[3..6] : Subject  {addonly} |
| address : String   {changeable} |
| phone : Integer   {changeable} |

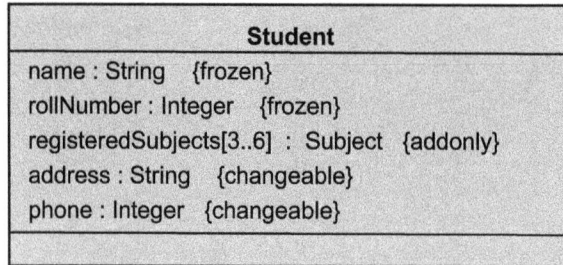

**Fig.3.7** A class with defined Properties

**Explanation:** The Fig.3.7 contains the definition of the class named Student. In this definition, the attributes are associated with defined properties. The attributes named, name and rollNumber are associated with the property frozen, because once a value is assigned to them, you cannot change. Obviously, the name and rollNumbers cannot be changed once values are assigned to them. The attribute named registeredSubjects has multiplicity. Its definition indicates that a student can register at least 3 subjects or at most 6 subjects for a semester (Let us assume). When a student registers for four subjects (for example), then he cannot remove it or modify it from the list of registered subjects. That is why it is associated with the defined property addonly. All the other attributes' values can be changed based on the situation. For example, the attributes address and phone number values can be changed depending on the situation, that is when a student moves to a new address or purchases a new SIM card.

## 3.6 Advanced Operations

You can always add new information to the operations. As we are  aware that the definition of an operation in any class is like any other ordinary function definition. An operation can have parameters whose values are passed from a caller, you call them as input parameters. An operation can have parameters whose values are set by the operation itself, you call them as output parameters. Apart from this, an operation can have parameters which act as both input and output parameters. The above information can be specified by using direction values which precede parameter definition. The     possible direction values are defined below:

❖ If the direction is **in:** An input parameter, it may not be modified.
❖ If the direction is **out:** An output parameter, it may be modified to communicate with caller.
❖ If the direction is **inout:** Both input and output parameter, can be input and may be modified.

**Example:**

| Rectangle |
|---|
| |
| findArea(in length : Float, in breadth : Float, out area : Float) |

**Explanation:** The above class named Rectangle contains an operation named findArea(), which computes the area of a rectangle when length and breadth dimensions are provided. Obviously, the parameters length and breadth are input parameters, and area will be an output parameter because its value is set by the operation.

There are four defined properties that you can associate with operations, they are:

❖ **isQuery**: If the operation is associated with this property, it means that execution of this operation will not have side effects, meaning the state of the system is unchanged.
❖ **sequential:** If the operation is associated with this property, it means that this operation is not protected against multiple threads or processes. The operation is or will be designed without concurrency control. Calling this operation concurrently might result in failures.
❖ **guarded:** If the operation is associated with this property, it means that this operation is protected against multiple threads or processes. The operation will automatically block until other instances of it have completed.
❖ **concurrent:** If the operation is associated with this property, it means that multiple threads or processes can execute the operation  at the same time guaranteeing its integrity. The operation is designed so that multiple calls to it can execute concurrently.

**Note**: The three properties (sequential, guarded, concurrent) address the concurrent semantics of your operation. These properties are relevant only for active objects, processes and threads.

## 3.7 Template Classes

In various object oriented programming languages you can write template classes, each of which defines a family of classes. The definition of template includes slots for classes, objects and values. These slots serve as template's parameters, which will be replaced by actual values when the template is bind. The ultimate result after template binding is a concrete class which can be used as any ordinary class. In UML terminology, template classes are called parameterized classes.

The following C++ code gives the way how templates can be used in class definition.

```
#include  <iostream.h>
..................
template<class T>
class  Stack
{
    T  list[100];
    int  top;
    public:
        Stack();    //Default constructor
        push(T);//Adds an element to the stack
        T  pop();    //Removes an element from the stack
};
```

The above code fragment in C++ defines a data structure named Stack using templates. The generic type T is the type of the elements of the Stack. You can associate any defined type with the generic type T while creating an object. You can instantiate this template such that Stack elements are float type as follows:-

Stack<float> stack1:

You can also model template classes in UML. The template class model is similar to any ordinary class model, but it contains a dotted rectangle on the upper right most corner containing template parameters.

**Examples:**

1.

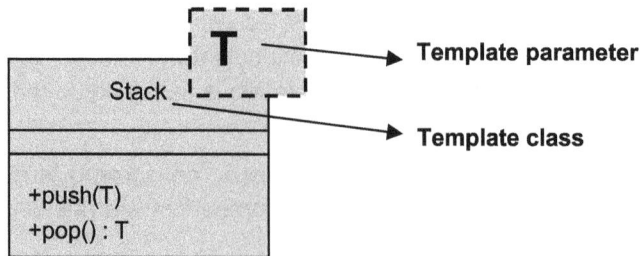

2.

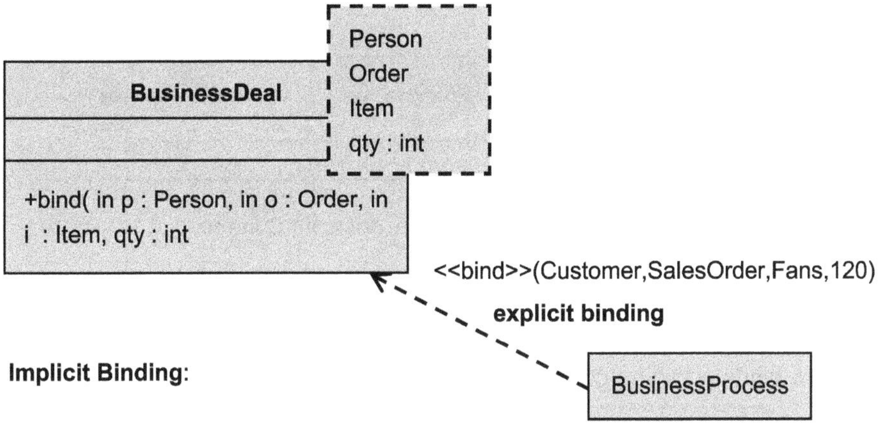


**Implicit Binding**:

BusinessDeal <Customer, SalesOrder, Fans, 120>

BusinessDeal<Supplier, PurchaseOrder, RawMaterial, 100>

BusinessDeal<Shipment,Invoice, PurchasedItems, 25>

**Fig.3.8** Template Class

**Note:** The above diagram specifies template class definition using UML. The template class name is BusinessDeal which has parameters such as Person, Order, Item and qty. When you implicitly bind this class with actual parameters, such as Customer, SalesOrder, Fans and 120, it means that it creates a class named businessDeal which include binding among a Customer, SalesOrder, Fans with quantity 120. Here, a sales transaction happened between a customer and a supplier for 120 fans. Similarly in the second binding, it infers that a purchase transaction happened between a Supplier and the Client for RawMaterial supply. In the third binding indicates shipment to a customer, where customer pays bill against the invoice for the shipped items.

The second way you can bind is by explicit means. Here another class is defined and this class binds the actual parameters with the template parameters to create a class named BusinessDeal. This binding is graphically indicated as a stereotype <<bind>> on a dependency relationship from another class to the template class as shown in the above diagram.

3. In this example, we consider a banking system, in which bank transactions happen between the account holder and the other client. These transactions could involve deposits, withdrawals, interbank transfer, loan payment, and loan receipt. You can create a generic class (template class) for the bank transaction and you can associate the relevant actual parameters to create a class named BankTransaction.

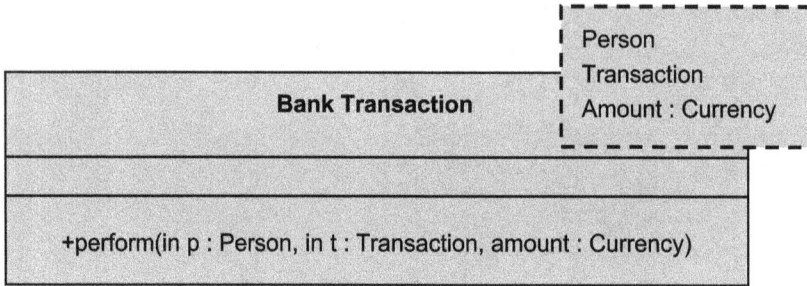

Fig.3.9 Another Template Class

The implicit binding can be given as:

BankTransaction<<Customer, deposit, 15000>

The above means that a customer has deposited 15000 in your account.

BankTransaction<<AccountHolder, withdrawal 25000>

The above means that you have withdrawn 25000 from your account.

BankTransaction<<AccountHolder, MakeDD, 12000>

The above means that you have raised a Demand Draft of 12000 from your account.

Apart from above implicit binding, you can do explicit binding by creating another class, named PerformTransaction which binds explicitly with the template class named BankTransaction. The explicit binding is self explanatory.

**Note:** Template classes are models of classes, which must be instantiated to produce a real class, which is then in turn instantiated to produce an object.

Hope you have understood the concept of modeling template classes using UML.

## 3.8 Standard Elements

We know that stereotypes are the extensibility mechanism by means of which you can create new building blocks in UML. Stereotypes are applied when there is no standard UML building block available for modeling certain elements that are part of your system. The UML defines four standard stereotypes that can be applied to classes. They are as follows:

❖ **metaclass:** This stereotype specifies that the class in which it is defined is a classifier whose objects are also classes.

❖ **powertype:** This stereotype specifies that the class in which it is defined is a classifier whose objects are the children of a given parent.

❖ **stereotype:** This stereotype specifies that the class in which it is defined is a classifier which itself is a stereotype that can be applied to create other new building blocks.

❖ **utility:** This stereotype specifies that the class in which it is defined is a classifier whose attributes and operations are all class scoped.

**Examples:**

**metaclass:** In object-oriented programming, a **metaclass** is a class whose instances are classes. Just as an ordinary class defines the behavior of certain objects, a metaclass defines the behavior of certain classes and their instances. A metaclass can implement a design pattern or describe a short hand for particular kinds of classes. Metaclasses are often used to describe frameworks.

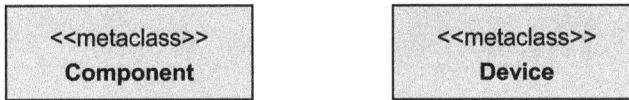

```
┌──────────────────┐        ┌──────────────────┐
│  <<metaclass>>   │        │  <<metaclass>>   │
│   Component      │        │    Device        │
└──────────────────┘        └──────────────────┘
```

**Fig.3.10** A Meta Class

**Note:** The Component is a metaclass, because Component gives a set of classes which are Components. For example, electronic components, electrical components and mechanical components are themselves components. Similarly Device is a metaclass whose instances are various types of devices, which are a type of classes, such as electronic devices, electrical devices, and mechanical devices etc. It means that the instances of Device are themselves classes of some type. For example, a PictureTube is a class whose instances are various PictureTubes. A PictureTube class is an instance of a metaclass named Device.

**powertype:** It is a keyword for a specific UML stereotype, and applies to a class. Powertype shows a classifier whose instances (objects) are children of the given parent. A powertype is a type the instances of which are subtypes of another type (called the partitioned type). Powertype and partitioned type are thus related indirectly through the entities that are instances of the former and, at the same time, subtypes of the latter.

**Note:** The powertype pattern can, in fact, be applied to just about every regular subtyping hierarchy. For example, a common example is that in the motor vehicle domain. The above shows the normal model, using inheritance (UML's generalization relationship), for a Vehicle with a subtype of Boat, an instance of which is also shown in this figure using regular UML notation. However, it is perhaps more accurate to introduce the class VehicleKind (of which Boat is just one instance), where VehicleKind categorizes Vehicle. Boat can then be instantiated to create objects such as B2:Boat. Since instantiation occurs at runtime, we can dynamically create other instances of VehicleKind, such as Plane or Car, in parallel to Boat in the above figure. We therefore propose that most   normal inheritance hierarchies in UML models can be easily modified to become powertype patterns, which thus represent features that belong to the powertype as well as those of the partitioned type.

**Fig.3.11(a)** A Powertype Pattern

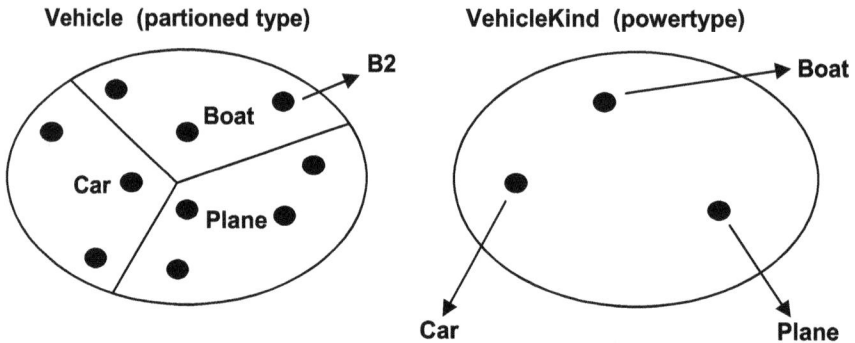

**Fig.3.11(b)** Powertype

**stereotype:** The intent of the stereotype pattern is to customize an element in the UML model for a particular usage. For example, the elements defined using the stereotype, <<metaclass>> are generic enough for large number of situations. Sometimes you may add details to a metaclass (generic class) so that it is optimized for a particular range of situations. We achieve this outcome by using stereotypes. This is applicable in situations where the metaclass element too generic and needs details to be added for a particular usage. In the following diagram, the Order is a metaclass, which is so generic, may include types such as sales order, purchase order, quotation, invoice, and goods receipts. You can attach a stereotype named purchase order so that your model represents the context of purchase orders in your system.

**Fig.3.12** Stereotype

**Note:** The Order class represents the UML metaclass that needs to be customized for a particular usage, let us say for the purpose of purchases. The stereotype class represents the optimized PurchaseOrder class.

**utility:** Utility is a stereotyped classifier representing a classifier that has no instances, but rather denotes a named collection of non-member attributes and operations, all of which are class-scoped. A class stereotyped with <<utility>> represents a class that provides utility services through static methods, just as Java's Math class.

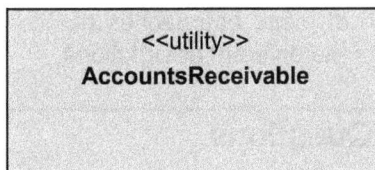

**Note:** AccountsReceivable is a utility class containing attributes and operations which are static. These static methods provide utility services for accounts receivables domain.

## 3.9 Modeling the Semantics of a Class

Generally, classes are used to model abstractions that are drawn from requirements document or from a problem statement for which you are developing a solution. Once you identify abstractions, the next task could be specifying their semantics, meaning, specifying what information they convey to the external world. You should decide what level of details of a model required to communicate effectively the intent of your model. You might require a less detailed model to communicate with end users. If the purpose of your model is to perform round trip engineering (forward and reverse engineering), then you definitely require a model with more details. The following steps are generally considered and followed while you are modeling the semantics of a class. Semantics means the information that a class conveys.

❖ Identify and specify responsibilities of the class. A responsibility is an obligation of a class. These responsibilities can be provided in a separate compartment attached to a class or a note is attached to a class containing textual information which is stereotyped as 'responsibility'.

❖ Specify the semantics of the class as a whole using structured text in a note which is stereotyped as 'semantics' and attach it with the class.

❖ Specify the body of each method either in the form a text or using a programming language in a note and associate it with the operation using dependency relationship.

❖ Describe the preconditions and post conditions of each operation, and also include the invariants of the class as a whole in the form of structured text in notes. These notes are stereotyped as precondition, postcondition, and invariant. These notes are attached to the operation or class by a dependency relationship.

❖ Draw a state chart (state machine) for the class. A state machine is a behavior that specifies the sequence of states an object goes through during its life time in response to internal or external events.

❖ Specify a collaboration that represents the class. A collaboration is a society of elements working together to accomplish a task. A collaboration has a structural part and behavioral part. You can use collaborations to fully express the complete semantics of a class.

**Note:** Some combination of these approaches mentioned above are used for modeling the semantics of the different abstractions.

## Essay Type Questions

1. Write short notes on classifiers.

2. Explain advanced classes with examples.

3. Briefly explain the following:
   (a) Advanced attributes     (b) Advanced operations

4. Explain template classes with examples.

5. Explain various steps involved in modeling the semantics of a class.

## Objective Type Questions

1. A classifier can be
   (a) class
   (b) interface
   (c) a signal
   (d) All

2. Which specifies an asynchronous communication that happens between instances while they interact.
   (a) interface
   (b) class
   (c) signal
   (d) component

3. ---------------------- indicates a physical computational resource that exists at run time
   (a) class
   (b) component
   (c) interface
   (d) node

4. A class scoped attribute
   (a) varies from instance to instance
   (b) holds good for the whole class
   (c) both a & b
   (d) none

5. An instance scoped attribute is
   (a) varies from instance to instance
   (b) holds good for the whole class
   (c) both a & b
   (d) none

6. A singleton class is a class with class multiplicity
   (a) more than one
   (b) zero or more
   (c) one
   (d) one or more

7. A class name in italics indicate
   (a) abstract class
   (b) singleton class
   (c) leaf class
   (d) None

8. The property that means that the attribute value can be changed.
   (a) addonly
   (b) frozen
   (c) changeable
   (d) All

9. The property that you cannot change the value of the attribute once it is initialized.
   (a) addonly
   (b) frozen
   (c) changeable
   (d) All

10. An input parameter, it may not be modified. The direction is
    (a) in
    (b) out
    (c) inout
    (d) All

11. An output parameter, it may be modified to communicate with caller. The direction is
    (a) in                              (b) out
    (c) inout                           (d) All

12. If the operation is not protected against multiple processes and threads , this property is
    (a) guarded                         (b) sequential
    (c) isQuery                         (d) concurrent

13. The property that multiple threads or processes can execute the operation at the same time guaranteeing its integrity is
    (a) guarded                         (b) sequential
    (c) isQuery                         (d) concurrent

14. A template class include slots for
    (a) classes                         (b) objects
    (c) values                          (d) All

15. The stereotyped bind dependency indicate
    (a) implicit binding                (b) explicit binding
    (c) both a & b                      (d) None

16. ---------------- stereotype specifies that the class in which it is defined is a classifier whose objects are also classes.
    (a) utility                         (b) powertype
    (c) metaclass                       (d) stereotype

17. ---------------- stereotype specifies that the class in which it is defined is a classifier whose attributes and operations are all class scoped.
    (a) utility                         (b) powertype
    (c) metaclass                       (d) stereotype

## Answers

| | | | | | |
|---|---|---|---|---|---|
| 1. (d) | 2. (c) | 3. (d) | 4. (b) | 5. (a) | 6. (c) |
| 7. (a) | 8. (c) | 9. (b) | 10. (a) | 11. (b) | 12. (b) |
| 13. (d) | 14. (d) | 15. (b) | 16. (c) | 17. (a) | |

# CHAPTER 4

# Advanced Relationships

A relationship is a connection between the things that constitute your model. In UML, the four important relationships are dependencies, generalizations, associations, and realizations. Graphically, these relationships are represented with different types of connecting lines. In this chapter we discuss advanced relationships, which specify some additional semantics to the normal relationships.

## 4.1 Dependency

A dependency relationship between two classifiers show that one classifier is dependent on the other, meaning the change in one will affect the other. In order to extend the semantics of this relationship, UML has a number of defined stereotypes. There are 17 stereotypes which are organized into six groups.

There are eight stereotypes that apply to dependency relationships among classes and objects in class diagrams.

**bind:** This stereotype specifies that the source class instantiates the target class which is a template class by binding actual parameters with the formal template parameters. The purpose of this dependency with bind stereotype is to create model elements from templates.

**derive**: This stereotype specifies that the source element may be computed from the target. If you have BirthDate, you can compute Age, Similarly, in a payroll system the NetSalary can be computed using BasicSalary.

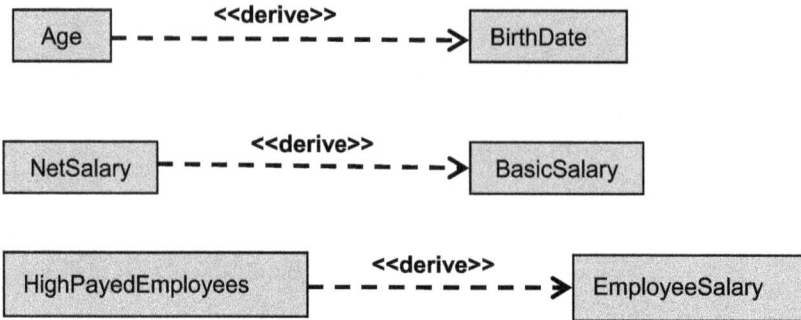

**Fig.4.1** Derive Dependency

**friend:** This stereotype specifies that the source is given special visibility into the target. The source classifier has access to the elements of the target classifier. A friend relationship grants the source access to the target regardless of the declared visibility.

**Example:**

**Note:** The HRD manager has access to every details of an employee.

**Fig.4.2** Friend Dependency

**instanceof:** This stereotype specifies that the source is the instance of the target.

**Example:**

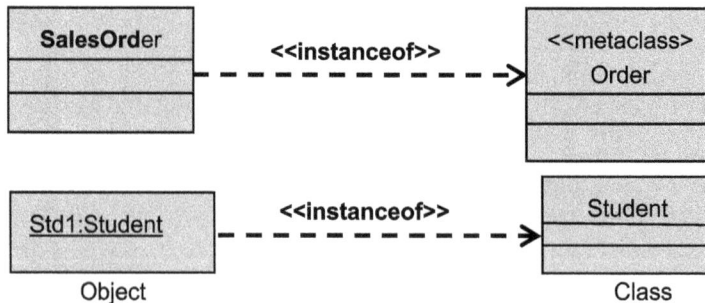

**instantiate:** This stereotype specifies that the source creates the instances of the target.

**Example:**

**Note:** While a HRD manager of any company is going for a recruitment drive, he advertizes for   various opportunities available in the company. In a way, we can say that he has created the instances of Opportunity class.

**powertype:** This stereotype specifies that the target is a powertype of the source. A powertype is a classifier whose objects are all the children of a given parent. Classifier powertype is a stereotyped classifier denoting that the classifier is a metatype, whose instances are subtypes of another type. Whereas dependency powertype is a stereotyped dependency whose source is a set of generalizations and whose target is a classifier specifying that the target is the powertype of the source.

**Example:**

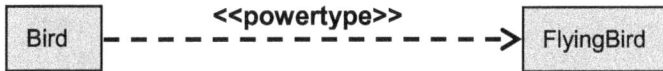

**Note:** The instances of the class named FlyingBird are subtypes of the class named Bird. It means that, all flying birds are a type of birds.

**refine:** This stereotype specifies that the source is at a fines degree of abstraction than the target. This refine dependency can be between the same class but at different levels of abstraction. While you are doing system analysis, you identify abstractions based on their responsibilities without bothering about their internal details. But, when you design, you may expand your class to contain attributes and operations. Though the class is same, it is in different levels of details.

**Example:**

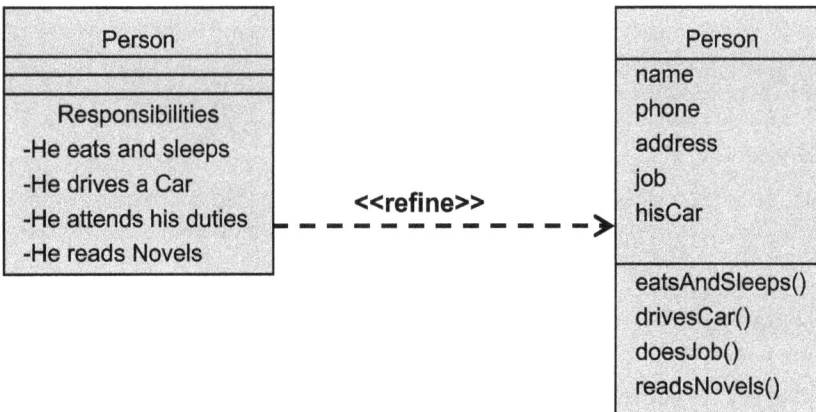

**Fig.4.3** Refine Dependency

**use:** This stereotype specifies that the semantics of the source element depends on the semantics of the public part of the target. This dependency is also called usage dependency, it is one in which the source classifier requires the presence of the target classifier for its correct implementation. The following diagram specifies dependency stereotyped with <<use>>, which describes that instances of Order class require instances of the OrderItem class for proper functioning.

**Example:**

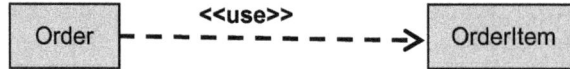

There are two other stereotypes which you can associate with dependency among packages to extend the semantics of your model. They are as follows:

**access:** This stereotype specifies that the source package is granted the right to refer the elements of the target package. This dependency means that objects from client package can access objects (public one) from supplier package.

**Example**:

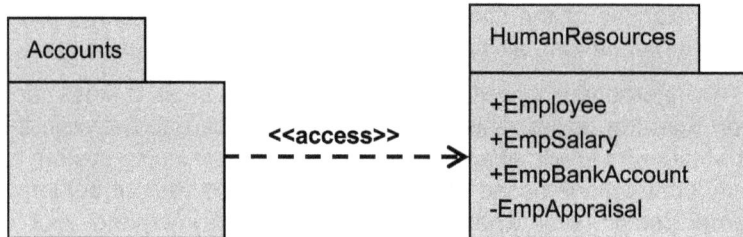

**Fig.4.4** Access Dependency

**Note:** The objects or the elements of the Accounts package can access the public part of HumanResources package. While you are accessing public elements of the package you need to fully qualify them with the name of the package. For example, the package Accounts can refer Employee class of the HumanResources package by using HumanResources::Employee. In the above figure, Accounts package cannot access the class EmpAppraisal as it is having private visibility.

**import:** This stereotype specifies that the public contents of the target package are added to the namespace of the source package. Here the source package can refer the public contents of the target package without qualifying them with the target package. For example, in the above diagram, if the dependency is stereotyped with <<import>>, then Accounts package can directly refer Employee class without qualifying it with the name of the target package.

There are two other stereotypes which you can associate with dependencies among use cases. They are as follows:

**extend:** This stereotype specifies that the target use case extends the behavior of the source use case.

**Example:**

**Note:** In the above figure, Verify Certificates is a source use case and Enroll in College is a target use case. The extend dependency between the above use cases imply that enrolling a student into a college must happen only after his relevant certificates are verified.

**include:** This stereotype specifies that the source use case incorporates the behavior of the target use case at a  location specified by the source.

**Example:**

**Note:** In the above figure, Enroll in University use case is a source use case and Enroll in Seminar is a target use case. A student who is enrolled in a university must also enroll himself for the seminars. Enrolling in the university incorporates enrolling for a seminar, where the student attends seminars as part of class work specified as curriculum by the university.

You may come across three more stereotypes associated with dependency relationship while you are modeling interactions among objects. The related stereotypes are as follows:

**become:** This stereotype specifies that the target is the same object as the source but at a later point in time and with possibly different values of attributes, state, or roles. The source object is transformed into the target object maintaining the same identity.

**Note:** In the above figure, the short listed candidate will become an employee when he is selected in the interview. A candidate before interview is a shortlisted one, after interview, if selected, he becomes an employee. That is, a candidate has become an employee with a different state and of course with a different role.

**call:** This stereotype specifies that the source operation invokes the target operation. Call is a stereotyped dependency whose source is an operation and whose target is also an operation. A call dependency specifies that the source invokes the target operation. A call dependency may connect a source operation to any target operation that is within scope including, but not limited to, operations of the enclosing classifier and operations of other visible classifiers.

**copy:** This stereotype specifies that the target is an exact, but an independent copy of the source. In this stereotyped dependency, source and target are different instances, but with the same values, same state and same role but with a distinct identity. In this relationship, the target is the exact copy of source. Future changes in source may not be reflected in the target.

**Note**: We use copy when you want to show the role, state, or attribute value of one object at different points in time or space.

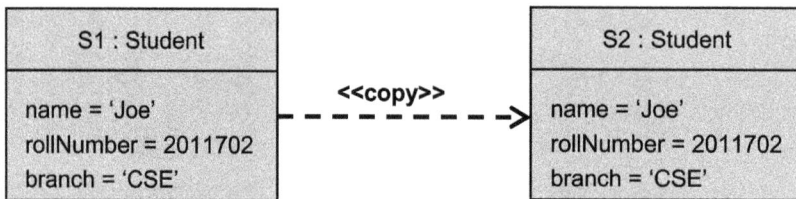

| S1 : Student | | S2 : Student |
|---|---|---|
| name = 'Joe'<br>rollNumber = 2011702<br>branch = 'CSE' | - - - <<copy>> - - -> | name = 'Joe'<br>rollNumber = 2011702<br>branch = 'CSE' |

There is only one stereotype you may come across in the context of state chart (state machine). It is described as follows:

**send :** This stereotype specifies that the source operation sends a target event. Generally a send dependency is indicated between a source which is an operation and a target which is a signal. This dependency stereotyped with send specifies that the source sends the target signal.

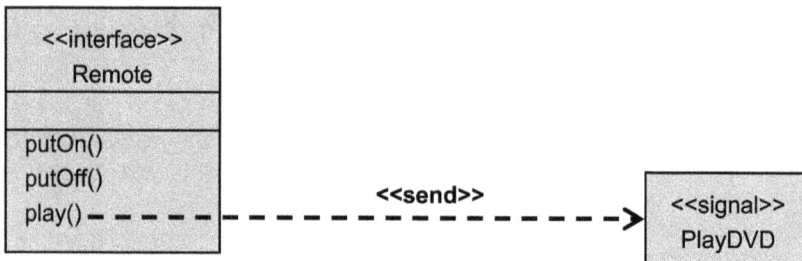

| <<interface>><br>Remote |
|---|
| putOn()<br>putOff()<br>play() - - - |

play() - - - - - - <<send>> - - - - - - -> | <<signal>><br>PlayDVD |

**Fig.4.5** Send Dependency

**Note:** In the above figure, the Remote interface has on operation play(), this operation sends a signal named PlayDVD. This signal goes to the DVD player and executes the implementation built inside DVD player for play() operation.

The last stereotype which you can associate with the dependency is <<trace>>.You generally use this stereotype for organizing and grouping elements into packages or subsystems.

**trace:** This stereotype specifies that the target is a historical ancestor of the source. You apply trace dependency to model relationships between elements belonging to different models. In this case each model may indicate different levels of details. For example, when you are doing system analysis you might have found a use case which depicts a particular service or a function of the system. This use case exists in the use case model. But when you design the system, the behavior expressed by this use case can be implemented by a set of various elements working together to accomplish this behavior specified by the use case. This group of elements working together can be expressed as a collaboration or as a package grouping all these elements. Here the package is in design model, and the corresponding use case is in use case model. Here the use case becomes the ancestor of the package. The dependency can be represented as follows:-

**Example:**

**Fig.4.6** Trace Dependency

## 4.2 Generalization

It is a relationship between a general thing (called super class or parent) and a specific thing (called child or sub class). This is also called inheritance relationship. In case of single inheritance, a child will have only one parent, whereas in multiple inheritance, a child will have more than one parent. The following figures give examples for generalization relationship.

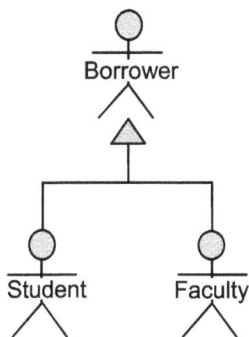

**Fig.4.7(a)** Single Inheritance

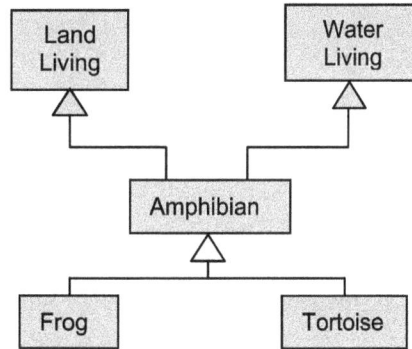

**Fig.4.7(b)** Multiple Inheritance

**Note:** In Fig.4.7(a), A borrower in a Library System, could be a student or a faculty. Borrower is more general, and student and faculty are more specific in their specification. In the Fig.4.7(b), Amphibian is both a land living and water living creature, whereas a frog is an amphibian.

Apart from plain generalization/specialization relationship, we may add additional semantics to make your model more informative. These additional semantics can be specified by associating generalization relationship with a stereotype and four other defined constraints in the UML. The following topic and diagrams describe these associated things with the generalization relationship.

**implementation:** This stereotype when associated with the generalization relationship specifies that the child inherits the entire implementation of the parent. As we are aware that in a generalization relationship, the child is substitutable wherever parent is referred. But in this case, the child though inherits implementation of parent, but does not make public, and it does not even support the interfaces realized by the parent. Because of this, the child is not substitutable. The parent retains the full right to make its implementation public or support its interfaces.

There are four standard constraints supported by UML that apply to generalization/specialization relationship. They are as follows:

**Complete:** If this constraint is associated with a generalization relationship, it implies that all the required children belonging to the parent are specified. The generalization is complete in the model, and no other additional children are permitted.

**Example:**

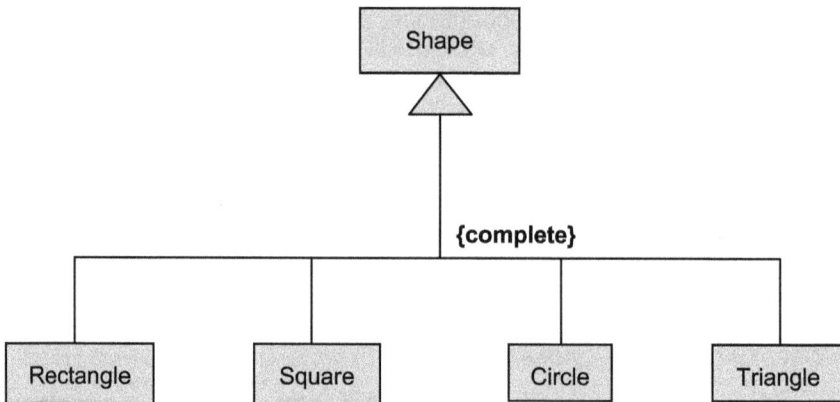

**Fig.4.8(a)** Complete Generalization

**incomplete:** If it is associated with generalization, it means that not all children of a parent specified. Additional children are allowed.

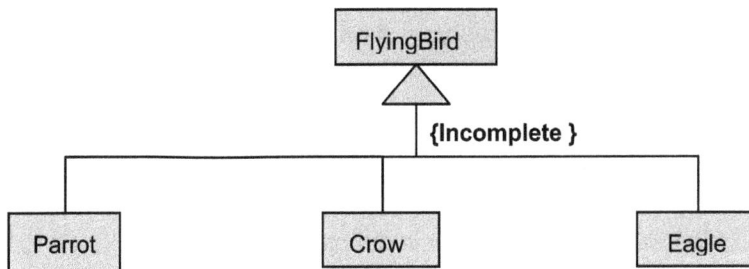

**Fig.4.8(b)** Incomplete Generalization

**Note:** The term incomplete partitioning applies to subgroups of a group. It means that not all of possible subgroups belonging to a group are included in the model. In other words, the group may have some members that don't belong to any of the modeled subgroups in generalization. The term complete portioning indicates that all subgroups belonging to a group are specified in the model and no other subgroup is permitted.

**disjoint:** If this constraint is associated with a generalization relationship, it means that, the objects of the parent have no more than one of the children as type. The term disjoint partitioning applies to two or more groups of things that are cleanly partitioned. In other words, no single thing can belong to more than one group at the same time. For example, dogs, pigs, and horses are disjoint sub groups. The following diagram illustrates the disjoint constraint applied to generalization.

**Example:**

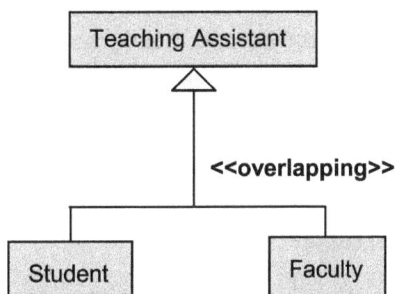

**Fig.4.9(a)** Disjoint Generalization          **Fig.4.9(b)** Overlapping generalization

**Overlapping:** If this constraint is associated with generalization, it means that objects of the parent may have more than one of the children as a type. It means that the sub groups are not cleanly partitioned and they might overlap causing an object of the parent may belong to more than one sub type.

**Note:** In the Fig.4.9(a), the constraint applied is disjoint, it means that a mammal can be a dog or can be a pig but not both. The instances of mammal can be of only one subtype. In the Fig.4.9(b), an instance of teaching assistant may include more than one subtype, meaning a teaching assistant can be a student studying some post graduate course, and also can be a faculty teaching for under graduate courses.

## 4.3 Association

An association between classifiers is a structural relationship, indicating how the objects of one thing are linked or connected with the objects of the other thing. Graphically, an association is represented as a solid line connecting the same or different classifiers. We have already discussed the adornments that apply to an association relationship. In the subsequent chapters we discuss navigation, qualification, and various flavours of aggregation. For example, a College class may have a one-to-many association with the Student class, expressing that each Student instance is associated with a College instance. In any association, especially the one we are discussing, given a Student, you can find the College in which he is studying. And also, given a College, you can navigate to all of its Students.

## 4.4 Navigation

In any association, such as College and Student, you can navigate from objects of one kind to the objects of the other kind. In any plain association, the navigation is bidirectional. When you are creating models, you may come across associations in which the navigation is unidirectional. You can represent the direction of navigation in an association by adorning the association with a directed arrowhead pointing to the direction of traversal. The unidirectional association happens between User objects and Password objects. Given a User you may find the corresponding Password, but not the reverse. An association between a Company and Client is also unidirectional. A Company is aware of Client, but the Client do not have any knowledge of the Company leading this association a unidirectional one.

**Examples:**

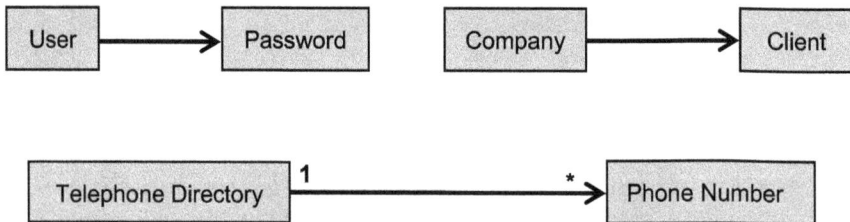

**Fig.4.10** Unidirectional Navigation

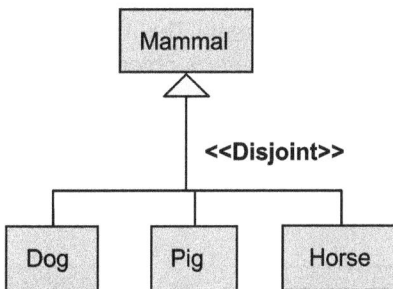

**Fig.4.8(b)** Incomplete Generalization

**Note:** The term incomplete partitioning applies to subgroups of a group. It means that not all of possible subgroups belonging to a group are included in the model. In other words, the group may have some members that don't belong to any of the modeled subgroups in generalization. The term complete portioning indicates that all subgroups belonging to a group are specified in the model and no other subgroup is permitted.

**disjoint:** If this constraint is associated with a generalization relationship, it means that, the objects of the parent have no more than one of the children as type. The term disjoint partitioning applies to two or more groups of things that are cleanly partitioned. In other words, no single thing can belong to more than one group at the same time. For example, dogs, pigs, and horses are disjoint sub groups. The following diagram illustrates the disjoint constraint applied to generalization.

**Example:**

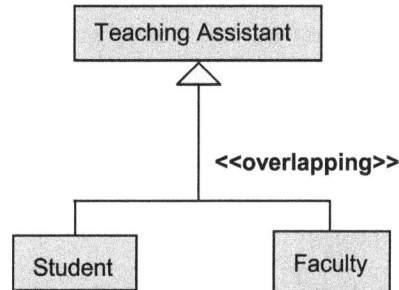

**Fig.4.9(a)** Disjoint Generalization    **Fig.4.9(b)** Overlapping generalization

**Overlapping:** If this constraint is associated with generalization, it means that objects of the parent may have more than one of the children as a type. It means that the sub groups are not cleanly partitioned and they might overlap causing an object of the parent may belong to more than one sub type.

**Note:** In the Fig.4.9(a), the constraint applied is disjoint, it means that a mammal can be a dog or can be a pig but not both. The instances of mammal can be of only one subtype. In the Fig.4.9(b), an instance of teaching assistant may include more than one subtype, meaning a teaching assistant can be a student studying some post graduate course, and also can be a faculty teaching for under graduate courses.

## 4.3 Association

An association between classifiers is a structural relationship, indicating how the objects of one thing are linked or connected with the objects of the other thing. Graphically, an association is represented as a solid line connecting the same or different classifiers. We have already discussed the adornments that apply to an association relationship. In the subsequent chapters we discuss navigation, qualification, and various flavours of aggregation. For example, a College class may have a one-to-many association with the Student class, expressing that each Student instance is associated with a College instance. In any association, especially the one we are discussing, given a Student, you can find the College in which he is studying. And also, given a College, you can navigate to all of its Students.

## 4.4 Navigation

In any association, such as College and Student, you can navigate from objects of one kind to the objects of the other kind. In any plain association, the navigation is bidirectional. When you are creating models, you may come across associations in which the navigation is unidirectional. You can represent the direction of navigation in an association by adorning the association with a directed arrowhead pointing to the direction of traversal. The unidirectional association happens between User objects and Password objects. Given a User you may find the corresponding Password, but not the reverse. An association between a Company and Client is also unidirectional. A Company is aware of Client, but the Client do not have any knowledge of the Company leading this association a unidirectional one.

**Examples:**

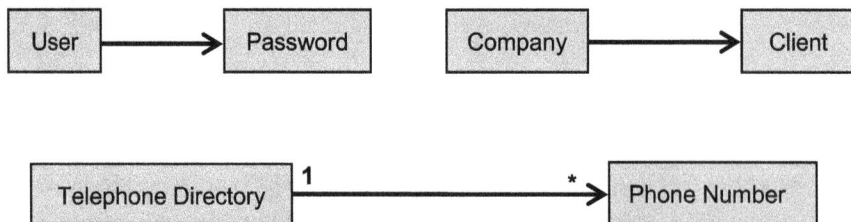

Fig.4.10 Unidirectional Navigation

## 4.5 Visibility

As we are aware that association also include navigation from one end of association to the other and vice versa, unless otherwise the navigation is unidirectional. You can associate visibility constraints with the objects participating in the association. These visibility constraints restrict the availability of objects to the outside of association. For example, in the following figure, there is an association between Bank Consortium, and Bank which is a bidirectional navigation. The association between Bank and its Policies is unidirectional, indicating that given a Bank you can navigate across its policies, but given policies you cannot identify a Bank, as policies are private to a Bank.

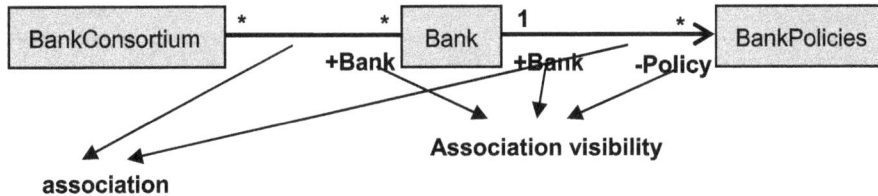

**Fig.4.11** Association Visibility

**Note:** You can specify three levels of visibility for the elements participating in an association. You can adorn visibility by appending a visibility symbol to a role name in an association. By default the visibility of a role is public, meaning this element is also available outside the association. Private visibility means that the objects at that end are not available outside the association. Similarly, protected visibility indicates that the objects at that end are not available outside the association, except for the children of the other end. In the above figure, the roles played by Bank Consortium and Bank are public, whereas the role Policy has private visibility, because policies are private to the Bank.

## 4.6 Qualification

In any typical association, you may come across a situation more often that given an object at one end, how do you identify an object or set of objects at the other end. Consider a problem of associating a Bank with a Person. Given a Bank object, you can identify Person objects relating to the bank by using the property called Account Number. In this case account number is the attribute of association, given an object of the class Bank, and the value of the account number, you can navigate one or more objects of the Person class. This association attribute is called qualifier. Graphically, you represent a qualifier as a small rectangle attached to the end of an association, placing the attributes in the rectangle.

Association qualification model relationships that involve "lookup", meaning, when navigating the relationship, you are looking for a particular object or set of objects. For example, a telephone directory consists of multiple entries, given a person's name, you can lookup the associated phone numbers. The following diagram indicates the applicability of qualification in an association.

**Fig.4.12** Association Qualification

## 4.7 Interface Specifier

An interface is a classifier containing a set of operations which specify a service of a class or a component. An interface always contains operations that are not implemented in it, but they are implemented in a class or in a component which is in relationship with the interface. In the context of an association between classes, a source class may choose only to present a part of its face. For example, in a university course registration system, a Student is a more generalized class, containing graduate and post graduate students. A post graduate student may play a role of a teaching assistant teaching for graduate students. The entire scenario can be depicted in the following figure.

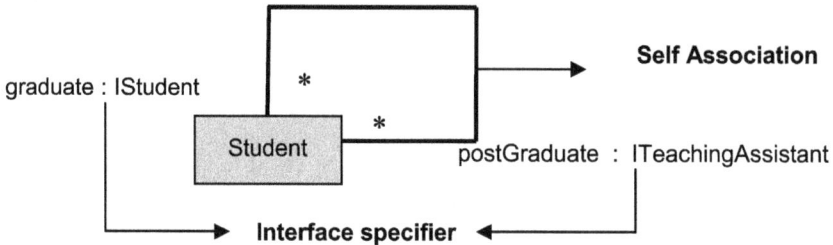

**Fig.4.13** Interface Specifier

**Note:** In the above figure, the Student classifier is in self association (an association with itself). The students registered could be graduate and post graduate students. However, the post graduate students have an option of getting a teaching assistant job where they teach for graduate students. The role of a graduate student is always a student, it means that it has an interface named IStudent for the self association. Whereas, the post graduate student, if he becomes a teaching assistant then he has an interface named ITeachingAssistant with that self association.

## 4.8 Composition

As we are aware that an aggregation relationship is an extension of association relationship, where you have a whole class and its children classes which are parts of its parent. An aggregation is basically a whole and part relationship. The best example for aggregation can be a Personal Computer, which has parts like mouse, keyboard, monitor, CPU, memory, Hard Disk etc. In aggregation the life spans of whole and parts are not tightly related, it means that even though the whole is destroyed, some parts still be useful. These parts can be used with other wholes.

An extension of aggregation is composition, where the life spans of whole and parts are tightly related, it means that when whole dies all its parts die or rendered useless. For example, human being and all his body parts are in composition relationship, when the man dies all his parts die, or become useless. Another example, suppose you have a dining table with four legs, the relationship between the table and its legs is a composition relationship. Because when dining table is destroyed, its legs are also destroyed. They have no purpose and rendered useless.

**Note:** We have already discussed extensively about composition relationship while we were discussing about various relationships supported by UML. We have already come across several examples for composition.

## 4.9 Association Classes

When you are modeling association between two classes, you may find that the association itself has some properties. For example, in an association between a Person class and a Company class, Company hires a person. This hiring by a company is an association which can be called Job. The Job is an association between a Person class and a Company class, which itself has some properties. Such associations with properties are called association classes.

Another example for an association could be an association between a software consultant and a client. Client might be wanting the Consultant to develop a software for him. Now the association between a Client and a Consultant becomes a software project which itself has some properties.

An association class is always linked with the association relationship by dotted lines. The following example specify association classes.

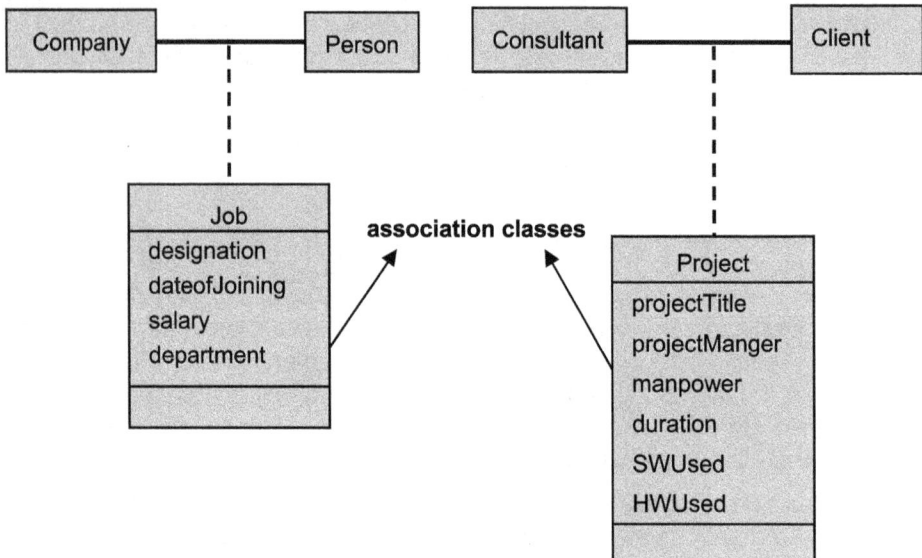

**Fig.4.14** Association Classes

## 4.10 Constraints

Most of the structural relationships can be sufficiently modeled with whatever we know about associations. However, there are some standard UML definitions by using with you can extend the intent of your model, or you add additional semantics to the model. There are five constraints defined in UML, which are applicable to association relationships, to specify additional meaning. The constraints are as follows:

**Implicit:** This constraint specifies that the association is only conceptual. For example, if you have an association between two parent classes, you can specify the same association between their children, as children inherit the relationships of parents. You can mark this relationship as implicit, because this relationship is derived from parents. An association with implicit constraint is never instantiated. This association is generally derived from a combination of other associations.

**Example: See Fig.4.15**

**Ordered:** There is a way to specify that the objects at one end of the association (the end where multiplicity is greater than one) are ordered or unordered. If you associate the constraint {ordered} with the association, the end where there is a set of objects are in an explicit order.

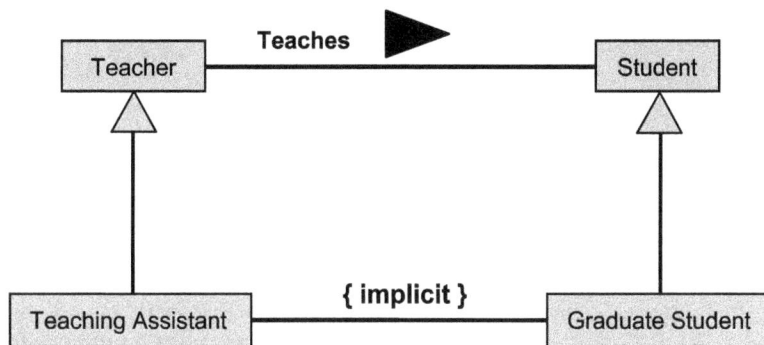

**Fig.4.15** Association with {implicit} constraint

**Example:**

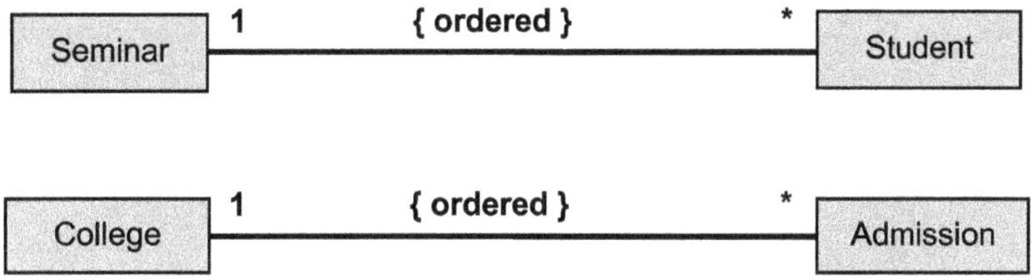

**Fig.4.16** Association with {ordered} Constraint.

**Note:** In the above Fig.4.16, the association is specified with ordered constraint. When a student enrols himself for a course in a university, he has to be added to the list for seminars on that course. The students are listed in first in first out order for seminars. Hence the association is added with a constraint {ordered}. In the second diagram there is an association between a College and student admissions in to the college. Students are admitted in to the college based on their rank in the common entrance examination. In a way it means that the admissions are ordered by rank. Hence an association between College and Admission are specified with the constraint {ordered}.

**Changeable:** This constraint specifies the changeability of the instances of association. Links between objects can be added, removed, or can be modified freely.

**addOnly :** This constraint specifies that new links may be added only, meaning a new link once added cannot be removed.

**Frozen:** This constraint specifies that a link once added, cannot be removed or cannot be modified.

## 4.11 Realization

It is the relationship between two classifiers, where one classifier specifies a contract or an obligation, and the other classifier guarantees. You may find realization between an interface and a class or a component. We know that an interface contains a set of operations without their implementations. These operations are implemented by an associated class or a component to the interface. An interface is a mechanism by means of which a service of a class or a component is specified. The relationship between the interface and its related class or a component is called realization. You may come across realization relationship between a use case and a collaboration. A use case specifies a service, or a contract which is guaranteed to be implemented by a society of elements and their interactions in the form of a collaboration. An interface can be realized by more than one component or class. A component or a class can realize more than one interface.

**Examples**:

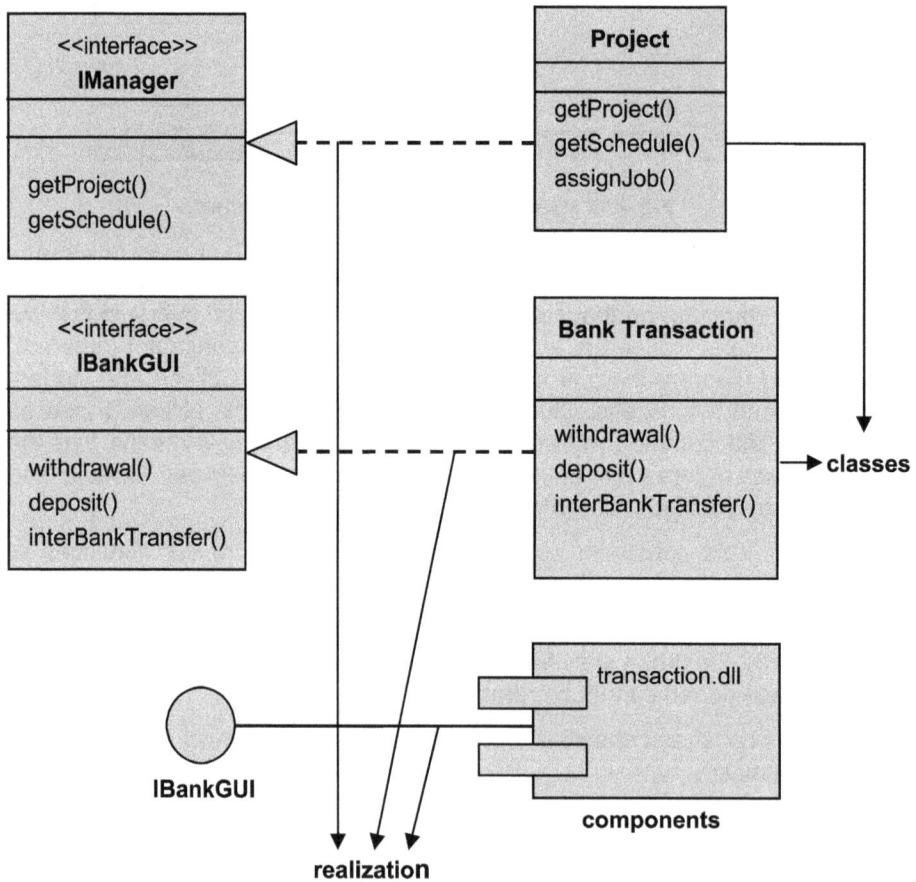

**Fig.4.17** Realization of an Interface

**Fig.4.18** Realization of a Use Case

## 4.12 Modeling Webs of Relationships

Suppose you are modeling a very complex system that works on a distributed platform, you might come across unmanageable number of use cases, classes, objects, interfaces, components and nodes. This model will become further complex, if you include relationships among these identified abstractions. You will be on a better side, if you develop a model based on balanced distribution of responsibilities, which will reduce the possibility of huge sized classifiers and also a large number of trivial sized classifiers. It could help you a lot, if you decompose your model into some independent views rather than having a single and a very complex graphical picture.

When you model these webs of relationships for a complex system, it is better if you fallow the sequence of steps as given below:

❖ Begin your model from use cases, identify the set of scenarios for each use case. In order to realize these use cases, find out the various abstractions and relationships.

❖ Start by modeling the structural relationships. Because the structural relationships identify the static structure of the system which may pave a way for understanding the system's architecture.

❖ Once you identify classifiers with balanced distribution of responsibilities, find for opportunities for generalization/specialization relationships. Push up the abstractions having common information as generalized ones, pull down abstractions having specific additional information as specialized ones. Do not hesitate to use multiple inheritance wherever possible.

❖ After identifying generalization relationships among abstractions, you go for dependencies. These dependencies identify semantic connection among various classifiers.

❖ After establishing a type of relationship among abstractions, start it with its basic form. Attach advanced features to make your model more clear and more informative. Apply these advanced semantics for expressing clearly and unambiguously the intent of your model.

❖ It is better if you do not model all kinds of relationships with their participating abstractions in a single diagram or view. Establish different views on the system, and then build relationships expressing the intended view of the system. You can have important relationships depicted in various individual diagrams.

If you want your model describing the complex webs of relationships, to be successful, the better approach is to build models in an incremental fashion. Of course, the modern software development approach is mostly iterative and incremental, it means, building models in an incremental fashion. For each iteration of your system development cycle, you extend the semantics of your model for deeper and better understanding of the intent of your model.

## Essay Type Questions

1. Explain briefly that eight stereotypes that apply to dependency relationship.
2. Write short notes on advanced generalization relationship with examples.
3. Briefly explain the following in advanced association relationship
   (a) Navigation   (b) Visibility   (c) Qualification
4. Explain association classes and association constraints.
5. Explain modeling webs of relationships with various steps involved.

## Objective Type Questions

1. The relationship between two classifiers where change in one affects the other is
   (a) Dependency                      (b) Association
   (c) Aggregation                     (d) Generalization
2. ------------------ stereotype specifies that the source element may be computed from the target
   (a) bind                            (b) derive
   (c) friend                          (d) instanceof
3. ------------------ stereotype specifies that the source is given special visibility into the target
   (a) bind                            (b) derive
   (c) friend                          (d) instanceof
4. The stereotype that specifies that the source creates the instances of the target
   (a) bind                            (b) derive
   (c) friend                          (d) instanciate

5. The stereotype which specifies that the source package is granted the right to refer the elements of the target package.

   (a) refine                    (b) instanciate
   (c) import                    (d) access

6. The stereotype which specifies that the public contents of the target package are added to the namespace of the source package

   (a) refine                    (b) instanciate
   (c) import                    (d) access

7. The stereotype which specifies that the target is an exact, but an independent copy of the source

   (a) call                      (b) copy
   (c) bind                      (d) import

8. The stereotype which specifies that the target is a historical ancestor of the source

   (a) copy                      (b) import
   (c) trace                     (d) extend

9. The constraint which  is associated with a generalization relationship, it implies that all the required children belonging to the parent are specified.

   (a) incomplete                (b) complete
   (c) implementation            (d) All the above

10. The constraint which is associated with a generalization relationship, it means that, the objects of the parent have no more than one of the children as type

   (a) overlapping               (b) disjoint
   (c) incomplete                (d) All the above

11. The constraint which  is associated with generalization, it means that objects of the parent may have more than one of the children as a type.

   (a) overlapping               (b) disjoint
   (c) incomplete                (d) All the above

12. In association relationship between bank and person the qualification is

   (a) account number            (b) account name
   (c) account holder address    (d) phone number

13. An association of the classifier with itself is called

   (a) interface                 (b) self association
   (c) navigation                (d) qualification

14. The relationship which is the extension of aggregation where as the life spans of whole and parts are tightly coupled

    (a) association                    (b) composition
    (c) navigation                     (d) aggregation

15. The constraint which specifies the changeability of the instances of association. Links between objects can be added, removed, or can be modified freely

    (a) implicit                       (b) explicit
    (c) changeable                     (d) All the above

16. The constraint in association which specifies that a link once added, cannot be removed or cannot be modified

    (a) changeable                     (b) implicit
    (c) extend                         (d) frozen

## Answers

| | | | | | |
|---|---|---|---|---|---|
| 1. (a) | 2. (b) | 3. (c) | 4. (d) | 5. (d) | 6. (c) |
| 7. (b) | 8. (c) | 9. (b) | 10. (b) | 11. (a) | 12. (a) |
| 13. (b) | 14. (b) | 15. (c) | 16. (d) | | |

# Interfaces, Types and Roles

An interface specifies a distinction between the specification of what an abstraction does and the implementation of how that abstraction does it. As we know that an interface is a collection of operations that are used to specify a service of a class or a component. An interface can be realized by more than one class or one component. Similarly more than one interface can be realized by a class or a component.

A type can be defined as a stereotype specifying a domain of objects, together with the operations applicable to the object. A role specifies the behavior of an entity that participates in a particular situation. We know that, graphically, an interface can be defined as a circle with its name. If you want to expand the details of an interface, it is defined as a stereotyped class with all its operations. An interface can also be used to specify a service of a use case or a subsystem.

Every interface must have a name that distinguishes it from other elements or other interfaces. An interface is graphically rendered as a circle with its name, the name of an interface may start with capital 'I' indicating that it is an interface. If you want to refer an interface that belongs to a package, you need to use a path name.

**Example**:

ISensor                                    Networking::IRouter

An interface is a named collection of operations. An interface may not have attributes as it does not represent any structure. An interface contains operations but not their implementation. When you want your interface in expanded form, you may give the details of operations it contains. These operations may be adorned with visibility properties (public, private, and protected), concurrency mechanisms and all extensibility mechanisms such as stereotypes, tagged values, and constraints. You can also associate signals with an interface.

An interface may participate in various relationships supported by UML. An interface may participate in generalization, association and dependency relationships. Apart from this, an interface can be a part of realization relationship. Realization is a semantic relationship between two classifiers where one classifier specifies a contract that another classifier guarantees to carry out.

We have seen enough of examples describing interfaces. The major purpose of an interface is to separate specification of a service with its implementation. An interface specifies a service, which is implemented by its associated class or a component. You can always change your implementation, may be for better performance, or for less memory requirements. This change in implementation may not have an impact on the interface, as long as its contract is unchanged.

**Example**:

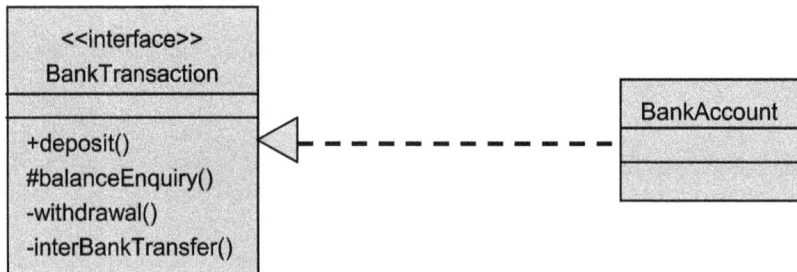

## 5.1 Types and Roles

A role is the named specific behavior of an entity participating in a particular context. A role may be static (e.g., an association end) or dynamic (e.g., a collaboration role). A single entity may play different roles based on context. Each role it plays can be considered as a face it is offering to the external world.

Each role can be considered as an interface, the entity is offering, based on the situation or the context of the system.

For example, consider a class named Person. When this class is in association with a Company class in which he is working. The role played by the Person in this context is employee. The below diagram depicts that aspect.

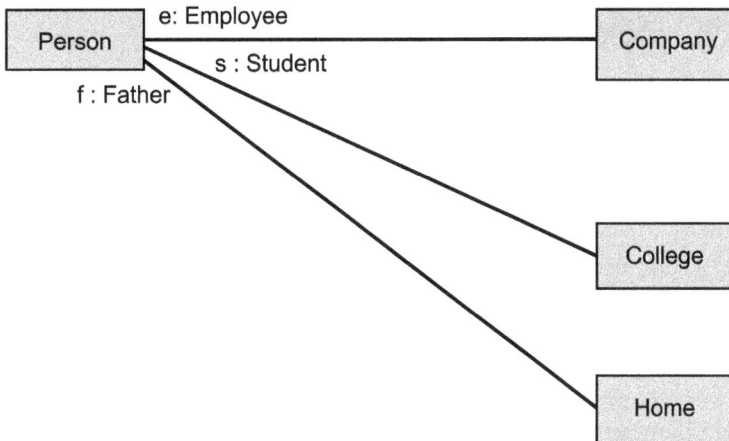

**Fig.5.1** Interfaces and Roles

**Explanation**: In the above figure the Person class is in association with three different classes based on the context of the system. Let us assume a case, where he is working in a Company, and he is married and a Father and also he is attending part time classes in a College. When you consider an association between Person and Company, he is playing a role called e which is of type Employee as long as he is with the Company. When he comes out of the Company and attends part time classes in a College, he plays a role called s which is of type Student. When he goes to Home, he plays a role called f which is of type Father. So, each role is a face the Person is offering to the external world based on the context in which he is involved.

The defined stereotype, Type can be used while you are modelling semantics of abstractions and their conformance to specific interfaces. Typically, Type is a stereotype of class that specifies the domain of objects with their operations that are applicable to objects of that Type. This Type definition has close similarity with the interface, except that the Type definition may include attributes, where as the interface will not include. Type specifies the behavior of an object without stating how it is implemented. An object is a member of a type if it. There are classes that have nothing but pure virtual functions. In Java such entities are not classes at all; they are a special language element called an interface. UML has followed the Java example and has created some special syntactic elements for such entities .The primary icon for an interface is just like a class except that it has a special denotation called a stereotype , the «type» string at the top of the class. When a stereotype is used above the name of a class it indicates that this class is a special kind of class that conforms to a rather rigid specification. The «type» stereotype indicates that the class is an interface. The type elements are modeled as classes with stereotype <<type>>.

**Note**: In most cases, the Type and Interface are interchangeable.

## 5.2 Modeling the Seams in a System

The major application of interfaces is, it helps in modelling the seams in a system composed of software components. These components could be the ones developed from scratch, or reusable ones from other systems, or they could be purchased from the software market. But, whatever be the type of components, you need to write code that attaches components together. In order to weave or physically integrate these components together, you need to understand the interfaces provided by each component. Interfaces help us to forge components together so that they work together to accomplish the very purpose of the system.

If you want to identify the seams in a system, you need to identify the lines of separation between components that are part of your system's architecture. The components on both sides of an interface should confirm to the contract specified by that interface. As long as this contract is intact, you can change components on one side without having any impact on components of the other side. This implements the clear line of demarcation that specification is independent of its implementation.

When you apply a component which is either bought from the market, or reused from other systems, you need to clearly understand the operations that are implemented by its associated interfaces. You might expect proper documentation mentioning all the details of operations and the interfaces it presents to the external world using which the components can be glued together to formulate your complete system.

**Note**: Most components that are available in the software market, such as COM+ and Java Beans provide a facility by using which you can programmatically query an interface to determine its operations. This helps in understanding the component fully and provides enough of information to physically integrate components so as to build your intended system.

In order to model the seams in a system, the following steps are followed:

❖ After you identify the collection of classes and components that constitute your system, identify those components or classes that tend to be coupled relative to other sets of classes and components.

❖ Identify classes and components that tend to change together. These classes and components should be grouped together as collaborations.

❖ Identify the operations and the signals that cross the boundaries of instances of one set of classes and components to the instances of other sets of classes and components.
❖ Group all these logically related sets of operations and signals as interfaces.
❖ For each identified collaboration in your system, identify the interfaces on which it depends on (imports) and the interfaces it provides to others (exports). Imports are modeled as dependency relationships, and exports are modeled as realization relationships.
❖ For each such interface, document the details of it. You can also document its dynamics by using pre and post conditions for each defined operation, and you can also apply use cases and state machines   to document the dynamics of the interface as a whole.

## 5.3 Modeling Static and Dynamic Types

Most object-oriented programming languages are statically typed, meaning the type of an object is bound at the time the object is created (an instance of a class is created). Once an object is created, it may play different roles based on the context of the system. Clients that use this object interact with the object through different sets of interfaces based on the role the object is playing at the context of the system. These different sets of interfaces which are based on the role object plays, might contain overlapping sets of operations.

You can model the static nature of an object by using a class diagram. When you model business objects belonging to a system, you must have to model their dynamic nature, because, these objects naturally change their roles during the workflows of the system. The following steps indicate how a dynamic type can be modeled:

❖ Identify the different possible types an object plays in the system. Each type is rendered as a class stereotyped as type, if you want to include both structure and behavior. Each type is rendered as an interface, if you just want to include only behavior.
❖ Model all the roles an object plays in a system during its life time. This can happen in two ways:
  ➤ In a class diagram, type each role that the class plays during its association with other classes. This will specify the face instances of that class in the context of its associated object.
  ➤ In a class diagram, specify the class-to-type relationships using generalization.
❖ In an interaction diagram, represent properly each instance of the dynamically typed class. Specify the role of that instance in square brackets below the object's name.

❖ To indicate the change in role of an object, graphically represent object once for each role it plays in an interaction, and connect these objects with a message stereotyped as <<become>>.

**Examples**:

1. The following figure shows the roles that instances of the class Person might play in the context of a human resource system

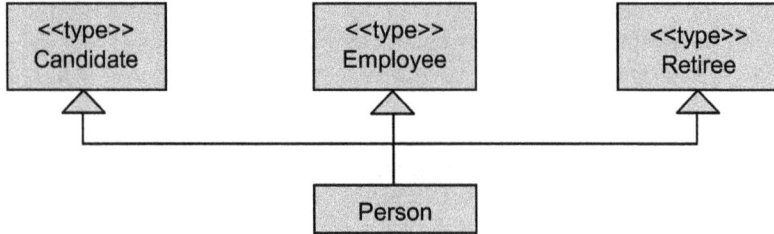

**Fig.5.2(a)** Modeling Static Types

**Note**: Instances of the Person class may be any of the three types–namely, Candidate, Employee, or Retiree.

2. The following figure shows the roles played by the instances of the class Student in a University Course Registration System.

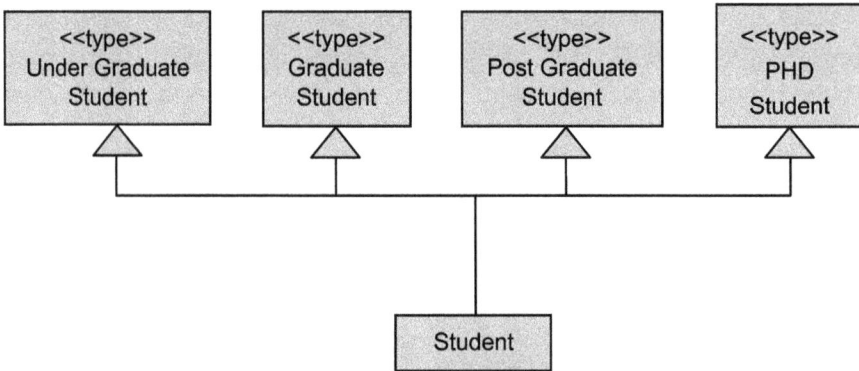

**Fig.5.2(b)** Modeling Static Types

**Note**: Instances of the Student class may be any of the four types-namely, Under Graduate Student, Graduate Student, Post Graduate Student, PHD Student.

3. The following diagram shows the dynamic nature of a Person's type. In this fragment of interaction diagram, the Person object changes its role from Candidate to Employee.

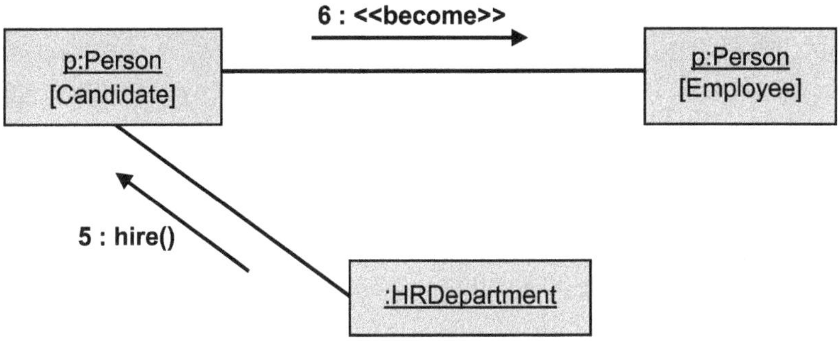

**Fig.5.3** Modeling Dynamic Types

**Note**: Before recruitment, the Person instance was a Candidate. Once the HR Department hires a Person, he becomes an Employee of the Company.

## Essay Type Questions

1. Explian modelling the seams in a system.
2. Describe modelling static and dynamic types.

## Objective Type Questions

1. ----------------- is a named collection of operations

   (a) interface                    (b) class
   (c) object                       (d) component

2. ------------------ can be defined as a stereotype specifying a domain of objects, together with the operations applicable to the object

   (a) Role                         (b) Type
   (c) Interface                    (d) All the above

3. ------------------- specifies the behavior of an entity that participates in a particular situation

   (a) Role                         (b) Type
   (c) Interface                    (d) All the above

4. An interface can be graphically rendered as

   (a) A circle with its name
   (b) A stereotyped class with all its operations
   (c) Both a and b
   (d) None of the above

5. An interface contains

   (a) operations                          (b) attributes
   (c) Both a & b                          (d) None

6. -------------------- helps in modelling the seams in a system composed of software components

   (a) operations                          (b) attributes
   (c) interface                           (d) class

7. -------------------- help us to forge components together so that they work together to accomplish the very purpose of the system

   (a) class                               (b) interface
   (c) role                                (d) category

8. Identify classes and components that tend to change together. These classes and components should be grouped together as -------------------

   (a) collaboration                       (b) use case
   (c) action state                        (d) None of the above

9. Static types can be modeled by using --------------------------- relationship

   (a) association                         (b) generalization
   (c) aggregation                         (d) dependency

10. Dynamic types can be modeled by using ----------------------

   (a) collaboration diagram               (b) class diagram
   (c) use case diagram                    (d) interface

## Answers

1. (a)    2. (b)    3. (a)    4. (c)    5. (a)    6. (c)
7. (d)    8. (a)    9. (b)    10. (a)

# CHAPTER 6

# Packages

In the UML, a package is a general purpose mechanism for organizing modeling elements into groups. When you are constructing models for a complex or large systems, you might have to maintain huge number of classes, interfaces, components, nodes, objects, diagrams and other elements. In order to handle such systems, it is mandatory to organize these elements into larger chunks. You use packages to group these semantically related elements so as to handle them as larger chunks. Packages help us to view or model the system at a higher level of abstraction (without much interior details). Packages are also very useful in modeling different views of your system's architecture.

Packages are UML constructs that organize model elements into groups, making your UML diagrams simpler and easier to understand. Package is graphically rendered as a tabbed folder. Packages can group any UML diagrams and also other packages. Mostly, packages are used to group use case diagrams and class diagrams because these diagrams have a tendency to grow during system development.

**LEARNING OBJECTIVES**

*After studying the chapter the students familiarize themselves with the following concepts:*

- Applications of Packages
- Importing and Exporting
- Standard Elements
- Modeling Groups
- Modeling Architectural Views

**Graphical Examples**

**Fig.6.1** Packages

**Note:** The above figure shows graphical representations for packages. The first figure is a package named Payment. The second figure is a package named Orders, which is in another package named Purchase.

## 6.1 Package Elements

A package may own other elements, such as classes, interfaces, components, nodes, collaborations, use cases, diagrams, and even other packages. If the package is destroyed, the associated elements that are declared in that package are also destroyed. All the elements declared inside the package should have unique names to distinguish each other. You can associate visibility for the package elements. You specify the visibility of an element owned by a package by prefixing the element's name with an appropriate visibility symbol. If the prefix is '+' symbol, the element has public visibility, meaning any other outside package can refer this element by qualifying it with its package name. If the prefix is '-', the element has private visibility, meaning this element is not available outside the package in which it is defined. If the prefix is '#', the element has protected visibility, meaning this element can be accessible to the children of the package in which it is defined.

**Note:** Packages that are friends to another may see all the elements of that package irrespective of their visibility.

**Example:**

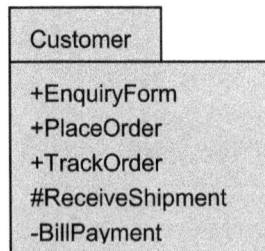

**Fig.6.2** Packages with Elements

## 6.2 Applications of Packages

When you are organizing functional models (behavioral aspects) of your system, use packages to model the real-world modules that form the structure of your system. When you are organizing source code, use packages to represent the different modules of the source code, such as:

- ❖ Presentation Module
- ❖ Controller Module
- ❖ Data Access Module
- ❖ Integration Module
- ❖ Business Services Module

When you are organizing components, use packages to group components based on ownership and reusability. Such as:

- ❖ Commercial Components (Purchased from the Market)
- ❖ Open Source Framework Components
- ❖ Custom built Framework Components
- ❖ Custom built Application Components

When organizing deployment models, use packages to represent the different types of deployment environments that you will be modeling. Such as:

- ❖ Development Environment
- ❖ Integration Test Environment
- ❖ System Test Environment
- ❖ Pre-production Environment
- ❖ Production Environment
- ❖ Post-production Environment

**Example:** A Schedule package belonging to University Course Registration System.

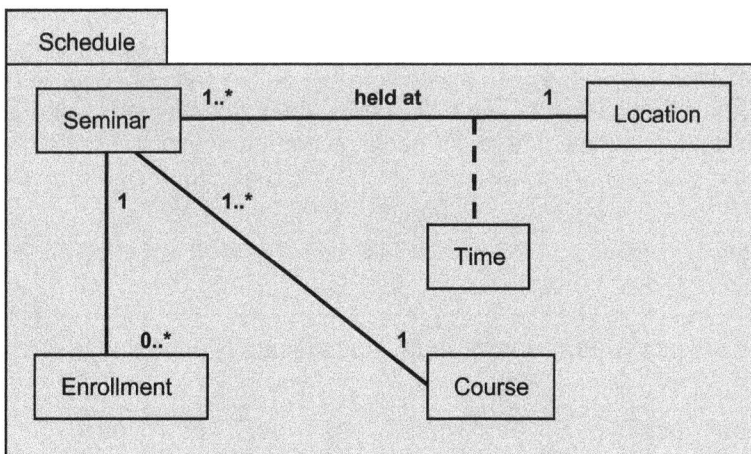

A High-Level Use case Diagram for University Information System. Packages are used here to group use cases.

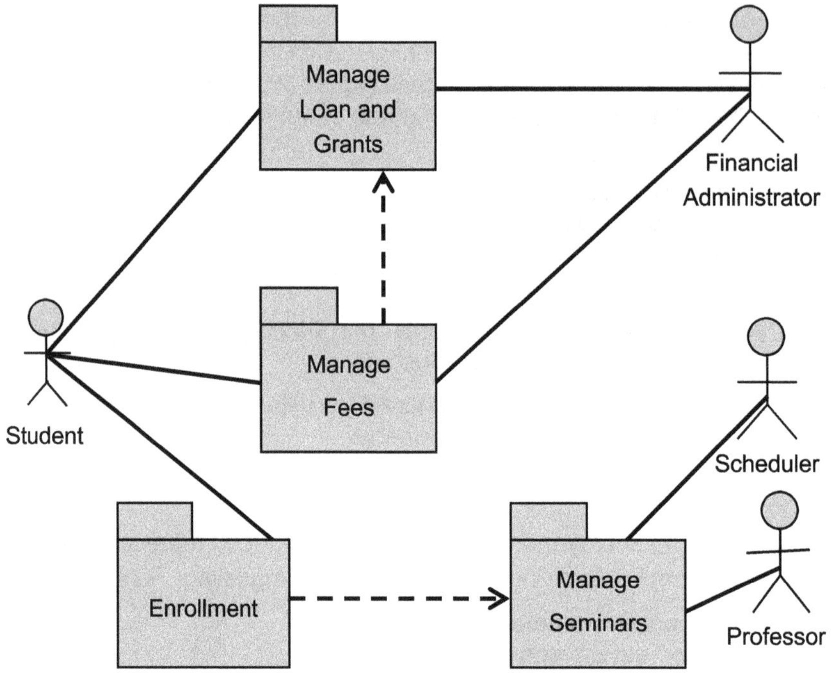

**Fig.6.3**   Packages enclosing Use Cases

## 6.3 Importing and Exporting

A package diagram is a graphical representation containing packages and their relationships. In package diagrams we mostly use dependency relationships among packages. Let us consider a situation where you have two classes side by side, then these classes can access or refer public parts of each. But if these classes are put into two differ rent packages, then these classes cannot accept their public parts, because here the package boundary avoids this. Still you can make one package to accept the public part of other package by using dependency relationships stereotyped with import and access.

The both stereotypes import and access specify that the source package has access to the contents of the target package. The import stereotype adds the contents of the target to the source's name space, so that when you refer target's elements you need not qualify their names with the name of the target package. When you use access stereotype, you have to explicitly qualify the elements belonging to the target package. But import stereotype is the mostly used one.

The public parts of a package are called its exports. These exports are visible only to the packages that import this package. Another important consideration when you discuss visibility of elements grouped as a package is: an element is visible within a package and it is also visible in all other packages nested inside the package. Nested packages can see everything that their containing packages can see.

Package diagrams can use packages containing use cases to illustrate the functionality of a software system. Package diagrams can use packages that represent the different layers of a software system to illustrate the layered architecture of a software system. The dependencies between these packages can be adorned with labels or stereotypes to indicate the communication mechanism between the layers. Package diagrams are typically used to depict the high-level organization of a software project.

**Examples:**

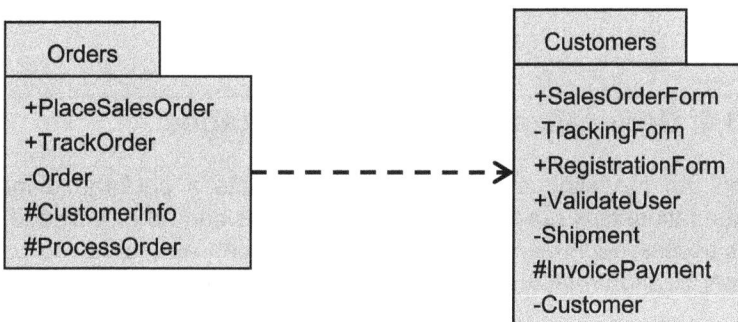

**Fig.6.4** Dependency among Packages

**Explanation:** In the above figure, there is dependency between Orders and Customers packages. Orders package contain the set of sales orders placed by various customers. Customers package contain all registered users who can place sales orders. Whenever a sales order is placed, the respective customer details have to be added to it, because of this, the Orders package depends on Customers package. In fact it is Customer who places sales orders. Each package is specified with their defined elements associated with their visibility.

**Explanation:** In the following diagram, package Mailing List UI (User interface) imports the package named Mailing List App (Application), and Mailing List App package imports Customers. All the public parts of a package are called exports. In the above packages all elements prefixed with '+' are exports of that package. The parts that one package exports are visible only to the contents of those packages that explicitly import the package. The elements of Mailing List UI package can access the public elements (exports) of Mailing List App, and similarly, Mailing List App package elements can access exports of Customers.

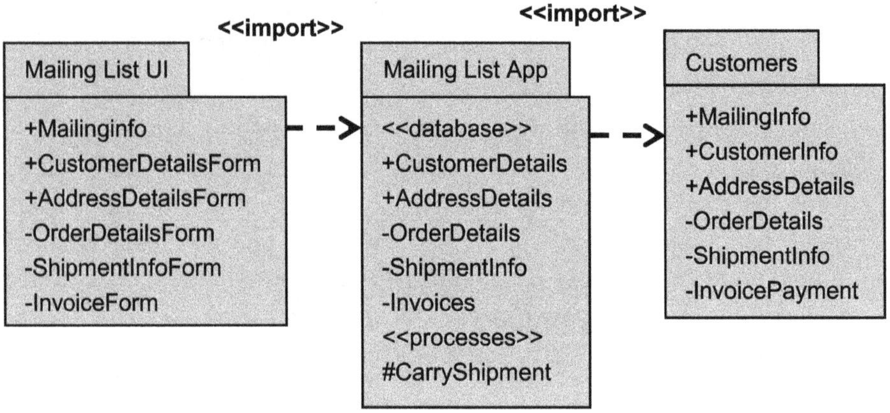

**Fig.6.5** Import Dependency

## 6.4 Generalization among Packages

While you are modeling a system, you can create a package diagrams to represent relationships among packages. Packages can be organized by using import or access dependency among them. You can also organize packages using generalization relationship, used to specify families of packages.

The generalization among packages is very similar to generalization among classes. As in classes, the specialized packages inherits public and protected parts from their generalized package and also can incorporate their own elements. Packages involved in generalization relationships follow the same type of substitutability as do classes. It means that, a specialized package can be used anywhere its associated generalized package is used.

## 6.5 Standard Elements

You can apply all extensibility mechanisms supported by UML to packages. More often we use tagged values to attach additional properties and details to the packages. You can specify new kinds of packages by applying stereotypes, such as building a package that encapsulate operating system services.

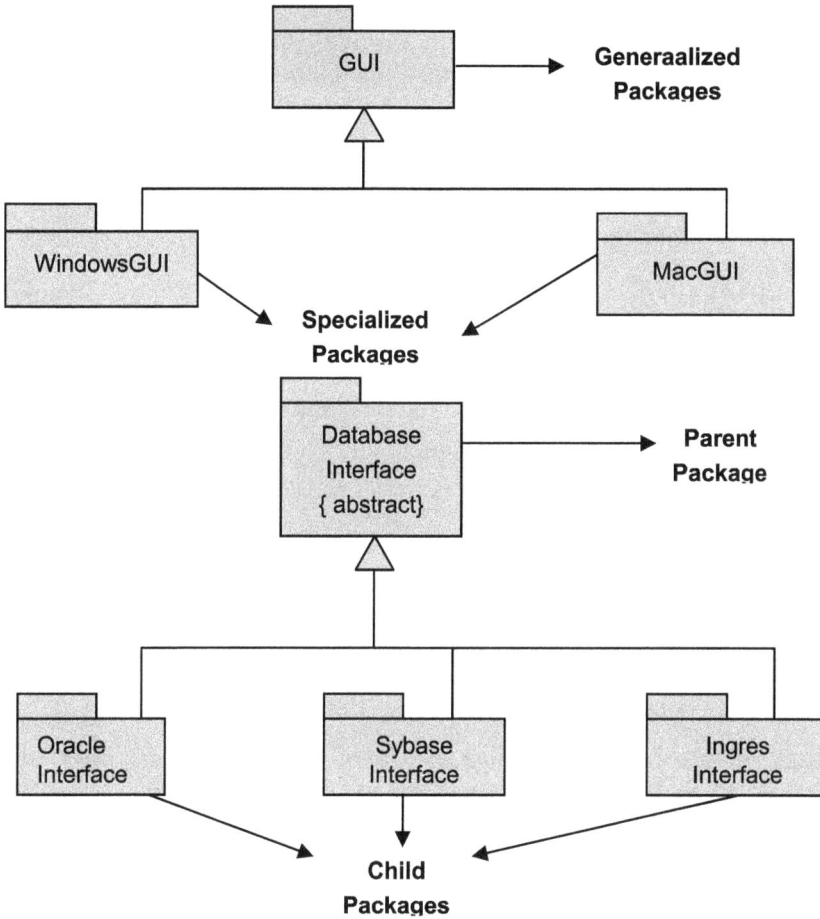

**Fig.6.6** Generalization among Packages

**Examples:**

Note: The package named Database Interface is an abstract one, which means it cannot have instances.

**Example:**

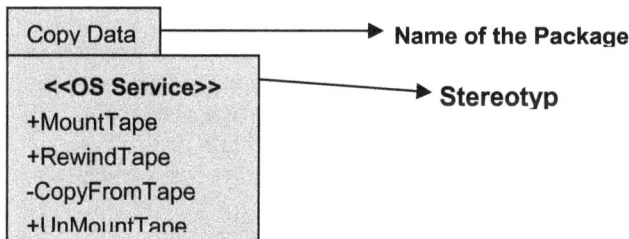

**Fig.6.7** A Stereotyped Package

**Note:** The above package includes the mechanism of copying data to a magnetic tape.

The UML defines five standard stereotypes that apply to packages:

- ❖ **façade:** Specifies a package that is only a view on some other package.
- ❖ **framework:** Specifies a package consisting mainly of patterns.
- ❖ **stub:** Specifies a package that serves as a proxy for the public contents of another package.
- ❖ **subsystem:** Specifies a package representing an independent part of the entire system being modeled.
- ❖ **system:** Specifies a package representing the entire system being modeled.

The UML does not provide icons for any of these stereotypes. In addition to these five package stereotypes, You can also use dependencies with the standard stereotype named import.

## 6.6 Modeling Groups of Elements

The major purpose of a package is to group modeling elements and manipulate them as a single set. For a trivial system, we might not need packages. For every other system, the modeling elements of your system, such as classes, interfaces, components, nodes, and even diagrams naturally form groups. These groups are modeled as packages in UML.

The major difference between classes and packages is, classes are abstractions found in your requirements document or problem statement, where as packages are the mechanisms of organizing elements into groups. A class can have instances, but a package cannot have instances. Generally, we use packages to group the same basic kind of modeling elements. But sometimes we may use packages to group different kinds of elements based on the context of the system.

The following, enumerates steps needed to model groups of elements (packages):

- ❖ Based on your system's architecture, formulate various views of it. Scan through the modeling elements in a particular architectural view, and identify elements that are semantically and conceptually related.
- ❖ Group all these semantically related elements into packages.
- ❖ After identifying packages, you need to establish the visibility properties for their elements. Find out elements in a package that should be accessible outside the package. Mark those elements as public and the remaining elements can be marked as private or protected.
- ❖ Develop a package diagram by explicitly connecting packages using import dependencies.
- ❖ Establish generalization/specialization relationship among packages by moving up generalized packages and pulling down specialized packages.

## 6.7 Modeling Architectural Views

It is mandatory to group related elements into packages in any complex model. Packages help us to have higher level of abstraction of your system's model. You can also apply packages to model different architectural views of your system. For each view, identify related elements and group them into a package. We know that a system's architecture can have five different views, such as a design view, a process view, an implementation view, a deployment view, and a use case view.

The following steps specify how to model architectural views:

❖ Identify the set of architectural views that are needed to model your system's context. At most you can have five different views as discussed above. In some trivial systems, we may not use all of these five architectural views.

❖ Group the elements and diagrams that are needed to visualize, specify, construct and document the semantics of each view into a package.

❖ If needed, further group these elements into lower level packages that become parts of our package used to represent our view.

**Graphical Example:**

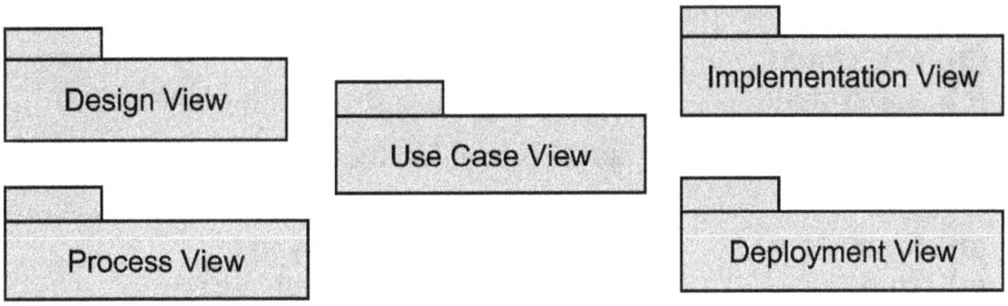

**Fig.6.8** Modeling Architectural Views

## Essay Type Questions

1. Briefly explain the following:
   (a) Applications of packages    ((b) Importing and Exporting packages

2. Explain briefly the following with various steps involved.
   (a) Modeling groups of elements    (b) Modeling architectural views.

## Objective Type Questions

1. A general purpose mechanism for organizing modeling elements into groups is called
   (a) package                      (b) interface
   (c) note                         (d) constraint

2.  ---------------------- are also very useful in modeling different views of your system's architecture.
    (a) interface                          (b) package
    (c) note                               (d) comment

3.  Package is graphically rendered as a --------------------
    (a) rectangle                          (b) cube
    (c) tabbed folder                      (d) square

4.  The visibility of the element in the package which can be referred by its child package is
    (a) public visibility                  (b) private visibility
    (c) protected visibility               (d) None

5.  A high level use case diagram may contain
    (a) packages                           (b) Actors
    (c) both a and b                       (d) none

6.  The standard stereotypes that apply to packages are
    (a) facade                             (b) framework
    (c) stub                               (d) All the above

7.  A package consisting mainly of patterns is stereotyped as
    (a) framework                          (b) stub
    (c) subsystem                          (d) None of the above

8.  A package that serves as a proxy for the public contents of another package
    (a) framework                          (b) system
    (c) stub                               (d) sub system

9.  Packages are applicable for
    (a) modeling groups of elements
    (b) modeling architectural views
    (c) both a & b
    (d) None of the above

## Answers

1. (a)     2. (b)     3. (c)     4. (c)     5. (c)     6. (d)
7. (a)     8. (c)     9. (c)

# CHAPTER 7

# Instances

The dictionary meaning of instance is a case or occurrence of anything. An instance is a concrete manifestation of an abstraction to which a set of operations may be applied and which may have a state that stores the effects of the operation. The terms "instance" and "object" are synonymous and are used interchangeably. You apply instances to model concrete or prototypical things. Most of the building blocks of UML may have instances, such as you can have use cases and use case instances, nodes and node instances, associations and association instances, collaborations and collaboration instances, classes and objects, components and component instances, and so on.

The UML provides a graphical representation for instances. Graphically an instance is rendered by underlining its name. This notation makes us to visualize named or anonymous instances based on the context of the system.

### LEARNING OBJECTIVES

*After studying the chapter the students familiarize themselves with the following concepts:*

- States and Operations
- Standard Elements
- Modeling Concrete Instances
- Modeling Prototypical Instances

**Examples:**

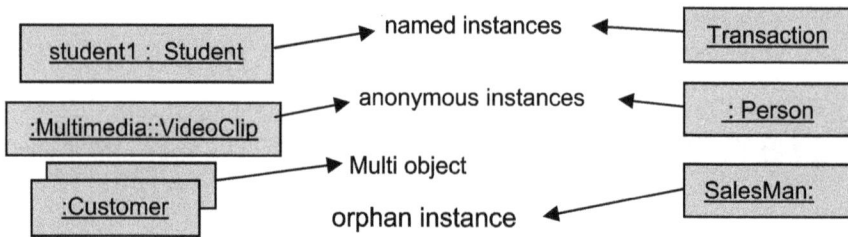

**Fig.7.1** Instances

**Explanation:** In the above diagram, the first figure represents the named instance. The object named student1 is an instance of the class named Student. The second figure specifies an instance without any name. Such unnamed instances are called anonymous instances. These type of instances are used when you require an instance without the need of its identity while you are building the model of a system. A multi object is used to model a set of objects, and an orphan instance is one whose associated class is unknown.

## 7.1 State and Operations

An object once created as an instance of a class, will have its own state. The state of an object is defined by its attributes defined in its class, and their values indicated in the object. It means that every object will have its own values for its properties defined in its class. Whatever values you specify for object's properties, it will indicate the state of the object at a given moment in time and space. As we are aware that the state of an object is not static. An object may change its state in its life time in response to the events that are happening on that object. This entire behavior of an object can be graphically described by using a state chart or a state machine. Let us consider the following examples to illustrate this.

**Explanation:** The Fig.7.2 describes a class named Customer, and its related instance named myCustomer. The object named myCustomer contains values for the properties defined in the Customer class. As we are aware that an object is a physical thing that takes up space in the real world. You can always perform certain things on an object. The things which you perform on an object are defined in its abstraction. For example, in the above figure, an abstraction named Customer defines an operation named placeOrder, and an object of the customer named myCustomer can perform this operation. It means that, myCustomer can place a sales order to an enterprise. It can be represented as myCustomer.placeOrder() . Similary, he can also track the sales order placed to know its current status. He can receive the shipment of his order, and pay the bill, which can be represented as myCustomer.receiveShipment(), and myCustomer.payBill().

**Example:**

| Customer |
|---|
| ID : String |
| name : String |
| phone : String |
| address : String |
| placeOrder() |
| trackOrder() |
| receiveShipment() |
| payBill() |

| myCustomer:Customer |
|---|
| ID = "432-511-91" |
| name = "Linn Roges" |
| phone = "09-040-99445687" |
| address = "Flat No. 212, Elm Street, Lincon's Road" |
| placeOrder() |
| trackOrder() |
| receiveShipment() |
| payBill() |

Class        Instance with attribute values

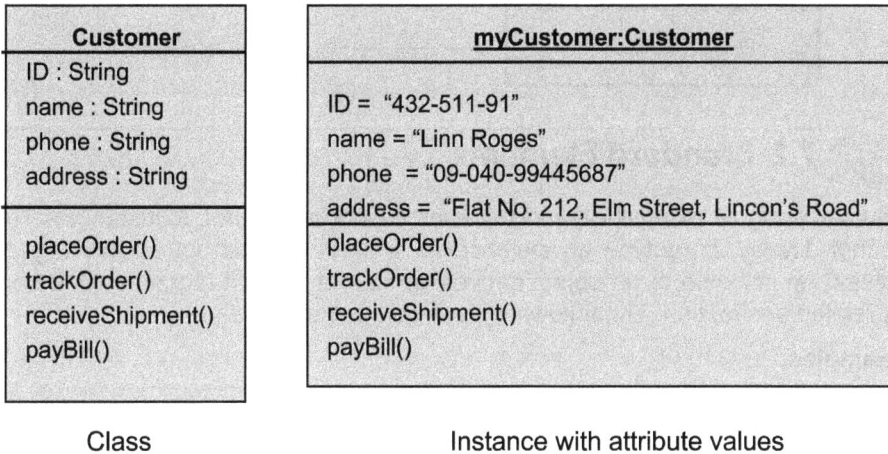

**Fig.7.2** Class and Object

You know that an object has behavior during which its state may change in response to internal or external events happening on it. When you model the behavior of an object, you might come across same objects but with different states based on the context of the system. You can explicitly specify the state of an object graphically, by writing the textual description of state and placed between square brackets below the name of the object. For example, when a customer places a sales order, it may be in a state pending or in a state under process, which can be graphically represented as:

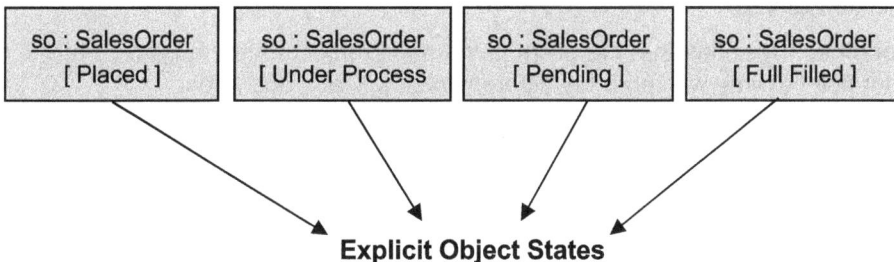

| so : SalesOrder | so : SalesOrder | so : SalesOrder | so : SalesOrder |
|---|---|---|---|
| [ Placed ] | [ Under Process ] | [ Pending ] | [ Full Filled ] |

**Explicit Object States**

**Fig.7.3** Objects with Explicit States

When you model a system, you may have to consider modeling system's process view. Any system's process view contain processes and threads. UML provides a distinct graphical representation to model active classes. An active class is a class whose objects or instances contain a thread or a process. Graphically, an active object is represented as any ordinary object, but with thick border as follows:

**Example**:

```
┌─────────────────────────┐
│    pl : ProcessLoans     │ ─────────────────▶    an active object
└─────────────────────────┘
```

## 7.2 Standard Elements

You can apply all extensibility mechanisms supported by UML to instances. You cannot directly stereotype an instance as well as you cannot specify tagged values. An instance or an object derives its stereotype and tagged values from its related abstraction. The following gives some of examples.

**Examples**:

```
┌─────────────────────┐    ┌─────────────────────┐    ┌─────────────────────┐
│    <<exception>>    │    │     <<signal>>      │    │    <<exception>>    │
│    e  :  Overflow   │    │   fa : FireAlarm    │    │  d  :  DividebyZero │
└─────────────────────┘    └─────────────────────┘    └─────────────────────┘
```

**Fig.7.4** Stereotyped Objects

The UML defines two standard stereotypes that are applicable to dependency relationships among objects and among classes. They are as follows:

**instanceof:** Specifies that client is an instance of supplier classifier.

**instantiate:** Specifies that the client classifier creates instances of supplier classifier.

The UML defines two stereotypes related to objects that apply to messages and transitions:

**become:** Specifies that the client is the same object as the supplier , but at a later point of time with possibly different values, state, and roles.

**copy:** Specifies that the client object is an exact but independent copy of the supplier.

The UML defines a standard constraints that applies to objects.

**transient:** Specifies that an instance of the role is created during execution of the interaction but is destroyed before completion of the interaction.

## 7.3 Modeling Concrete Instances

A concrete instance is the thing that exists in the real world. The task of modelling concrete instances make us to visualize real life things. For example, you cannot see physically the Customer class which is a conceptual one, but an instance of a Customer can be seen or can be felt or understood as a representation of that instance in your system.

Let us consider an example, where we model the hardware topology on which your system operates in an organization. This modeling includes identifying instances of nodes which have physical existence during run time. You model nodes and their inter connections by using a deployment diagram. In a way, you are modeling concrete instances of nodes that establish a hardware platform on which you system can be installed and can operate.

Similarly, if you want to model components that constitute your system, you use component diagrams. Component diagrams represent various components that are installed on the nodes and indicate inter relationships among them. As we know that a component is a physical replaceable part of the system, when you model them, you are modeling concrete instances in a system, because instances of components are real life things belonging to the nodes on which they are installed, and work together to accomplish a task.

When you are debugging a system developed using object oriented methodologies, you come across objects and their structural relationships in the form of object diagrams. So, an object diagram represents the model of the concrete instances belonging to a system you are modeling.

The following section discusses various steps needed to model concrete instances:

❖ Identify all the necessary instances to visualize, specify, construct , or document the problem you are modeling.
❖ Represent these objects graphically as instances. Give each object a name to identify it, you may face situations where you need not know the name of the object based on the context of the system you are modeling, in such cases represent instances as anonymous instances.
❖ While you are modeling, expose all the relevant information about instances such as, attributes with their values, and all extensibility mechanisms associated with them.
❖ Express all these identified instances and their relationships by using object diagrams or other diagrams to indicate the intent of your model.

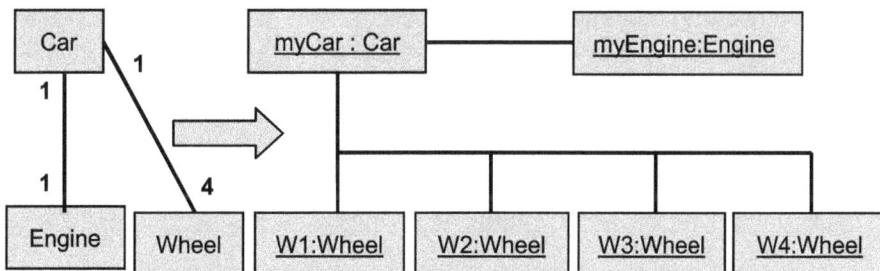

Class Diagram                              Its associated Object Diagram

For example, an instance diagram (object diagram) is an instance of a class diagram. The following figure specifies how a class diagram can be used to build its related object diagram.

**Explanation:** The above diagram is a model of concrete instances for a car class diagram.

## 7.4 Modeling Prototypical Instances

The major application of instances is to model dynamic interactions among the objects. While you model these interactions, you might not use concrete instances that exist in the real world. Rather, you use conceptual objects to model these interactions, which are essentially proxies for real life objects. These objects are called prototypical objects and these are roles to which concrete instances confirm.

**Note**: Concrete objects appear in static places, such as object diagrams, component diagrams, and deployment diagrams. Prototypical objects appear in such places as interaction diagrams and activity diagrams.

The following steps are followed while you are modeling prototypical instances:

❖ Identify those instances that can appear in interactions or activity diagrams. Include all these prototypical instances that are necessary to visualize, specify, construct, or document the system which you are modeling.

❖ Represent all these prototypical instances by using UML graphical notations that are used for instances. Give each object a name to distinguish it from others. If there is no meaningful name or the name of an instance is not required for modeling that context of the system, render it as an anonymous object.

❖ For each instance, identify and expose all the properties with their values that are required to model your system.

❖ Identify these instances with their associated relationships. Graphically represent these in an interaction diagram or an activity diagram.

The following diagram shows an interaction diagram illustrating a partial scenario for using a ceiling fan. This example is a collaboration, containing a society of roles and other elements that work together to accomplish a purpose. Collaborations have two aspects, such as structural and dynamic aspects. The structural aspect of a collaboration is represented by the classifier roles and their relationships. The dynamic aspect of a collaboration can be represented by interactions among prototypical instances.

**Example:**

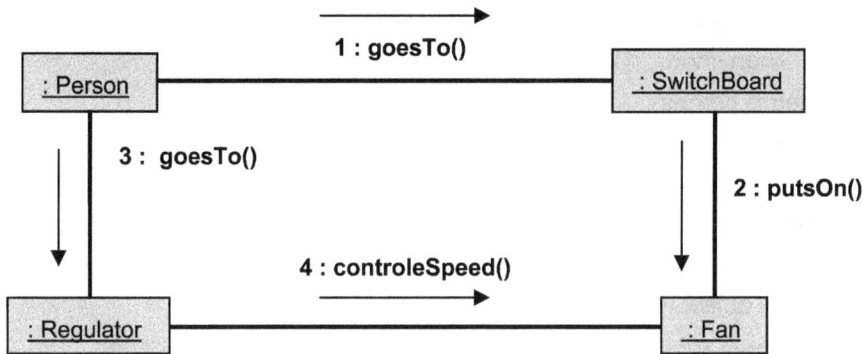

**Fig.7.5** Modeling a Collaboration

## Essay Type Questions

1. Explain various steps involved in modeling concrete instances.

2. Explain various steps involved in modeling prototypical instances with an example.

## Objective Type Questions

1. A concrete manifestation of an abstraction is called

    (a) instance
    (b) class
    (c) object
    (d) both a & c

2. The following cannot have instances

    (a) abstract class
    (b) leaf class
    (c) use case
    (d) component

3. An instance is graphically rendered as

    (a) tabbed folder
    (b) underlining its name
    (c) a circle
    (d) a cube

4. An instance which does not have name is called

    (a) named instance
    (b) orphan instance
    (c) anonymous instance
    (d) multi object

5. An instance which does not have its associated class specification is called

    (a) named instance
    (b) orphan instance
    (c) anonymous instance
    (d) multi object

6. An instance which is having multiple copies is called

   (a) named instance          (b) orphan instance
   (c) anonymous instance       (d) multi object

7. System's process view contains

   (a) Active classes           (b) processes
   (c) threads                  (d) All the above

8. An active object is graphically rendered as

   (a) Node                     (b) component
   (c) an object with thick border  (d) cube

9. -------------- specifies that client is an instance of supplier classifier

   (a) instantiate              (b) instance of
   (c) become                   (d) copy

10. The stereotype that specifies the client is the same object as the supplier, but at a later point of time with possibly different values, state and roles.

   (a) transient                (b) copy
   (c) instance                 (d) become

11. The instance that exists in the real world is

   (a) instance                 (b) object
   (c) concrete instance        (d) exception

12. The instances which are really proxies for real life objects are called

   (a) prototypical instance    (b) concrete instance
   (c) object                   (d) class

13. The following objects are static

   (a) prototypical objects     (b) interaction diagrams
   (c) concrete objects         (d) All the above

14. The following objects are dynamic

   (a) prototypical objects     (b) interaction diagrams
   (c) concrete objects         (d) All the above

15. concrete objects appear in places such as

   (a) object diagrams          (b) component diagrams
   (c) deployment diagrams      (d) All the above

## Answers

1. (d)    2. (a)    3. (b)    4. (c)    5. (b)    6. (d)
7. (d)    8. (c)    9. (b)    10. (d)   11. (c)   12. (a)
13. (c)   14. (a)   15. (d)

# CHAPTER 8

# Object Diagrams

Object diagrams are used to model the instances of the things that appear in class diagrams. In fact, an object diagram itself is an instance of a class diagram. An object diagram is a snapshot of a set of objects and their relationships at a particular instant of time. An object diagram in the UML, is a diagram that shows a complete or partial view of the structure of a modeled system at a specific point of time. Typically, an object diagram focuses on some set of instances and attributes with their values, and the links between the instances that constitute your system. Graphically, a link is shown as a solid line, and represents an instance of an association between the relevant classifiers. Usually, object diagrams are helpful in modeling the static design view or the static process view of a system.

Object diagrams, sometimes referred as instance diagrams, are useful for exploring real world examples of objects and the relationships between them. Though the class diagrams describes this information, it may be in too abstract form. An object diagram can be a better option for explaining complex relationships between classes. Object diagrams are used for modeling your system's structure. You can apply object diagrams for constructing the system through forward and reverse engineering.

An object diagram commonly contains objects, links, notes, and constraints. It may also contain packages or subsystems, when you want to model the system at a higher level of abstraction. Sometimes an object diagram may include classes for the purpose of visualizing classes that lay behind each instance. An object diagram mostly contains objects and their connecting links. Your object diagram may include concrete or prototypical instances. If a component diagram, or a deployment diagram contains only instances without any information about messages, then they can be called object diagrams.

**Examples:**

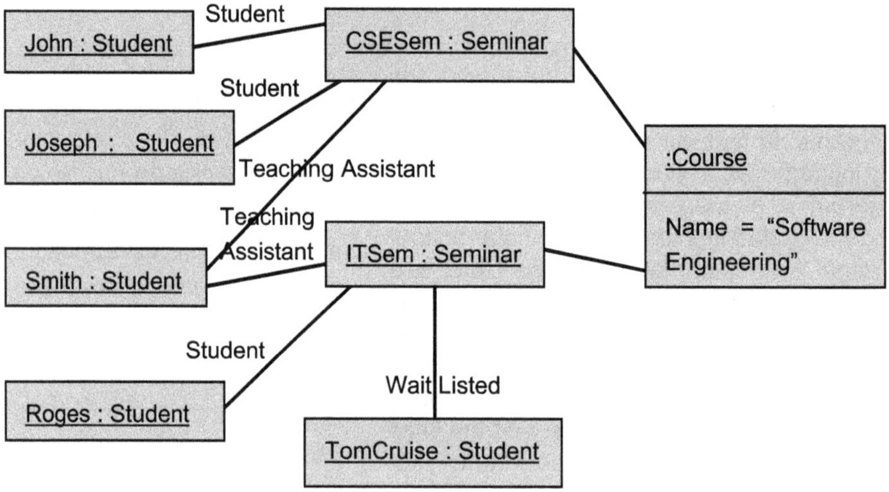

**Fig.8.1** Object Diagram

**Explanation:** In the figure 8.1, John and Joseph are students who attend CSE seminars. Whereas student named Roges attends IT seminar and Smith is a teaching assistant who attends both the seminars. Tom cruise is a student who is on the waiting list for IT seminar. Both the seminars are on course named Software Engineering.

## 8.1 Common Uses of Object Diagrams

Object diagrams primarily indicate the functional requirements of a system. Functional requirements are the services that a system provides to its end users. Object diagrams are helpful in modeling static data structures, which are used in constructing a system. These diagrams are used to model the static design view or the static process view of a system. The typical application of an object diagram is to model object structures. An object diagram represents a static frame in the dynamic storyboard represented by an interaction diagram.

**Note:** When you take photographs of a marriage party, these photographs are object diagrams, and the video of the marriage party represent interaction diagram. Object diagram deals with the static aspects and interaction diagram deals with the dynamic aspects of the system. Hope you have understood the difference between an object   diagram and an interaction diagram.

**So, the purpose of an object diagram can be summarized as follows:**

- ❖ They are used to specify the object's relationships of a system.
- ❖ They specify the static view of an interaction among objects.
- ❖ They are useful in understanding objects' behavior and their relationships from a practical perspective.
- ❖ They are used for forward and reverse engineering.

We have already discussed that an object diagram is an instance of a class diagram. It implies that an object diagram consists of instances of things used in a class diagram. So, both diagrams are made of same basic elements but in different form. In class diagram elements are in abstract form to represent the blue print and in object diagram the elements are in concrete form to represent the real world object. The following topic discusses the various considerations to make before constructing an object diagram:

- ❖ The object diagram should have a meaningful name to indicate its purpose.
- ❖ The most important elements are to be identified.
- ❖ The association among objects should be clarified.
- ❖ Values of different elements need to be captured to include in the object diagram.
- ❖ Add proper notes at points where more clarity is required.

## 8.2 Modeling Object Structures

When you freeze a running system, it represents the system at a moment of time, containing a set of objects, each in a state, and each in a particular relationship to other objects. Object diagrams are used to model object structures which results in modeling complex data structures required for constructing system. To model object structures, the steps below are followed:

- ❖ Identify the mechanism in the system you want to model. Generally, a mechanism represents a function or a part of the behavior of the system. Specify the society of classes, interfaces, and other things that represent an interaction which results into the system's behavior.
- ❖ For each mechanism, establish the corresponding collaboration. Identify the classes, interfaces, and other elements with their relationships that participate in this collaboration.
- ❖ Consider various scenarios that go through this mechanism. For each scenario, freeze it at a moment in time, and represent each object that participates in the mechanism.
- ❖ In order to understand the scenario, expose the state and attribute values of each object that participates in the scenario.
- ❖ Expose the links among objects that participate in the scenario, to represent instances of associations among them.

**Example:**

The following diagram is an example of an object diagram. It represents the Order Management System. The following diagram is an instance of the system at a particular time of purchase. It has the objects, such as Customer, Order, SpecialOrder, and NormalOrder.

Now the customer object (C) is associated with three order objects (O1, O2 and O3). These order objects are associated with special order and normal order objects (S1, S2 and N1). The customer is having the following three orders with different numbers (12, 32 and 40) for the particular time considered. For orders the values are 12, 32, and 40 which implies that the objects are having these values for the particular moment (here the particular time when the purchase is made is considered as the moment) when the instance is captured. The same is for special order and normal order objects which are having number of orders as 20, 30 and 60. If a different time of purchase is considered then these values will change accordingly.

So the following object diagram has been drawn considering all the points mentioned above:

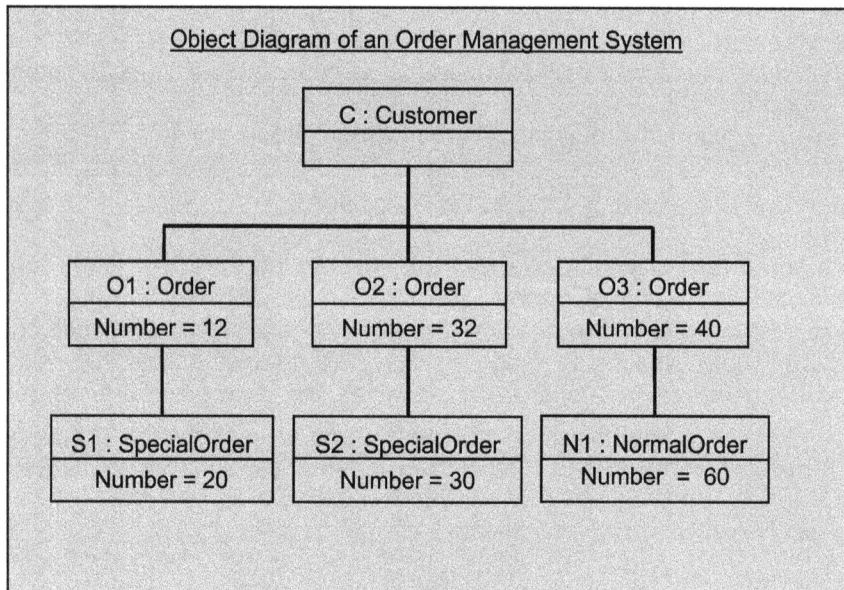

**Fig.8.2** Modeling Object Structures

In brief, we can use object diagrams for

❖ Making the prototype of a system.
❖ Reverse engineering.
❖ Modeling complex data structures.
❖ Understanding the system from practical perspective.

# 8.3 Forward and Reverse Engineering

Forward engineering (generating code from a UML model) an object diagram is of limited value. In any object oriented system, instances are created and destroyed by the application during its execution. Because of this, it is not possible to instantiate these objects from outside. This is very much true of object diagrams containing instances of classes.

If your object diagram contains either instances of components or instances of nodes, then we call them component, and deployment diagrams. Component instances and node instances live outside the running system, so, helpful in some degree of forward engineering.

Reverse engineering (creating a model from code) an object diagram is a different thing.

**The steps mentioned below are followed while you reverse engineer an object diagram:**

❖ Choose the thing you want to reverse engineer. Typically, you set your context relative to an instance of one particular class.

❖ Using a tool, simply walk through the code and stop execution at a certain moment in time.

❖ Identify the set of objects that collaborate in that context and place them in an object diagram.

❖ For better understanding of the context at a moment in time, expose the states and values of properties of all objects that are participating in the context.

❖ For better understanding of the semantics of the context, identify and specify the links that exist among these objects.

❖ If your object diagram becomes complex, prune certain objects that may not have any influence on the context of your system. If your diagram is too simple, expand the neighboring objects and expose each object's state more deeply.

# Essay Type Questions

1. Depict modeling object structures with an example.

2. Describe the task of forward and reverse engineering for object diagrams.

# Objective Type Questions

1. ---------------- model the instances of the things that appear in class diagrams.

   (a) component diagram        (b) object diagram
   (c) deployment diagrams       (d) All the above

2. An instance of an association between the classifiers is called

    (a) qualifier                          (b) component
    (c) node                              (d) link

3. -------------- diagrams are helpful in modeling the static design view and static process view of the system

    (a) object diagram              (b) class diagram
    (c) both a & b                  (d) None

4. An object diagram commonly contains

    (a) objects                     (b) links
    (c) notes                     (d) All the above

5. An object diagram representing model at higher level of abstraction may contain

    (a) packages               (b) subsystems
    (c) both a & b                  (d) none

6. Object diagrams primarily indicate

    (a) Functional requirements     (b) system services
    (c) both a & b                  (d) None

7. The purpose of the object diagram is

    (a) to specify the static view     (b) object's behaviour
    (c) forward & reverse engineering     (d) All the above

8. The considerations to be made before modeling an object diagram

    (a) Identifying most important elements
    (b) clarifying associations among objects
    (c) Adding notes wherever clarity required
    (d) All the above

9. The following diagram specifies object structures

    (a) object diagram              (b) class diagram
    (c) component diagram        (d) deployment diagram

10. Forward engineering an object diagram is of limited value because

    (a) instances cannot be created from outside (b) classes are complex

    (c) reverse engineering cannot happen     (d) All the above.

## Answers

    1. (b)     2. (d)     3. (c)     4. (d)     5. (c)     6. (c)
    7. (d)     8. (d)     9. (a)     10. (a)

# Basic Behavioral Modeling Interactions

In the UML, you model the dynamic aspects of the system by using interactions. In every system you model, you find objects that constitute your system, interact with each other by passing messages. An interaction typically includes a set of messages exchanged among a set of objects within a context to accomplish a purpose. You apply interactions to model dynamic aspects of your system which comprises a society of objects working together to carry out some behavior of your system. Interactions normally include prototypical instances of classes, interfaces, components, nodes and use cases.

Interaction diagram is used to describe some type of interactions among the different elements in the model. So this interaction is a part of dynamic behavior of the system. This interactive behavior is represented in UML by two diagrams known as Sequence diagram and Collaboration diagram. The basic purposes of both the diagrams are similar. Sequence diagram emphasizes on time sequence of messages and collaboration diagram emphasizes on the structural organization of the objects that send and receive messages.

Interactions in a system happen, when participating objects send and receive messages. Mostly, messages involve

**LEARNING OBJECTIVES**

*After studying the chapter the students familiarize themselves with the following concepts:*

- Modeling Flow of Control
- Use cases
- Flow of Events and Scenarios
- Organizing Use cases
- Modeling Use cases and Collaborations
- Use case Diagrams and their Uses
- Modeling the Context of a System
- Modeling the Requirements of a System
- Forward and Reverse Engineering

invocation of an operation or the sending of a signal. You apply interactions to model the flow of control within an operation, a class, a component, a use case, or the system as a whole.

**So the purposes of interaction diagrams are:**

❖ To capture dynamic behavior of a system.
❖ To describe the message flow in a system.
❖ To describe structural organization of the objects.
❖ To describe interaction among objects.

The following diagram discusses a basic interaction in a university registration system:

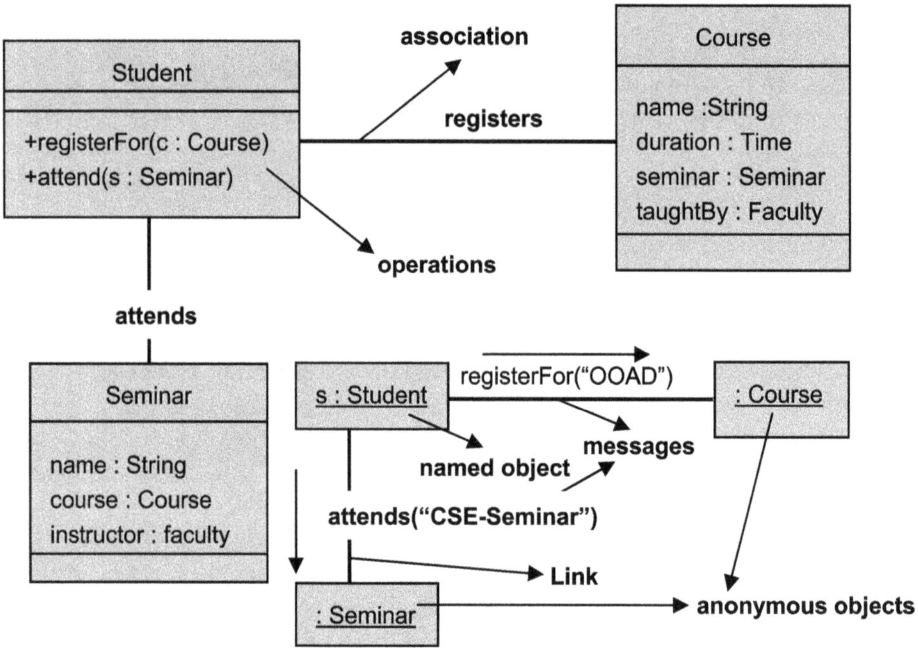

**Fig.9.1** Associations and Links

A link is an instance of an association and specifies a path along which objects can exchange messages between each other. You can add more semantics to a link by using the following standard stereotypes.

❖ **association:** Specifies that the corresponding object is visible by association.
❖ **self:** Specifies that the corresponding object is visible because it is the dispatcher of the operation.
❖ **global:** Specifies that the corresponding object is visible because it is in an enclosing scope.

❖ **local:** Specifies that the corresponding object is visible because it is in a local scope.

❖ **Parameter:** Specifies that the corresponding object is visible because it is a parameter.

A link can also be adorned with association name, association role name, navigation and aggregation. Multiplicity in association cannot be applied to links. When objects interact they pass messages among themselves. This message passing may result into an executable actions. In the UML, you can model the following kinds of actions.

❖ **Call:** Invokes an operation on an object.
❖ **Return:** Returns a value to the caller.
❖ **Send:** Sends a signal to an object.
❖ **Create:** Creates an object.
❖ **Destroy:** Destroys an object.

**Example:**

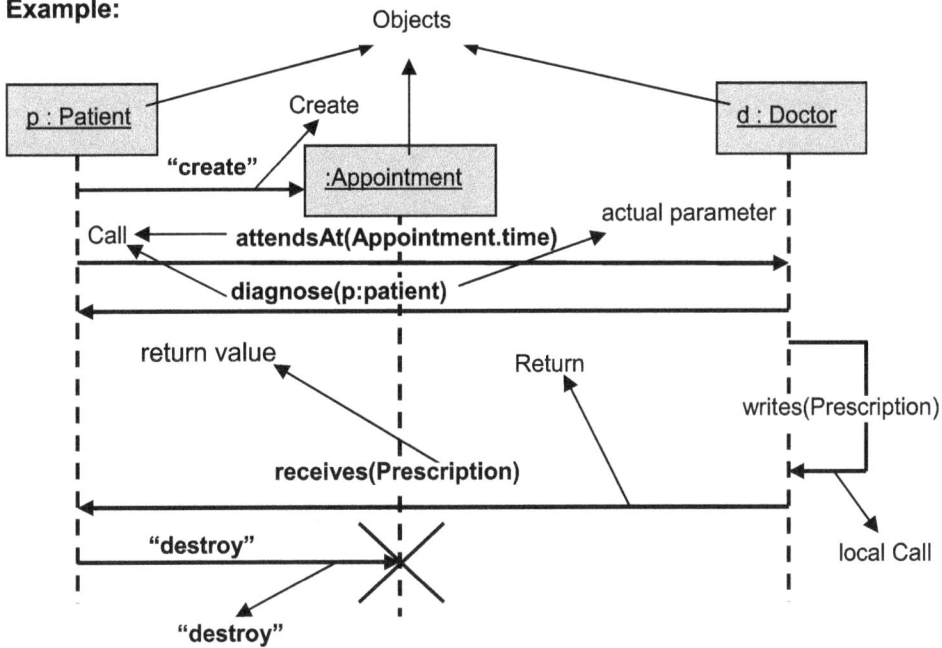

**Fig.9.2** Messages

**Explanation:** The above diagram is a sequence diagram indicating object interactions when a patient visits a doctor by taking appointment. In this sequence an object of Appointment is created and destroyed after doctor's diagnosis of the patient. The messages passed between objects and all kinds of actions that can happen as part of an interaction are specified.

## 9.1 Creation and Destruction

Generally, the objects that are participating in an interaction exists for the entire duration of the interaction. In some interactions new objects can be created and old objects can be destroyed. Similarly, the links among objects may come and go during an interaction. In order to specify these creations and destructions that happen in an interaction, you attach the following constraints with the elements.

❖ **new:** Specifies that the object or the link is created during the interaction.
❖ **destroyed:** Specifies that the object or the link is destroyed before the completion of the interaction.
❖ **transient:** Specifies that the instance or link is created during the interaction but is destroyed before the completion of the interaction.

## 9.2 Modeling a Flow of Control

The major application of interactions is to model the flow of control that characterizes the behavior of a system as a whole. The following sequence of steps are followed while you are modeling a flow of control:

❖ Specify the context for the interaction, whether it is the system as a whole, a class, or an individual operation.
❖ Identify objects that are participating in an interaction. Specify attribute values, state and role of each object in the interaction.
❖ If your target is to model structural organization of objects, identify the links that connect them based on the path of communication in the specified interaction. Adorn the links with UML's standard stereotypes or standard constraints.
❖ If your target is to model time ordering of messages, identify objects that are participating in an interaction with their life lines emanating from them. Specify the messages that pass between objects in the order of their time of occurrence. Specify parameters and return values to convey detailed information pertaining to the interaction.
❖ Adorn each object participating in the interaction, with its role and state at every moment of interaction.

As we have already discussed that the purpose of interaction diagrams are to capture the dynamic aspect of a system. We have two types of interaction diagrams in UML. One is sequence diagram and the other is a collaboration diagram. The sequence diagram captures the time sequence of message flow from one object to another and the collaboration diagram describes the organization of objects in a system taking part in the message flow. You need to do the following clearly before drawing interaction diagrams.

❖ Identify all objects taking part in the interaction.
❖ Identify all message flows among the objects.
❖ Identify the sequence or order in which the messages are flowing.
❖ Identify how the participating objects are organized.

The following topic discusses the interaction diagrams developed for the purpose of modeling Order Management System. The first one is a sequence diagram and the second one is a collaboration diagram.

**The Sequence Diagram:** The sequence diagram is having three objects (Customer, Order, and Special Order). The following diagram shows the message sequence for special order and provides information about the time sequence of message flows. Here, the message flow is nothing but a method call of an object.

**Sequence Diagram of an Order Management System**

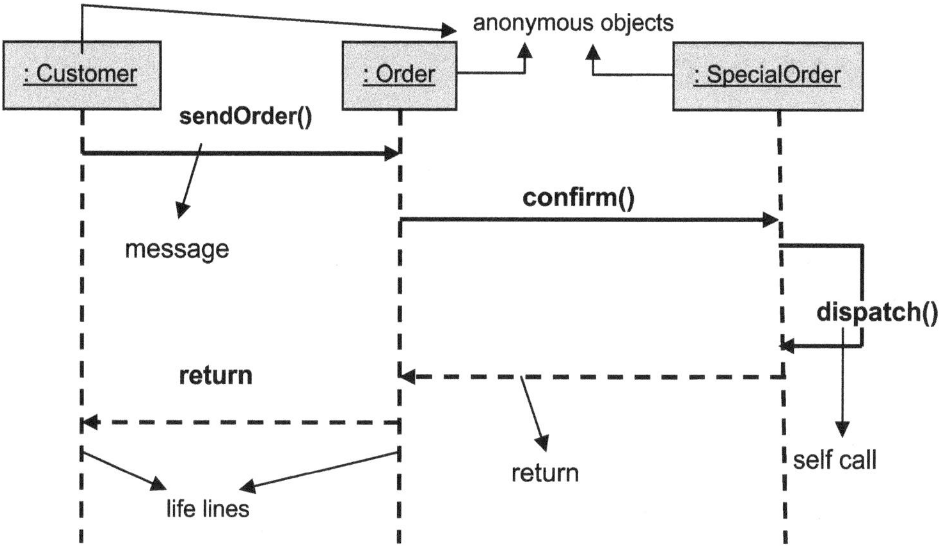

**Fig.9.3** Sequence Diagram

**Collaboration Diagram of an Order Management System**

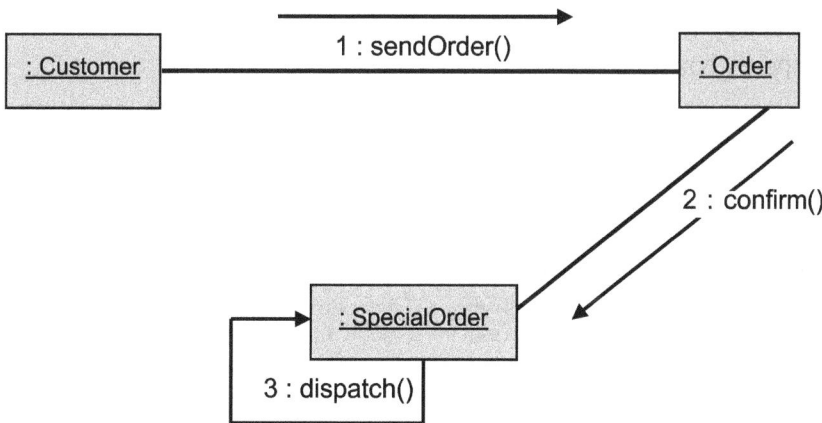

**Fig.9.4** Collaboration Diagram

**Explanation:** The first call is sendOrder() which is a method of Order object. The next call is confirm(), which is a method of SpecialOrder object and the last call is dispatch(), which is a method of SpecialOrder object. So here the diagram is mainly describing the method calls from one object to another and this is also the actual scenario when the system is running.

You can briefly say the following are the usages of interaction diagrams:
  ❖ They help in modeling flow of control by time sequence.
  ❖ They help in modeling flow of control by structural organizations.
  ❖ They help in forward engineering.
  ❖ They help in reverse engineering.

## 9.3 Use Cases

Every system you develop must be utilized for the purpose to which it is developed. In order to get the services of the system, the system has to be interacted with either human users or with some other automated systems. A use case specifies the part of the behavior or the entire behavior of the system. The elements which interact with the system and exists outside the boundary of the system are called actors. An actor can be a human user or an automated system.

You apply use cases to capture the functions of the system you are developing. You do not specify here, how these functions or behaviors are implemented. The major applications of use cases are described as follows:-

  ❖ They help in having good understanding of the system among end users and domain experts.
  ❖ They help in validating the system's architecture as it evolves during system development.

Use cases are realized by corresponding collaborations. A collaboration is a collection of elements that work together to accomplish the intended purpose of each use case. Use cases specify the desired behavior of the system, but they do not specify how this behavior is implemented.

A use case describes a set of sequences, which represent the interaction between actors and the system itself. These behaviors represented by use cases are system level functions. Use cases help us to visualize, specify, construct, and document the intended behavior of your system during requirements capture and system analysis. Typically, a use case involves the interaction between an actor and the system. You can apply use cases to model the behavior of a system, subsystem, a class, and even an interface. Usually, a use case is graphically represented as a solid ellipse with the name specified, and an actor is graphically represented as a stick symbol.

**Example**:

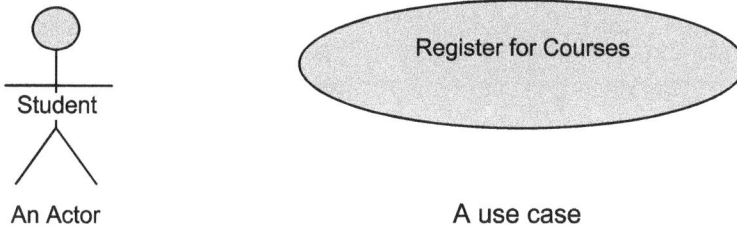

An Actor                              A use case

**Fig.9.5**  Use Case and Actor

A use case is a description of a set of sequences of actions, including variants, that a system performs to yield an observable result of value to an actor. Graphically, a use case is rendered as an ellipse. Every use case must have a name which distinguishes it from other use cases. A use case may have simple name or path name when it belongs to a package.

**Example**:

**Use case Names:**

**Simple Name:**                    **Path-Name Package Name:: Use case Name**

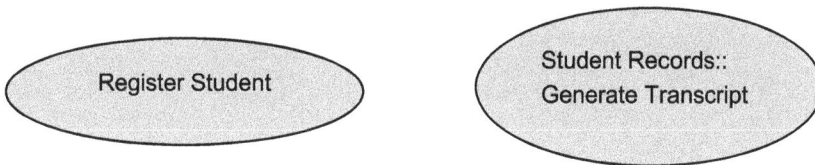

**Fig.9.6**  Use Case Names

An actor interacts with the system through use cases. Normally, an actor can be a human, a hardware device, or another automated system that interacts with your system. Actor can have instances. An instance of an actor represents an individual interacting with the system in a specific way. Though you model actors in a system, they are not actually part of the system, they live outside the system. Actors are connected to use cases only by association. A connection between an actor and a use case indicates communication between them in the form of sending and receiving messages. You can organize actors by using generalization/specialization relationships as follows:

**Example:**

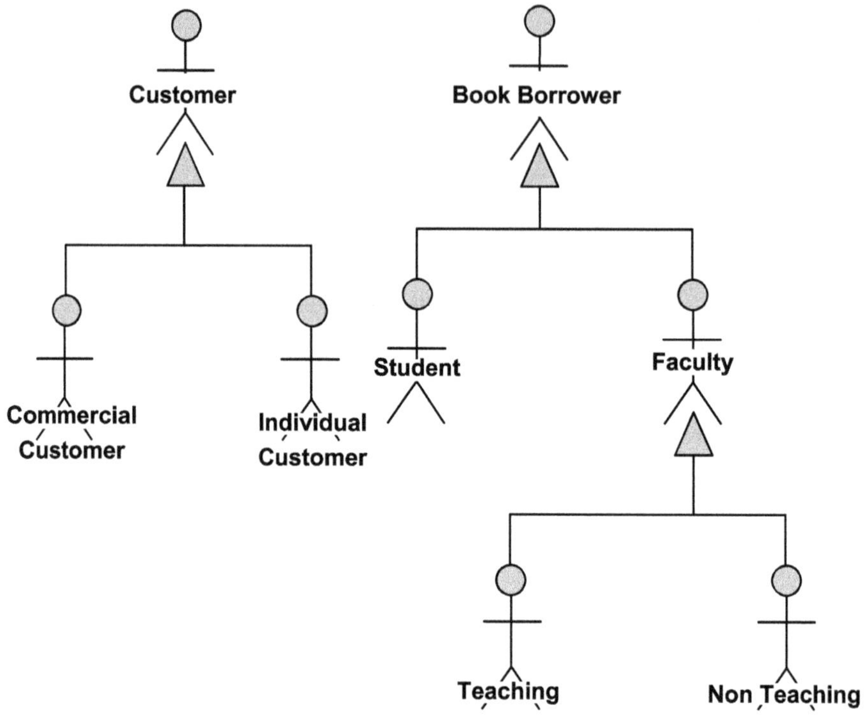

**Fig.9.7** Generalization among Actors

## 9.4 Use Cases and Flow of Events

A use case describes what a system, a subsystem, a class, or an interface does without specifying how it does. You can specify the behaviour of a use case in the form of flow of events. When you are using these flow of events, you should specify when the use case starts and ends, when the use case interacts with the actors, and the basic flow and alternate flows of the behavior. Let us consider a fragment of the model of a university course registration system to illustrate flow of events in a use case. The typical actors and use cases for the specified system can be described as follows:

| Actors | Use Cases |
|---|---|
| Registrar | Maintain the Curriculum |
| Professor | Request Course Roster |
| Student | Maintain Schedule |
| Billing System | Receive Billing info. from registration |

When you are modeling your system, you should document flow of events for each use case from an actor point of view. This document should describe all the details of the system that are provided to the actor when the use case is executed. The typical contents of this documentation include how the use case starts and ends, normal flow of events, alternate flow of events, and exceptional flow of events. Let us consider the use case Maintain the Curriculum interacted by the actor named Registrar. The flow of events for this use case can be specified as follows:

❖ The use case begins when the Registrar logs into the University Course registration System.
❖ The system prompts the Registrar to select the semester after validating the entered password.
❖ Once the Registrar enters the desired semester, the system prompts the user to select the desired activity, there are four possible activities; Add, Delete, Review, and Quit.

  ➢ If the activity selected is Add, a sub flow for adding a new course is performed.
  ➢ If the activity selected is Delete, a sub flow for deleting existing course is performed.
  ➢ If the activity selected is Review, a sub flow for reviewing curriculum is performed.
  ➢ If the activity selected is Quit , then the use case ends.

## 9.5 Use Cases and Scenarios

The flow of events that represent a use case can be modeled graphically as interaction diagrams. You may model a sequence diagram for main or normal flow of events, and a separate sequence diagram for each alternate flow of events. Usually, a use case can be graphically described by a set of sequences, where each sequence represents a flow of events. Each of these sequences can be called scenarios. A scenario is a sequence of actions that illustrates behavior. For each use case, you find primary scenarios which define essential sequences, and secondary scenarios which define alternative sequences.

Scenarios specify behavior of a use case not graphically, but by description using normal and informal structured text with conditions and pseudo code. A scenario typically specifies:

❖ How and when the use case starts and ends.
❖ Interactions with the actors and the exchange of objects during such an interaction.
❖ Flow of events, such as main/typical events that specify successful flow, alternative flow of events that specify   successful   flow, and exceptional flows that specify failure flows.

**Example**:  In a human resources system, for the Hire Employee use case, the following scenarios may apply:

Main success scenario:  Hire a person from another company.

Alternative success scenario:   Transfer the person from within the same company from another division.

Exceptional failure scenario: No qualified person could be hired.

## 9.6  Conditions and Quality Requirements that apply to Use Cases

**Entry and Exit Conditions**

❖ Entry conditions describe the environment under which the use case is invoked.

❖ Exit conditions reflect the impact of the use case on the environment through its execution.

**Quality Requirements**

❖ Describe quality attributes in terms of a specific functionality. For example, requires system response in < 30 seconds.

## 9.7  Relationships for Organizing Use Cases

You can group semantically related use cases in packages as you do in case of classes. You can organize use cases by applying relationships such as generalization, include and extend dependency among them.

**include**: Common behavior of more than one use case is referenced as a separate instance to avoid repetition.

**extend:** Implicit integration of the behavior of another use case by declaring the extension points/events in the base use case.

**Note**: Use cases are classifiers, so, they can have attributes and operations just as in case of classes. The objects that constitute your use case can be considered as attributes of the use case. The various scenarios or flow of events can be considered as operations of a use case. These objects and flow of events are used in your interaction diagrams depicting the behavior of the use case.

## 9.8  Identifying Actors, Use Cases, and Scenarios

**Actors**

❖ Define system boundary to identify actors correctly.

❖ Identify users and systems that depend on the system's primary and secondary functionalities.
❖ Identify hardware and software platforms with which the system interacts.
❖ Select entities that play distinctly different roles in the system.
❖ Identify as actors, the external entities with common goals and direct interaction with the system.
❖ Denote actors as nouns.

### Use Cases

❖ **Business/Domain Use Cases:** Interactions between users and the business (or domain).
❖ **System Use Cases**: Interactions between users and the system. One business use case contains a set of system use cases.
❖ To name the use cases, give it a verb name to show the action that must be performed. Describe a transaction completely, without the description of user interface.
❖ Capture use cases during requirements elaboration.
❖ Use cases are not mapped one-to-one to requirements. Each requirement must be covered by at least one use case. However, use cases may contain many requirements.
❖ Use scenarios to model assumptions and define system scope.
❖ List exceptions separately.

### Scenarios

❖ Extract the functionality that is available to each actor.
❖ Establish specific instances and not general descriptions.
❖ Denote situations in the current and future systems.
❖ Identify

> ➢ Tasks to be performed by the user and the system .
> ➢ Flow of information to the user and to the system .
> ➢ Events that are conveyed to the user and to the system .
> ➢ For the events flow, name steps in active voice.

## 9.9 Use Cases and Collaborations

A use case describes the intended behavior of the system, sub system, class, or an interface. A use case does not specify how that behavior is implemented. It means that there is a clear separation between the specification of the behaviour of the system and its implementation. A use case specifies the behavior. This behavior can be implemented by a society of objects and other elements that work together. This society of elements is named as a collaboration. This relationship can be modeled as follows:

**Example**:

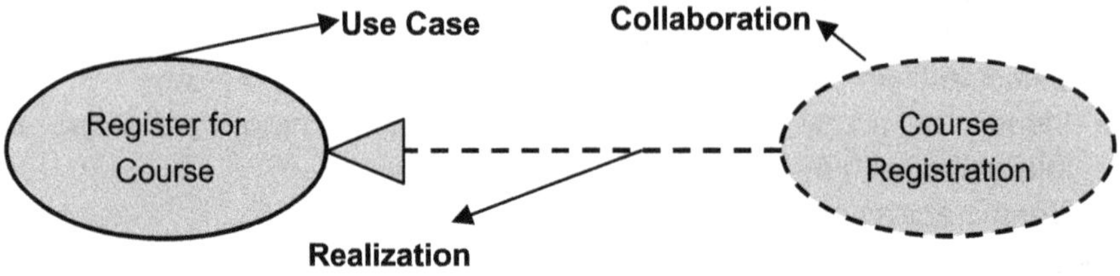

**Fig.9.8** Use Case and Collaboration

## 9.10  Organizing Use Cases

You can organize use cases in the following ways:

❖ You can organize use cases by grouping them in packages as you group classes when you organize them.

❖ You can organize use cases by using Generalization/Specialization relationship.

❖ You can organize use cases by using extend and include relationships among them.

Generalization among use cases is same as generalization among classes. Here it means:

❖ The child use case inherits the behavior and meaning of the parent use case.

❖ The child may add to or override the behavior of its parent.

❖ The child is substitutable any where the parent appears.

❖ Both the parent and the child may have concrete instances.

**Example**:  In a banking system you might validate the user by using password verification or by doing retina scan, because the retina pattern differs from person to person and you can also use thumb impressions. This can be modeled as follows:

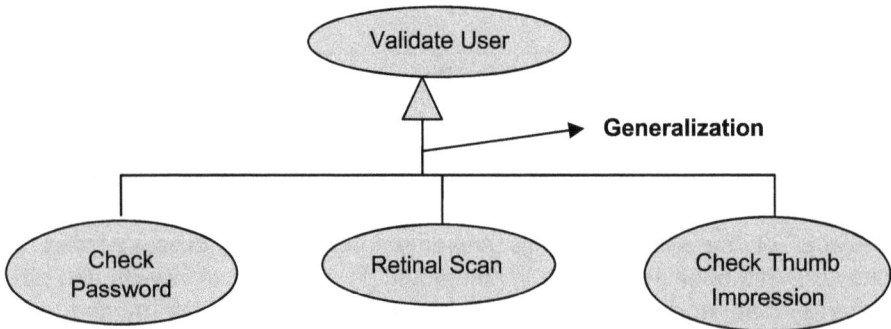

**Fig.9.9** Generalization among Use Cases

**Note:** In the above figure, Validate User use case is the parent use case, where as the use cases, Check Password, Retinal Scan, and Check Thumb Impression are children. Here, it means that you can verify the user by using any of the methods such as, checking password, checking thumb impression, or by scanning the retina.

**include:** This relationship among use cases is used to factor common behavior. The use case pulls such behavior from other use cases that it includes. This is a kind of link that relates use cases.

**Examples**:

1. The following figure gives a model from purchase order system, where material is purchased by enterprise from various vendors. The purchase may happen in two ways:

    (a) Purchasing it by paying invoice amount after the material is shipped to the enterprise's location.
    (b) The another way is to purchase the material by placing an order, online. The supplier (vendor) might have implemented a web commerce application using with a customer can place purchase orders using internet.

**Note**: Whatever way you use for purchasing, you need to do purchase valuation, meaning, what are the items/material to be purchased, in what quantity, and calculating the total price including any kinds of discounts. In the following figure, both invoice purchase and online purchase include the scenarios defined by purchase valuation. The include link avoids the duplication of scenarios in multiple use cases.

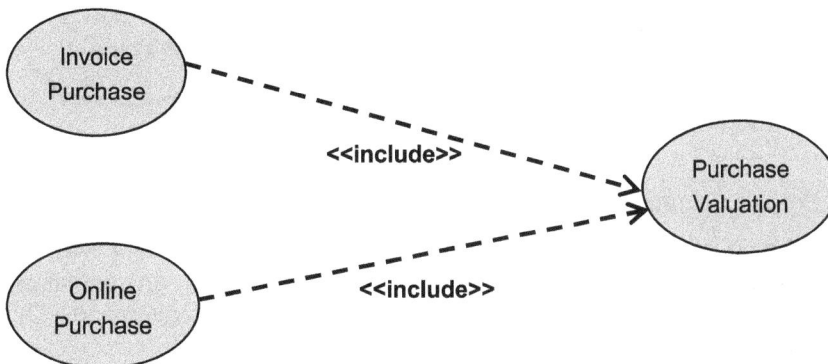

**Fig.9.10(a)** Use Cases with include Relationship

2. This is a fragment from student's course registration system's model. After registering in a university, the student may choose courses, or modify existing course selection information. Whenever a student selects a list of courses or modifies the existing selected courses, he is verified

whether he is a registered student or not. Only registered students can select/modify courses. The following figure illustrates that.

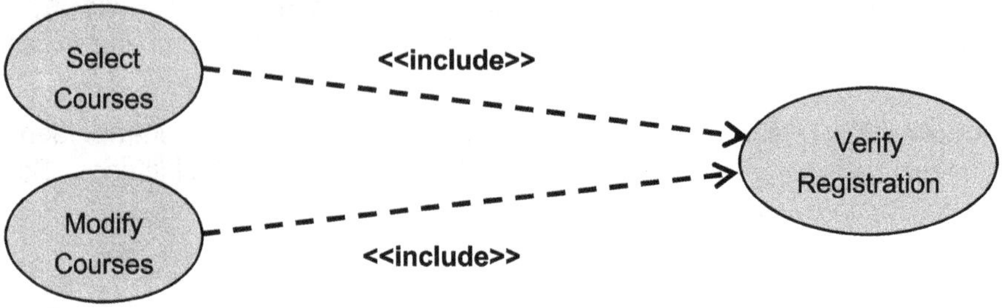

**Fig.9.10(b)**  Use Cases with include Relationship

**extend**: This relationship among use cases is used to factor variants. The use case pushes such behavior into other use cases that extend it. This relationship describes a variation on behavior at extension points in the extended use case.

**Examples**:

1. In the figure below, Search by Name extends Search at the name extension point and Search by Email extends Search at the Email extension point.

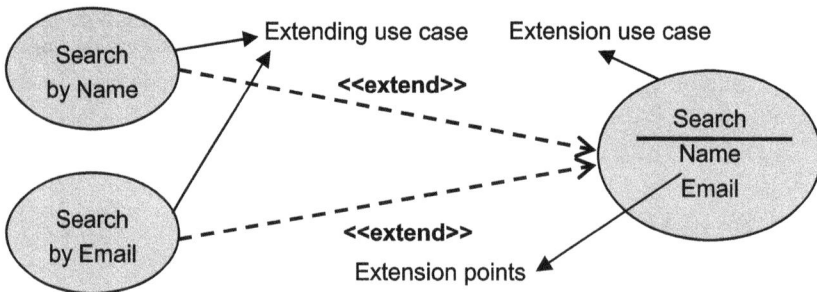

**Fig.9.11(a)**  Use Cases with extend Relationship

2. The figure below illustrates a fragment of model for Student Registration System. Here, managing Student Registration is an extension of Registering New Student or Modifying existing Registration. This is graphically described below:

**Note**: Use cases are classifiers similar to classes. They too may have attributes and operations. Here, the attributes of a use case are the objects that are involved to carry the behavior specified by the use case. The operations of a use case are the actions of the system that describe a flow of events. These objects and operations may be used in interaction diagrams to model the behavior as specified by a use case. You can also describe the behavior specified by a use case using state machines.

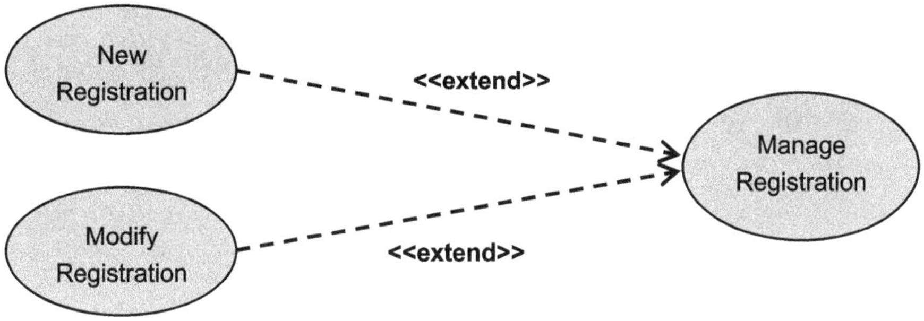

**Fig.9.11(b)** Use Cases with extend Relationship

## 9.11 Modeling the Behavior

The major purpose of a use case is to model the behavior of an element. This element could be a system as a whole, a sub system, or a class. While you are modeling this behavior, you only think of what the element does but not how it does it. You apply use cases to elements for three reasons, and they are as follows:

❖ Use cases provide a way for domain experts. Use cases describe external view of the system to communicate with the end users. The internal view of use cases are under stood by the developers.
❖ Use cases provide a way for developers to understand an element and visualize how to implement its behavior.
❖ Use cases are helpful in developing test cases, test procedures to test the system.

  The steps mentioned below are followed while you are modeling the behavior of an element.

❖ Identify the actors that interact with the element. Potential actors are those who perform functions of the element.
❖ Organize these identified actors in the form of Generalization/ Specialization relationships.
❖ Identify the primary ways actors behave when they are interacting with the element.
❖ Identify the exceptional ways actors behave when they are interacting with the elements.
❖ Represent these behaviors in the form of use cases. Organize use cases by using generalization, include, or extend relationships. Here, include factors out common behavior and exclude factors out exceptional behavior.

**Example:** The figure below discusses a fragment of the model for Student's Course Registration System.

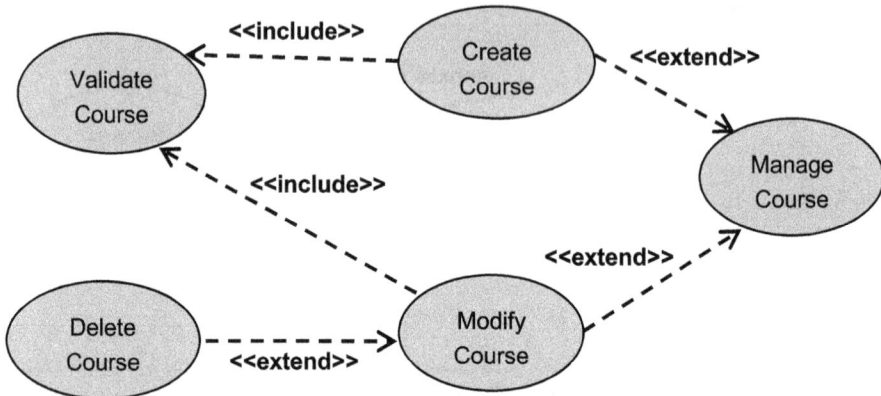

**Fig.9.12** Modeling the Behavior

**Explanation:** Here, Modify Course use case is an extension of Delete Course use case. The use cases named Create Course and Modify Course include use case Validate Course as common behavior. The use case Manage Course extends use cases Create Course and Modify Course. For each of these use cases, you can specify the behavior, either by using text, state machine, or by using interactions.

## 9.12 Use Case Diagrams

Use case diagrams model the dynamic aspects of a system. Each use case diagram contain a set of use cases and actors and their relationships. Use case diagrams typically model the use case view of the system. Use case diagrams are used for:

- ❖ Modeling the context of an element (system, subsystem, or class) .
- ❖ Modeling requirements of an element (system, subsystem, or class) .
- ❖ Testing executable systems through forward and reverse engineering.

A use case diagram commonly contains use cases, actors and relationships, such as association, dependency, and generalization. You can also include notes and constraints in use case diagrams. Use case diagrams may also contain packages containing groups of elements. Use case diagrams may also include instances of use cases, especially when you are modelling an executing system. Use cases are used in every software intensive projects. They are helpful in exposing system requirements and in planning a project. Most of the use cases are defined initially, but the software development process is iterative and incremental, you may find more use cases as the project continues.

While you are modeling a system's behavior using use case diagrams, start by listing a sequence of steps the actors might take in order to complete a set of services specified by the system. Each service may be modeled as a use case associated with the relevant actor for that service. For example, a customer placing an order for purchasing items with an organization may have the following sequence of steps:

- ❖ Browse items catalog and choose items to be purchased.
- ❖ Contact sales department.
- ❖ Submit sales order to sales representative.
- ❖ Supply shipping information by warehouse clerk.
- ❖ Supply payment information by sales representative.
- ❖ Receive confirmation from sales person.

The corresponding use case diagram for the above process could be as follows:

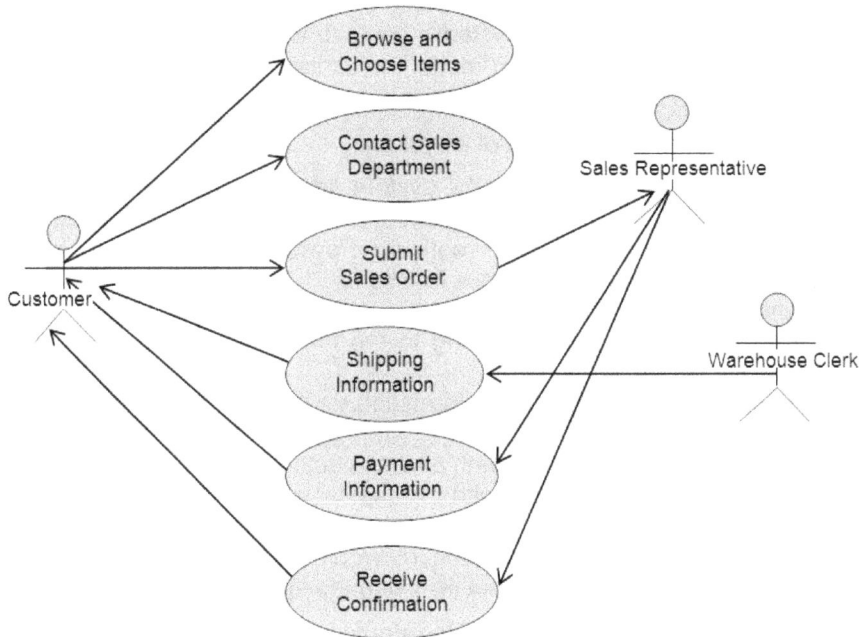

## 9.13 Common Uses of Use Case Diagrams

The major use of use case diagrams is to model the static use case view of the system. The purpose of this view is, it supports the behavior of the system. In fact, this diagram describes the externally visible services that the system provides in the context of its environment. You typically apply use case diagrams for the following purposes:

**To model the context of a system:** Here, you model the system by drawing a boundary around the whole system. Then, identify which actors lie outside the system and interact with it. When you model the context of a system by using use case diagrams, you specify actors and their roles.

**To model the requirements of a system:** Here, you model the requirements of the system. You apply use case diagrams to specify what the system does as seen by the outside view. Here, use case diagrams are applied to specify the desired behavior of a system as seen by the end user without being bothering about how this behavior is implemented.

## 9.14 Modeling the Context of a System

When you model any given system, you find some things that live inside the system, and some things live outside it. The inside things carry on the behavior as expected by the outside things. All those things that lie out side and interact with the system constitute   the system's context. It is typically an environment in which the system lives. You can model the context of a system by using use case diagrams with major emphasis on the actors that surround the system.

The steps in modeling the context of a system:

* ❖ Identify actors that surround the system. Identify, who require help from the system, who execute the system's functions, who interact with external hardware and/or software systems, and who perform administration and maintenance functions.
* ❖ Identify generalization/specialization hierarchy among the actors. Organize these actors according to the inheritance relationship among them.
* ❖ You can augment additional information for better clarity of the model by providing stereotypes for actors.
* ❖ Populate use case diagram with all these actors.
* ❖ Populate use case diagram with the use cases placed within the system's boundary.
* ❖ Specify paths of communication between actors that lie out side the system with the use cases that lie inside the system.

Let us consider University Course Registration system as an example. Here, students register for courses. Let us describe the requirements for computerizing university course registration. The specification of requirements can be as follows:

* ❖ The Registrar sets up the curriculum for a semester. One course may have multiple course offerings.
* ❖ Students select at least four courses (primary courses) and at most six courses (two alternate courses).
* ❖ Once a student registers for a semester, the billing system is notified so that student can be billed.
* ❖ After a student is registered, he/she may use the system to add/drop courses for a period of time.
* ❖ Professors use the system to receive their course offering rosters.
* ❖ Users of this system are assigned passwords which are used for logon validation.

Based on the requirements of the above system, the actors named, Registrar, Professor, Billing System, and Student. The associated needs of each actor are as follows:

❖ Registrar maintains curriculum.
❖ Professors request rosters.
❖ Students involve in maintaining schedule, and in registering courses.
❖ Billing system receives billing information from registration.

The related use case diagram is:

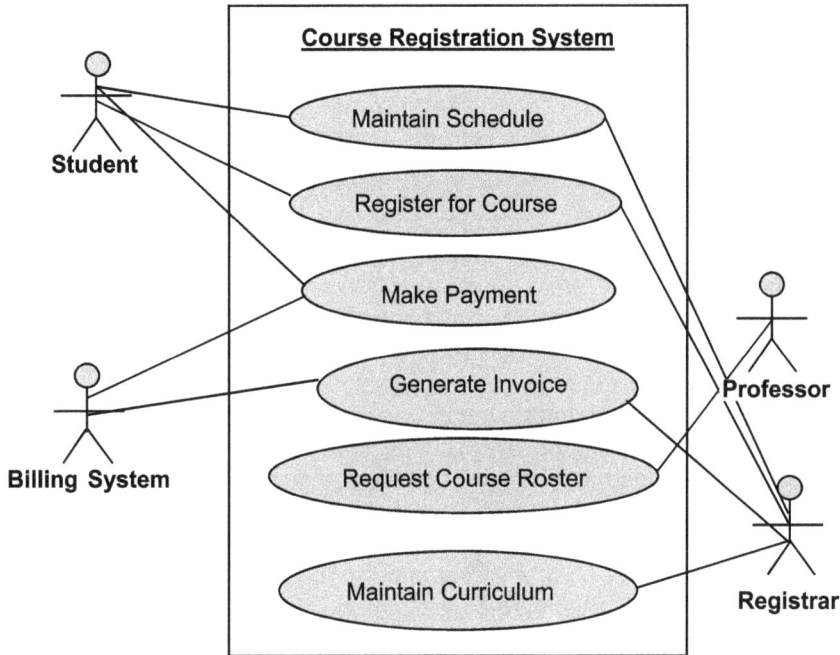

**Fig.9.13** Modeling the Context of a System

**Explanation:** Student and Registrar are involved in registering for courses. Student and Registrar are involved in maintaining course schedule. Registrar and Billing System are involved in generating invoices for the purpose of billing Student. Student and Billing System are involved in making payment for course billing. Professor requests course rosters and Registrar maintains curriculum. The generalization among the above actors are indicated below:

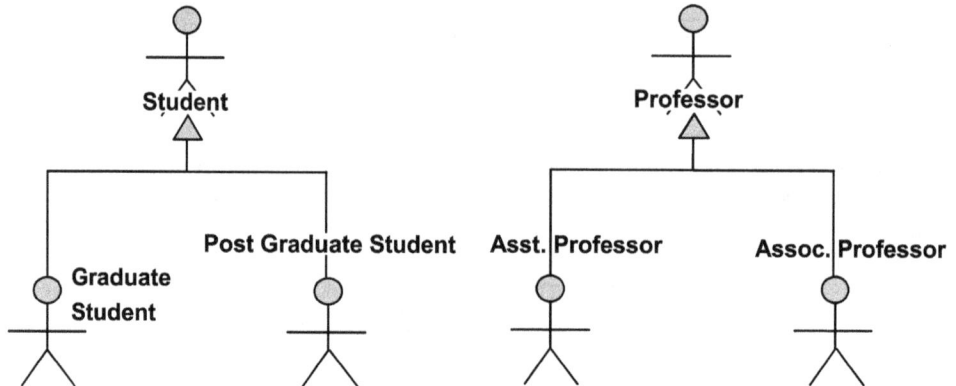

## 9.15 Modeling the Requirements of a System

Requirements specify the services a system offers to the end users. Requirements specify the behavior of a system as expected by the external actors lying outside the system boundary. Generally, system's requirements are an initial document prepared by the customer and given to the client who implements the system. They specify the entire behavior and functionality of the system as required by the customer. The understanding of requirements grows as your system evolves during its iterative and incremental development. If you want to use a system handed over to you, you definitely need to know how it behaves in order to use it properly. Functional requirements can be expressed in plain text or by using expressions in a formal language. In UML, system's requirements can be graphically expressed using use case diagrams. So, use case diagrams become means of communication between the customer and the developer for understanding the requirements of a system.

The steps required to model the requirements of a system are as follows:

❖ Identify the actors which are external and surround the system. These actors establish the system's context.
❖ Identify the behavior each external actor expects from the system.
❖ Represent all these behaviors of the system as use cases.
❖ Establish, use cases which contain common behavior and use cases which contain variant behavior.
❖ Model a use case diagram by using use cases and actors and their relationships.
❖ You can always attach notes to these use cases which describe nonfunctional requirements.

The below figure expands the previous use case diagram. This diagram does not specify the relationships between the use cases and actors. Compared to the previous use case diagram, this diagram contain some additional use cases which are invisible to the customer, yet essential behaviors of the system. This diagram describes functional requirements of a system to start with. This diagram is useful for end users and domain experts, and developers to understand the system's behavior. In a way, now we have a graphical representation of a system's requirements.

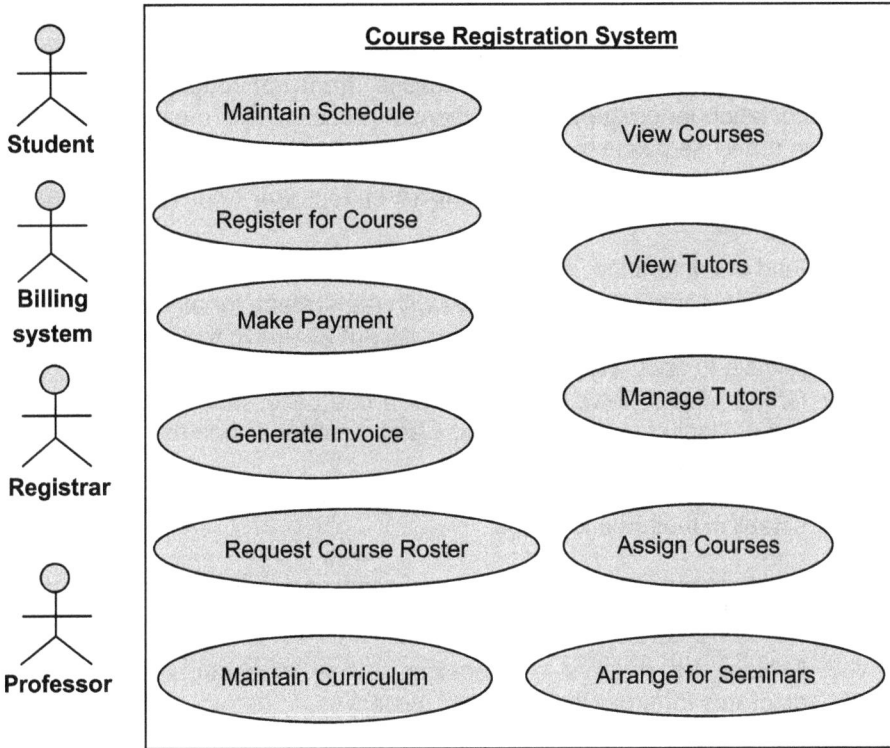

## 9.16  Forward and Reverse Engineering

The UML's diagrams, such as class, component, and state chart diagrams have analogs in the executable system. Because of this, forward and reverse engineering can be applied on them. Use case diagrams are different, because they describe how an element behaves, not how that behavior is implemented, so it cannot be directly forward or reverse engineered.

A use case diagram can be forward engineered for not to generate code but to generate test cases. As we are aware each use case specifies a behavior of a system. This behavior can be tested during system development. A well defined use case may specify a test's initial state and its success criteria. The below mentioned steps are followed to forward engineer a use case diagram:-

❖ Identify normal flow of events and exceptional flow of events for each use case in the use case diagram.

❖ Generate a test case for each flow. The flow's preconditions form the test's initial state and post conditions form its success criteria.

❖ Whenever you release the element to which the use case diagram applies, use tools to run these tests.

Reverse engineering a use case diagram may not be possible automatically, because we cannot derive specification from its implementation using tools. Still there is a way of getting use cases from its implementation in an implementation language by using manual process. This means from the code you can draw use cases by hand.

**The below mentioned steps are followed when you reverse engineer a use case diagram:**

❖ Find out actors that interact with the system.

❖ Consider how an actor interacts with the system, for all identified actors.

❖ Trace the primary and alternative flow of events in the executable system relative to each actor.

❖ Group related flows in the form of a use case. Model common flows by using include relationships, and model variants using extend relationships.

❖ Use these actors and use cases to develop a use case diagram, and establish their relationships.

## Essay Type Questions

1. Explain the process of modeling a flow of control. Draw interaction diagrams for order management system.

2. Briefly explain the following with examples.
   (a) use cases      (b) use cases and flow of events.

3. Explain how to identify actors, use cases and scenarios.

4. Write short notes on organizing use cases.

5. Explain how to model the behavior using use case diagrams.

6. Explain how to model the context of a system with various steps involved and with examples.

7. Explain how to model the requirements of a system with various steps involved and with examples.

## Objective Type Questions

1. Dynamic aspects of the system can be modeled by using
   (a) interactions            (b) classes
   (c) object diagram          (d) components

2. Interactions normally include

   (a) objects                          (b) interfaces
   (c) components                       (d) All the above

3. The diagram that emphasizes on time sequence of messages

   (a) collaboration diagram            (b) sequence diagram
   (c) component diagram                (d) object diagram

4. The diagram that emphasizes on the structural organization of the objects that send and receive messages

   (a) collaboration diagram            (b) sequence diagram
   (c) component diagram                (d) object diagram

5. You apply interactions to model the flow of control within

   (a) operation                        (b) class
   (c) component                        (d) All the above

6. Mostly, messages involve

   (a) invocation of operation          (b) sending a signal
   (c) both a & b                       (d) None

7. The purpose of an interaction diagram is

   (a) To capture dynamic behavior of a system
   (b) To describe the message flow in a system
   (c) To describe structural organization of the objects
   (d) All the above

8. ------------------ standard stereotype  specifies that the corresponding object is visible by association.

   (a) global                           (b) association
   (c) local                            (d) self

9. ------------------  standard stereotype specifies that the corresponding object is visible because it is the dispatcher of the operation

   (a) global                           (b) association
   (c) local                            (d) self

10. ----------------- standard stereotype specifies that the corresponding object is visible because it is in a local scope.

   (a) global                           (b) association
   (c) local                            (d) self

11. ---------------- is the action that invokes an operation on an object

   (a) call                             (b) return
   (c) send                             (d) create

12. ------------------ is the action that sends a signal to an object

    (a) call                          (b) return
    (c) send                          (d) create

13. ----------------- is the action that creates an object

    (a) call                          (b) return
    (c) send                          (d) create

14. ------------------ constraint that pecifies that the instance or link is created during the interaction but is destroyed before the completion of the interaction

    (a) new                           (b) transient
    (c) destroy                       (d) All the above

15. Modeling flow of control happens through

    (a) objects                       (b) sequence diagram
    (c) collaboration diagram         (d) both b & c

16. You need to do the following clearly before drawing interaction diagrams

    (a) Identify all objects taking part in the interaction
    (b) Identify all message flows among the objects
    (c) Identify how the participating objects are organized
    (d) All the above

17. The usage of interaction diagram is

    (a) They help in modelling flow of control by time sequence
    (b) They help in forward & reverse engineering
    (c) both a & b
    (d) None

18. ------------- specifies the part of the behavior or the entire behavior of the system

    (a) class                         (b) use case
    (c) interface                     (d) object

19. The major applications of use cases are

    (a) They help in having good understanding of the system among end users and domain experts
    (b) They help in validating the system's architecture as it evolves during system development
    (c) both a & b
    (d) None

20. An actor is graphically rendered as

    (a) dotted ellipse                (b) solid ellipse
    (c) cube                          (d) stick symbol

21. An actor typically represents
    (a) A person interacting with the system
    (b) Another automated system interacting with the system
    (c) both a & b
    (d) None

22. The flow of events that represent a use case can be modeled graphically as
    (a) object diagrams                (b) class diagrams
    (c) interaction diagrams           (d) component diagrams

23. --------------- conditions describe the environment under which the use case is invoked
    (a) entry                          (b) exit
    (c) cancel                         (d) exception

24. Use cases are generally realized by
    (a) classes                        (b) collaborations
    (c) objects                        (d) Nodes

25. ------------- relationship among use cases is used to factor common behavior
    (a) generalization                 (b) association
    (c) include                        (d) extend

## Answers

| | | | | | |
|---|---|---|---|---|---|
| 1. (a) | 2. (d) | 3. (b) | 4. (a) | 5. (d) | 6. (c) |
| 7. (d) | 8. (b) | 9. (d) | 10. (c) | 11. (a) | 12. (c) |
| 13. (d) | 14. (b) | 15. (d) | 16. (d) | 17. (c) | 18. (b) |
| 19. (c) | 20. (d) | 21. (c) | 22. (c) | 23. (a) | 24. (b) |
| 25. (c) | | | | | |

# CHAPTER 10

# Interaction Diagrams

Interaction diagrams such as sequence diagrams and collaboration diagrams in UML are used for modeling dynamic aspects of a system. An interaction diagram shows interaction among objects that constitute your system. Objects can interact with each other by sending and receiving messages. The definitions of interaction diagrams are given below:

❖ A sequence diagram is an interaction diagram that emphasizes the time ordering of messages.

❖ A collaboration diagram is an interaction diagram that emphasizes the structural organization of the objects that participate in an interaction, by sending and receiving messages.

Both of these interaction diagrams are equivalent, meaning, they convey the same information. These diagrams are isomorphic, in the sense if you have one diagram you can generate the other one without loosing any information. That is, if you have sequence diagram you can generate collaboration diagram and if you have collaboration diagram you can generate sequence diagram.

Interaction diagrams are helpful in modeling dynamic aspects of a system. This includes modelling instances of classes, interfaces, components, and nodes that are in your system along with the messages that are dispatched among them. Interaction diagrams are applicable not only for modeling dynamic aspects of the system but also for constructing executable systems through forward and reverse engineering. Interaction diagrams commonly contain objects, links among objects, and messages that are dispatched, in addition, it may contain notes and constraints.

## 10.1 Sequence Diagrams

A sequence diagram describes the time ordering of messages. This diagram contains objects and their interactions in the form of messages. Each object in a sequential diagram has a life line emanating from it indicating its life span in an interaction.

**Example**: Here we discuss an issue of faculty recruitment in any college. The entire faculty recruitment process can be expressed in the form of the following steps:

❖ Whenever there is a requirement for faculty, the HOD (Head of the Department) approaches the principal.
❖ Principal gives an advertisement.
❖ Applicant after reading the advertisement applies for the post.
❖ College sends call letters to the short listed candidates specifying the date and time of interview.
❖ Applicants attend interview, and college conducts interviews.
❖ Appointments will be given to the selected candidates.
❖ The applicant becomes the faculty of the college after accepting the appointment.

The entire faculty recruitment process can be expressed in the form of a sequence diagram as follows:

Sequence Diagram for faculty recruitment

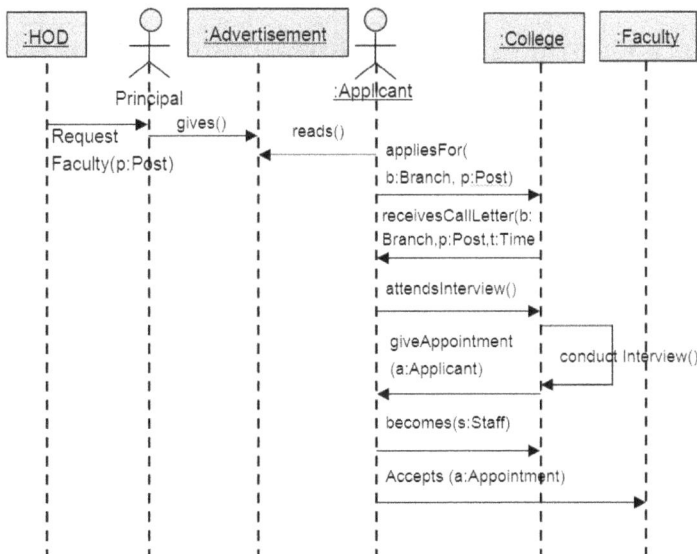

## 10.2 Collaboration Diagrams

A collaboration diagram describes the structural organization of objects that participate in an interaction. You model a collaboration diagram by first placing the objects that interact, then connecting these objects through the links, finally, these links are adorned with the messages that objects send and receive.

**Example**:

Collaboration Diagram for faculty recruitment

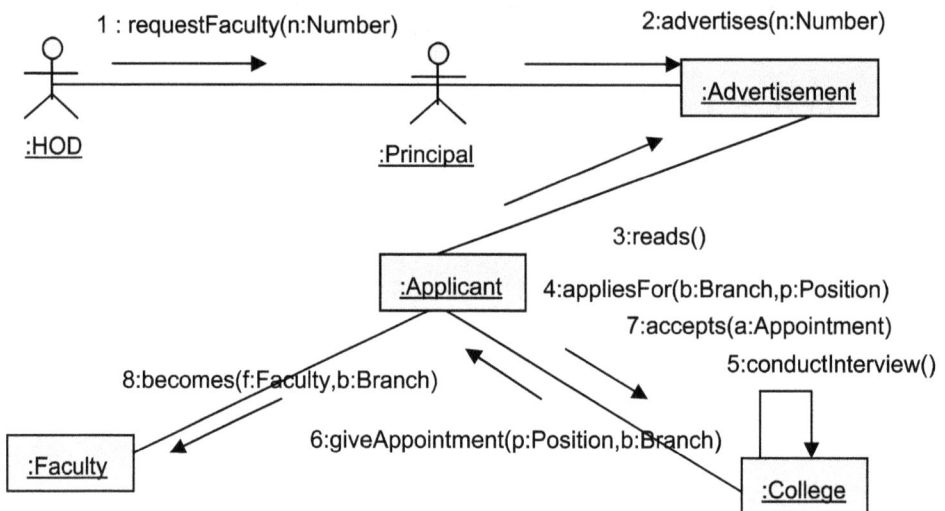

## 10.3 Common Uses of Interaction Diagrams

Interaction diagrams are used to model the dynamic aspects of a system. It may involve interactions among instances, including instances of classes, active classes, interfaces, components, and nodes. Interaction diagrams can model the whole system, a subsystem, an operation, or a class. Interaction diagrams can model various scenarios belonging to use cases and also collaborations including a society of objects. You typically apply interaction diagrams in two ways:

❖ To model flows of control by time ordering of messages (Sequence diagram).

❖ To model flows of control by organization of objects that send and receive messages (Collaboration diagram).

## 10.4 Modeling Flows of Control by Time Ordering

If you model flow of control using time ordering of messages, it results into an interaction diagram named sequence diagram. The following steps are followed while you model a flow control by time ordering:-

❖ Find out whether you are modeling interactions for a whole system, a sub system, an operation, a class, a scenario in an use case, or a scenario in a collaboration.

❖ Identify the objects that participate in an interaction which you are modeling. Place instances based on their importance from left to right in an order.

❖ Establish the life line for each object. In most of the cases objects remain in the entire interaction. But in some cases, new objects might get created during an interaction and also existing objects might get killed during an interaction. The birth and death of objects are modeled using stereotyped messages in an interaction.

❖ Indicate interactions among objects in the form of messages between the life lines of objects from top to bottom. In order to explain an interaction you may show properties such as parameters in a message.

❖ Adorn each object's life line with its focus of control.

❖ Specify time and space constraints needed in an interaction using messages.

❖ Attach pre and post conditions to each message to clearly specify flow of control.

A sequence diagram can model only one control flow. When you are modeling interactions, you may have to develop several interaction diagrams, some of which model primary flows of control, and some model alternative as well as exceptional flows of control. You can name a sequence diagram to distinguish it from other sequence diagrams. You can organize these sequence diagrams in the form of packages.

**Note**: While you want to model the objects that change their states, roles, and attribute values during an interaction. There are two ways you can do that as follows:

❖ The same object may appear multiple times in a sequence diagram with different states, different roles, and different values of attributes. The change in object can be specified by using **become** a stereotyped dependency.

❖ You can model changing state by placing it directly on the object's life line.

## 10.5 Modeling Flows of Control by Organization

You can model flow of control by using structural organization of objects that participate in an interaction and the messages that are send and received in that interaction. These messages could be numbered based on their order of occurrence and the direction of occurrence can also be specified. This interaction diagram is called collaboration diagram. You apply collaboration diagrams to model the whole system, subsystem, an operation, a class, or a flow in a use case. The following steps are followed while you model a flow of control by organization:

❖ You establish the context of interaction. Whether you are modeling a system, a subsystem, an operation, a class, a scenario in a use case, or in a collaboration.

❖ Identify the objects that play roles in an interaction. Put them as vertices in a collaboration diagram. Place the important objects at the center, and their neighbors at the outside of a collaboration diagram.

❖ Connect the objects that interact by using a message with a suitable sequence number specifying the order of occurrence.

❖ If the state, role, and attributes of an object change during an interaction, place a duplicate object on the collaboration diagram with these new values and connect them by a message stereotyped as **become** or **copy**.

❖ Establish the links among these objects through which messages pass. Identify association links first, because they represent structural connections. Identify other links adorning them with suitable path stereotypes specifying how these objects are related.

❖ Specify a sequence number for each message in the order of its occurrence during objects' interactions.

❖ You can adorn each message with time or space constraints.

❖ You can associate pre and post conditions to each message.

## 10.6  Forward and Reverse Engineering

As we know forward engineering is the process of converting a model in UML into code in an implementation language. Similarly, reverse engineering is the process of converting code in an implementation language into an equivalent model in UML. Forward and reverse engineering is possible in case of sequence and collaboration diagrams using tools, if the context of these diagrams is an operation. We are aware that sequence diagrams or collaboration diagrams can be modelled for indicating the behavior of an operation also.

## Essay Type Questions

1. What are interaction diagrams? Specify common uses. Explain them with examples.

2. Specify various steps involved in modeling flows of control by time ordering.

3. Specify various steps involved in modeling flows of control by organization.

## Objective Type Questions

1. Both of these interaction diagrams are
   - (a) isomorphic
   - (c) convey the same information
   - (b) equivalent
   - (d) All the above

2. An interaction diagram typically contains
   - (a) objects
   - (c) messages
   - (b) links
   - (d) All the above

3. Life line in sequence diagram indicate
   - (a) life span of a class
   - (c) life span of an interface
   - (b) life span of an object
   - (d) All the above

4. In a collaboration diagram the links between objects are adorned with
   - (a) classes
   - (c) both a & b
   - (b) objects
   - (d) messages

5. Interaction diagrams involve instances of
   - (a) classes
   - (c) nodes
   - (b) components
   - (d) All the above

6. Forward and reverse engineering is possible in case of sequence and collaboration diagrams using tools, if the context of these diagrams is
   - (a) attribute
   - (c) both a & b
   - (b) operation
   - (d) None

## Answers

1. (d)      2. (d)      3. (b)      4. (d)      5. (d)      6. (b)

# Activity Diagrams

Activity diagrams are used to model the dynamic aspects of a system. An activity diagram shows a flow of control from activity to activity. An activity is a non atomic execution within a state machine. Activities result into some action made up of executable atomic computations that result in a change in state of the system or the return of a value.

**Actions include:**

❖ Calling another operation.
❖ Sending a signal.
❖ Creating or destroying an object. Or
❖ Some pure computation such as evaluating an expression.

An activity diagram describes the flow of control (and data) through the various stages (action/activity states) of a procedure (operation/use case).

The common uses of activity diagrams are as follows:

❖ They describe algorithmic aspects of an operation of an object.
❖ They describe flow of control as well as flow of data through the system.
❖ They describe the actions of a use case.
❖ An activity diagram can be owned by an object or by a group of objects.

Activity diagrams are also useful for constructing executable systems through forward and reverse engineering. An activity diagram commonly contain:

❖ Activity states and action states.

**LEARNING OBJECTIVES**

*After studying the chapter the students familiarize themselves with the following concepts:*

◆ Action and Activity States
◆ Transitions and Branching
◆ Forking and Joining
◆ Swim Lanes
◆ Object Flow
◆ Uses of Activity Diagrams
◆ Modeling Work Flow
◆ Modeling an Operation

❖ State transitions.
❖ Branching.
❖ Forking and Joining.
❖ Swimlanes.

## 11.1 Action States

Action states are typically executable atomic computations of the system, each representing the execution of an action. These actions include, evaluating an expression, calling an operation of an object, sending a signal to an object, or even create or destroy an object. An action state is graphically represented as follows:

**Examples:**

**Fig.11.1** Action States

Properties of an action state can be described as follows:

❖ Action states cannot be decomposed.
❖ Action states are atomic, in the sense, action state is not interrupted.
❖ Action state consumes insignificant execution time.

## 11.2 Activity States

An activity state can be further decomposed. An activity state may contain other activity states as well as action states. An activity can be represented by other activity diagrams. Activity states are not atomic, meaning they can be interrupted. Activity state in general, takes significant duration to complete. Both action states and activity states are represented in a similar fashion. But activity states may have additional information such as entry and exit actions.

**Example:**

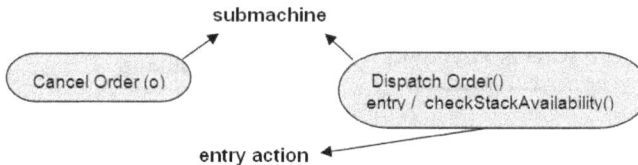

**Fig.11.2** Activity States

## 11.3 Transitions

When an action or activity of a state completes, flow of control passes immediately to the next action or activity state. This state transition is indicated by a directed line as follows:

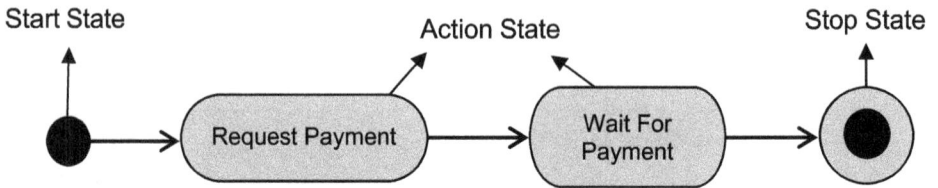

**Fig.11.3(a)**  Trigger less Transitions

**Fig.11.3(b)**  An Action on a Transition

**Note**: An action on transition may trigger an event. In the Fig.11.3(b), a transition from activity Process Payment to Clear Debt will trigger an event that updates the cash balance.

## 11.4 Branching

When you are modeling a flow of control using activity diagrams, simple and sequential transitions are common. But sometimes you may include a branch which specifies alternate paths taken based on some Boolean expression. You represent a branch as a diamond.

**Example**:

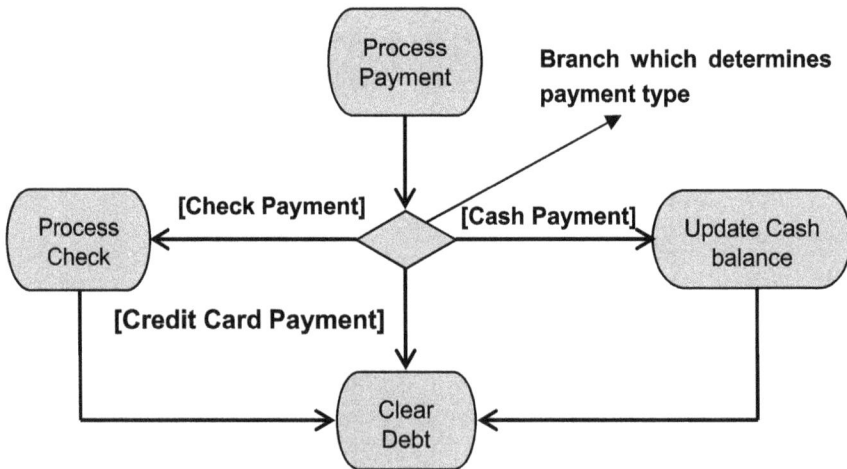

**Fig.11.4** Branching

## 11.5  Forking and Joining

When you are modeling work flows of business processes using activity diagrams, you might encounter work flows that are parallel. In UML, a synchronization bar is used to specify the forking and joining of these concurrent flows of control. Graphically, a synchronization bar is rendered as a thick horizontal or vertical line. A fork may have one incoming transition and two or more outgoing transitions where each represents an independent flow of control. A join may have two or more incoming transitions and one out going transition.

Sometimes it makes sense to allow a number of activities to run in parallel. A transition can be split into multiple paths and multiple paths combined into a single transition by using a synchronization bar. Where the paths split is known as a fork, and where the paths meet is known as a join. A synchronization bar may have one entry transition and two or more exit transitions, or multiple entry transitions and one exit transition.

**Note**: Joins and Forks must balance each other, it means that the number of flows that leave a Fork must match the number of flows that enter its corresponding Join. Activities that are in the concurrent flows of control can communicate with one another by means of sending and receiving signals. You can model this style of communication by using active objects.

**Examples**:

1. The following Fig.(11.5) specifies an activity diagram involved in University Course Registration System. This diagram contains Forks, Joins and Branching. It is required that about 25 students can register for a course. If the number of students registered are less than 25, the registration process for that course continues otherwise the registration for the course is closed.

2. The following Fig.(11.6) describes the business level activity diagram for the library system. Here, we consider two actors dealing with the system, they are Library member and Librarian. A member can borrow a book by searching for it on book shelf in the library. Similarly members can return borrowed books to the librarian. These members must stand in a queue if there are more members trying to borrow and return books. The librarian after recording the borrowed or the returned book proceeds with the next member in the queue.

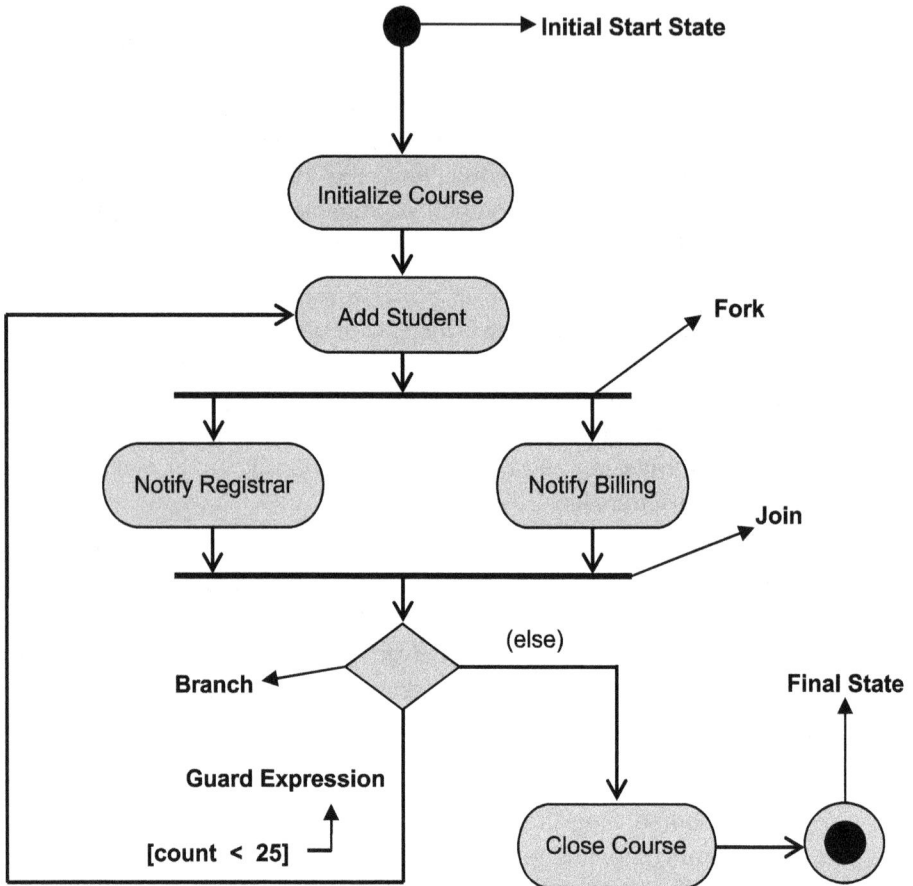

**Fig.11.5** An Activity Diagram

## 11.6 Swimlanes

When you are modeling work flows of business processes, the activity states in an activity diagram can be partitioned into groups. Each group represents either an actor or a business organization responsible for those activities. Each group is called a swimlane because these groups are divided from their neighbors by a vertical solid line. If an activity diagram is partitioned into swimlanes, every activity belongs to exactly one swimlane, but transitions may occur across lanes.

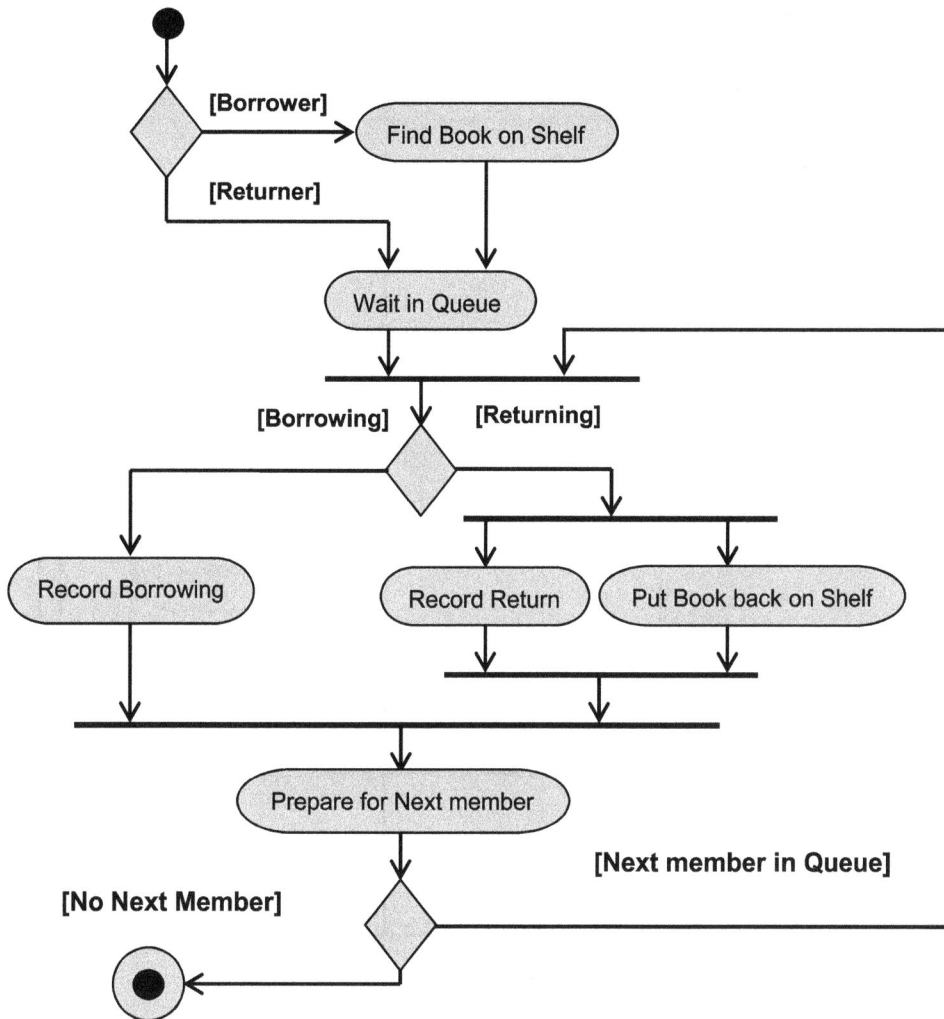

**Fig.11.6** An Activity Diagram of the Library

**Examples**:

1. This diagram shows the activity diagram across swimlanes for ATM machine's withdrawal transaction.

2. The following diagram describes the activity diagram for University Course Registration system across swimlanes.

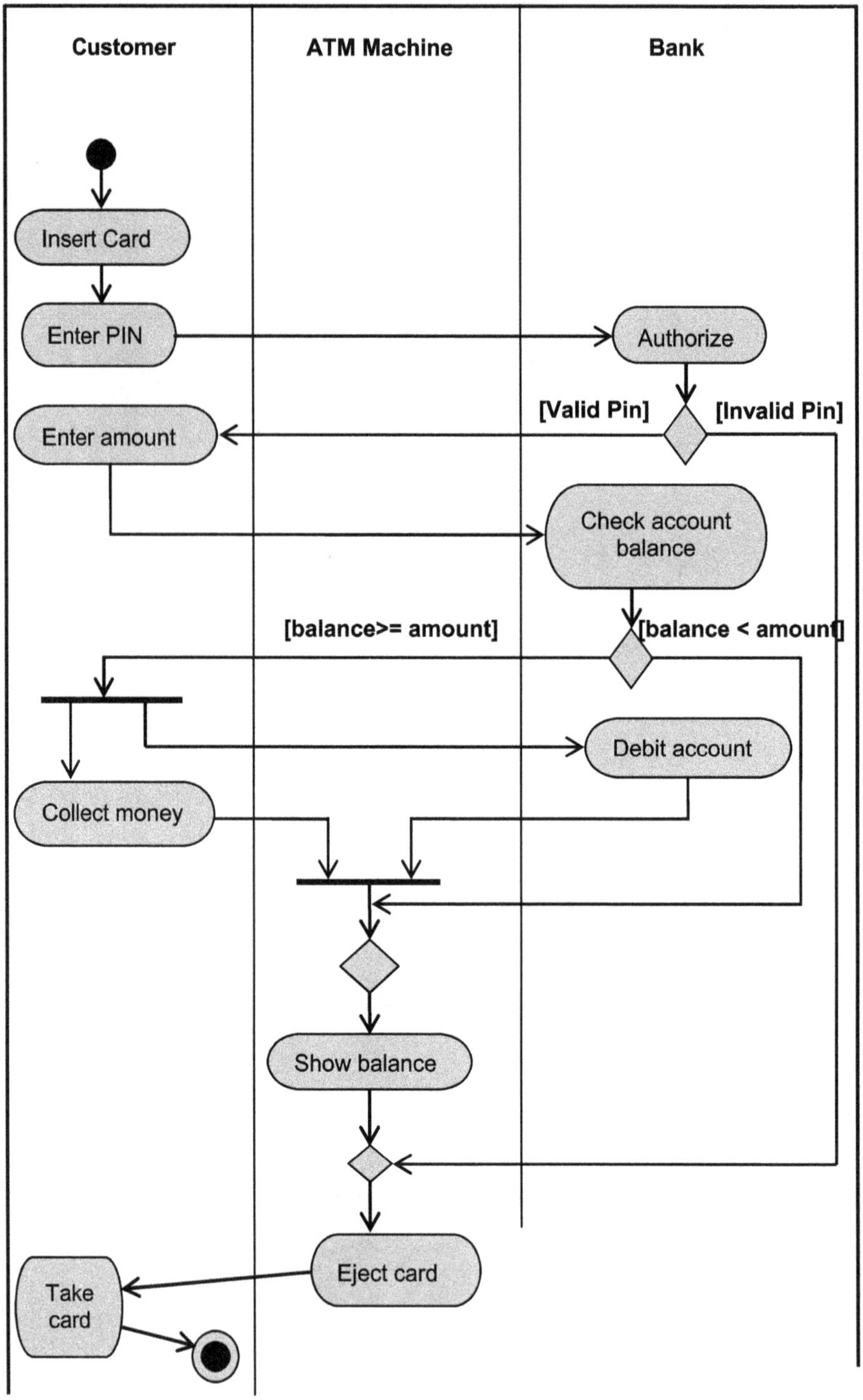
Customer
ATM Machine
Bank
Insert Card
Enter PIN
Authorize
[Valid Pin]
[Invalid Pin]
Enter amount
Check account balance
[balance>= amount]
[balance < amount]
Debit account
Collect money
Show balance
Eject card
Take card

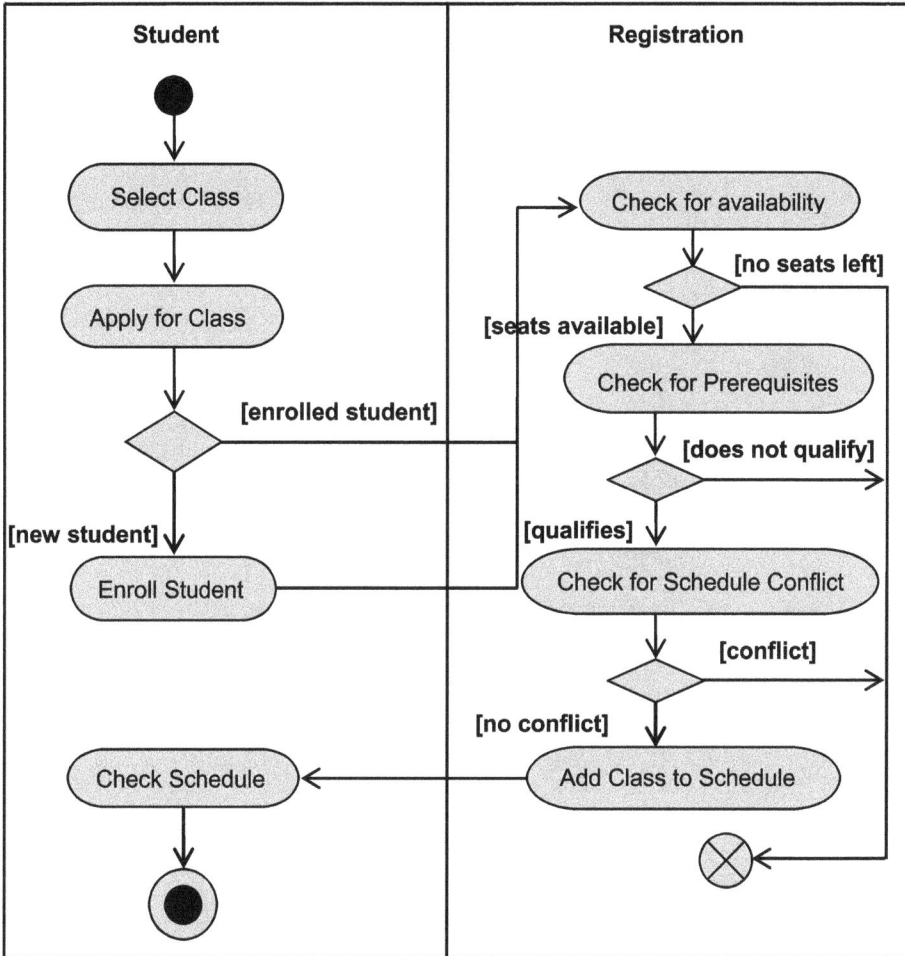

**Fig.11.7**  An Activity Diagram with Swimlanes

## 11.7 Object Flow

Objects can be involved in the flow of control described by an activity diagram. Consider the following example which involves work flow of processing an order. Your problem space include class such as Order. Objects of this class are created during control flow by activity such as Request Service. Other activities such as Take Order, Fill Order and Deliver Order may modify the object named Order. These activities change the state of this object.

You can specify these things in an activity diagram by placing these objects in the diagram, connected using a dependency relationship to the activity or transiition that creates, destroys, or modifies them. This kind of specification is called an Object Flow because it includes the participation of an object in a flow of control. You can also specify how an object can be modified. You can show how its role, state and attribute values change. The state of an object in an activity diagram can be specified by naming it in brackets below the object's name. Similarly you can specify attribute values by placing them in a compartment below the object's name.

**Example**: The following figure describes an activity diagram for Service Order Processing System with swimlanes as well as with object flow.

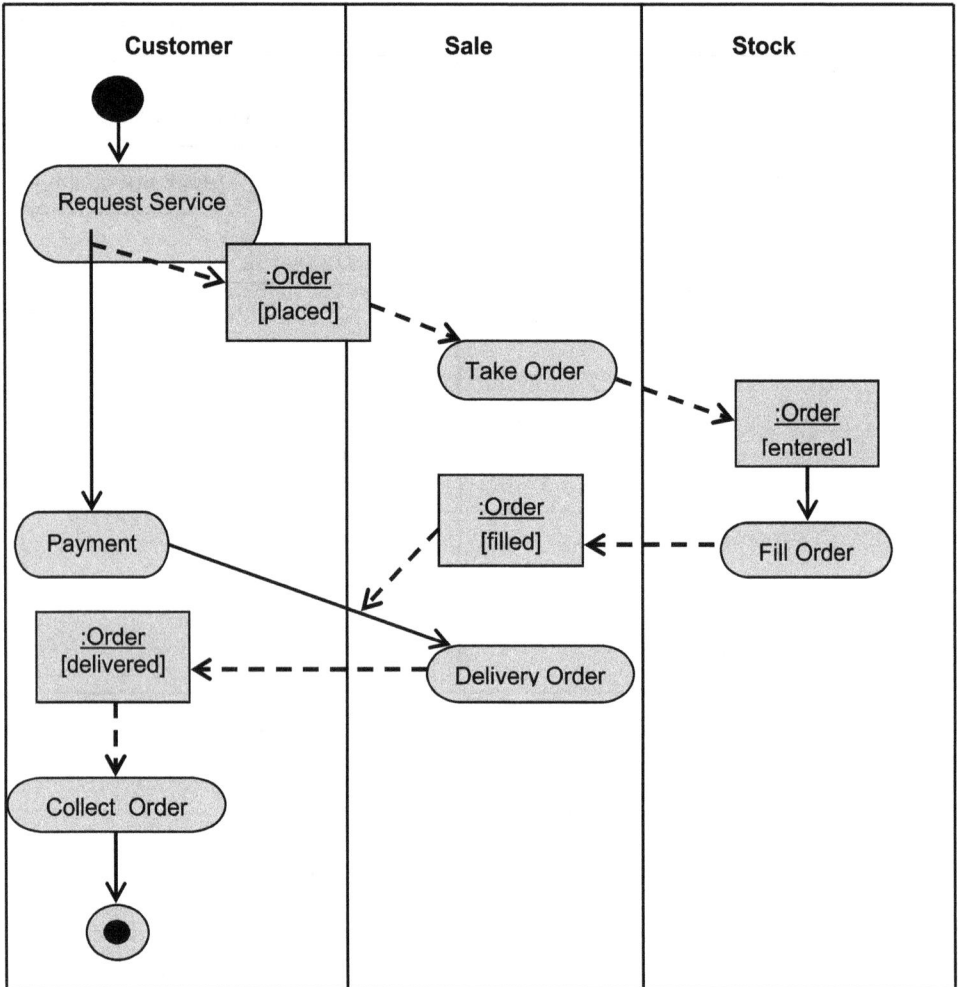

**Fig.11.8**  An Activity Diagram with Object Flow

## 11.8  Common uses of Activity Diagrams

Activity diagrams are used to model the dynamic aspects of a system. These dynamic aspects may involve the activities relating to classes (may also include active classes), interfaces, components and nodes. You may use activity diagrams to model the behavior of a whole system, a subsytem, an operation or a class. Activity diagrams can be used to model various scenarios belonging to use cases and to model collaborations. As we are aware that a collaboration models the dynamic aspects of a socioety of objects. Typically, activity diagrams are used in two ways such as:

❖ To model a work flow.
❖ To model an operation.

To model a work flow, we concentrate on activities as viewed by actors who interact with the system. Work flows represent business processes that involve the system you are developing. Here, activity diagrams may involve modeling of object flows.

To model an operation, we apply activity diagrams as flow charts to describe the details of the computation involved in the operation. These activity diagrams commonly contain branches, forks and joins. An activity diagram depicting an operation involves parameters of an operation as well as its local objects.

## 11.9  Modeling a Workflow

No software system lives in isolation. It involves various actors that interact with the system. These actors can be human users or automated systems. Any task the software implements may include various business processes. These business processes constitute work flows in a system which can be modeled by activity diagrams. For example, if you are modeling a Sales Order Processing System, you may come across some automated systems such as Marketing and Ware House Systems and some human systems belonging to Sales, Marketing and Shipping Departments that interact with your system. Activity diagrams are used to model the business processes which involve these human and automated systems that interact with your system. The following enumerates various steps in modeling a workflow:

❖ Establish the workflow you are modeling. You may require more than one diagram to model workflows.

❖ For each workflow, select the important business objects that participate in the workflow. While developing an activity diagram, create swimlane for each business object.

❖ Establish pre and post conditions of the workflow you are modeling. This will model the boundaries of your workflow.

❖ For each workflow, establish actions and activities that take place. Model your workflow as an activity diagram consisting action states and activity states.

❖ Represent graphically the transitions that connect these action and activity states that constitute your workflow. Initially consider sequential workflows followed by branching, then only, consider forking and joining.

❖ If any objects are involved in the workflow, model them as activity diagrams with object flows. You can specify the modification of these objects during workflows to specify the intent of object flows.

# 11.10 Modeling an Operation

An activity diagram can be used to model the behavior of an element. You can associate activity diagrams to classes, interfaces, components, nodes, use cases, collaborations, and operations. An activity diagram which models the behavior of an operation is simply a flow chart describing actions of that operation. The following enumerates the steps in modeling an operation using activity diagrams:

❖ Collect the information relating to an operation you are modeling. These might be:

➤ Operation's parameters and return types.

➤ The attributes of the related class.

➤ The neighboring classes.

❖ Find out pre and post conditions relating to the operation you are modeling.

❖ Graphically represent the activities and actions that take part in an operation as an activity diagram with the corresponding action and activity states.

❖ Apply branching to an activity diagram to indicate conditional paths and iterations.

❖ Use forking and joining in an activity diagram to specify concurrent flows of control.

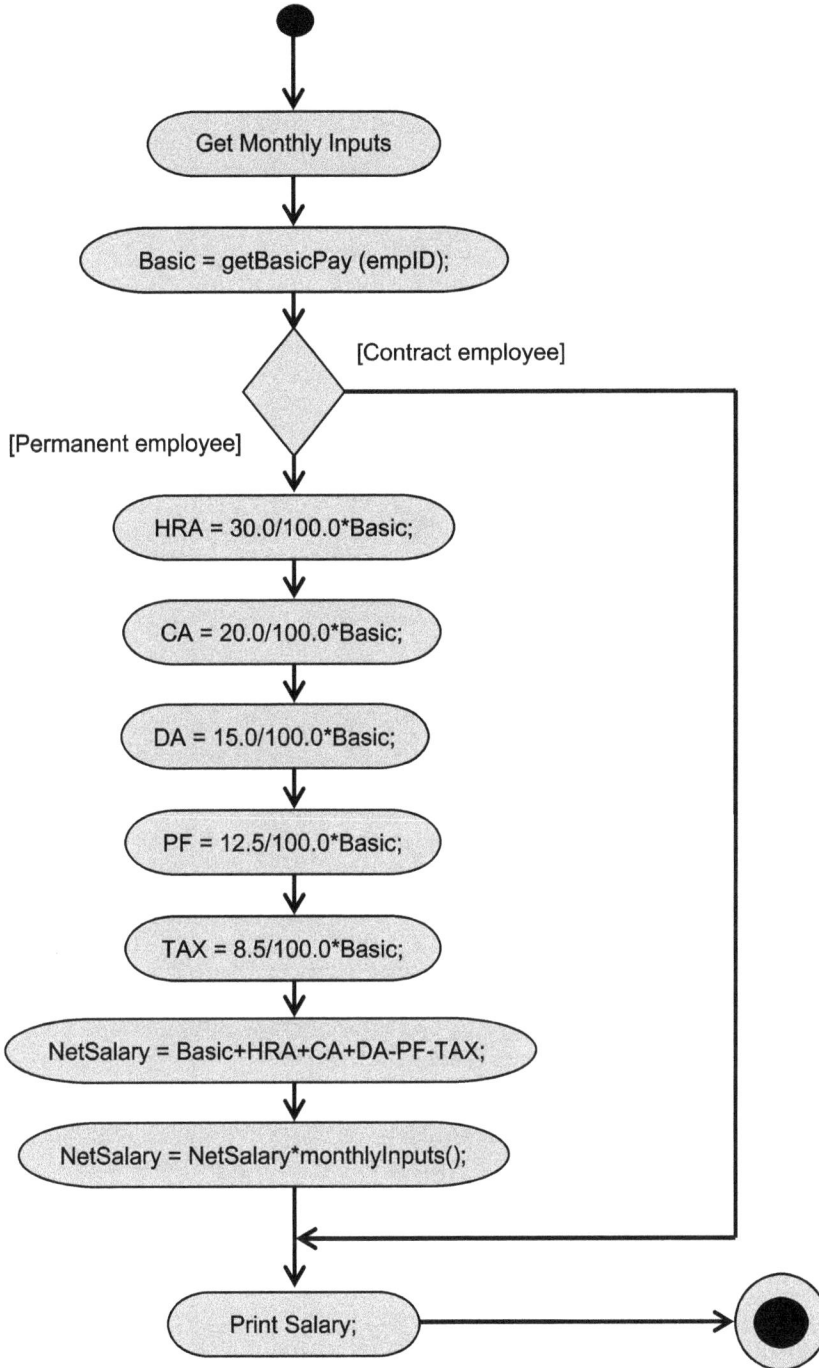

**Fig.11.9**  Activity Diagram for getManthlySalary() Operation

**Example**: The Fig(11.9) is an activity diagram for an operation in a payroll system which computes monthly salary for each employee in the organization and prints the same. This operation uses a function named getBasicPay() by accepting employee ID as its parameter and returns his basic pay. Based on the basic pay all other components of the net salary are computed depending on their respective percentages. Then the net salary is computed by adding basic pay, HRA, CA, DA and subtracting PF and TAX as follows:

HRA (House rent Allowance) = 30% of Basic;

CA (Conveyance Allowance) = 20% of Basic;

DA (Dearness Allowance) = 15% of Basic;

PF (Provident Fund) = 12.5% of Basic;

TAX = (Tax on Income) = 8.5% of Basic;

The total number of working days in a month are calculated. The number of working days an employee has attended for a month are computed after considering any leave facilities. These values are provided by a function named getMonthlyInputs(). Then the net salary is computed as follows:

Net Salary = Basic + HRA + CA + DA − PF − TAX;

Net Salary = Net Salary * (Number of days employee has attended/Number of working days in a month);

An employee can be a contract employee or a permanent employee. Net salary is not computed for a contract employee, basic pay is payed as consolidated amount. An operation named computeSalary() which accepts employee ID as its parameter and computes net salary for a month and prints the same can be modeled as an activity diagram in Fig.(11.9).

## 11.11 Forward and Reverse Engineering

Forward engineering (The creation of code from a model) is applicable to activity diagrams if the context of the diagram is an operation. If you forward engineer the above activity diagram with the implementation language of C++, the following code for the operation get MonthlySalary() is generated.

```
void Employee::getMonthlySalary (char empID[])
{
  int workingDays, attendedDays;
  getMonthlyInputs (&workingDays,&attendedDays,empID);
  float Basic = getBasicPay (empID);
  char empType = getEmpType (empID);
  if (empType == 'P')   // Permanent Employee
  {
    float HRA  = 30.0/100.0 * Basic;
    float CA   = 20.0/100.0 * Basic;
    float DA   = 15.0/100.0 * Basic;
    float PF   = 12.5/100.0 * Basic;
    float TAX  = 8.5/100.0 * Basic;
    float netSalary = Basic+HRA+CA+DA-PF-TAX;
  }
  else    float netSalary = Basic;

  netSalary = attendedDays/workingDays * netSalary;
  printf("The net salary = %10.2f\n", netSalary);
  return;
}
```

Reverse Engineering (The creation of a model from code) is also applicable to activity diagrams if the context is the code for the body of an operation.

## Essay Type Questions

1. Write short notes on the following:
   (a) Activity states  (b) Transitions (c) Branching  (d) Forking and Joining

2. Draw an activity diagram of the library application

3. Explain swim lanes with an example activity diagram

4. Explain object flow with an example activity diagram

5. Explain the various steps involved in modeling a work flow by using an activity diagram

6. Explain briefly the following
   (a) Modeling an operation
   (b) Forward and reverse engineering of activity diagrams

## Objective Type Questions

1. A non atomic execution within a state machine is called
   - (a) action state
   - (b) activity
   - (c) collaboration
   - (d) composite state

2. Actions include
   - (a) Calling another operation
   - (b) Sending a signal
   - (c) Creating or destroying an object
   - (d) All

3. The common uses of activity diagrams are
   - (a) They describe algorithmic aspects of an operation of an object.
   - (b) They describe the actions of a use case
   - (c) both a & b
   - (d) none

4. An activity diagram commonly contain
   - (a) State transitions
   - (b) branching
   - (c) forking and joining
   - (d) All the above

5. Action states are
   - (a) cannot be decomposed
   - (b) atomic
   - (c) both a & b
   - (d) none

6. The state that can be interrupted
   - (a) action state
   - (b) activity state
   - (c) both a & b
   - (d) none

7. --------------- specifies alternate paths taken based on some Boolean expression
   - (a) branching
   - (b) forking
   - (c) joining
   - (d) All the above

8. A branch is graphically rendered as
   - (a) cube
   - (b) square
   - (c) diamond
   - (d) rectangle.

9. The decomposition of a single work flow into multiple and parallel work flows is called
   - (a) joining
   - (b) branching
   - (c) forking
   - (d) none of the above

10. A solid filled in circle in activity diagram indicates
    - (a) initial start state
    - (b) final state
    - (c) branching
    - (d) forking

11. The partitioning of activity states in an activity diagram is called

    (a)  forking                         (b)  branching
    (c)  swim lanes                   (d)  All the above

12. The uses of an activity diagram are

    (a)  To model a work flow          (b)  To model an operation
    (c)  both a & b                     (d)  none

13. The information collected during modeling of an operation include

    (a)  Operation's parameters and return types
    (b)  The attributes of the related class
    (c)  The neighboring classes
    (d)  All the above

14. Forward engineering  is applicable to activity diagrams if the context of the diagram is

    (a)  operation                     (b)  attribute
    (c)  use case                    (d)  collaboration

## Answers

| | | | | | |
|---|---|---|---|---|---|
| 1. (b) | 2. (d) | 3. (c) | 4. (d) | 5. (c) | 6. (b) |
| 7. (a) | 8. (c) | 9. (c) | 10. (a) | 11. (c) | 12. (c) |
| 13. (d) | 14. (a) | | | | |

# CHAPTER 12

# Events and Signals

Look at the world around you. You find things that are happening. The things that happen are called events. An event represents the specification of a significant occurrence that has location in time and space. When you are modeling state machines, you use events to model state transitions triggered by the occurrence of events. There are four types of events specified as follows:

❖ Signal events.
❖ Call events.
❖ Time events (passing of time).
❖ Change events (change in state).

Events can be synchronous or asynchronous. Modeling events comes when you model Processes and Threads. An event can trigger state changes. Any processing that happens in a system is triggered by events. An event might be:-

❖ A user clicking an icon or a graphical object.
❖ A signal from a sensor triggered by some physical event.
❖ A signal from another system.
❖ A signal from a timer:
❖ A time out.
❖ An alarm going off.
❖ A change in condition.
❖ Power On or Off.

An event can appear synchronously or asynchronously. In case of asynchronous events, the sender does not wait until the receiver received the event or reacted on it. In case of synchronous events, the sender waits until the receiver reacted on the event.

**LEARNING OBJECTIVES**

*After studying the chapter the students familiarize themselves with the following concepts:*

• Events and kinds of Events
• Sending and Receiving Events
• Modeling Signals
• Modeling Exceptions

**Synchronous Events**:
- ❖ Call event: triggered by call.
- ❖ Exception event: triggered by called object at return.

**Asynchronous Events**

- ❖ Signal event: signal sent by other object.
- ❖ Change event: triggered by side effects on object attributes.
- ❖ Time event: spontaneously triggered by a guard expression over time.

## 12.1 Events

In the UML, you can model four different types of events. They are:

- ❖ **Change Events** occur when a condition is satisfied. Example:   when (balance < 0).
- ❖ **Signal Events** occur when there is receipt of an explicit (real time) signal from one object to another.
- ❖ **Call Events** occur when there is receipt of a call for an operation by an object.
- ❖ **Time Events** occur there is passage of a designated time period. Example: after (10 minutes).

**Example:**

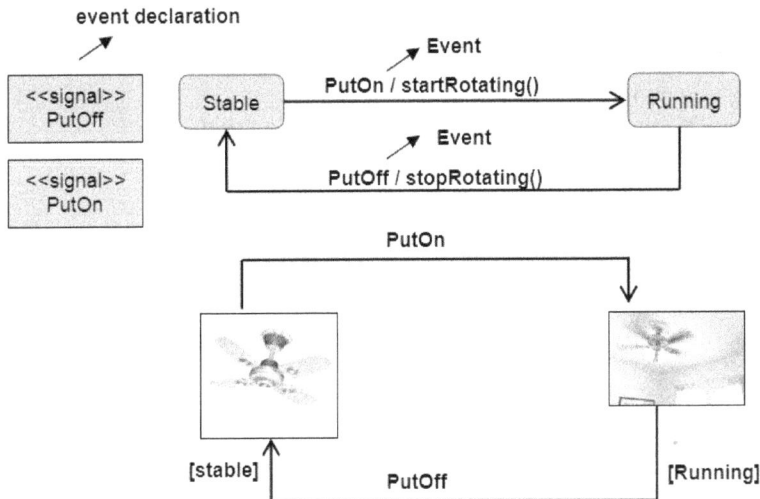

**Fig.12.1** Events for Ceiling Fan Operation

**Note**: PutOn and PutOff are the two events that can happen on a ceiling Fan. Initially the Fan is in the Stable state, when PutOn event happens the ceiling Fan changes its state from Stable to Rotating. While the Fan is in Rotating state, if PutOff event happens, then the Fan goes to Stable state. In the UML, the signals PutOn and PutOff are modeled as stereotyped classes as shown in the diagram.

## 12.2 Kinds of Events

Events can be external or internal. External events are the events that happen between the system and its interacting actors.

Examples:
- ❖ Pushing a button.
- ❖ Interrupt from a temperature sensor.
- ❖ Fire alarm from a smoke detector.

Internal events are the events that happen among a society of objects that live inside the system.

Examples:
- ❖ An Overflow exception.
- ❖ An Underflow exception.
- ❖ Divide by Zero exception.

## 12.3 Signals

A signal is a named element send by one object and asynchronously received by another object. Exceptions are the best examples for internal signals, which are supported by almost all implementation languages supporting object oriented concepts. Signals are graphically rendered as stereotyped classes. Similar to classes, the signals have some following commonalities:

- ❖ Signals can have instances.
- ❖ Signals may involve in generalization relationship.
- ❖ Signals may have attributes and operations.

**Note:** The attributes of a signal serve as its parameters.

A signal may be sent as the action of a state transition or the sending of a message in an interaction. When an operation belonging to a class or an interface is executed, signals may be sent. In the UML, you model signals that can be sent by an operation by using dependency relationship stereotyped as <<send>>.

**Examples:**

1.

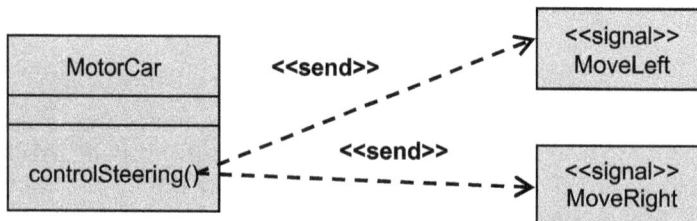

**Fig.12.2** Signals send by an Operation

**Note**: In the above diagram the class MotorCar has an operation named controlSteering() by means of which the direction of the wheels can be changed. A wheel can be moved right or left depending on the steering movement. If MoveRight and MoveLeft are the signals that represent the direction of wheels' movement, then execution of the operation controlSteering() sends these two signals.

**2.**

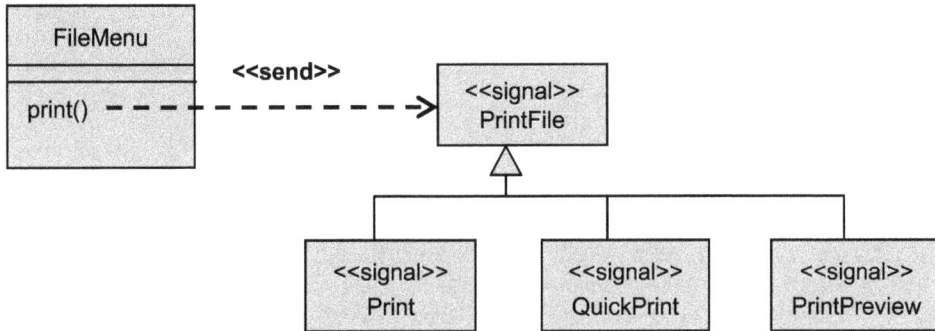

**Fig.12.3** Signal send by Print Operation

**Note:** In the Fig.12.3 we have File Menu containing operations such as New (creating new file), Open (opening an existing file), Save (saving a file), SaveAs (saving a file with a different name), Print (for printing a file) etc. The print operation sends a general signal named PrintFile. This signal can be of three specialized signals named Print, QuickPrint or PrintPreview.

## 12.4 Call Events

A call event represents the execution of an operation that could trigger state transition in a state machine. A call event is a synchronous event, where the sender waits for the response from the receiver.

**Examples**:

1. Any system if it is shutdown it will be in Idle state. When it is started up it will be in an Active state to do some task. Shutdown and Startup operations are Call events.The following diagram describes the call events and state transitions of the system.

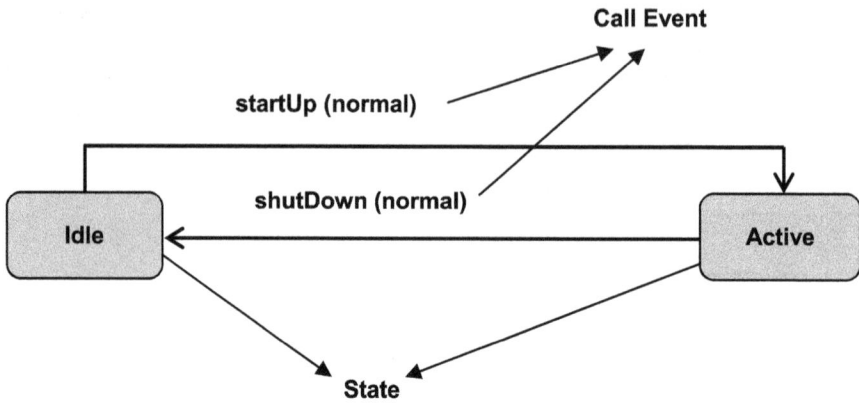

2. We consider here, Water which is currently in the Liquid State, when heated up to temperature equal to 100 degrees centigrade Water becomes Vapor a Gaseous Sate. This process can be pictorially represented as a Call Event.

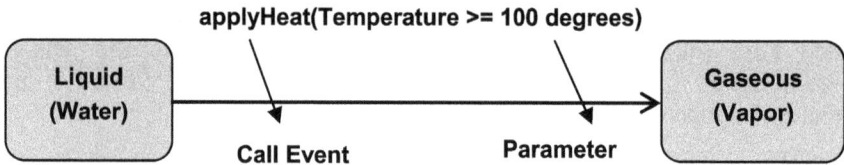

3. When you are watching a TV, you may change channel by using remote or directly. When channel is changed, depending on the channel number the relevant TV Program is shown on TV. This can be described as a Call Event as follows:

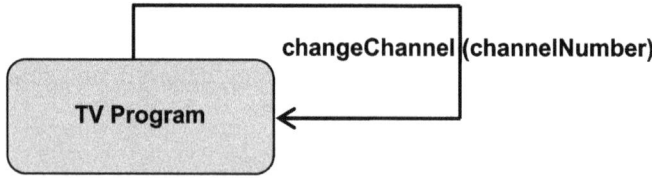

**Fig.12.4** Call Events

## 12.5  Time Events

A time event is an event that represents the passing of time. You model time events by using the key word **after** followed by an expression that evaluates to a period of time. Such expressions can be simple or complex.

**Examples**:

1. Initially when the baby is born it will be in Infant state. After some time, say after five years, the baby changes its state to Child and may go to school. This can be pictorially represented as above:

2. If there is no interaction with the computer for some time, the screen may go blank to save the life time of the computer screen. If there is no response from the user for about 20 minutes, the screen goes blank, whenever any button is pressed, the screen is displayed again.

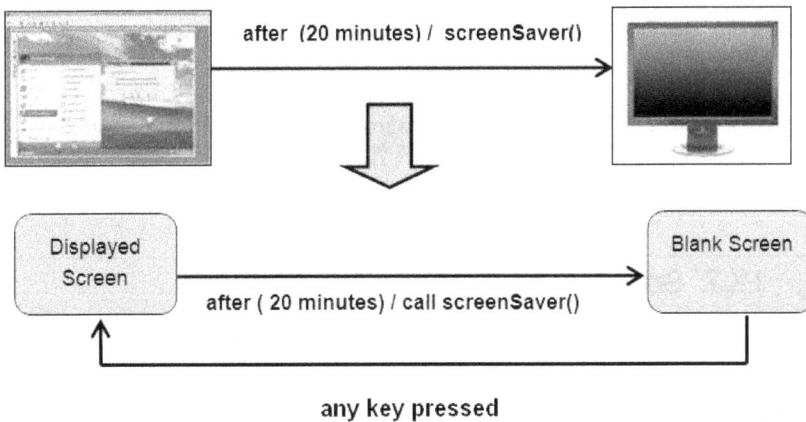

**Fig.12.5**  Time Events

## 12.6  Change Events

Change event is an event that represents a change in state or the satisfaction of some condition. In the UML, change events can be modeled by using the keyword **when** followed by some Boolean expression.

**Examples:**

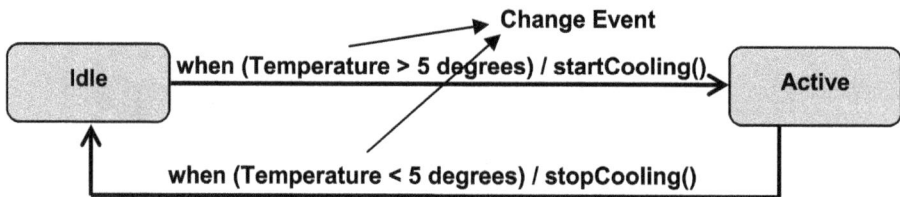

**Note**: In the above diagram, the time piece, when it is working, was set for an alarm at 05:45 early in the morning. The time at which the time piece has to give alarm is set by using change event if it is modeled using the UML.

    **2.** The functioning of a Home Refrigerator can be described by using change events. The temperature in the Refrigerator is maintained at five degrees centigrade. The following diagram describes change events. Assume the Refrigerator to have two different states Idle and Active.

**Fig.12.6** Change Events

## 12.7 Sending and Receiving Events

Signal events and Call events involve at least two objects, one is a sender and another is a receiver. During Signal event, the sender object sends a Signal and the Receiver object receives it. During Call event, the sender object executes an operation belonging to the receiver. A Signal event is asynchronous where as a Call event is synchronous.

**Note**: If one object sends a Signal to a set of objects, it is called Multicasting. If an object sends a Signal to any object in the system that is listening is called Broadcasting.

    In the UML, you model the named Signals that an object may receive by naming them in an extra compartment of the class (usually an active class) as shown below:

**Examples:**

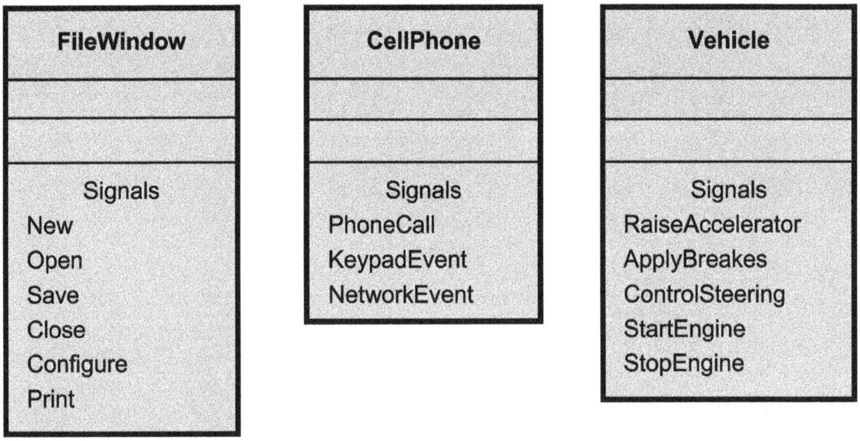

| FileWindow | CellPhone | Vehicle |
|---|---|---|
| | | |
| | | |
| Signals | Signals | Signals |
| New | PhoneCall | RaiseAccelerator |
| Open | KeypadEvent | ApplyBreakes |
| Save | NetworkEvent | ControlSteering |
| Close | | StartEngine |
| Configure | | StopEngine |
| Print | | |

**Fig.12.7** Active Classes with Receiving Signals

**Explanation:**

In the Fig.12.7, active classes with their receiving Signals are specified. FileWindow class can receive signals such as New (for creating a new file), Open (for opening an existing file), Save (for saving the current file), Close (for closing the current file), and Print (for printing the currently opened file).

Similarly, a class named CellPhone can receive Signals such as PhoneCall (for receiving random phone call), KeypadEvent (for using the Cell Phone), and NetworkEvent (when call moves from one call to another call over network).

Lastly, the Vehicle class can receive various Signals for its operation when a person drives it. The Signals can be StartEngine (for starting the engine of the Vehicle), StopEngine (for stopping engine of the Vehicle when parked), RaiseAccelerator (to increase the speed of the Vehicle), ApplyBreaks (for slowing down the Vehicle), and ControlSteering (for changing the direction of the moving Vehicle).

# 12.8 Modeling a Family of Signals

As you model any event driven systems, you find signal events tend to form a hierarchy. In signal events' hierarchy, you may find generalized signal events at the higher position and specialized signal events at the lower position in the hierarchy.

**Steps in Modeling a family of Signals:**

❖ Find out all signal events to which a given set of active objects respond.

❖ Find common signals and classify them as generalized and specialized ones. Elevate generalized ones, and lower specialized ones.

❖ If the state machines of these active objects contain polymorphism, introduce intermediate abstract signals in the hierarchy.

**Examples:** All signals that happen while you are driving a motor car can be modeled as a family of signals depicted below:

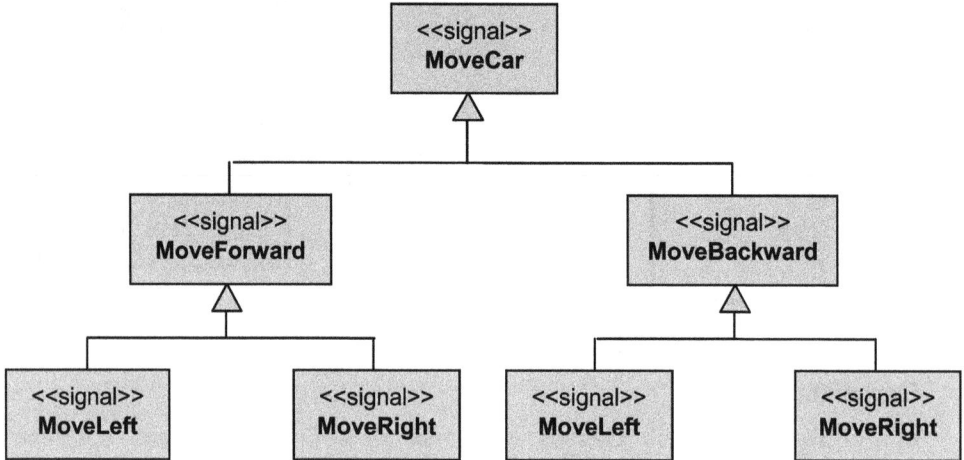

**Fig.12.8** Modeling a Family of Signals

**2.** You can model a family of signals an active object may receive as follows:

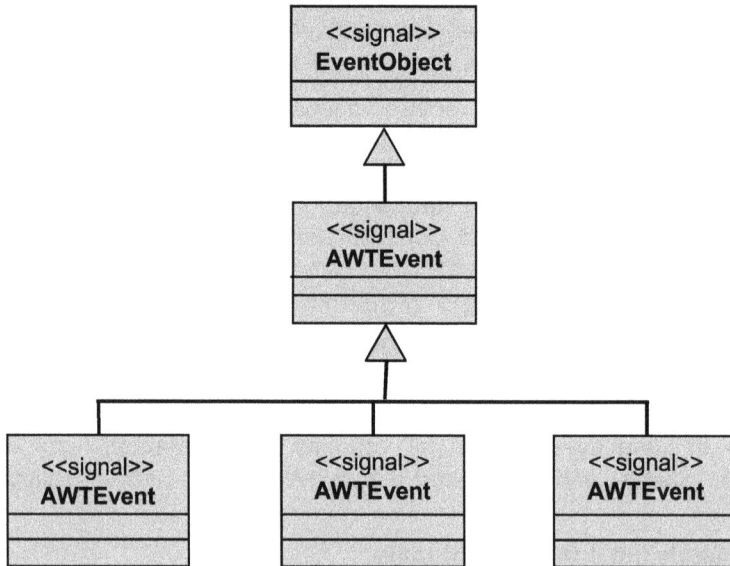

**Fig.12.9** Modeling a Family of Signals

## 12.9 Modeling Exceptions

When you model classes and interfaces in the UML, the operations they contain are quite evident. When you are modeling the behavior of a system, you may have to model the exceptions that these operations raise. In the UML, exceptions are modeled as stereotyped classes. When you model signals, you specify the signals an active object receives, whereas, when you model exceptions, you specify exceptions that an object may raise through its operations.

**The following steps are followed while modeling exceptions:**

❖ Find out exceptions that can be raised by each operation belonging to classes and interfaces that constitute your system.

❖ Arrange these exceptions as a hierarchy. Place above, the generalized ones and place below, the specialized ones. Attach new intermediate exceptions whenever they are needed.

❖ For each operation you identify, model the exceptions it can raise by using send dependencies from the operation to its exceptions.

**Examples:**

**Explanation**: The diagram 12.10 and 12.11 contains a hierarchy of exceptions that happen in an ATM transaction. If the PIN entered by the user is invalid, an InvalidPIN exception is raised. If the account chosen is invalid, an InvalidAccount exception is raised. While you are transferring funds or performing withdrawals, if the balance is not sufficient, an InsufficientBalance exception is raised. All these exceptions are InvalidTransaction exception types. It means that InvalidTransaction is a generalized exception while other exceptions, such as InvalidPIN, InvalidAccount, and InsufficientBalance are specialized ones.

1.

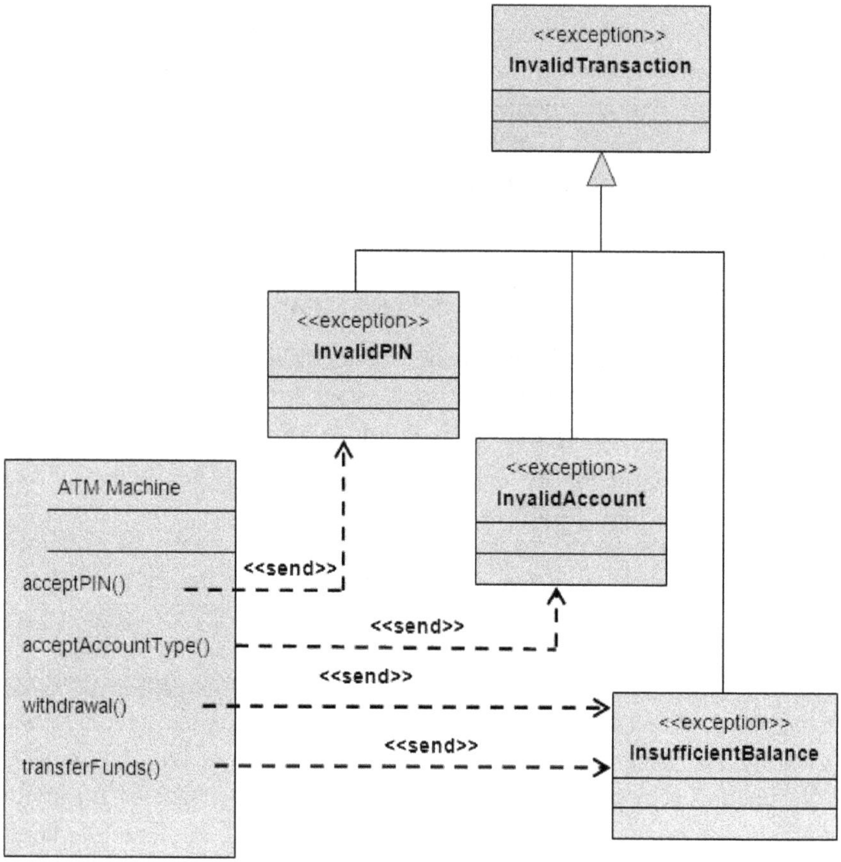

**Fig.12.10** Modeling a Family of Exceptions

2.

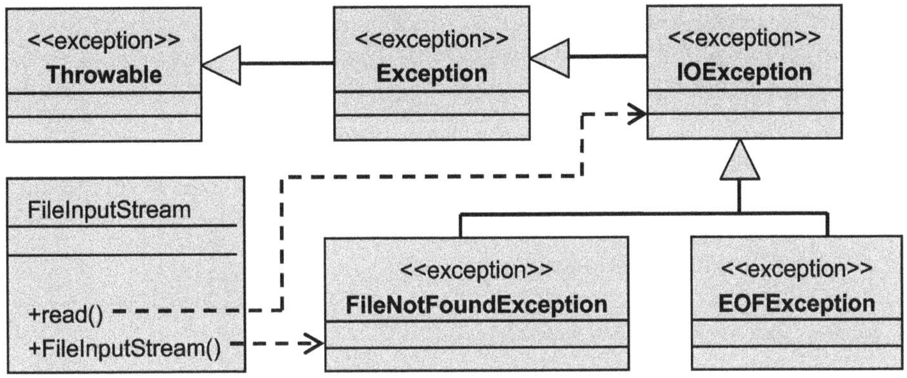

**Fig.12.11** Modeling a Family of Exceptions

## Essay Type Questions

1. Explain all the four types of events with suitable examples.
2. Explain the below briefly
   (a) Modeling a family of signals    (b) Modeling exceptions

## Objective Type Questions

1. The events are
   (a)  signal event                      (b)  call event
   (c)  time event                        (d)  All the above

2. The synchronous event is
   (a)  signal event                      (b)  call event
   (c)  time event                        (d)  change event

3. The asynchronous event is
   (a)  signal event                      (b)  change event
   (c)  both a & b                        (d)  call event

4. ------------ event occurs when a condition is satisfied
   (a)  change event                      (b)  call event
   (c)  signal event                      (d)  All the above

5. -------------- event occurs there is passage of a designated time period
   (a)  call event                        (b)  time event
   (c)  signal event                      (d)  None

6. External events are

    (a)   pushing a button
    (b)   fire alarm from smoke detector
    (c)   both a & b
    (d)   none

7. --------------- is the internal event

    (a)   Pushing a button
    (b)   Interrupt from a temperature sensor
    (c)   Fire alarm from a smoke detector
    (d)   Divide by Zero exception

8. Signals are graphically rendered as--------------

    (a)  stereotyped class          (b)  stereotyped interface
    (c)  stereotyped object        (d)  none

9. System Shutdown and Startup operations are

    (a)  signal event              (b)  time event
    (c)  call event               (d)  exception event

10. **when (05:45 AM) /giveAlarm()** is a

    (a)  signal event              (b)  change event
    (c)  call event               (d)  none

11. Exceptions are modeled as

    (a)  stereotyped class          (b)  interfaces
    (c)  objects                 (d)  time constraint

## Answers

| 1. (d) | 2. (b) | 3. (c) | 4. (a) | 5. (b) | 6. (c) |
|--------|--------|--------|--------|--------|--------|
| 7. (d) | 8. (a) | 9. (c) | 10. (b) | 11. (a) | |

# State Machine

In the UML, you model the behavior of group of objects that work together in the form of interactions. A state machine models the behavior of an object. A state machine contains a sequence of states an object goes through in its life time in response to events. A state machine depicts the various states an object goes through, and transitions among those states. State machine describes the change of object over time. State machines are very useful to model concurrent and real-time systems.

The state of an object is defined as a situation or condition during which it satisfies some condition, performs some activity, or waits for some event. You can represent a state machine in two ways:

- ❖ By using an activity diagram that describes the flow of control from activity to activity.
- ❖ By using a state chart diagram that describes the states of an object and transitions among these states.

A state machine is used to model the dynamic aspects of a system. A state machine models the life time of a single instance. This instance can be an instance of a class, a use case, or an entire system.

**Example**: The following Fig.(13.1) gives the state machine for Soda Vending Machine.

An object during its life time may get exposed to various events, such as follows:

- ❖ A Signal.
- ❖ The execution of an operation.
- ❖ The creation or destruction of an instance.

❖ The passage of time.
❖ The change in state or some condition.

When an object is exposed to above events, it may respond by performing an action. This action may result in change in state, or the return of a value. The UML provides various graphical symbols for states, transitions, events, and actions.

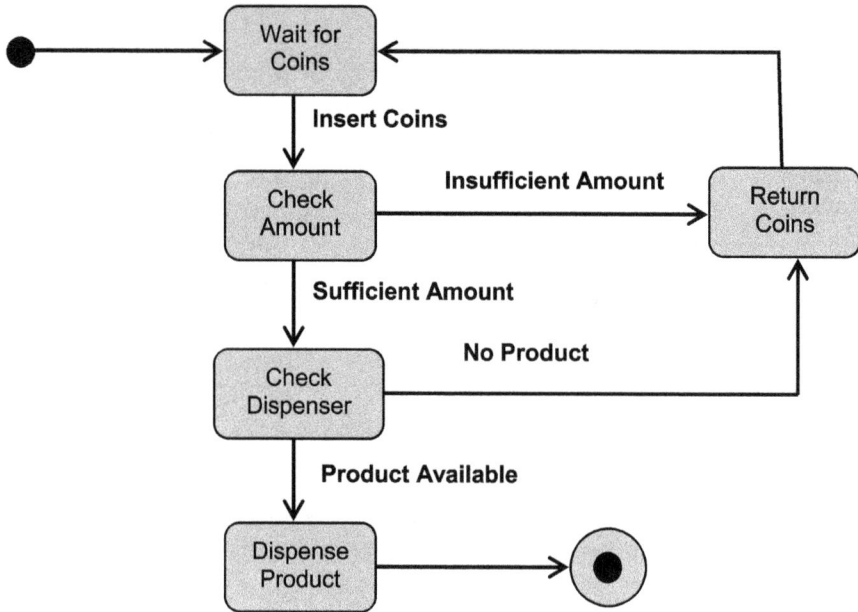

**Fig.13.1** State Machine for Soda Vending Machine

You use state machines to model the behavior of elements such as, a class, a use case, or an entire system. You can visualize state machines by using activity diagrams or by using state chart diagrams. In the formal case, the focus is on the activities that take place within the object. In the later case, the focus is on the event ordered behavior of an object.

A state machine typically contains states, transitions, events, and actions. The UML provides graphical representations for all of them. They are defined as follows:

A **state** is a condition or a situation in the life time of an object during which it satisfies some condition, performs some activity or waits for some event.

A **transition** is the connection between two states of an object, indicating that the object in the first state will enter the second state when an event occurs.

**Note**: A transition can be trigger less, where transition takes place without the occurrence of any event.

An **event** is the specification of something that happens, which has a location in time and space.

An **activity** is a non atomic execution.

An **action** is an atomic execution that causes change in state or return of some value.

In the UML, graphically, a state is rendered as a rectangle with rounded corners and a transition is rendered as a solid directed line.

While you are modeling a system's behavior, you may encounter objects whose current behavior depends on their past behavior. For example, consider a ceiling Fan, you can perform speed control on the Fan by using regulator while the Fan is in Running state, but not in Stationary state.

The behavior of objects that must respond to events or whose current behavior depends on their past can be best modeled by using state machine. You also use state machines to model the behavior of the entire system.

**Example**:

The following diagram shows a state machine for selecting and scheduling courses in a University. This state machine starts with unscheduled state and ends with a scheduled state. This diagram contains various states and their transitions to schedule a course.

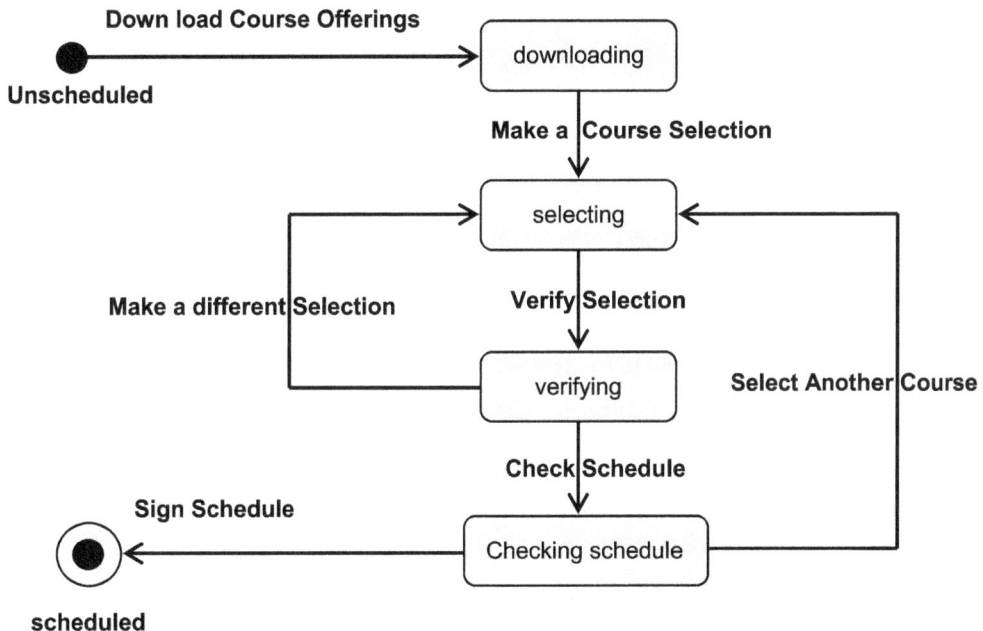

**Fig.13.2**  A State Machine for University Course Selection

A state inside any state machine has the following parts:

1. **Name:** It is a textual string that distinguishes a state from other states.

2. **Entry/exit actions**: Actions performed on entering and exiting the state.

3. **Internal Transitions**: Transitions that do not cause change in state.

4. **Substates**: States inside states.

5. **Deferred Events**: The events that are not handled in the current state of the object but handled later in another state.

## 13.1 Initial and Final States

There are two special states that may be defined for an object's state machine. There is the initial state which indicates the default starting place for the state machine. Initial state is represented as a filled black circle. There is the final state which indicates that the execution of the state machine has been completed. A final state is represented as a filled black circle surrounded by an unfilled circle. These states are actually pseudo states.

## 13.2 Transitions

A transition is the link between two states which indicates an object in the first state enters into the second state when an event occurs or some condition is satisfied. When a transition fires, an object in its source state enters into the specified target state. A transition has the following five parts:

1. **Source State:** It is the state that the object is currently in. A transition to another state may occur due to an event or when a guard condition is met.

2. **Event trigger:** It is the event, which is received by an object that results in state transition.

3. **Guard condition:** It is a Boolean expression that is evaluated when the transition is triggered by the reception of the event trigger. The transition fires when the guard condition evaluates to true otherwise not.

4. **Action:** It is an executable atomic computation which may act on the object that owns the state machine.

5. **Target State:** It is the state reached by an object after the state transition.

**Note:** A transition may have multiple sources, which represents **join**. A transition may have multiple targets, which represents **fork**.

The following diagram describes a state machine that models the login part of the Online Banking System.

**Fig.13.3**  A State Machine

## 13.3 Advanced States and Transitions

An advanced state contains the following definitions.

❖ Entry and exit actions occur on state entry or exit. These are useful when there are multiple transitions in to or out of a state.
❖ Internal transitions do not fire entry and exit transitions. If there are no entry and exit transitions, then internal transitions become self transitions.
❖ Activities execute while an object is in a state. They are non-atomic and non-instantaneous.
❖ Deferred events are remembered and processed later.

**Example**:

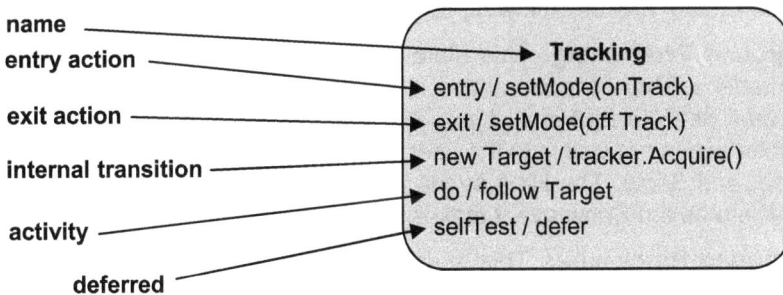

**Fig.13.4**  An Advanced State

## 13.4 Sub States

A sub state is a state that is nested inside another state. Sub states help us to model the complex behavior of a system. A state that has sub states(nested states) is called a composite state. A composite state may contain either concurrent or sequential sub states. You can have nesting of states to any level.

## 13.5 Advanced State Diagrams

The UML allows you to include one or more state diagrams inside a single state. These state diagrams indicate sequential or concurrent state diagrams. Let us consider a system which has two states namely, Idle and Active states. When the system is in the Active state, each object and sub system has its own state, and the state diagram for each element may be shown inside the Active state of the system. The Active state of the system under consideration is described pictorially as follows:-

The state has three compartments. The top compartment indicates the name of the state. The middle compartment of the state contain transitions for the following events:

- ❖ **Entry:** The action performed when an element enters the state.
- ❖ **Exit:** The action performed when an element leaves the state.
- ❖ **do:** An action to be performed while an element is in that state.

When the example system indicated below enters the Active state, a message is logged using the LogMessage action. When this system exits the Active state, the user's time and date is retrieved using the GetDateAndTime action. Finally, the system continuously monitors its usage using the MonitorUsage action.

The bottom compartment of this state may contain one or more nested state diagrams separated by dashed lines with a title describing the element to which the state diagram belongs. When a state becomes the current state of an element, all its nested state diagrams become active. The Active state of this example system has the following concurrent state diagrams:-

**Foreground Processing:** This state diagram describes the life cycle of the user interface. There are two states, such as Shown and Hidden. In the Shown state, the User Interface is visible to the user, where as in the Hidden state the User Interface is not visible to the user. This state diagram has two events, such as Hide, and Show. The Hide event makes the User Interface invisible to the user, where as the Show event makes the User Interface visible to the user.

**Background Processing:** This state diagram describes the life cycle of how the system works when the user interacts with the system. There are two states, named Idle, and Busy states. During the **Idle** state, our system is not handling any user request. During the **Busy** state, our system is handling user requests. There are two events in this state diagram. The DoProcessing event makes the system Busy handling user requests. Whereas the ProcessingComplete event makes the system Idle waiting for user requests. The entire processing can be modeled as follows by using UML:

**Example:**

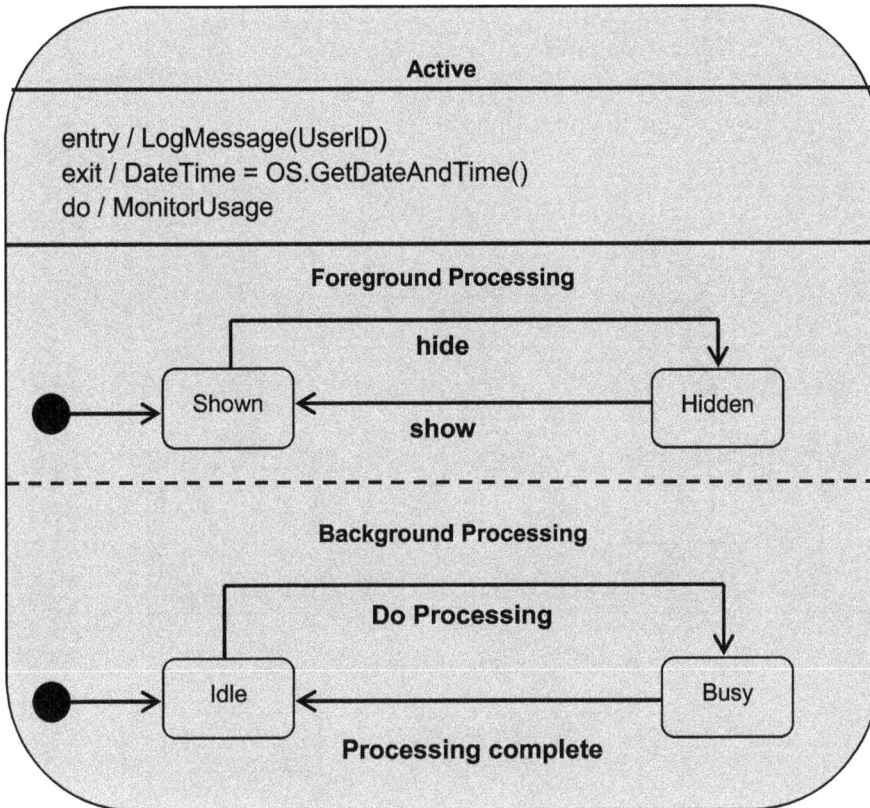

**Fig.13.5** An Advanced State Machine with Concurrent Sub States

**Note:** In the diagram 13.5, Foreground and Background Processing happen simultaneously.

**Example:** In this example, Fig.(13.6) we consider state diagrams relating a telephone operation. A telephone can be in two different states, one is in Idle state where nothing happens, another is in Active state where the telephone is used for the purpose of talking.

## 13.6 Nested States

When state transition diagrams become large and complex, we use nested states to simplify diagrams. We define super states which enclose sub states.

Such states are called nested or composite states. A composite state can be broken down into sub states. State machines for sub states can be drawn either within the state or as a separate diagram.

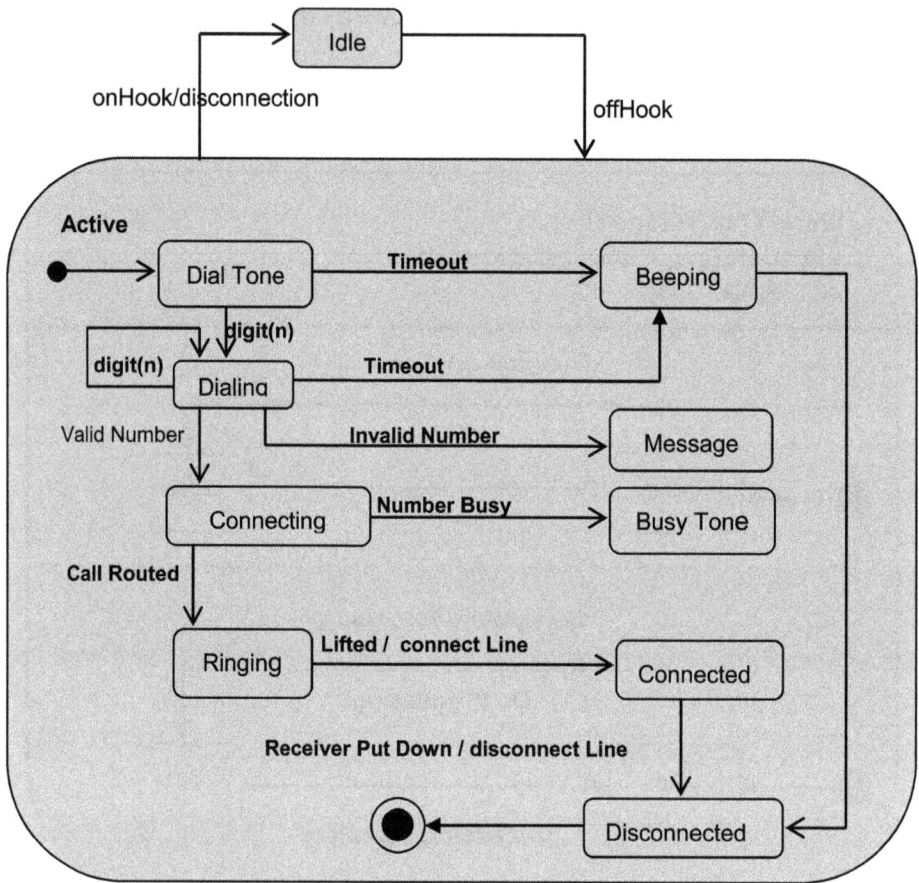

**Fig.13.6** An Advanced State Machine with Sequential Sub States

## 13.7 History States

When a state transition enters into a composite state, the associated nested state machine starts all over again at its initial state. But in some cases, you may have to model state machines in such a way that it remembers the last sub state that was active before leaving the composite state. You can model this in a state machine by using history states. History states make an object to remember in which sub state it was before leaving the composite state. There are two ways of specifying history as follows:

❖ **Shallow history:** remembers only the outermost nested    state, and is indicated by the symbol H.

❖ **Deep history:** remembers an innermost nested state to any depth, and is indicated by the symbol H*.

**Example:** We demonstrate history states in the case of a washing machine as follows. A washing machine may be in two major states, such as Paused and Runnable states. A washing machine when in Paused state, does nothing, but when in Runnable state, it does washing. When it is in the Runnable state, it cycles around the sub states such as Stopped, Filling, Washing, and Spinning. A washing machine can only start running if the door is closed and it will pause immediately when the door is opened. A washing machine runs to a program. The machine restarts the program from the state when it left, whenever it re-enters the Runnable state. The machine should remember where it was up to and continue at the point in the cycle when the door was opened. It is like the machine keeps an internal memory or history of where it was up to. This can be modeled using a special symbol called the history state, such that when the state is re-entered the history state remembers the sub state that was active before the enclosing state was exited.

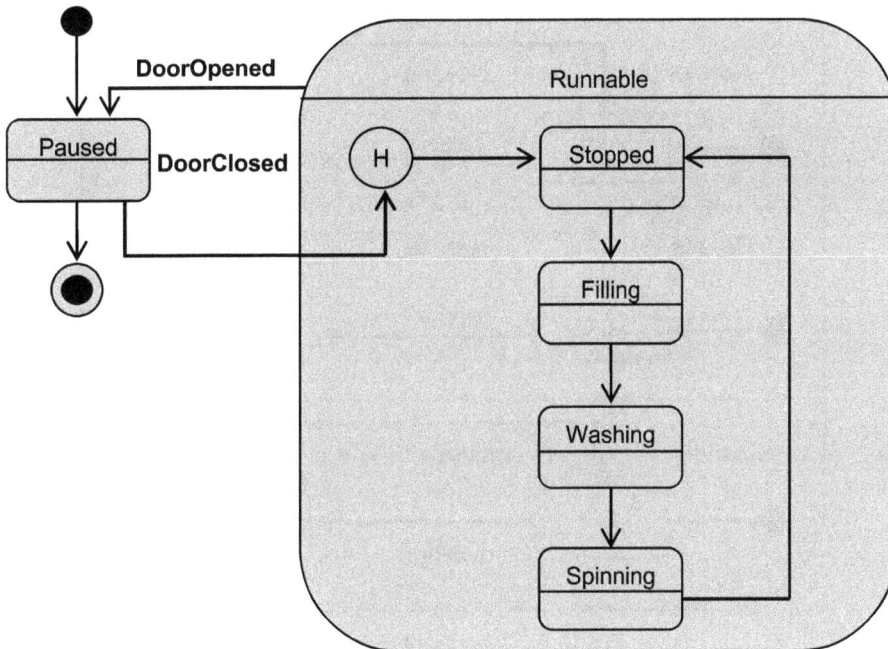

**Fig.13.7** Using History State

## 13.8 Concurrent Sub States

In the above example we have seen sequential sub states specifying sub states of the washing machine's state named Runnable. In the following, we see state machines of sub states that execute simultaneously. Consider an example of driving motor vehicle. This vehicle when it is in Driving state, it may have sub states such as Accelerator, Breaks, and Steering whose state machines are executed concurrently. This can be described as follows:

**Example:**

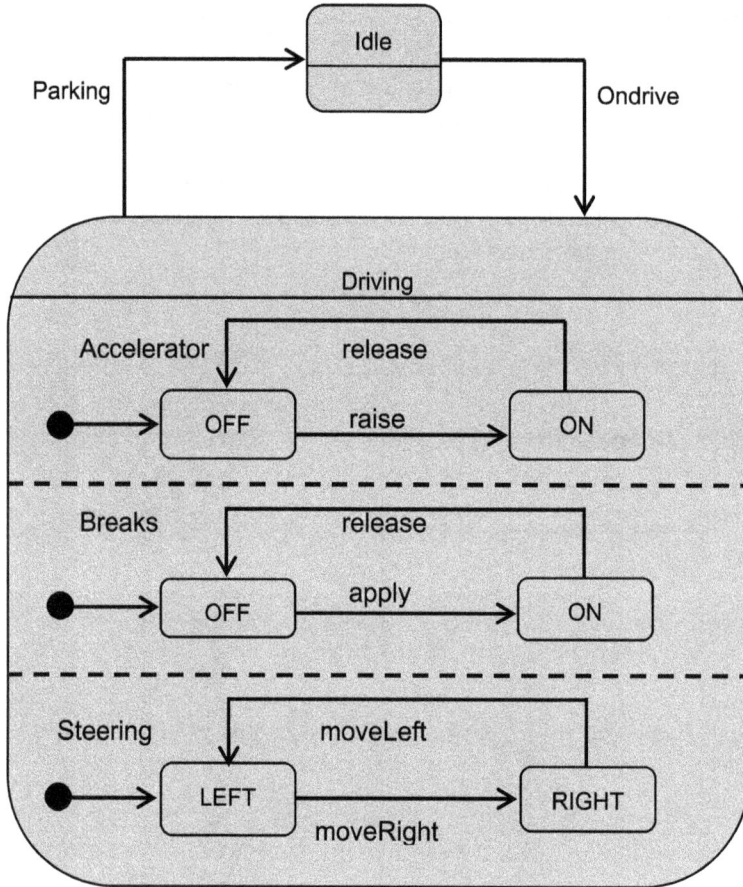

**Fig.13.8**  Concurrent Sub States

## 13.9 Modeling the Life Time of an Object

We generally apply state machines to model the life time of an object, such as, instances of classes, use cases, and the whole system. A state machine models the behavior of a single object over its life time. When you apply state machine, you specify three things:

* ❖ The events to which the object can respond
* ❖ The response to those events and
* ❖ The impact of the past on current behavior

**The steps followed while you model the life time of an object:**

* ❖ Find out for which your state machine is applicable, such as for classes, use cases, or the entire system.
    * ❖ If the purpose is to model the behavior of a class or use case, then identify the neighboring classes which are included in generalization, association, or dependency relationship. These neighbors can become targets for actions and can be included in guard conditions.
    * ❖ If the purpose is to model the system as a whole, concentrate only on the behavior of the system. This behavior could be the result of a society of objects working together.
* ❖ Identify objects that may have complex behavior.
* ❖ Determine the initial and final states of the object and also specify their pre and post conditions.
* ❖ Identify the events that affect the object.
* ❖ Working from the initial state, trace the impact of events and identify intermediate states. List out events which can trigger transitions. Connect these states with transitions and also add actions to these transitions.
* ❖ Identify entry and exit actions for each state.
* ❖ If the state is a complex one, model it as a composite state with its associated sub states.
* ❖ Establish whether all the events specified in an object are matching with the events specified by its interfaces.
* ❖ Check whether all actions specified in the state machine are in accordance with the relationships, methods, and operations of the enclosing object.
* ❖ Once you model a state machine, trace through it to check the expected events and their responses. During this process, identify non reachable states and the states at which the machine may get struck.
* ❖ After you change your state machine, recheck it by tracing through it, so as to ensure that you have not changed the object's semantics.

**Note**: When you model embedded system's state machines, they may not contain final states, as they are intended to run continuously.

## ⟩ Essay Type Questions

1. Explain various parts of a transition with an example.
2. Describe advanced state diagrams with examples.
3. Briefly explain the below:
   (a) History states   (b) Concurrent sub states
4. Explain the various steps involved in modeling the life time of an object.

> **Objective Type Questions**

1. State machines are very useful to model --------------- systems.

   (a) concurrent system (b) real-time system
   (c) both a and b (d) static systems

2. State machine can be represented as

   (a) Activity diagram (b) state chart diagram
   (c) class diagram (d) both a & b

3. The parts of a state in state machine

   (a) name (b) entry/exit condition
   (c) internal transition (d) All the above

4. Transitions that do not cause change in state are

   (a) internal transitions (b) name
   (c) deferred event (d) none

5. The events that are not handled in the current state of the object but handled later in another state are

   (a) deferred event (b) call event
   (c) time event (d) signal event

6. It is the state that the object is currently in

   (a) target state (b) event trigger
   (c) source state (d) guard condition

7. It is a Boolean expression that is evaluated when the transition is triggered by the reception of the event trigger.

   (a) target state (b) event trigger
   (c) source state (d) guard condition

8. -------------------- is the state reached by an object after the state transition

   (a) target state (b) source state
   (c) guard condition (d) event trigger

9. selfTest/defer in an advanced state specifies

   (a) entry action (b) exit action
   (c) deferred event (d) transition

10. do/follow target in an advanced state specifies

    (a) activity (b) Internal transition
    (c) entry action (d) exit action

11. The state that is nested inside another state

    (a) advanced state (b) sub state
    (c) composite state (d) All the above

12. --------------- remembers only the outermost nested    state, and is indicated by the symbol H.

    (a) deep history                      (b) shallow history
    (c) advanced state                    (d) nested state

13. --------------- remembers an innermost nested state to any depth, and is indicated by the symbol H*

    (a) deep history                      (b) shallow history
    (c) advanced state                    (d) nested state

14. While you apply state machine you specify

    (a) The events to which the object can respond
    (b) The response to those events
    (c) The impact of the past on current behaviour
    (d) All the above

## Answers

| | | | | | |
|---|---|---|---|---|---|
| 1. (c) | 2. (d) | 3. (d) | 4. (a) | 5. (a) | 6. (c) |
| 7. (d) | 8. (a) | 9. (c) | 10. (a) | 11. (b) | 12. (b) |
| 13. (a) | 14. (d) | | | | |

# Processes and Threads

Look at the world around you, you find it very busy containing several events that are happening. Among the things that are happening around, you may find some of the things happening at the same time. When you are modeling a real life system, you have to consider its process view that includes threads and processes.

A process is a program in execution. It can be defined as a group of instructions that are executed by a processor. A process is a heavy weight flow that can execute concurrently with other processes. A thread can be defined as a block of code that can execute concurrently with other threads in the same process. A thread is a light weight flow that represents a single sequential flow of instructions. Generally, all the threads in a process run simultaneously, and can access the same objects to implement their functionality. Threads communicate among themselves through shared objects.

Unlike in sequential systems, communication and synchronization are more complex in concurrent systems. You need to be extra cautious while you are modeling control flows of a concurrent system. If you specify too many concurrent flows, it may lead to system thrashing. If you specify insufficient concurrent flows, it does not optimize the system's throughput.

In the UML, each independent flow of control is modeled as an active object. An active object (an instance of an active class) specifies the concurrent behavior of real world objects. Active objects own threads or

**LEARNING OBJECTIVES**

*After studying the chapter the students familiarize themselves with the following concepts:*

- Active Classes
- Extensibility Mechanisms
- Communication and Synchronization
- Process View
- Modeling Multiple Flows of Control
- Inter process Communication

processes and can initiate control activities. Active classes can be implemented by heavyweight processes with their own address space or by lightweight threads sharing the same address space. When active objects collaborate, they may communicate among themselves by passing messages, which you call it as inter process communication. Several object oriented implementation languages, such as Java, C++, and Smalltalk directly support the concept of an active object.

An active class is graphically rendered as similar to any ordinary class, but with thick border. We are aware that active objects communicate with each other by using signals. These signals, an active object receives, can be specified in a separate compartment for an active class. Processes and threads are graphically rendered as stereotyped active classes.

**Example:** The following diagram shows the detailed UML model of a process and a thread and their relationship using the class diagram. We use UML stereotypes for defining a process and a thread namely <<process>> and <<thread>>. The stereotypes defined active classes of process and thread namely the classes Process and Thread. The active class Process contains multiple instances of the active class Thread.

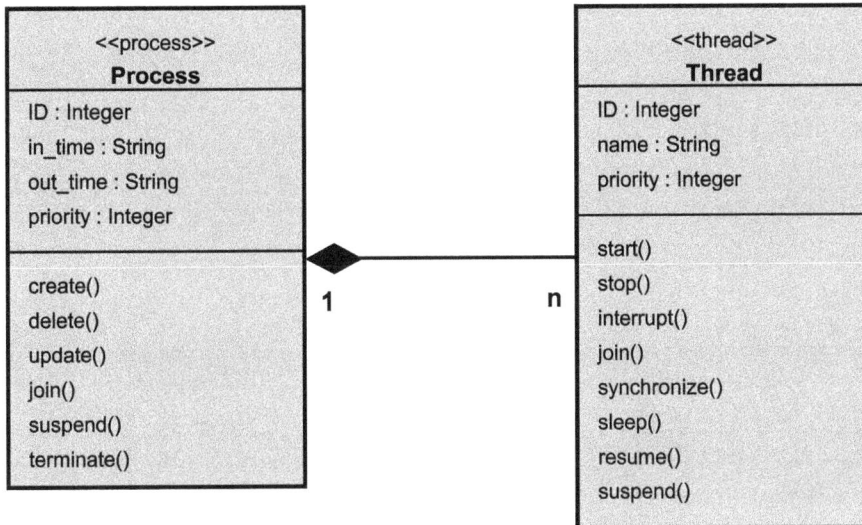

| <<process>> **Process** | <<thread>> **Thread** |
|---|---|
| ID : Integer<br>in_time : String<br>out_time : String<br>priority : Integer | ID : Integer<br>name : String<br>priority : Integer |
| create()<br>delete()<br>update()<br>join()<br>suspend()<br>terminate() | start()<br>stop()<br>interrupt()<br>join()<br>synchronize()<br>sleep()<br>resume()<br>suspend() |

Relationship: 1 ◆——— n

**Fig.14.1** UML definition of Process and Thread

**Another Example**: Consider an ATM Machine, where asynchronous events must be handled coming from three different sources, such as:

❖ The user of the system
❖ The ATM devices (for example: in the case of a jam in the cash dispenser)
❖ The ATM network (in the case of a shutdown directive from the network)

To handle these asynchronous events, we can define three separate threads of execution within the ATM itself, as shown below using active classes.

## 14.1 Flows of Control

In a sequential system, there is only one flow of control that can take place at a time. A sequential program starts flow of control at the beginning of the program and processes events one after another. The events are processed one event at a time discarding any concurrent external events. When a sequential program is executed, there will be execution flow from one statement to another in sequential order. During this flow, there may be actions that branch, loop and jump about. There would be a single flow of execution in a sequential system.

In a concurrent system, there are multiple simultaneous flows of control. You can achieve concurrency in these systems in the following three ways:

❖ By distributing active objects across multiple nodes
❖ By placing active objects on nodes having multiple processors
❖ By a combination of both of the above.

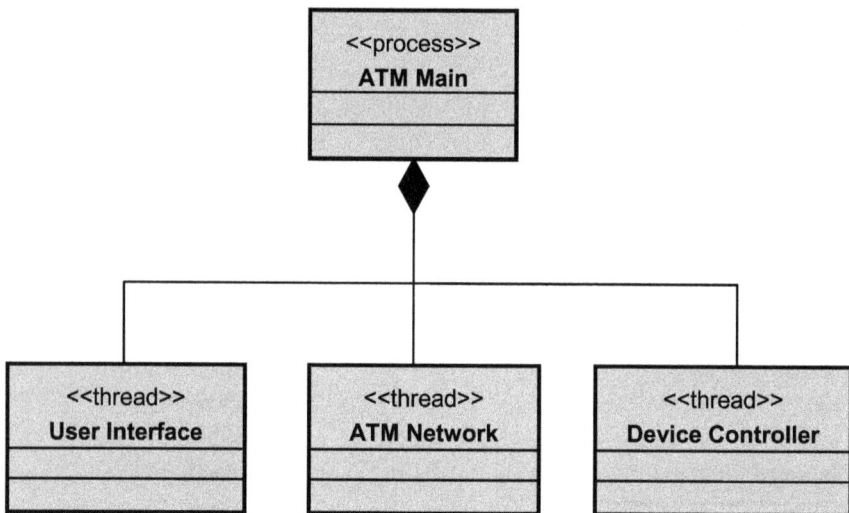

**Fig.14.2** Processes and Threads within ATM

## 14.2 Active Classes

An active class represents an independent flow of control which can initiate control activity. Where as a plain class cannot independently initiate control activity. Plain classes are considered passive because they rely on an external event to initiate control activity. Active classes are helpful in modeling families of processes or threads. An active object (an instance of an active class) initiates a process or thread. You can model concurrent systems by using active objects, each of which represents an independent flow of control. A flow of control is started when an active object is created and it is terminated when the active object is destroyed.

**Active classes have several similar properties as plain classes have, such as:**

- ❖ Active classes may have instances called active objects.
- ❖ Active classes may have attributes and operations.
- ❖ Active classes may participate in dependency, generalization, and association relationships.
- ❖ Active classes may use extensibility mechanisms, such as, stereotypes, tagged values, and constraints.
- ❖ Active classes may realize interfaces.
- ❖ Active classes may be realized by collaborations.
- ❖ Active classes' behaviors can be specified by using state machines.

**Note:** You can model the collaboration of active and passive objects (plain objects) with interaction diagrams (sequence or collaboration diagrams).

## 14.3 Extensibility Mechanisms

- ❖ You can use tagged values to extend active class properties, such as, specifying the scheduling policy.
  The standard stereotypes that apply to active classes are:
  - ❖ Process – Specifies a heavy weight flow.
  - ❖ Thread – Specifies a light weight flow.
  Processes and threads are handled differently by the operating system:-
- ❖ Each process runs in its own independent address space.
- ❖ Thread is hidden inside a process, and runs in the associated address space of the process.

**Note**: A process or thread can never be nested inside one another. All the threads that live inside a process are peers of one another.

When we say that a process is a heavyweight, we mean that is known to the operating system itself and runs independently in its own memory address space. When we refer to a thread as lightweight, it means that while a thread may be known to the operating system itself, more often it is hidden inside a process and runs inside the memory address space of the enclosing process.

## 14.4 Communication

In any system, interactions between active and passive objects happen by passing messages. You can expect four possible types of interactions, they are:

- ❖ Passive object to passive object.
- ❖ Active object to active object.
- ❖ Active object to passive object.
- ❖ Passive object to active object.

### Passive to Passive

A message may be passed from one passive object to another. This interaction could be because of invocation of an operation.

### Active to Active

A message may be passed from one active object to another. This interaction results in inter process communication which can be synchronous or asynchronous. During synchronous communication, the caller waits for the receiver to accept the call and respond. During asynchronous communication, the caller never waits for the receiver. This is called mailbox semantics, because the two objects are not synchronized and one object drops off a message for another object.

**Note**: Graphically, synchronous message is rendered as a full arrow, and asynchronous message as a half arrow.

### Active to Passive

A message may be passed from an active object to a passive object. If more than one active object tries to communicate with a passive object at the same time, difficulty may arise. In this situation, you have to model the synchronization very carefully.

### Passive to Active

A message may be passed from a passive object to an active object. This has same semantics as an active object passing a message to another active object.

**Example:** While you are modeling communication among objects (active and passive), the messages are the means of communication. Messages are displayed as a line with an arrow that points in the direction in which it is sent. The following diagram shows the communication diagram that represents a banking scenario in which a bank customer applies for a loan. The following process is adopted for loan sanction:

❖ A customer fills up an application for the loan and gives it to a Bank Teller.

❖ The Bank Teller sends the application to the Bank Manager for the purpose of loan processing and waits for the Manager to finish.

❖ The bank manager starts the credit check program, enters the data, and waits for the Credit Agency to send the results.

❖ The Bank Manager receives a response from the Credit Agency and sends a message to the Bank Teller that states the decision.

❖ The Bank Teller sends a message to the customer that states whether the loan was approved.

❖ The Bank Manager closes the Credit Agency program and the customer completes the transaction.

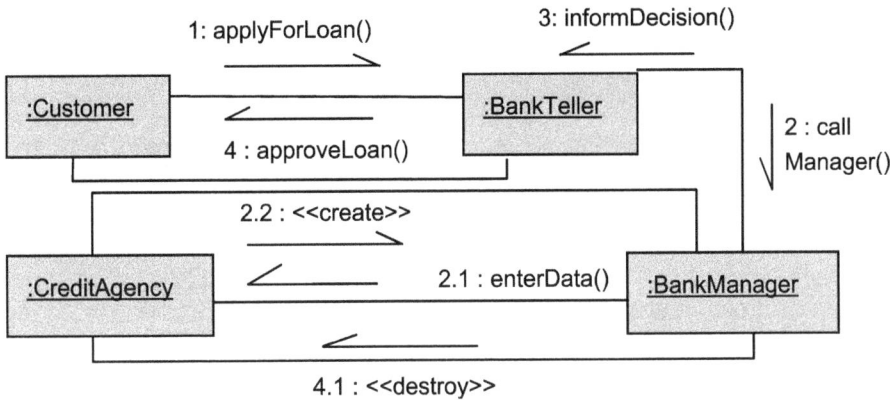

**Fig.14.3** Communication

## 14.5 Synchronization

A problem with synchronization arises when there is more than one flow of control in an object at the same time. This creates the risk of corrupting the state of the object. This type of problem is called mutual exclusion. The UML provides three ways to deal with this type of problem, where an object is treated as a critical region. They are as follows:

- ❖ Sequential
- ❖ Guarded
- ❖ Concurrent

**Sequential:** Callers should coordinate with each other in such a way so that there is only one flow in the object at a time. But in the presence of multiple flows of control, the semantics and integrity of the object cannot be guaranteed.

**Guarded:** In this case there are multiple flows of control. All calls to operations are sequentialized so that only one operation at a time can be invoked on the object. In this case the semantics and the integrity of the object is guaranteed.

**Concurrent:** Even in the presence of multiple flows of control, the state of the object is not corrupted. Because, operations are treated as atomic.

You can attach these properties to operations in the form of specifying constraints.

**Example**:

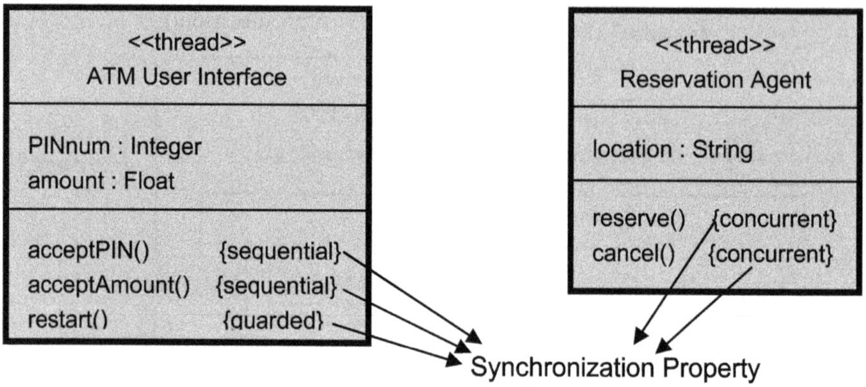

**Fig.14.4** Active Classes with Synchronization Properties

## 14.6 Process View

Active objects describe completely a system's process view. The process view of a system contains threads and processes that form the system. This view mainly addresses the performance, scalability, and throughput of the system. This view majorly focuses on the active classes that represent the threads and processes.

## 14.7 Modeling Multiple Flows of Control

It is difficult to build a system which contains multiple flows of control. You need to consider the following to build a system:

❖ You have to divide work properly across concurrent active objects.
❖ You have to devise the right mechanisms for communications and synchronizations among objects
(active as well as passive).
❖ You have to ensure that objects behave properly in the presence of multiple flows.

You can model how these flows interact with one another. You can capture their static semantics through class diagrams, and dynamic semantics through interaction diagrams involving active classes and active objects.

**Steps followed for modeling multiple flows of control:**

❖ Identify concurrent flows of control, and specify each flow as an active class.
❖ Group the common sets of active objects into an active class.

❖ Identify responsibilities and distribute them evenly among the active classes. Identify other active or passive classes with which each class collaborates. Ensure that each class has the right set of attributes, operations, and signals.

❖ Capture the static semantics of your system, from class diagrams mostly involving active classes.

❖ Capture the dynamic semantics of your system illustrating how classes collaborate with one another through interaction diagrams mainly involving active objects.

❖ Understand the communication among active objects. Establish appropriately the messaging between them, whether synchronous or asynchronous.

❖ Understand the synchronization among these objects (active or passive).

❖ Apply operation semantics appropriately, such as, sequential, guarded, or concurrent.

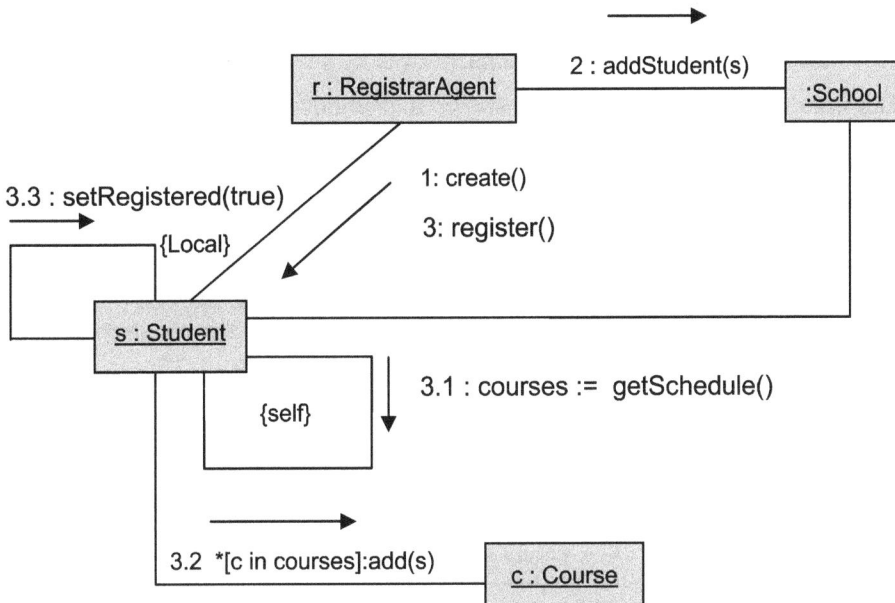

**Fig.14.5** Modeling Flows of Control

**Example**: The above diagram specifies the model of various flows of control involved in a School Registration System.

## 14.8 Inter Process Communication

When you model multiple flows of control in your system, you should understand how objects belonging to different flows communicate with one another. Objects may communicate via signals or call events across threads or processes either synchronously or asynchronously. You know that, threads live in the same address space whereas processes live in separate address spaces.

**Note**: In a distributed system, inter process communication may happen among processes that live on separate nodes.

There are two different approaches for inter process communication:
- ❖ By message passing, which can be modeled as asynchronous events.
- ❖ By remote procedure calls, which can be modeled as synchronous events.

**The various steps followed in modeling inter process communication:**
- ❖ First, model the multiple flows of control.
- ❖ Identify which active objects represent processes and which represent threads. Model them using the appropriate stereotype.
- ❖ Model messaging among objects as asynchronous communication. Model remote procedure calls as synchronous communication.
- ❖ Specify additional information for communication among objects either by using notes or by collaborations.

**Example**: The following diagram shows a distributed reservation system with processes spread across four nodes. Communication among the ReservationAgent, TicketingManager, and HotelAgent is asynchronous. Modeled with a note, communication is described as building on a Java Beans messaging service. Communication between the TripPlanner and the ReservationSystem is synchronous. The semantics of their interaction is found in the collaboration named CORBA ORB. The TripPlanner acts as a client, and the ReservationAgent acts as a server. By zooming into the collaboration, you will find the details of how this server and client collaborate.

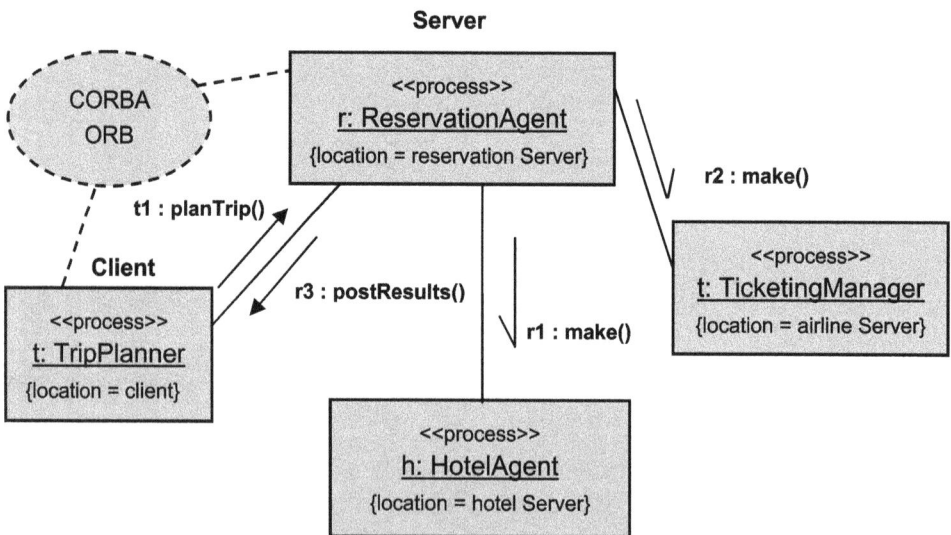

**Fig.14.6** Modeling Inter Process Communication

## Essay Type Questions

1. Mention four types of interactions that happen between passive and active objects by passing messages.

2. Write short notes on synchronization.

3. Explain the steps involved for modeling multiple flows of control using an example.

4. Write short notes on inter process communication with an example.

## Objective Type Questions

1. A program in execution is called
   (a) process                      (b) thread
   (c) both a & b                    ((d) none

2. --------------- is the light weight flow
   (a) process                      (b) thread
   (c) both a & b                    ((d) none

3. In the UML, each independent flow of control is modeled as
   (a) active object                (b) passive object
   (c) static class                 ((d) Interface

4. Processes and threads are graphically rendered as
   (a) stereotyped interface        (b) stereotyped static class
   (c) stereotyped active class     (d) All the above

5. The sources of asynchronous events that the ATM machine receives
   (a) The user of the system       (b) The ATM devices
   (c) The ATM network              (d) All the above

6. The ways of achieving concurrency in a system
   (a) By distributing active objects across multiple nodes
   (b) By placing active objects on nodes having multiple processors
   (c) both a & b
   (d) None

7. Active classes' behaviors can be specified by using ---------------
   (a) class diagram                (b) object diagram
   (c) state machine                (d) component diagram

8. The interaction between one active object to another active object is called
   (a) inter process communication  (b) activity diagram
   (c) action states                (d) none

9. Asynchronous message is graphically rendered as
   - (a) full arrow
   - (b) half arrow
   - (c) cube
   - (d) tabbed folder

10. The ways of dealing with mutual exclusion problem
    - (a) Sequential
    - (b) Guarded
    - (c) Concurrent
    - (d) All the above

11. The synchronizing property where in the presence of multiple flows of control, the state of the object is not corrupted. Because, operations are treated as atomic
    - (a) Sequential
    - (b) Guarded
    - (c) Concurrent
    - (d) All the above

12. The approaches for inter process communication are
    - (a) By message passing, which can be modeled as asynchronous events
    - (b) By remote procedure calls, which can be modeled as synchronous events
    - (c) both (a) & (b)
    - (d) None

## Answers

| 1. (c) | 2. (b) | 3. (a) | 4. (c) | 5. (d) | 6. (c) |
|--------|--------|--------|--------|--------|--------|
| 7. (c) | 8. (a) | 9. (b) | 10. (d) | 11. (c) | 12. (c) |

# CHAPTER 15

# Time and Space

Look at the world around you, you find several events happening. Some of the events may happen at unpredictable times. You find some of the events connected or associated in a strange way. Some of the events may expect specific responses at specific times.

In network oriented or distributed systems, the system resources may be distributed at different physical locations around the globe. Sometimes these resources may migrate from one physical location to another. These resource migrations may raise issues such as, latency, synchronization, security and quality of service.

Modeling time and space is an essential aspect of real time and distributed systems. You use several UML features to model these systems, such as, timing marks, time expressions, timing constraints, and tagged values, such as locations.

**LEARNING OBJECTIVES**

*After studying the chapter, the students familiarize themselves with the following concepts:*

♦ Real-time Systems
♦ Distributed Systems
♦ Modeling Timing Constraints
♦ Modeling the Distribution
♦ Modeling the Migration of Objects.

## 15.1 Real Time Systems

A real time system is one in which certain behavior is to be carried out at a precise time within a predictable duration. The major characteristic of any real time system is timeliness. The correctness of any real time system is not only judged by what the system does, but mostly by quality aspects of the service delivery, meaning the timeliness of the service. You can associate a rule such as "A late answer is wrong answer" with any real time system. While you are modeling real time systems, you should show concern toward deadlines and durations which describe non functional aspects of processing. Generally, the metrics of any real time system include the following:

❖ The system should perform its intended function in a predictable manner, while supporting other functions.

❖ The timing requirements of the system must be satisfied during its utilization. We define timing requirements of a system by scheduling them for the system.

❖ A system may not meet all deadlines when it is overloaded by events, but still, it should guarantee deadlines of the selected critical tasks.

The major emphasis in modeling any real time system includes modeling duration and timing constraints. When modeling a real-time system, or even a time bound business process, you may have to consider the length of time it takes to perform actions. You do it by setting a duration constraint for a message. To model real time systems, the UML has provisions for graphically representing timing marks, time expressions, and timing constraints. Timing requirements in the UML can be specified using:

❖ Timing marks.
❖ Time expressions.
❖ Timing constraints.

**Timing Marks:** Timing marks denote the time at which a message or an event occurs. Graphically, it is formed as an expression from the name given to the message.

**Examples:**

1. a: getStudent(college). In this example, 'a' is timing mark and getStudent() is a message.
2. message:sendTime() – Time that the message is send.
3. message:receiveTime() – Time that the message is received.

**Note:** Where 'message' is the name of the message.

**Time Expressions:** Time expression is an expression that evaluates to an absolute or relative value of time.

**Examples:**

1. {a.executionTime < 10ms}.
2. After { 500 ms }.
3. when (t = 08:00).

**Timing Constraints:** Timing constraint expresses a constraint based on the absolute or relative value of time. It is a semantic statement about the relative or absolute value of time. A timing constraint is rendered similar to any constraint.

**Examples:**

1. {a.responseTime < 20 ms}.
2. {b.sendTime() – a.receiveTime() < 10 ms}.

**Time in Sequence Diagrams:** UML uses timing constraints to model time in sequence diagrams, such as, absolute time of an event, relative time between events, and time to perform action. Name messages, and use names in specifying timing constraints, such as {a.timeOfAction() < 50 ms}. A timing constraint that specifies response time can be modeled as, {responseTime ( j.receiveTime() – i.sendTime() ) < 5 sec }, If you want to specify response time for a transaction request in case of an ATM system, which is less than five seconds.

**Types of Timing:**

A synchronous message, but the sending object gives up on the message if the receiving object is not ready to accept it.

**Example**: timing constraint {wait = 0}.

A synchronous message, but the sender waits only for a specified period for the receiver to get ready to accept the message.

**Example:** timing constraint {wait = 50 ms}.

**Example for Modeling Time:**

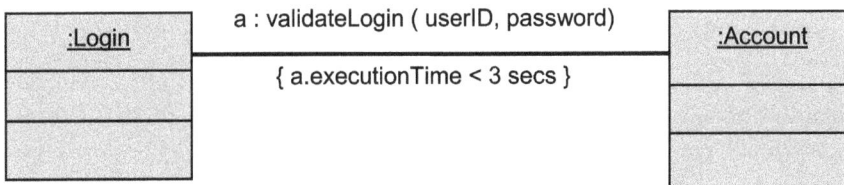

**Fig.15.1** Specifying Timing Constraints

**Note: 'a'** is the timing mark. The timing mark makes it easier to refer to that message elsewhere in the sequence diagram. The expression between { } is a constraint.

## 15.2 Modeling Time

Real time systems are time critical systems, meaning, events may happen any time, but response to them must happen at predictable absolute or relative times. These real time systems can be classified into two categories, **hard real time** and **near real time** systems. Hard real time systems expect the required behavior within nanoseconds or milliseconds. Near real time systems expect the predictable behavior in seconds or longer.

We know that the behavior of a system can be represented as an interaction among objects that pass messages among them. If it is a time critical system (real time), each message is given a name indicating timing mark. A timing mark is an expression formed from the name of a message in an interaction. Once a name is given to a message you can refer these functions of the message, such as, **startTime**, **stopTime**, and **executionTime**. You can use these functions to specify time expressions. In order to model the timing behavior of your system, you specify timing constraints using time expressions. Timing constraints can be placed adjacent to the messages, or can be attached by using dependency relationships.

**Note:** You can associate time expressions to operations. These time expressions specify the time complexity of the attached operations. Time complexity for an operation specifies time budget for it. By knowing time budgets for each operation, you can calculate the time complexity of an entire transaction.

**Example:**

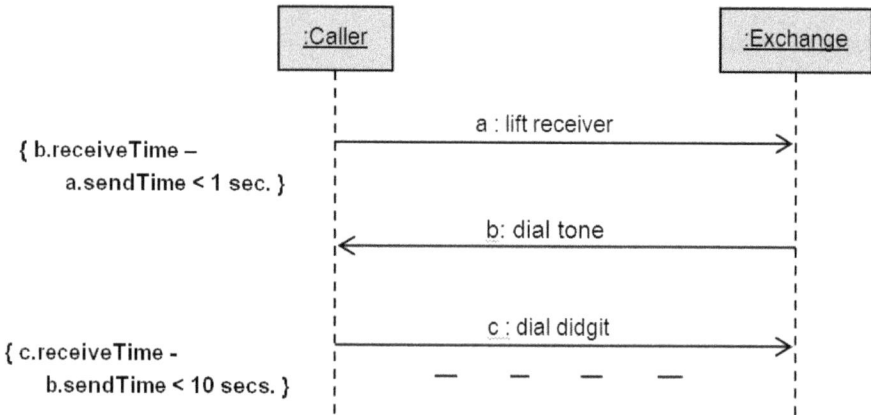

**Fig.15.2** Sequence Diagram with Time Information

## 15.3 Distributed Systems

A distributed system is one in which components may be physically distributed across nodes. These nodes can be different processors physically located at the same location, or computers that are geographically distributed across the globe. The UML provides graphical representation for modeling distributed systems by using the word **location** to specify the physical location of a system's component. **Location** is the placement of a component on a node. Graphically, location is rendered as a tagged value.

**Example:**

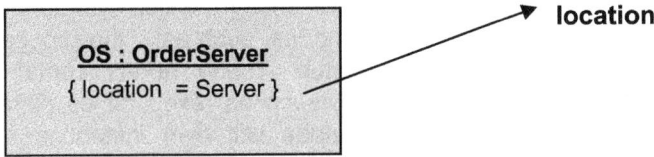

**Fig.15.3** Specifying Location of a Component

**Note:** Distributed systems contain their components that are physically scattered across the nodes of a system. Components are generally fixed on nodes on which they are loaded. Sometimes, components may migrate from one location to another, that is from one node to another node.

The following example gives you an idea how real time and distributed systems can be modeled by using timing constraints and locations. This example represents operations of an online book store. It has three objects, such as Client, BookServer, and BookWarehouse and the interaction among them can be specified as follows, using a sequence diagram.

**Example:**

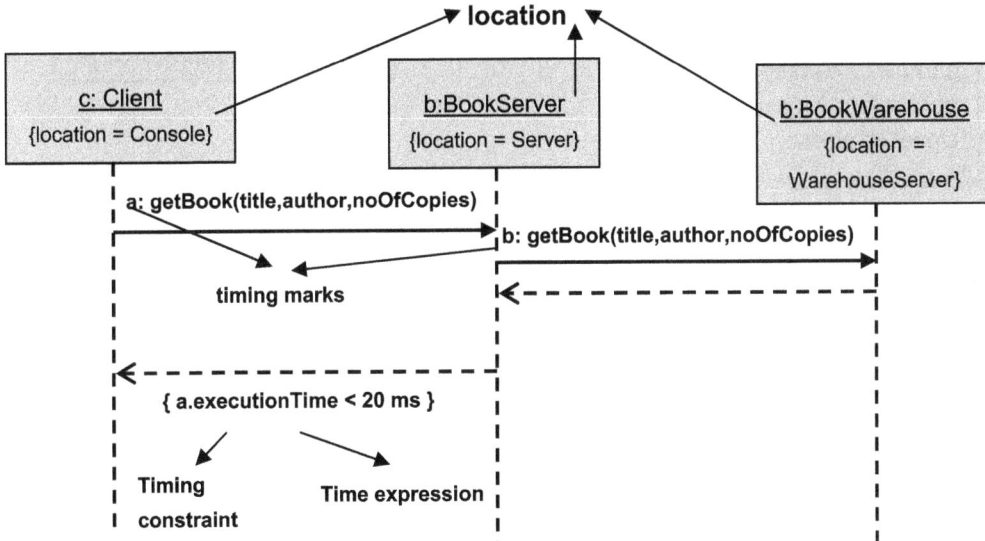

**Fig.15.4** Modeling Timing Constraints and Location

## 15.4 Location

In the UML, the deployment diagram representing the deployment view of the system contains the topology of various nodes, such as, the processors and devices on which your system executes. These nodes contain various components that constitute your system, such as, executables, libraries and database tables. Each instance of a node will own instances of related components. You can model the location of components in two ways. First, by nesting the components in an extra compartment of a related node. Second, by using the tagged value **location** to indicate the node on which the component instance resides.

**Example:**

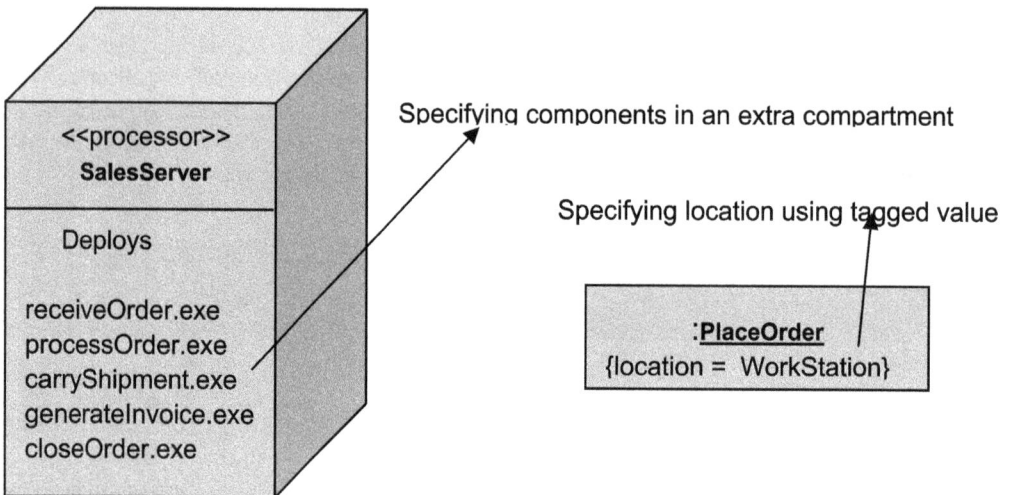

Specifying components in an extra compartment

Specifying location using tagged value

**Fig.15.5** Specifying Location

Components and classes may be manifested as artifacts. For example, in the following figure, class **LoadAgent** is manifested by the artifact **initializer.exe** that lives on the node of type **Router.**

You can model the location of an artifact in two ways in the UML. First, as shown for the **Router**, you can physically nest the element (textually or graphically) in an extra compartment in its enclosing node. Second, you can use a dependency with the keyword **«deploy»** from the artifact to the node that contains it.

**Example:**

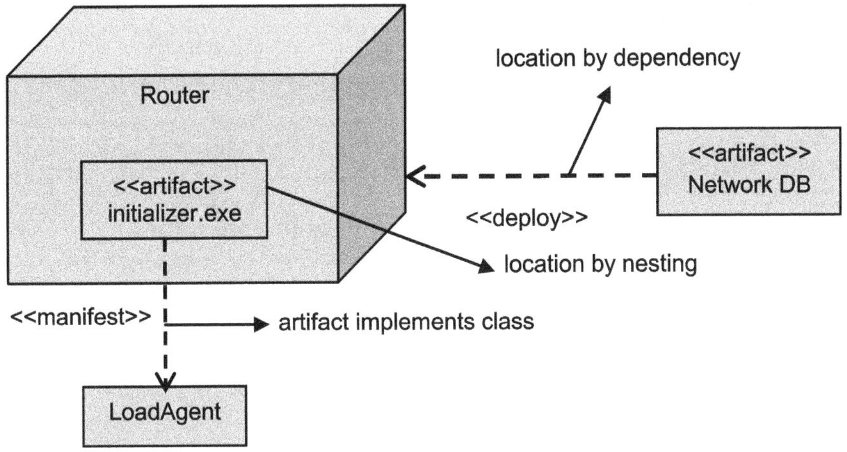

**Fig.15.6** Modeling Location

**Note:** Modeling the location of a component by using tagged values is very much useful when you want to show the redistribution of a component over time. The migration of a component from one location to another location can be specified by using **become** message.

## 15.5 Modeling Timing Constraints

You apply timing constraints to model time critical properties of any real time system. There are three primary time critical properties that can be modeled by using the UML. They are as follows:

❖ Modeling the absolute time of an event.

❖ Modeling the relative time between events.

❖ Modeling the time taken for carrying out an action.

**The various steps followed while modeling timing constraints:**

❖ In an interaction, find out whether an event must start at some instance of time. Model this time instance as a timing constraint on the message.

❖ In an interaction, for each sequence of messages, find out whether there is any maximum relative time for that sequence. Model this relative time as a timing constraint on the sequence.

❖ Identify time critical operations in a class. For each such operation, identify time of execution or the time complexity. Model these time complexities as timing constraints on the operations.

**Example:**

**{ a.startTime every 10 secs }**

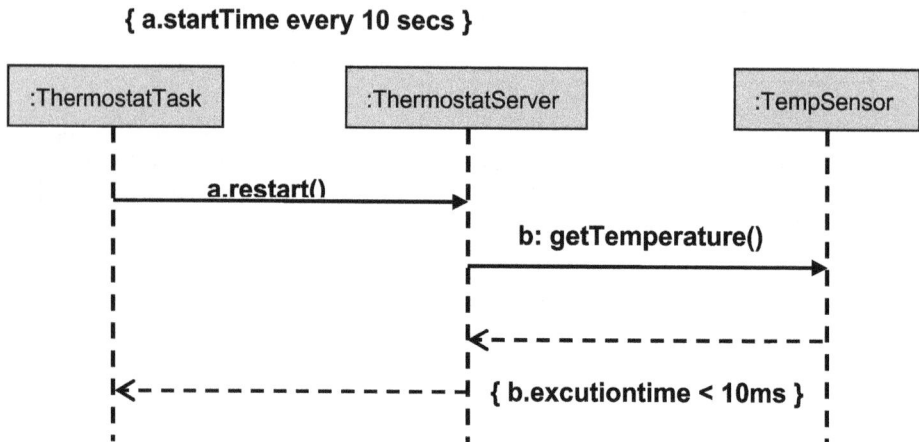

**Fig.15.7** Modeling Timing Constraint

The above figure represents the functioning of a Thermostat which maintains the temperature in a house at a comfortable level. This thermostat restarts for every 10 seconds and reads the temperature in a house. Based on the temperature, the thermostat either cools or heats the house.

The timing mark **'a'** which restarts for every 10 seconds is indicated as a timing constraint **{a.startTime every 10 seconds}** which describes that the thermostat restarts for every 10 seconds.

Similarly, the timing constraint **{ b.executionTime <10ms }** indicates the time required to read the temperature of the house. If the execution time exceeds 10 ms, it means that there is a problem with the temperature sensor.

## 15.6 Modeling the Distribution of Objects

The model of the topology of any distributed system represents the physical placement of components and instances across the various nodes the system constitutes. If you are interested in the configuration management of the system, you are concerned with the distribution of components such as, executables, libraries, and tables. If your emphasis is on the functionality, scalability, and throughput of the system, you will be more concerned with modeling the distribution of objects.

The distribution of objects has to be handled carefully, otherwise it may lead to the problems of concurrency and system's poor performance. The following systematic steps are followed while you are modeling the distribution of objects:

❖ For each object that is in your system, find its location and consider all its neighbors and their locations. In a tightly coupled system, the neighboring objects are close by. Whereas, in a loosely coupled system, the objects are physically distant. It is better to assign objects closer to the actors that interact with them.

❖ Establish patterns of interaction among sets of objects. Keep the objects in the same set that have higher interaction in order to reduce the cost of communication. Keep the objects in separate sets that have very low level of interaction.

❖ Distribute your objects properly across the system so as to balance the load of each node.

❖ Redistribute your objects appropriately considering the issues such as, security, volatility, and quality of service.

❖ Graphically represent this distribution of objects across the system in any of the following ways:

  ◆ In the form of a deployment diagram by nesting objects on the nodes.

  ◆ By specifying the locations of the objects using tagged values.

**Example:**

The following figure describes an object diagram that models the distribution of objects in an Order Processing system. Any sales order is placed on a work station client. So, the Order object resides on a WorkStation.

The Order is received by the Sales department of an organization at the Client location of the Sales department. So, the Sales object resides on Client node.

The SalesPerson object that processes the Sales Order will be at location Server. During the processing of the Sales order the items for which order is placed are identified. So, the Item object is located on Server.

Once the items in a sales order are identified, they are checked for their availability in the warehouse. So, the object ItemTable is placed on DataWarehouse node which contains the information about various items available.

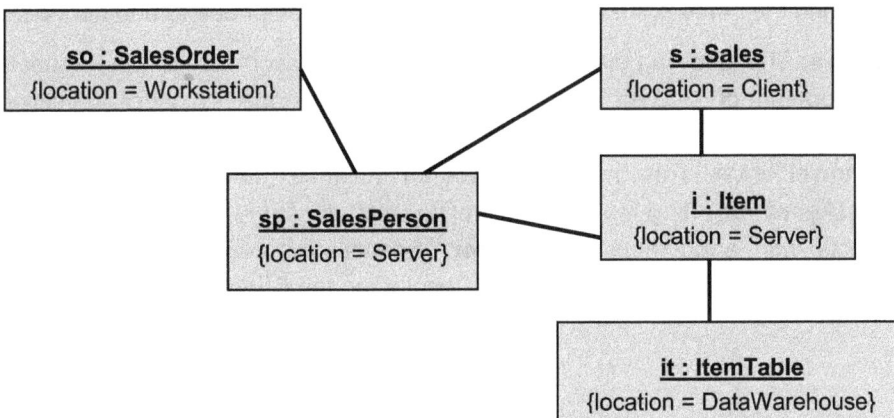

**Fig.15.8** Modeling the Distribution of Objects

## 15.7  Modeling Objects that Migrate

Generally, in many distributed systems, components and objects once loaded on the system, they remain there for their lifetime. They never leave the node on which they were born. There are some distributed systems, where objects move around. This may happen because of the two reasons discussed below:-

❖ First, you find objects moving closer to actors and other objects they work with for better interaction.

❖ Second, objects may migrate because of the failure of a node or connection or to balance the load across the multiple nodes of the system.

Migration of objects in a system is a bigger problem than distribution of objects, because migration raises problems of synchronization and preservation of identity. The following steps are followed for modeling the migration of objects:

❖ Select the mechanisms for transporting objects which are likely to migrate across nodes.

❖ Use tagged values to indicate location of an object on a node.

❖ For objects that are migrating across nodes, use stereotypes such as **become** and **copy** to indicate new locations.

❖ Take precautions to preserve the issues of synchronization and identity of objects that migrate across nodes.

Here, synchronization means keeping object's state consistent when object migrates across nodes. The issue of preserving identity of an object means, preserving the name of the object as it migrates from one node to another node.

**Example:** The following diagram indicates a collaboration diagram that models the migration of a Web agent that moves from node to node, collecting information and bidding on resources in order to automatically deliver a lowest-cost travel ticket. This diagram shows an instance (named t) of the class **TravelAgent** migrating from one server to another. Along the way, the object interacts with anonymous **Auctioneer** instances at each node, eventually delivering a bid for the **Itinerary** object, located on the **Clientserver**.

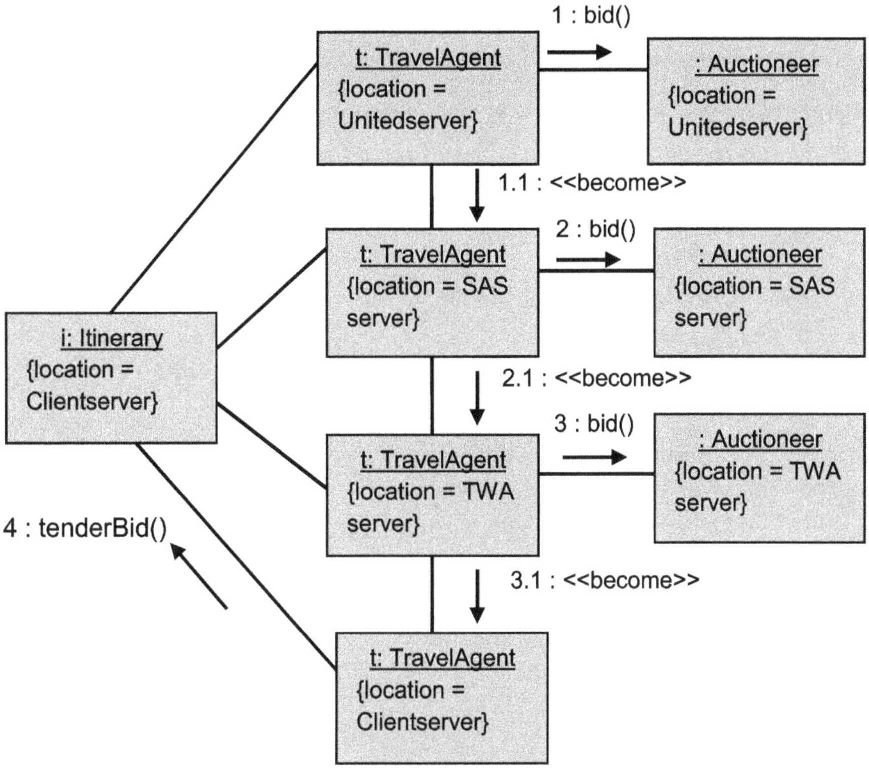

**Fig.15.9** Modeling Objects that Migrate

## Essay Type Questions

1. Explain timing marks, time expressions, and timing constraints with examples.
2. Write short notes on distributed systems.
3. Explain briefly the following:
   (a) Modeling Location    (b) Modeling timing constraints.
4. Explain how to model the distribution of objects with an example.
5. Explain how to model the objects that migrate with an example.

## Objective Type Questions

1. The issues raised by resource migration in a distributed system are
   (a) latency
   (b) synchronization
   (c) security and quality of service
   (d) All the above

2. The system that depends on the timeliness of the services is called
   (a) real time system
   (b) client/server system
   (c) distributed system
   (d) none

3. Timing requirements in the UML can be specified using
   (a) Timing marks
   (b) Time expressions
   (c) Timing constraints
   (d) All the above

4. message:sendTime()
   (a) Time that the message is send
   (b) Time that the message is received
   (c) timing mark
   (d) time expression

5. After { 500 ms }. Is a
   (a) Time that the message is send
   (b) Time that the message is received
   (c) timing mark
   (d) time expression

6. A real time system where responses are in nanoseconds are called
   (a) near real time system
   (b) hard real time system
   (c) both a & b
   (d) none

7. These are the functions of message
   (a) executionTime()
   (b) startTime() & stopTime()
   (c) both a & b
   (d) none

8. The system in which components may be physically distributed across nodes
   (a) real time systems
   (b) distributed systems
   (c) both a & b
   (d) none

9. Graphically the location of the component is rendered as
   (a) constraint
   (b) stereotype
   (c) tagged value
   (d) none

10. Locations of components can be specified as
    (a) tagged values
    (b) extra compartment
    (c) stereotypes
    (d) both a & b

11. The primary time critical properties that can be modeled by using the UML

   (a) Modeling the absolute time of an event
   (b) Modeling the relative time between events
   (c) Modeling the time taken for carrying out an action
   (d) All the above

12. You will be more concerned with modeling the distribution of objects when the emphasis is on

   (a) functionality               (b) scalability
   (c) throughput                (d) All the above

13. Migration of the objects happen because of

   (a) objects moving closer to actors and other objects they work with for better interaction
   (b) the failure of a node or connection or to balance the load across the multiple nodes of the system
   (c) both a & b
   (d) none

## Answers

| | | | | | |
|---|---|---|---|---|---|
| 1. (d) | 2. (a) | 3. (d) | 4. (a) | 5. (d) | 6. (b) |
| 7. (c) | 8. (b) | 9. (c) | 10. (d) | 11. (d) | 12. (d) |
| 13. (c) | | | | | |

# CHAPTER 16

# Statechart Diagrams

A statechart diagram shows a state machine which is used to model the dynamic aspects of a system. You can model the behavior of an object in its life time either by using activity diagrams or by using statechart diagrams. Here, an activity diagram describes flow of control from activity to activity, where as a statechart diagram shows flow of control as state transitions among states.

**LEARNING OBJECTIVES**

After studying the chapter, the students familiarize them-selves with the following concepts:

♦ Terms and Concepts

♦ Modeling Reactive Objects

♦ Implementing State chart

Statechart diagrams describe states and their transitions due to external or internal events in the life time of an object. Mostly, statechart diagrams are used to model the behavior of reactive objects in their lifetimes. A reactive object behaves based on the response to an internal or an external event that happens on it. A reactive object's current behaviour depends on its past behavior, that is, past responses based on past events.

**Note:** You can associate statechart diagrams to classes, use cases, and even to entire systems.

The most important purpose of a statechart diagram is to model behavior of an object in its life time from its creation to termination. Though, statechart diagrams are useful for constructing executable systems through forward and reverse engineering, the main purpose is to model reactive systems. The following gives the summary of purposes of statechart diagrams:

❖ They are used to model dynamic aspects of a system.
❖ They are used to model life time behavior of reactive objects and reactive systems.
❖ They are used to model the behavior of an object in its lifetime.
❖ They are used to define state machines.

**Example:** In this example, we discuss statechart diagram for **Order** object. The first state is an idle state from where the process starts. The next states arrive because of the events, such as **send request, confirm request,** and **dispatch order.** These events cause state transitions for **order** object. The following statechart diagram graphically describes the life cycle of **order** object. This diagram depicts normal and abnormal exits that can happen in the system. When the entire life cycle is complete, then we can consider the completion of an associated transaction. The diagram also includes the dummy initial and final states.

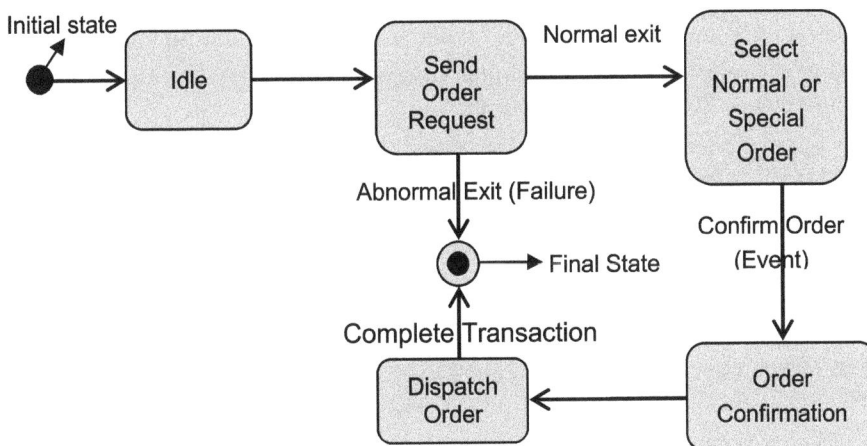

**Fig.16.1** State Chart Diagram for Order Management System

## 16.1 Terms and Concepts

A **statechart diagram** shows a state machine, describing the flow of control from state to state. A **state machine** is a behavior that specifies the sequences of states an object goes through during its life time in response to events, together with its responses to those events. A **state** is a condition or situation in the life of an object during which it satisfies some condition, performs some activity, or waits for some event. An **event** is the specification of a significant occurrence that has a location in time and space. In the context of state machines, an event is an occurrence of a stimulus that can trigger a state transition. A **transition** is a relationship between two states indicating that an object in the first state will perform certain actions and enter the second state when a specified event occurs and specified conditions are satisfied. An **activity** is ongoing non atomic execution within a state machine. An **action** is an executable atomic computation that results in a change in state of the model or the return of a value.

## 16.2 Common Contents

Statechart diagrams commonly contain:

❖ Simple states, Nested states and Composite states.
❖ Internal, External and Complex Transitions.
❖ Includes Events and Actions.
❖ Contains Notes and Constraints.

## 16.3 Common Uses

Statechart diagrams are mainly used to model dynamic aspects of a system. Statechart diagram is used to model event ordered behavior of any object which is part of a system's architecture, including classes (including active classes), interfaces, components, and nodes.

You apply statechart diagrams to model dynamic aspects of a system, a subsystem, a class, or a use case. You typically use statechart diagrams to model reactive objects. A reactive object can be considered as an event driven object whose behavior depends on the external or internal events that happen on it. A reactive object sits idle waiting for an event. When it receives an event, it responses, then again it sits idle for the next event to happen. When you develop a model for a reactive object, it focuses, on the states of the object, the events that trigger state transitions, and the actions that occur on each state change.

So, the common uses of statechart diagrams are summarized as follows:

❖ To model dynamic aspects of a system.
❖ To model sequence of states an object goes through in its life time, in response to internal or external events.
❖ To model reactive systems. Reactive systems consist of reactive objects.
❖ To identify events responsible for state changes.
❖ To carry on forward and reverse engineering tasks.

## 16.4 Modeling Reactive Objects

The UML Statechart Diagram is a tool for specifying the dynamic behavior of reactive objects. Reactive objects are objects that respond to events sent from other objects. The response of the reactive object to an event depends on what state the object is in at the time that the event occurred. Interaction diagrams model the behavior of a society of objects working together, where as a statechart diagram models the behavior of a single object over its lifetime.

You specify the following aspects, when you model the behavior of a reactive object:

❖ The states in which the object might live in its life time.
❖ The events that trigger state transitions.
❖ The actions that happen on each state change.
❖ The typical process of modeling the behavior of a reactive object involves the modeling of its life time, starting from its creation to until its destruction, indicating all the stable states through which the object goes through. Stable state represents a condition in which an object may exist for some identifiable period of time. The following things may happen when an event occurs:
❖ When an event occurs, the object may move from state to state (a transition).
❖ Events may also trigger self-and internal transitions, in which the source and the target of the transition are the same state.
❖ In reaction to an event or a state change, the object may respond by dispatching an action.

**Note**: When you model the behavior of a reactive object, you can specify its action by associating it with a transition or state change. A state machine whose actions are attached to transitions is called a **Mealy machine**. Whereas, a state machine whose actions are associated with states is called a **Moore machine**. Generally, when you develop statechart diagrams, you use a combination of **Mealy** and **Moore** machines.

**Example**: The following diagram gives you the statechart diagram for a simplified STD for a telephone line.

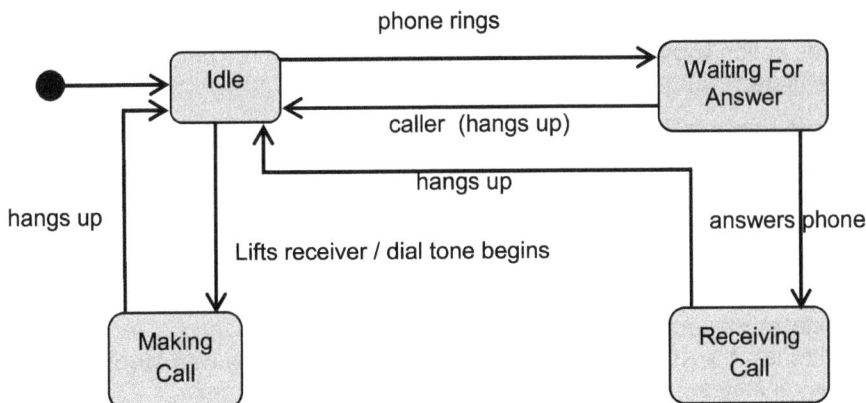

**Fig.16.2** Statechart Diagram for a Telephone Line

**Another Example:** The following diagram specifies the statechart for a **stack** class.

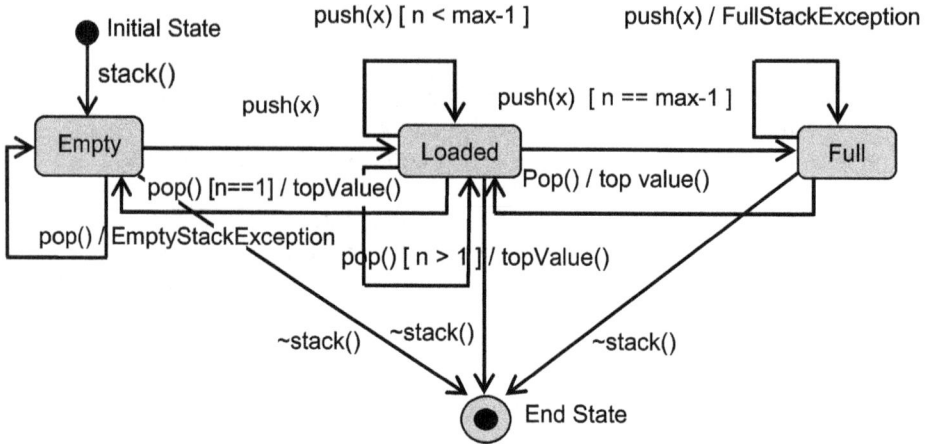

**Fig.16.3**  Statechart Diagram for a Stack Class

**Explanation**: The above diagram indicates the Statechart of a **stack** class. It has three states, namely, **Empty**, **Loaded**, and **Full** respectively. It also has dummy **start** and **end** states. You can carry five operations on a **stack** class. They are, **stack(), ~stack(), push(), pop()** and **topValue().** The transitions from **source** state to **target** state are labeled with **event [guard condition] / action** , which means that , when **source** state detects the **event** and **guard condition** is also satisfied, a transition will occur by executing **action.** For instance, the transition **pop()[n==1]/topvalue()** from **Loaded** state to **Empty** state, means that, when **pop()** event happens on **Loaded**  state, if **guard condition** *"n==1"* **is** true, then this transition happens. This is to say, the stack object first executes action **topvalue(),** and implement the transition from **Loaded** state to **Empty** state.

**The various steps involved in modeling a reactive object are as follows:**

* Identify the purpose of your state chart. Meaning, whether you are using it for modeling the dynamic aspects of a class, a use case, or the system as a whole.
* Identify the initial and the final states of your reactive object which you want to model. Specify the pre and post conditions of the initial and final states respectively.
* Identify the stable states the object may be in. Begin with identifying high-level states.
* Identify the partial ordering of stable states that an object goes through during the life time of the object.

❖ Identify the events that may trigger state transitions.

❖ Associate actions to these transitions (as in a Mealy machine) and/or to these states (as in a Moore machine).

❖ Simplify your state chart diagram by using substates, branches, forks, joins, and history states.

❖ Verify whether all states that constitute your state chart diagram are reachable by means of some combination of events.

❖ Verify whether any state is a dead end. A dead end is a state from which there can be no state transitions out of that state. Avoid dead ends in any state chart diagram.

❖ Check the statechart diagram considering each state, and their responses against expected sequences of events.

**Example**: The following diagram shows a statechart for parsing a simple context free language, such as, stream in or stream out messages to XML. The machine is designed to parse a stream of characters that match the syntax:

message : '<' string'>' string';'

The first string represents a tag, where as the second string represents the body of the message. Given a stream of characters, only well-formed messages that follow this syntax may be accepted. In this figure, there are only three stable states for this state machine, they are **Waiting**, **GettingToken** and **GettingBody**. This statechart is designed as a Mealy machine with actions tied to transitions. There is only one event in this state machine, that is the invocation of **put** operation with the parameter 'c', which is a character.

This state machine, while it is in the **Waiting** state throws away any character that does not designate the start of a token (as specified by the guard condition). When the start of a token is received, the state of the object changes to **GettingToken**. While in that state, the machine saves any character that does not designate the end of a token (as specified by the guard condition ). When the end of a token is received, the state of the object changes to **GettingBody**. While in that state, the machine saves any character that does not designate the end of a message body (as specified by the guard condition). When the end of a message is received, the state of the object changes to **Waiting,** and a value is returned indicating that the message has been parsed (and the machine is ready to receive another message).

The diagram below indicates a statechart for the above machine:

**Note:** This statechart specifies a machine that runs continuously. So, there is no final state.

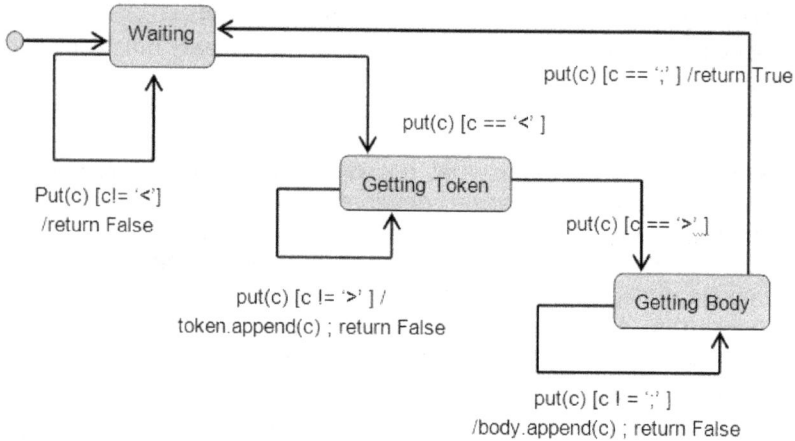

**Fig.16.4** Modeling Reactive Objects

# 16.5 Forward Engineering

It is the process of creating code from the model. Forward engineering is possible for statechart diagram, if the context of the diagram is a class. If the forward engineering tool is applied for the previous statechart diagram, the following Java code for the class MessageParser is generated.

**Another Example:** In this example also we discuss statechart diagram for a class and the code generated for forward engineering task. The following discusses how UML diagram can be transformed into Java code if the diagram is a statechart.

**UML to Java Transformation rules for a Statechart:**

| UML | Java Transformation |
|---|---|
| State | Scalar Variable or Object |
| Event | Object or Method |
| Action | Simple statement or Method |
| Entry/Exit Actions | Objects or Methods |

Most of the class diagram concepts have a one-to-one mapping with the programming language concepts so the class diagram implementation is relatively straight forward. Class diagrams can be implemented directly in a programming language supported concepts like classes and objects, composition and inheritance.

**Java Code**:

```
class   MessageParser   {
public
      boolean    put ( char c ) {
      switch  (state)
      { case  Waiting   :          if ( c == '<' ) {
                                   state = GettingToken;
                                   token = new StringBuffer();
                                   body = new StringBuffer();
                                   }
                                   break;
          case  GettingToken :     if ( c == '>')
                                     state = GettingBody;
                                   else  token.append(c);
                                   break;
          case GettingBody :       if ( c == ';' )
                                       state = Waiting;
                                   else  body.append(c);
                                   return True;
      }    //end of switch
    return False; // end of function put()
    }
    StringBuffer  getToken()
     {
                    return token;
     }
    StringBuffer  getBody()
     {
                    return  body;
     }

private
              ;
    final  static  int  Waiting = 0;
    final  static  int  GettingToken = 1;
    final  static  int  GettingBody = 2;
    int state = Waiting;
    StringBuffer  token, body;
```

The transformation rules for class diagram are summarized as follows:

**UML to Java Transformation rules for a Class**:

| UML | Java Transformation |
|---|---|
| Class | Class |
| Interface | Interface |
| Attribute | Attribute |
| Properties on Attributes | Attribute Modifiers |
| Operation | Method |
| Properties on Operations | Method Modifiers |
| Realization between classes and Interfaces | Implements |
| Generalization between classes and Interfaces | Extends |
| Association between classes | Reference attributes in both classes |

Let us consider an example of implementing statechart for an air conditioner.

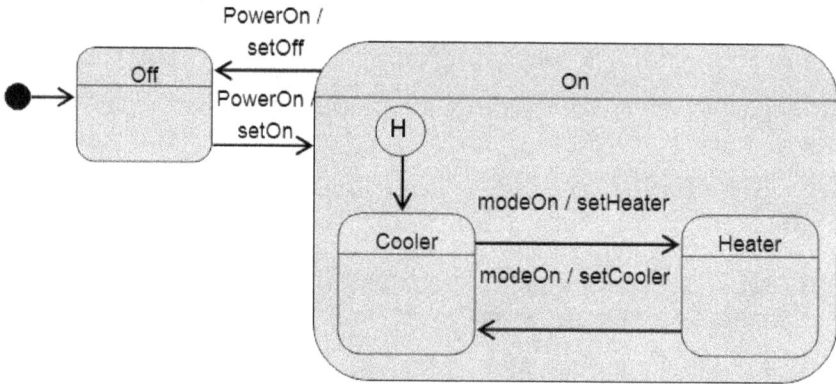

**Fig.16.5** Statechart for an Air Conditioner

## 16.6 Approach to Implement above Statechart

Mostly statecharts are implemented by using the switch statement. Based on the current active state, it jumps to the corresponding code for processing the event. States are represented as data values, where a single scalar variable stores the current active state. Each event is implemented by one switch statement. The state variable is used as a discriminator in the switch statement. The correct case is selected based on the value of the state variable. Each case clause in the switch statement can implement the various actions and activities for the specific state. All the behavior of the statechart is put in one single class. The code generated by this approach for the air conditioner statechart is shown below:

**Generated Java Code:**

```
class AirConditiner { // context class
public static final int Off = 1;
public static final int On = 2;
public static final int Cooler = 3;
public static final int Heater = 4;
public int State;              // state variable
public int on_subState;
AirConditioner ()
{                             //constructor
        State = Off;
        on_subState = Cooler ;
 }
public void  modeOn()
{                             // event method
        switch (State)
        {
                case Off : break;
                case Cooler :
                    setHeater ; // action
                                    // exit actions
                    on_subState = Heater ;
                    State = on_subState;
                        // entry actions
                    break;
                case Heater :
                    setCooler ; // action
                                    // exit actions
                    on_subState = Cooler;
                    State = on_subState;
                        // entry actions
                    break;
                default :  break;

        }
}
```

```
public void powerOn()
{      // event method
           switch (State)
           {
              case Off :
                      setOn;                    // action
                                                // exit actions
                          State = on_subState;
                                                // entry actions
                      break;

              case Cooler :
                      setOff;                   // action
                                                // exit actions
                          State = Off;
                                                // entry actions
                      break;

              case Heater :
                      setOff;                   // action
                                                // exit actions
                          State = Off;
                                                // entry actions
                      break;

              default :  break;

           }
}
           ------------------------
} // end of class definition
```

## 16.7 Reverse Engineering

It is the process of creating statechart diagram from the code. Though reverse engineering among statecharts is theoretically possible, it is practically not useful. A designer may have an idea of what constitutes a meaningful state. But reverse engineering tools do not have the capacity to generate meaningful states that constitute a statechart diagram.

## Essay Type Questions

1. Explain state chart diagrams. Draw a state chart diagram for order management system.
2. Explain modelling reactive objects with suitable examples.
3. Describe forward engineering with state chart diagrams with a suitable example.

## Objective Type Questions

1. Modeling the behavior of reactive objects in their lifetimes is done by
   - (a) activity diagram
   - (b) state chart diagram
   - (c) class diagram
   - (d) object diagram

2. State chart diagrams can be associated to
   - (a) classes
   - (b) use cases
   - (c) entire system
   - (d) all the above

3. The major purpose of the state chart diagram is
   - (a) to model dynamic aspects of a system
   - (b) to model the behavior of an object in its lifetime
   - (c) to define state machines
   - (d) All the above

4. ------------ is a condition or situation in the life of an object during which it satisfies some condition, performs some activity, or waits for some event.
   - (a) A state
   - (b) A transition
   - (c) An activity
   - (d) An action

5. ------------ is a relationship between two states indicating that an object in the first state will perform certain actions and enter the second state when a specified event occurs and specified conditions are satisfied.
   - (a) A state
   - (b) A transition
   - (c) An activity
   - (d) An action

6. ------------ is ongoing non atomic execution within a state machine
   - (a) A state
   - (b) A transition
   - (c) An activity
   - (d) An action

7. ------------ is an executable atomic computation that results in a change in state of the model or the return of a value.
   - (a) A state
   - (b) A transition
   - (c) An activity
   - (d) An action

8. A state chart diagram commonly contains

    (a)  states                                (b)  transitions
    (c)  events & actions                      (d)  All the above

9. The common use of state chart diagram is

    (a)  To model dynamic aspects of a system
    (b)  To identify events responsible for state changes
    (c)  To carry on forward and reverse engineering tasks
    (d)  All the above

10. The thing that  may happen when an event occurs:

    (a)  A state transition
    (b)  the object may respond by dispatching an action.
    (c)  both (a) & (b)
    (d)  none

11. A state machine whose actions are attached to transitions is called

    (a)  Moore machine                         (b)  Mealy machine
    (c)  activity                              (d)  action

12. A  state machine whose actions are associated with states is called

    (a)  Moore machine                         (b)  Mealy machine
    (c)  activity                              (d)  action

13. Forward engineering is possible for state chart diagram, if the context of the diagram is

    (a)  class                                 (b)  object
    (c)  component                             (d)  node

## Answers

| 1. (b) | 2. (d) | 3. (d) | 4. (a) | 5. (b) | 6. (c) |
|--------|--------|--------|--------|--------|--------|
| 7. (d) | 8. (d) | 9. (d) | 10. (c) | 11. (b) | 12. (a) |
| 13. (a) | | | | | |

# CHAPTER 17

# Architectural Modeling Components

Components are the important building blocks in modeling the physical aspects of a system. A component can be defined as a physical and replaceable part of a software intensive system. A component may confirm to a set of interfaces. A component may realize a set of interfaces. The internals of a component are hidden, but it has well defined provided interfaces through which its functions can be accessed. A component can have a required interface which defines what functions or services the component requires from other components. A larger component can be constructed from assembling smaller components by connecting them through their interfaces.

**Note:** A complete software oriented system can be considered as a component.

The UML uses components to model the physical things that reside on nodes. Nodes are the physical parts of the system's architecture. The physical things that may reside on a node are, executables, libraries, tables, files, and documents. A component is, typically, a physical representation of logical things, such as classes, interfaces, and collaborations.

We know that a Motor Car can be constructed or built by assembling components which are independent. These components can be car tiers, body, engine, doors, breaks, gears, and steering etc. All these components need not be

**LEARNING OBJECTIVES**

*After studying the chapter, the students familiarize themselves with the following concepts:*

- Components and Classes
- Aspects of a Component
- Components and Interfaces
- Organizing Components
- Modeling Executables and Libraries
- Modeling Tables, Files, and Documents
- Modeling an API

manufactured by a single vendor. Similarly, a software intensive and object oriented system can be developed by integrating components which can be glued together through their well defined interfaces. These components are always replaceable whenever there is such requirement. You can always replace older components with newer and compatible ones.

When you are building a software intensive system, you do logical, structural and behavioral modeling of the system. Logical model specify the vocabulary of your system domain. Structural and behavioral models specify how the various things in the system collaborate.

The logical things that are part of the logical model live in the conceptual world. The physical things that are part of the physical aspects of the system live in real world. A real world is the world of bits. These physical things which are part of your system, reside on nodes which are physical. These nodes form the physical architecture of the system. These physical components are executed directly or indirectly to participate in system's execution.

The physical things that form part of the system are modeled as components by using the UML. You can associate a set of interfaces either to classes or to components. These interfaces are useful in gluing various components together to formulate bigger components, subsystems, or systems. These interfaces bridge your physical and logical models.

**Example**: While you are building the logical models of a system, you may specify classes and interfaces realized by those classes. When you are building physical models, the same interfaces can be realized by physical components. The concept of the component is directly supported by various operating systems and programming languages.

Software components such as, Object libraries, executables, COM+ components, and Enterprise Java Beans can be directly represented as components in the UML. In the UML, you can represent components such as tables, files, and documents that participate in an executing system. Graphically, a component is rendered as a rectangle with tabs.

**Examples**:

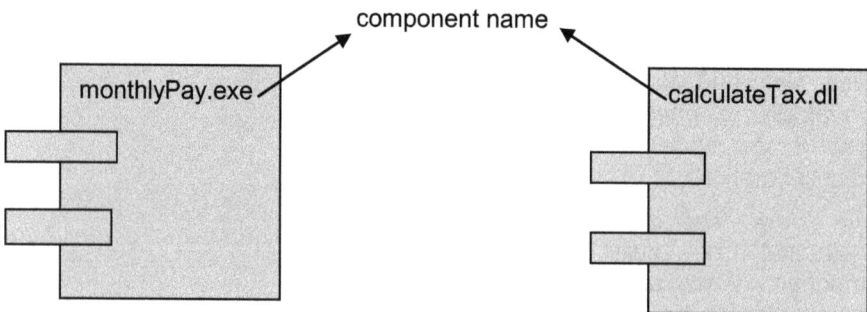

**Fig.17.1** Specifying a Component

## 17.1 Component Names

Every component must have a unique name that distinguishes it from other components. A component may have a simple name. Sometimes a component may have a path name, when the component is placed in a package.

**Examples**:

Simple Name

Extended Name

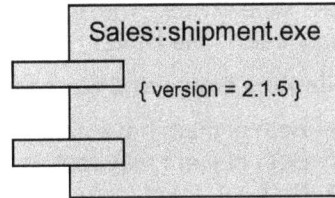

invoice.java

Sales::shipment.exe

{ version = 2.1.5 }

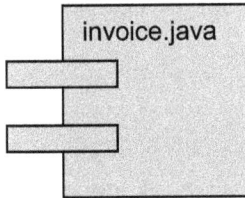

**Fig.17.2(a)**  A Source Code File        **Fig.17.2(b)**  An Executable File

**Explanation**: The component named **invoice.java** represents a java source code file. Whereas **shipment.exe** is an executable file embedded in a package named **Sales.** While you are giving a name for such component, you associate the component name with the package name as shown. The component's version is specified by using tagged values.

**Note** : Typically, component name is a short noun or a noun phrase drawn from the vocabulary of the implementation.

## 17.2 Components and Classes

As we are aware that a component represents physical aspects of a system. Generally, a component definition uses words like **binary** and **replaceable**. A binary component is an executable one which is compiled, not source code. A binary component is a component which is ready to run with no assembly required. If a component is replaceable, it means that, a new component can be substituted in place of an old one without affecting the working environment. The new component may have different implementation, but it should provide the same API (Application Programming Interface) as the old one. You can say that a component obliges to carry on a contract promising to provide a given API.

While implementing the system, a class can be coded in any object oriented programming language. The code containing the class when compiled becomes a component. Sometimes   a component may be a huge aggregation of classes hidden behind a relatively simple API. These classes may be implemented in the same or other languages and placed at the same or other physical locations.

A component is a code module. A component is a physical analog of a set of related classes. A component has a higher level of abstraction than a class. Usually, a component is implemented by one or more classes (or objects) at runtime. So, a component eventually encompasses a large portion of a system.

In the UML, you can model classes and components in a similar fashion. So, there are certain similarities between classes and components apart from certain differences. The following section discuses issues of classes versus components in the UML.

**Similarities between Classes and Components**:

❖ Both of them have names to distinguish.
❖ Both of them may realize a set of interfaces.
❖ Both of them may participate in relationships such as dependency, generalization, and association.
❖ Both of them may be nested.
❖ Both of them may have instances.
❖ Both of them may participate in interactions.

Though a component and a class representation in the UML have above mentioned similarities, they do have certain well defined differences. The following section discusses their differences.

**Differences between Classes and Components:**

❖ Classes represent logical things, where as components represent physical things of a system. Components may be deployed and may live on nodes, but classes may not.
❖ Components represent the physical analogs of otherwise logical elements, such as classes, interfaces, or collaborations. The physical components are at a higher level of abstraction than their associated logical elements.
❖ You can refer or access attributes and operations of a class directly. Whereas, operations of a component are can only be reachable through their interfaces.

You can make the following understandings based on the differences between classes and components when they are modeled by using the UML.

Based on the above mentioned first difference, you can make the following conclusions. When you are modeling a system, you should decide whether to represent a thing as a class or as a component. If the thing you are modeling lives directly on a node, use a component, otherwise use a class.

Based on the second difference, you can understand the established relationships among classes and components. A component can be the physical implementation of otherwise logical elements such as classes, interfaces, and collaborations. The relationship between a component and the classes it implements can be shown explicitly as follows:

❖ By using dependency relationships directed towards classes from the associated component.
❖ By placing these relationships in the component as a part of its specification.

**Example**:

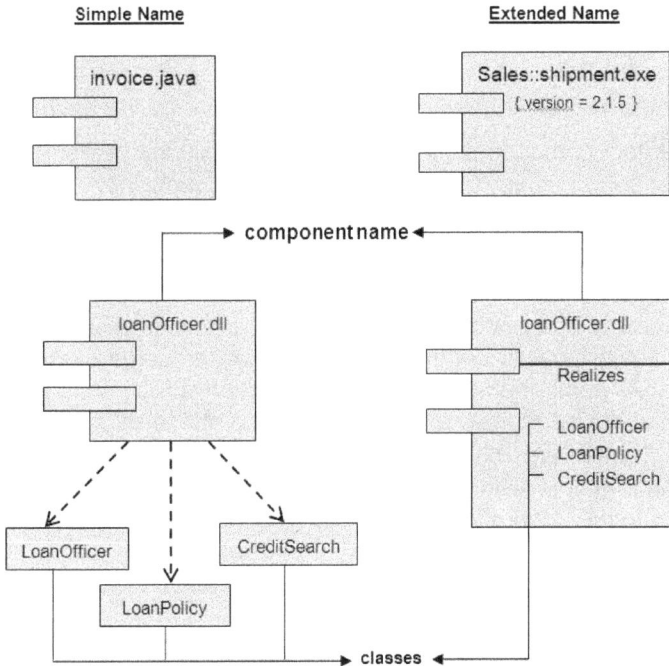

**Fig.17.3** Components and Classes

   Based on the third difference, you can understand how interfaces bridge components and classes. Classes and components may both realize an interface, but a component's services are usually available only through its interfaces.

**Note**: While you are modeling components, you can specify attributes and operations for them. It mostly happens in cases when you are modeling reflective systems. Reflective systems are the systems which manipulate their own components.

## 17.3  Aspects of a Component

❖ Every component has a specification.

❖ Every componesnt has an implementation.
❖ Every component confirms to a set of standards.
❖ Every component can be packaged into modules.
❖ Every component can be deployed on nodes.

A component in the UML represents a modular part of a system. A component encapsulates its content and its manifestation is replaceable within its environment. A component's behaviour can be specified in terms of its associated interfaces. A component can be replaced by another if their interfaces are identical. It is similar to plug-and-play capability of component based systems and promotes building a new software oriented system by assembling components. In this case the software components are reusable. There is no restriction on the level of abstraction of a component. A component can be as small as a multiplier of numbers, or as large as the entire system.

**Note:** A larger component can always be built by assembling smaller components across their interfaces. You can graphically represent these assemblies by using component diagrams.

A component can be further explained as one that is composed of one or more classes, or other components and is intended to support a constructed unit of functionality of a system. Multiple components can utilize the same class. A class utilized in multiple components maintains the same semantics in all of its contexts. A component diagram graphically represents the higher-level interaction and dependencies among software components that constitute your system. A component diagram captures the physical structure of the implementation and is built as part of architectural specification. Component diagrams are developed by architects and programmers. Component diagrams are used for the purposes, such as organizing source code, constructing executable releases, and specifying the physical database, etc.

## 17.4 Components and Interfaces

Components may both provide and require interfaces. An interface is a collection of operations that are used to specify a service of a class or a component. Most of the component based operating system facilities, such as COM, DCOM, COM+, CORBA, and EJB (Enterprise Java Beans) use interfaces as glues to bind components together. The relationship between an interface and its associated component can be specified in one of the following two ways:

❖ The component that realizes the interface is connected to the interface using an elided realization relationship (using the lollipop notation).

❖ In this case, the interface is rendered in its expanded form where all its operations are revealed.

Any other component that wants to access the services of the component is modeled as connection to the interface using a dependency relationship. An interface associated with a component can be of the following two types:

**export interface:** It is an interface that a component realizes. This is an interface that the component provides as a service to other components. A component may provide many export interfaces.

**Import interface:** It is the interface any other component uses. This is the interface that a component confirms to and so build on. A component may confirm to many import interfaces.

**Note:** A component may both import and export interfaces. A given interface may be exported by one component and imported by another.

**Examples:**

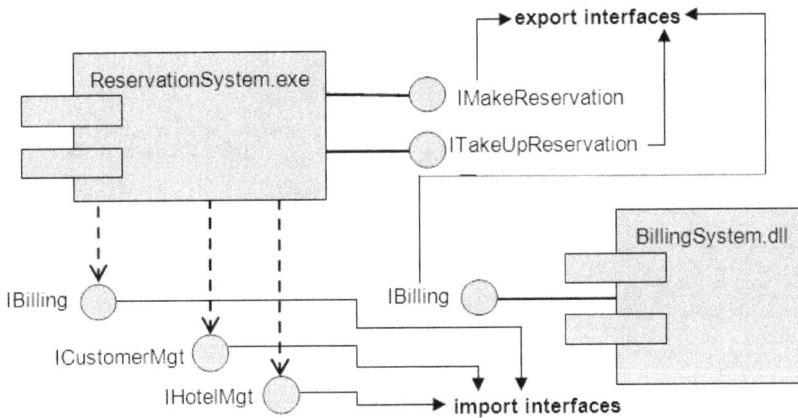

**Fig.17.4** Components and Interfaces

**Interface Specification in elided Form:**

**Note:** Interfaces span across logical and physical boundaries. The same interface that is realized and implemented by a component can be realized by an another class.

The purposes of an interface in a component specification can be summarized as follows:

❖ An interface provides services to other components.
❖ An interface request services from other components.
❖ An interface is a named collection of one or more methods, and zero or more attributes.
❖ An interface may contain synchronous and/or asynchronous operations.
❖ Interfaces bridge the components when they are assembled.
❖ An interface fully isolates a component's internals from its environment.

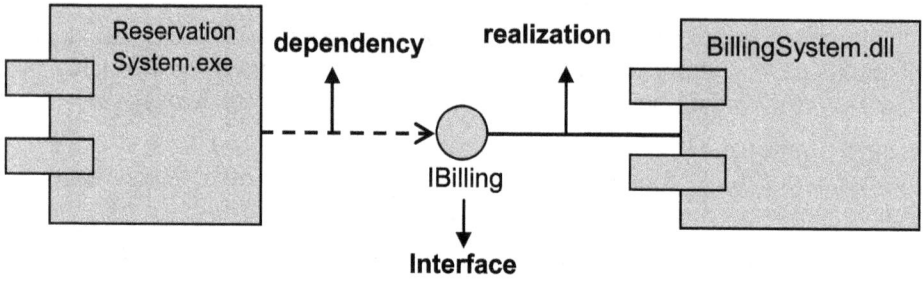

**Interface Specification in expanded Form:**

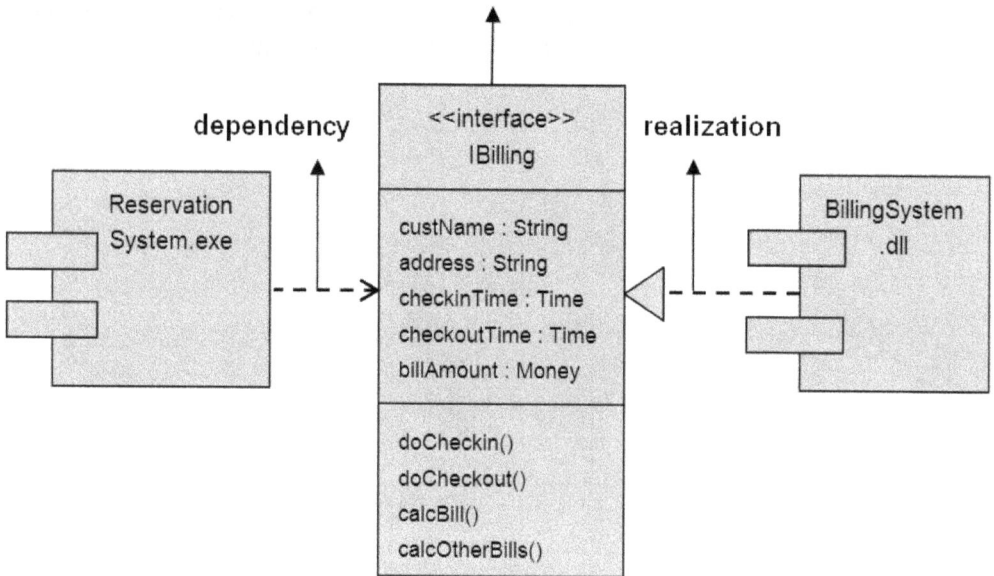

**Fig.17.5** Interface Specifications

## 17.5 Component Intent

The primary purpose of any component based system is to build the system (software intensive) by assembling replaceable parts (components). You can build a system by connecting components through their interfaces. You can evolve the system by adding new components or replacing older ones without rebuilding the system.

Typically, a component can be defined as a physical and replaceable part of a system that confirms to and provides the realization of a set of interfaces. You can attribute the following four properties to any component definition.

**First:** A component is a physical thing that exists in the real world, that is in the world of bits. It cannot exist in the world of concepts.

**Second:** A component is replaceable. It is possible to replace a component with another component that confirms to the same interfaces, in a similar fashion of replacing a car tier with a different one. These insertions and replacements of components in a runtime system is transparent to the component user.

**Third:** A component is a part of a system, meaning it rarely stands alone. Generally, in a system, a given component collaborates with other components, which form the physical architecture of the system. A component can be reused across many systems. So, a component represents a fundamental building block using which any software intensive system can be built.

**Note**: A subsystem may be a component at a higher level. Similarly, a system itself becomes a component for a bigger and higher level system.

**Fourth:** A component may confirm to a set of interfaces. Similarly, a component may realize a set of interfaces.

## 17.6 Types of Components

There are three distinguishable kinds of components in the UML, they are as follows:

**Deployment Components:** These components form the executable system. They can be as follows:

❖ Dynamic Libraries (with the extension.dll).
❖ Executables (with the extension .exe).

**Note**: The definition of a component in the UML is broad enough to include classic object models, such as COM, DCOM, COM+, CORBA, and EJB (Enterprise Java Beans). A component definition in the UML will also involve dynamic web pages, database tables, and other executables.

**Work Product Components:** These components are not part of the executable system, but are the products of development of an executable system. These components can be source code files, document files, and data files from which the deployment components are created.

**Execution Components:** These are the components that are created as a result of an executing system. They can be as follows:-

❖ .exe files, developed for carrying certain tasks.
❖ Components such as COM+ object which is an instance of a DLL component.

All executable and standard library files form executable components of a system implementation.

## 17.7 Organizing Components

As you go on modeling the system by identifying components, you find that some of the components tend to be conceptually and semantically related. You can organize components in the following ways and means:

* ❖ You can organize components by grouping similar components in packages.
* ❖ You can organize components by gluing them through export and import interfaces.
* ❖ You can also organize components by using relationships among them such as, dependency, generalization, association, and realization.

## 17.8 Standard Elements

You can apply all kinds of UML's extensibility mechanisms to model components. For example, they are as follows:

* ❖ You can use tagged values to specify additional component properties. These properties can be version number, author name, submitted date etc. of a developed component.
* ❖ You use stereotypes to extend the definition of components. A new and a non standard component such as operating system specific one can be modeled by using stereotypes.

The UML supports five standard stereotypes that are applicable to components.

**Table 17.1** Stereotypes

| S.No. | Stereotype Name | Explanation |
|---|---|---|
| 1. | executable | Specifies a component that may be deployed and executed on a node. |
| 2. | library | Specifies a static or dynamic object library. |
| 3. | table | Specifies a component that represents a database table. |
| 4. | file | Specifies a component that represents a document containing source code or data. |
| 5. | document | Specifies a component that represents a document. |

## 17.9 Modeling Executables and Libraries

The major purpose of using components is to model deployment components that make up implementation of your system. If your system consists a single executable, you do not require component modeling. On the other hand, if your system is composed of several executables and several libraries, you need to do component modeling to better understand the system. During your system development, as your system evolves, your component modeling helps in version control and configuration management of various parts that form your system.

The component models you build, depends on how you are physically implementing your system. The way you physically implement your system depends on the following technical considerations:

- ❖ Your choice of component-based operating system facilities.
- ❖ Your configuration management issues.
- ❖ Reusability of your components.

**The steps followed to model executables and libraries:**

- ❖ Initially, partition your physical system into parts it contains. Then consider the impact of technical, reusability, and configuration management issues in the system.
- ❖ Identify executables and libraries that form your system. Model these executables and libraries as components. If you find a new type of component, which cannot be modeled by using available standard elements, model them by using appropriate stereotypes.
- ❖ If your emphasis is on managing seams in your system, model the required interfaces. Some of these interfaces are realized by some components and some other interfaces are used by some other components.
- ❖ Model the relationships among these executables, libraries, and interfaces. This model expresses the intent of your system. Dependency relationships among these components indicate the impact of changes.

**Example:** Here we discuss a set of components and their relationships drawn from Sales Order Processing System. The executable component is processSalesOrder.exe and shipment.exe and there are several standard library components such as customer.dll, salesOrder.dll, items.dll, warehouseItems.dll, invoicePayment.dll, closeOrder.dll etc. The following diagram give you the details of modeling executables and their related libraries.

**Explanation**: The below diagram describes the executables and libraries that form part of a Sales Order Processing System. The executable component processSalesOrder.exe is used to process the customer raised sales order against the items he has ordered for. The salesOrder.dll library component verifies the availability of items by using customer.dll and items.dll library components. The items listed in the sales order are verified against their physical availability in the warehouse by using warehouseItems.dll library component. Once there is the availability of Items, then shipment of these items is to deliver to the customer is carried out by using the executable component shipment.exe. After shipment, the customer pays for the delivery of items by means of invoicePayment.dll library component. Once the payment is over, then the sales order is closed by invoking closeOrder.dll library component.

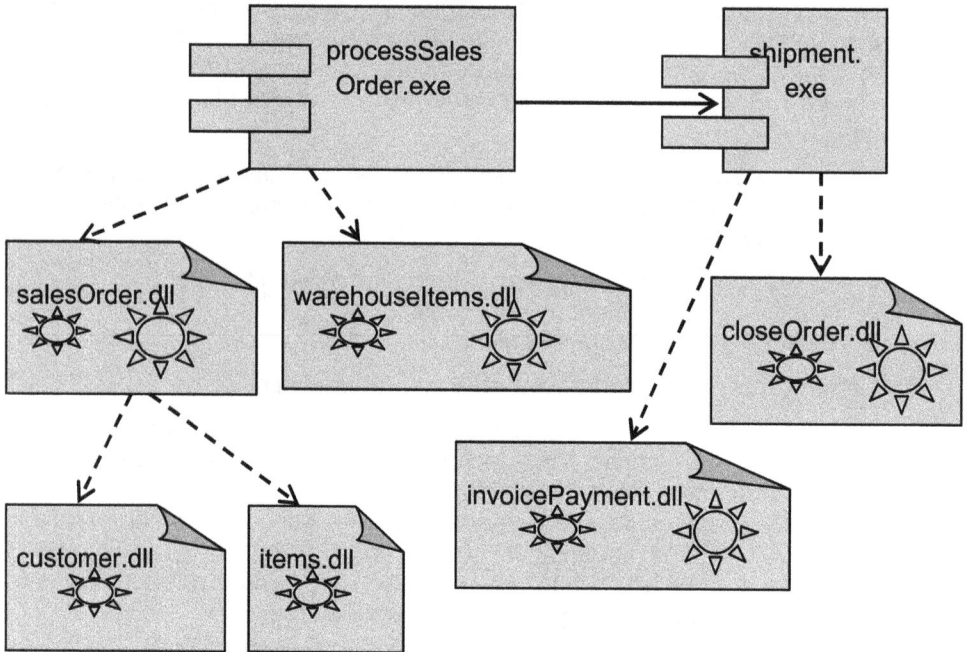

**Fig.17.6** Modeling Executables and Libraries

**Note:** You show dependency between two components, if one component imports interfaces exported by another component.

As your model grows to bigger in size, you may find certain components tend to cluster to form groups. These clustered components are conceptually and semantically related. These clusters of components can be modeled using packages.

If your system can be a quite huge distributed system with physical architecture spreading across several computers which are geographically distributed at different physical locations. If you have to develop component models for such kind of systems, you need to understand the component distribution across various nodes. It means that you need to collect information about the physical placement of components over the nodes.

## 17.10  Modeling Tables, Files and Documents

Apart from executables and libraries, there are other  deployment components which are critical for the physical deployment of your system. They are, data files, help documents, scripts, log files, initialization files, and installation/ removal files. You can model these artifacts by using components in the UML.

**Steps Required to Model Tables, Files and Documents:**

❖ Identify other things    of your system that are not executables and libraries, but are part of the physical implementation of your system.

❖ The things that are identified above can be modeled as components in the UML. If the things are new and cannot be represented by using standard definitions for components, use appropriate stereotypes to represent them.

❖ Model the relationships among these components and other components, such as executables, libraries, and interfaces in your system. You can identify the impact of change on components which are related by dependency relationship.

**Example:**

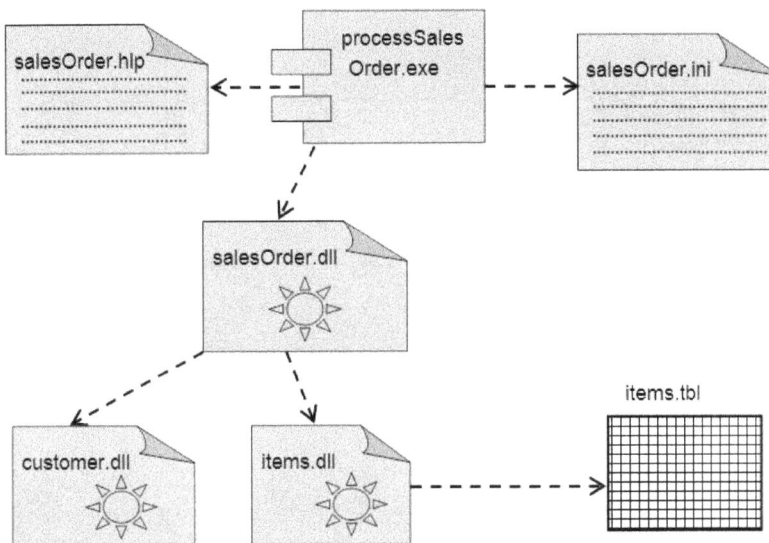

**Fig.17.7**   Modeling Tables, Files, and Documents

**Explanation**: In the above diagram, the component salesOrder.ini represents initialization file, the component salesOrder.hlp represents a help document, the component processSalesOrder.exe represents an executable, and all other components with dll extension represent libraries and the component items.tbl represents a data base table that contain data about various items that can be sold by a sales organization to its customers.

## 17.11 Modeling an API

If you are building a system by assembling components, you need APIs (Application Programming Interfaces) to glue these components together. APIs are programmatic seams which are modeled using interfaces and components. An API is essentially an interface that is realized by one or more components.

**The Steps followed while Modeling an API:**

❖ Establish the programmatic seams across components of your system. Model each seam as an interface and collect the attributes and operations that form this edge.

❖ Based on the given context of the system, identify only those properties of the interface to be exposed. Hide all other properties. The hidden properties are specified in the interface for further reference as needed.

❖ Model the realization of each API to the extent of showing the configuration of a specific implementation of your system.

**Example**: The following figure exposes the APIs for the student executable component. There are four interfaces that form the API of the executable as shown.

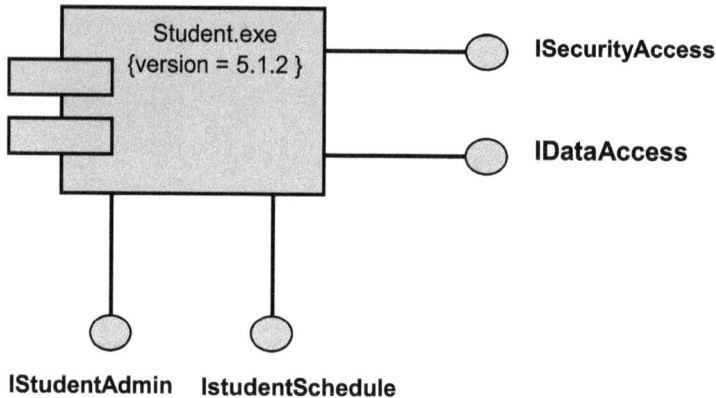

**Fig.17.8**  Modeling an API

## 17.12  Modeling Source Code

You can use components to model the configuration of your source code files which are used to generate components that implement your system. Source code components represent the work product components of your system development process. Modeling the source components graphically is useful for knowing the compilation dependencies among them to formulate your system implementation. Mostly, source code components are used to store the details of your classes, interfaces, collaborations, and other logical elements. By using tools you can transform these components into physical or binary components.

**Steps Required to Model Source Code:**

❖ Identify all the files that are used to store the details of logical elements of your system. Model these files as components in the UML. Establish dependency relationships among the components based on their compilation dependencies.

❖ If you are willing to use these models for configuration management and version control, use tagged values to specify additional information such as version number, author name, and check in/ check out information for each file.

❖ Use your development tools to manage the relationships among these files. Apply the UML only to visualize and document these relationships.

**Example**: The following diagram models the source code components. There is source code file named calcMonthlyPay.cpp, which is used to calculate monthly payment for an employee given monthly inputs. There is a header file named monthlyInputs.h contains all monthly inputs for an employee in a month. There is another header file named numbersToFigures.h which converts salary data into textual information. The header file named taxDetails.h include all tax information. The header file named attendanceReg.h contain information about employee's monthly attendance. These relationships are modeled as below:

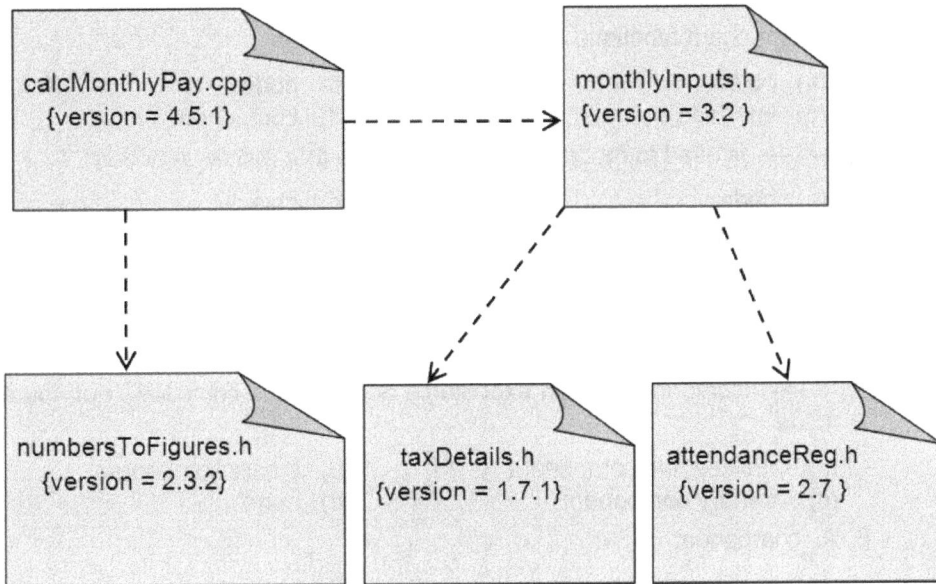

**Fig.17.9**   Modeling Source Code

**Note:** As your model grows bigger, you find many source code files tend to form clusters that are conceptually and semantically related. These groups of source code files are placed in separate directories for better identification. These clusters of source code files are modeled by using packages in the UML.

## Essay Type Questions

1. Write short notes on components versus classes.

2. Explain in brief components and interfaces.

3. Explain modeling executables and libraries with the steps followed.

4. Write brief notes on the following:-
   (a) Modeling tables, files, and documents.
   (b) Modeling an API
   (c) Modeling source code.

## Objective Type Questions

1. A physical and replaceable part of a software intensive system is
   (a) object                          (b) class
   (c) component                       (d) node

2. A component functions can be accessed through
   (a) object                          (b) node
   (c) interface                       (d) component

3. ---------- is used to model the physical things that reside on nodes
   (a) node                            (b) object
   (c) component                       (d) package

4. A component is graphically rendered as
   (a) A rectangle with tabs           (b) cube
   (c) A rectangle with compartments   (d) dotted ellipse

5. ---------- component is an executable one which is compiled , not source code
   (a) replaceable component           (b) binary component
   (c) ternary component               (d) none

6. A component is
   (a) a code module
   (b) a physical analog of a set of related classes
   (c) both a & b
   (d) none

7. Similarities between Classes and Components
   (a) Both of them may realize a set of interfaces.
   (b) Both of them may have instances
   (c) Both of them may participate in interactions
   (d) All the above

8. The following specifies the difference between components and classes

    (a)  Classes represent logical things, where as components represent physical things of a system
    (b)  Components represent the physical analogs of otherwise logical elements
    (c)  In classes attributes & operations are accessed directly, where as we need interfaces to access a component.
    (d)  All the above

9. An export interface in components is

    (a)  It is an interface that a component realizes
    (b)  This is an interface that the component provides as a service to other components
    (c)  both a & b
    (d)  none

10. An import interface in components is

    (a)  It is the interface any other component uses
    (b)  This is the interface that a component confirms to and so build on
    (c)  None
    (d)  both a & b

11. Interface specification can be in

    (a)  elided form                    (b)  expanded form
    (c)  both a & b                      (d)  none

12. ---------- bridge the components when they are assembled.

    (a)  classes                        (b)  objects
    (c)  nodes                          (d)  interfaces

13. These are the properties of the component

    (a)  A component is a physical thing that exists in the real world
    (b)  A component is a part of the system and is replaceable
    (c)  both a & b
    (d)  none

14. This is not a type of component in UML

    (a)  deployment components          (b)  execution components

    (c)  work product components        (d)  real time components

15. The number of standard stereotypes that are applicable to components

    (a)  4                              (b)  3
    (c)  5                              (d)  8

16. The stereotype that specifies a component that may be deployed and executed on a node
    (a) library      (b) table
    (c) executable      (d) file

17. The stereotype that specifies a component that represents a database table
    (a) library      (b) table
    (c) executable      (d) file

18. The stereotype that specifies a component that represents a document containing source code or data.
    (a) library      (b) table
    (c) executable      (d) file

19. If one component imports interfaces exported by another component. Then they have the relationship named.
    (a) generalization      (b) realization
    (c) dependency      (d) All the above

20. The steps followed while Modeling an API
    (a) Establish the programmatic seams across components of your system
    (b) Based on the given context of the system, identify only those properties of the interface to be exposed
    (c) both a & b
    (d) none

## Answers

1. (c)   2. (c)   3. (c)   4. (a)   5. (b)   6. (c)
7. (d)   8. (d)   9. (c)   10. (d)   11. (c)   12. (d)
13. (c)   14. (d)   15. (c)   16. (c)   17. (b)   18. (d)
19. (c)   20. (c)

# Architectural Modeling Deployment

Nodes, just like components live in the real world and are important building blocks for modeling physical aspects of a system. A node is a physical element that exists at run time and represents a computational resource having some memory and some processing capability. Nodes can be personal computers, work stations, networks, network nodes, mainframes, sensors, printing devices, PDA (Personal Digital Assistances) or servers.

Nodes are used to model the physical layout or the hardware topology of a system. This hardware topology describes the configuration of runtime processing nodes and the artifacts that are deployed on them. It is a platform on which your system is installed and executes. A node is typically a processor or a device on which components of your system can be deployed. Nodes can contain other nodes or software artifacts (software components).

Any software intensive system encompasses both software and hardware. The software components that are deployed on nodes form system's software architecture. The nodes that are connected, form system's hardware architecture. When you are modeling the physical architecture of a software intensive system, you need to consider both its physical and logical aspects. The logical aspects include the

**LEARNING OBJECTIVES**

*After studying the chapter, the students familiarize themselves with the following concepts:*

- Nodes andComponents
- Organizing nodes
- Modeling processors and Devices
- Modeling the Distribution of Components

things such as classes, interfaces, collaborations, interactions, and state machines. The physical aspects include components which are physical analogs of logical things and nodes which are the hardware on which these components are deployed and execute. A node is graphically rendered as a cube associated with a name.

**Example**:

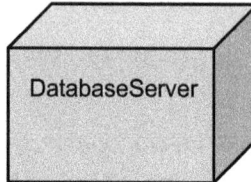

**Fig.18.1**   A Node named Database Server

**Note:** The UML though intended for modeling software intensive systems, it can be applied even for modeling hardware systems. The UML is sufficiently expressive for modeling the topologies of various types of systems such as stand alone, embedded, client/server, and distributed systems.

## 18.1  Node Names

Every node must have a name to distinguish it from other nodes. The name can be a simple name or a path name. An extended node is indicated with a path name where the name of the node is prefixed with the name of the package in which the node lives. A node typically contains its name, however, you can specify additional information using tagged values. You can use additional compartments to mention additional details such as the components deployed on that node.

**Examples:**

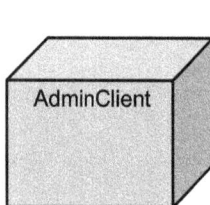

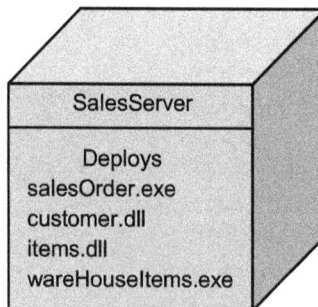

**Simple Names:**                                              **Extended Node Name:**

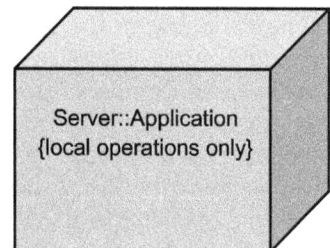

**Fig.18.2** Simple and Extended Nodes

**Explanation**: In the above diagram, AdminClient is a node which represents a personal computer or a workstation. The SalesServer node represents Server system to carry operations in a sales department. This node deploys executable components such as salesOrder.exe, wareHouseItems.exe, customer.dll, and items.dll. The node named Application is part of a package named Server, so, the node name is prefixed with package name. This node is used only for local operations as specified by using tagged values in the node specification.

**Note:** In practice, node names are short nouns or noun phrases drawn from the vocabulary of implementation.

## 18.2  Nodes and Components

In many ways, nodes are very much similar to components. The following section specifies the similarities between them.

**Node and Component Similarities:**

❖ Both of them have names.
❖ Both of them may participate in dependency, generalization, and association relationships.
❖ Both of them can be nested.
❖ Both of them may have instances.
❖ Both of them may participate in interactions.

Apart from the above similarities, they do have some significant differences.

**Node and Component Differences:**

❖ Components directly participate in system execution. Nodes are the computational things that execute components deployed on them.

❖ Components are physical representations of logical elements such as classes and collaborations. However nodes are physical things that represent the deployment of components.

You can conclude the following based on the above mentioned differences.

The **first** difference infers the understanding that nodes execute components and components are deployed on nodes and are executed by nodes.

The **second** difference concludes a relationship among classes, components, and nodes. A component is a physical analog of logical elements such as classes and collaborations. A node is a physical location where components are deployed. You can implement a class by using one or more components. A component may be deployed on one or more nodes. The relationship between a node and the components that are deployed on it can be expressed graphically in the following ways:

❖ By using a dependency relationship between a node and its components.

❖ By keeping them in a separate compartment as part of the node's specification.

**Example**

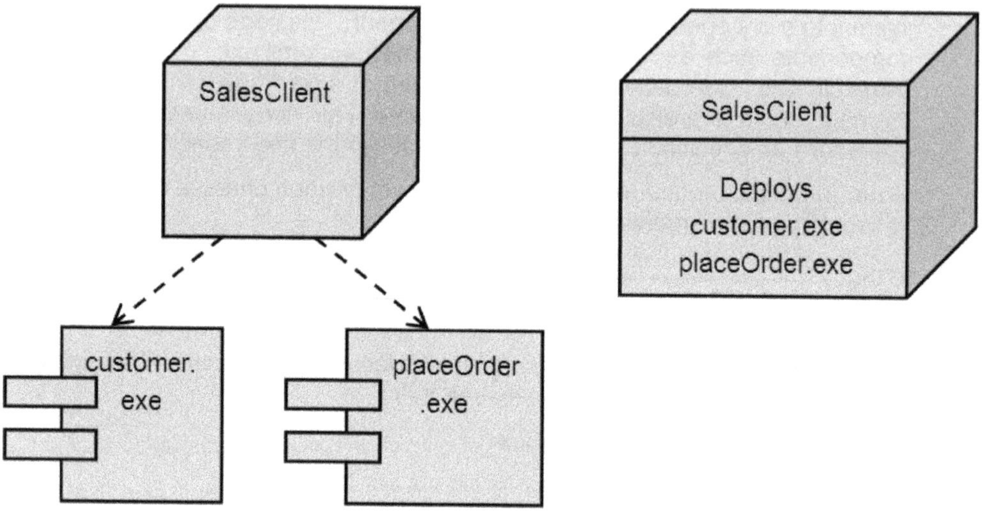

**Fig.18.3** Nodes and Components

**Explanation:** In the above diagram node and components deployed on it are shown. In the first case, the executable components such as customer.exe and placeOrder.exe which are deployed on the node named SalesClient are indicated with dependency relationships. In the second case, the components are placed on the node specification in a separate compartment as shown.

**Note**: You can specify attributes and operations for a node. For example, you can specify attributes like **processSpeed**, **memory**, and operations like **turnOn, turnOff**, and **suspend**.

The deployment of components over nodes show how different architectural elements are distributed, deployed and connected. The connectors (links) between nodes or node instances represent network connections with specific protocols. The purposes of nodes in deployment can be summarized as follows:

* ❖ Nodes are used to model the physical/hardware aspects of a system.
* ❖ A node is typically a computational resource.
* ❖ Nodes are used to model the hardware topology of a system.
* ❖ Nodes can be tailored to any specific kind of devices using stereotypes.
* ❖ Nodes can be parts of packages.
* ❖ Nodes execute components.

You can graphically represent the deployed components on a node by placing the components over a node.

Example:

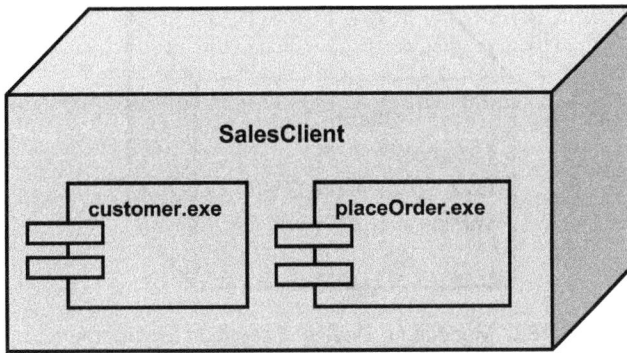

**Fig.18.4** Components Deployed over Nodes

There are two types of nodes such as device nodes and execution environments.

❖ A device represents a hardware part. It is a physical resource that acts as an interface to the real world upon which UML artifacts (components) may be deployed for execution. Devices can be complex, meaning a device may consists of other devices.

❖ An execution environment represents software containers such as JVM (Java Virtual Machine), EJB (Enterprise Java Beans) containers, application servers, portal servers etc. It is a node which offers an execution environment for the execution of components that are deployed on it.

Execution environments can be nested, meaning you can have execution environments embedded inside another execution environment. Nodes can be connected by means of communication links to establish network structured distributed systems. A communication path is an association between two deployment targets by means of which you can exchange signals and messages.

You can model devices in the UML in several different ways, such as:

❖ Name a device using the type and make, for instance **IBM RS6000, HP 9000**.
❖ Name a device using its intended function, for instance **Database Server, High Speed Switch**.
❖ Name a device using the operating system deployed on it, for instance **Linux Server, Solaris Server**.

Use tagged values to specify device characteristics or execution environment, for instance:

**Example**:

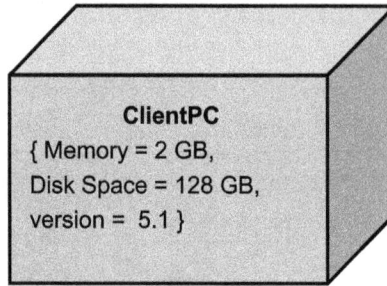

**Fig.18.5** Modeling a Device/ Execution Environment

## 18.3 Organizing Nodes

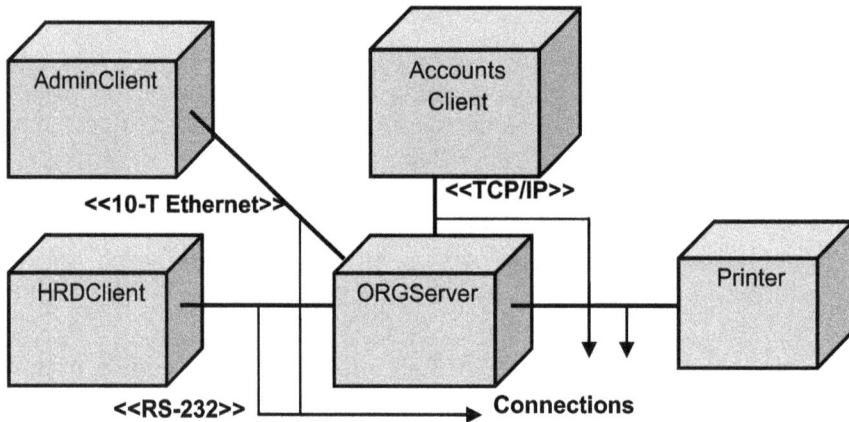

**Fig.18.6** Modeling Connections

Nodes that constitute the physical architecture of your system can be organized as follows:

❖ You can group them in packages based on conceptual and semantic similarities.
❖ You can organize them by using relationships such as dependency, generalization, and association among them.

The most general kind of relationship you use among nodes is an association. The association among nodes represents a physical connection among nodes, such as Ethernet connection, TCP/IP connection, a serial line, or a shared bus. You can also use associations to model indirect connections, such as a satellite link between distant processors.

**Example**:

While you are modeling associations among nodes, you can include information about roles, multiplicity, and constraints as you do with classes. You can stereotype these associations among nodes to model new kinds of connections as shown above, such as <<RS-232>> serial connection.

## 18.4 Modeling Processors and Devices

The major applicability of nodes is to model the processors and devices that form the hardware topology of systems like, a stand-alone, embedded, client/server, or distributed system. All extensibility mechanisms supported by the UML are applicable to nodes. You can use tagged values to specify additional information relating to the node under consideration. You can apply stereotypes to model new and specific kinds of processors and devices. A processor is a node that possesses processing capability, it means that it can execute a component deployed on it. Most often, a device may not have processing capability, but acts an interface to the real world.

**Example:**

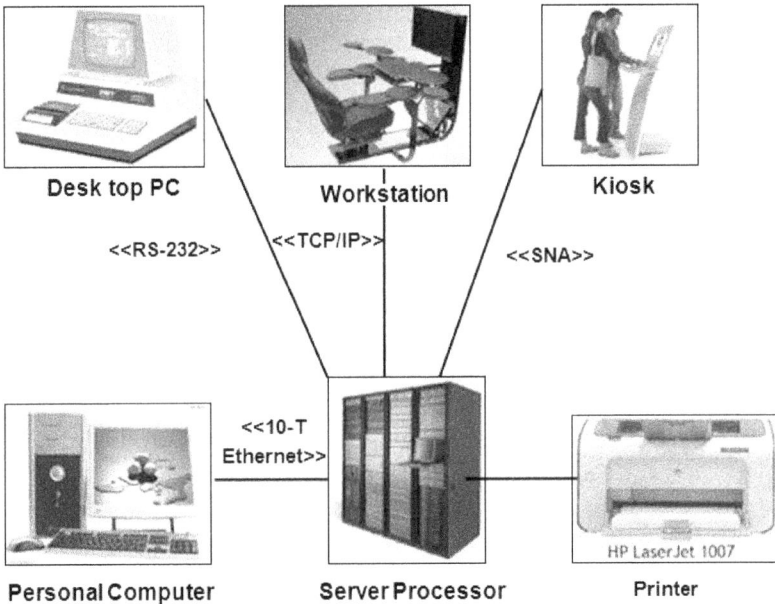

**Fig.18.7** Processors and Devices

### Steps in Modeling Processors and Devices:

❖ Look into your deployment view of your system. Identify the all computational elements that form parts of your physical system. Model each of these computational elements as nodes of the system.

❖ From the above mentioned step, the elements identified can be modeled as standard stereotypes if they represent commonly used processors and devices. If these computational elements are not of standard type, then specify an appropriate stereotype with an icon for each.

❖ Once the node is identified in the model, identify what attributes and operations that might belong to the node.

## 18.5 Modeling the Distribution of Components

When you model the topology of a system, it gives an idea of how the components are physically distributed across the nodes that constitute the physical architecture of a system.

### Steps in Modeling the distribution of Components:

❖ Identify the components that your system may contain. For each component, identify the node on which it has to be deployed. Allocate these components on to a relevant node.

❖ Identify the duplicate locations where components reside. It is common in the system, where the same kind of component may reside on multiple nodes simultaneously.

❖ Represent graphically the allocation of components to various nodes. You may adopt three ways of specifying these allocations.

 ♦ Do not make visible these allocations. It is better, if you keep information about allocations in node's specification as part of the back plane of your model.

 ♦ Relationships to connect each node with the components it deploys.

 ♦ Specify all the components deployed on a node in a separate compartment of the node.

**Explanation:** The below diagram depicts the allocation of components across nodes based on the third approach as discussed above. Here, the location of various executable components are specified. This diagram is an object diagram specifying instances of nodes and their inter relationships. In this case, the Printer and AdminClient instances are anonymous and other two instances are named such as **a** for AccountClient and **o** for ORGServer (Organization Server). Each node in this figure is rendered with an additional compartment showing the components it deploys. The ORGServer object is also rendered with attributes such as processorSpeed and memory and with operations such as startUp() and shutDown().

**Note:** The distribution of components across nodes need not be static. During system execution, there can be dynamic migration of components from node to node. In the UML, you have all facilities to model the migration of components across nodes. The migration of components may happen in systems involving clustered servers and replicated databases.

**Example:**

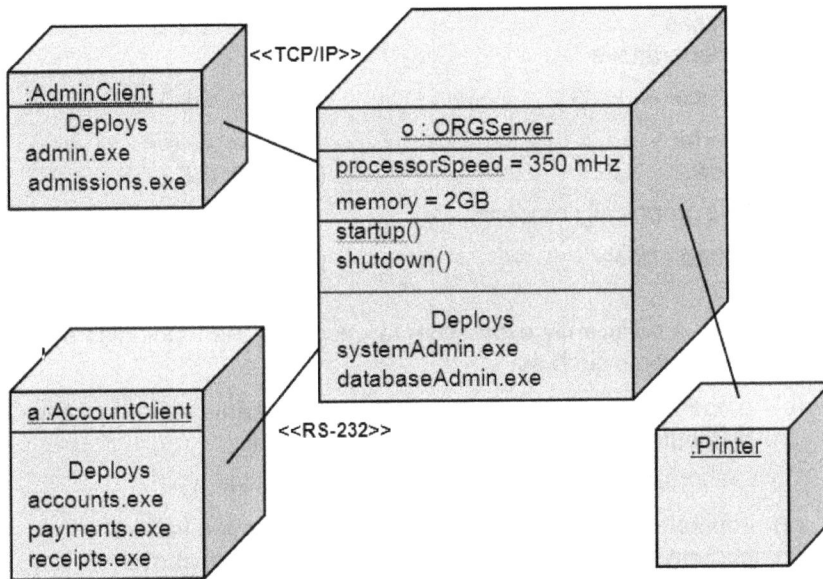

**Fig.18.8** Modeling the Distribution of Components

## Essay Type Questions

1. Compare and contrast Nodes and Components.
2. Explain the below briefly:

   (a) Distribution of components.

   (b) Modeling processors and Devices.

## Objective Type Questions

1. ---------------- is a physical element that exists at run time and represents a computational resource having some memory and some processing capability

   (a) component                 (b) node

   (c) class                     (d) object

2. The thing that models the physical layout or the hardware topology of a system
   (a) node                          (b) component
   (c) interface                     (d) package

3. The logical aspects of a system include the things such as
   (a) classes                       (b) interfaces
   (c) collaborations                (d) All

4. The physical aspects of a system include the things such as
   (a) interface                     (b) component
   (c) node                          (d) both b & c

5. A node is graphically rendered as
   (a) dotted ellipse                (b) rectangle
   (c) cube                          (d) solid ellipse

6. The UML is sufficiently expressive for modeling the topologies of various types of systems such as
   (a) embedded systems             (b) client /server systems
   (c) distributed systems          (d) All

7. The components deployed on node can be specified as
   (a) separate compartment          (b) tagged values
   (c) stereotypes                   (d) All the above

8. Similarities between nodes and components include
   (a) they can participate in interactions
   (b) they can have instances
   (c) both a & b
   (d) nodes execute the components

9. The relationship between a node and the components that are deployed on it can be expressed graphically in
   (a) By using a dependency relationship between a node and its components
   (b) By keeping them in a separate compartment as part of the node's specification
   (c) both a & b
   (d) None

10. .--------------- is the attribute of a node
   (a) processSpeed                  (b) turnOn
   (c) turnoff                       (d) All the above

11. A node contain operations such as          (d)
   (a) turnOn                        (b) turnoff
   (c) suspend                       (d) All the above

12. The purposes of nodes in deployment can be specified as

    (a)  A node is typically a computational resource
    (b)  Nodes execute components

    (c)  Nodes are used to model the hardware topology of a system
    (d)  All the above

## Answers

| 1. (b) | 2. (b) | 3. (d) | 4. (d) | 5. (c) | 6. (d) |
|--------|--------|--------|--------|--------|--------|
| 7. (d) | 8. (c) | 9. (c) | 10. (a) | 11. (d) | 12. (d) |

> **CHAPTER 19**

# Architectural Modeling Component Diagrams

Component diagrams are the diagrams mainly applied for modeling the physical aspects of object-oriented systems. A component diagram shows the organization and relationships mostly dependencies among a set of components. Component diagrams are helpful in modeling the static implementation view of a system. This involves modeling components that reside on nodes. Component diagrams are similar to class diagrams but focuses on a system's components. Component diagrams not only applicable to model component-based systems, but also useful for constructing executable systems, by means of forward and reverse engineering.

As we are aware that new systems can be built by assembling existing components. Component diagrams typically represent these assemblies. Component diagrams illustrate the pieces of software and embedded controllers etc. that make up a system. A component diagram is at a higher level of abstraction than a class diagram. So, component diagrams are used to visualize the organization and relationships among components in a system. These diagrams are also used to make executable systems. You use the component diagrams to visualize the static aspects of the physical components and their relationships and to specify their details for system construction.

**Explanation**: The Fig.19.1 depicts a component diagram derived from a University Registration System. It has two

**LEARNING OBJECTIVES**

*After studying the chapter, the students familiarize themselves with the following concepts:*

♦ Concepts, Contents, and Uses
♦ Modeling Source Code
♦ Modeling Executable Release
♦ Modeling a Physical Database
♦ Modeling Adaptable Systems

executable components named **billing.exe** and **register.exe**, and it has four library components named **course.dll**, **people.dll**, **student.dll**, and **professor.dll**. It has two database tables to store persistently the data about students as well professors using **student.tbl** and **professor.tbl**.

**Examples:**
**1.**

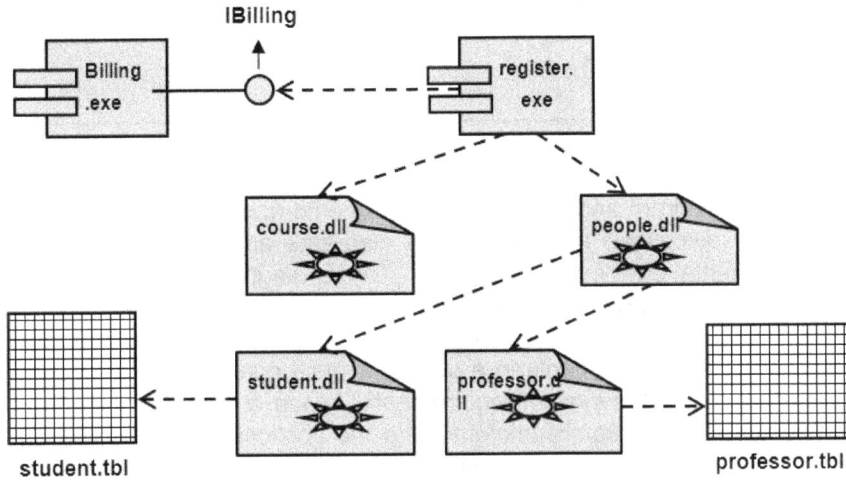

**Fig.19.1** A Component Diagram

**2.**

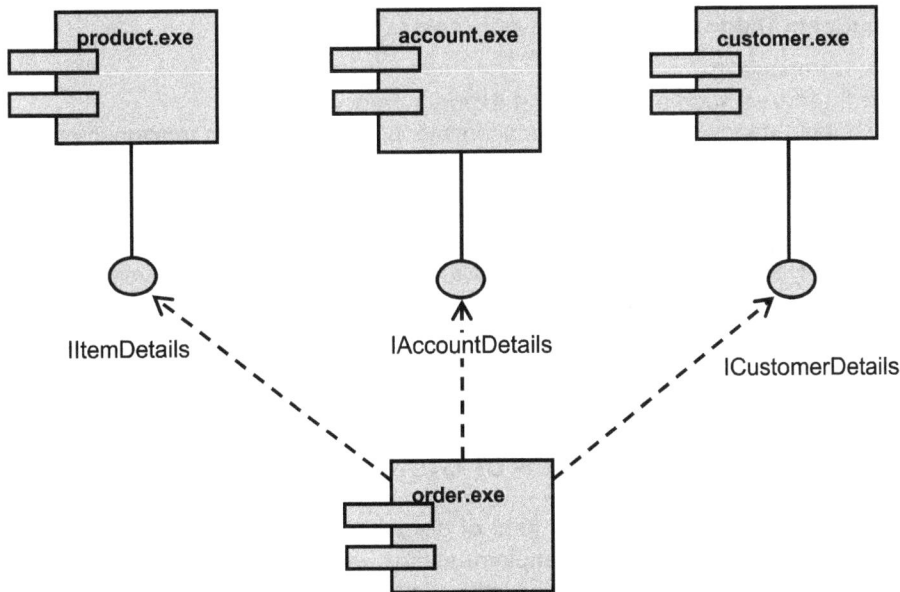

**Fig.19.2** A Component Diagram

**Explanation:** The Fig.19.2 depicts a component diagram containing four executable components. It is taken from Sales Order Processing System. It has three interfaces. IItemDetails interface is an export interface for the component product.exe and an import interface for the component order.exe. Similarly, IAccountDetails interface is an export interface for the component account.exe and an import interface for the component order.exe and the interface ICustomerDetails is an export interface for the component customer.exe and an import interface for the component order.exe. The rest of the component diagram is self explanatory.

# 19.1 Concepts and Contents

A component diagram shows a set of components and their relationships. We have already discussed that component diagrams are used to visualize the static implementation view of a system. These diagrams show the physical components of a system. We can say that component diagrams describe the organization of the components in a system. Organization can be described as the location of the components in a system. These components are organized in a way that meets the system requirements. These components are libraries, files, executables etc. Before implementing the application, these components are to be organized. This component organization is also designed separately as a part of project execution. Component diagrams are very important from implementation perspective. So the implementation team of an application should have a proper knowledge of the component details.

**Component Diagrams Commonly Contain:**

- ❖ Components.
- ❖ Interfaces such as import and export interfaces.
- ❖ Dependency, generalization, association, and realization relationships.
- ❖ Notes and Constraints.

Component diagrams my include packages or subsystems when you want to group conceptually and semantically related components. Sometimes your component diagram may contain instances. For example, when you want to visualize one instance of a family of component based systems.

**Note**: A component diagram can be considered as a special kind of class diagram that emphasizes on a system's components.

# 19.2 Common Uses of Component Diagrams

Component diagram is a special kind of diagram in UML. You use component diagrams to model the static implementation view of a system. This view primarily supports the configuration management of system's parts during the development of any software intensive system. Component diagrams may not describe the functionality of the system but it describes the components used to make those functionalities. Component diagrams can also be described as a static implementation view of a system. Static implementation represents the organization and relationships of the components at a particular moment. A single component diagram cannot represent the entire system but a collection of diagrams are used to represent the whole.

Component diagrams describe the physical artifacts of a system. These artifacts include files, executables, libraries etc. Generally, component diagrams are used during the implementation phase. But it is modeled in advance to better visualize the implementation details. When the system artifacts are ready, component diagrams gives an idea of the implementation. You cannot implement a system efficiently without component diagrams. Component diagrams are also helpful in improving system's performance and maintenance.

The following artifacts are to be identified before you draw a component diagram:

- ❖ Files used in the system.
- ❖ Libraries and other artifacts relevant to the application.
- ❖ Relationships among the artifacts.

Component diagrams are modeled after all the relevant artifacts are identified. There are four major uses of component diagrams, which are described as follows:

**To Model Source Code:** Source code files are work-product components. As components evolve, you need to modify source code files and test them to rebuild your system. Component diagrams are used to model the configuration management of these files as the system evolves.

**To Model Executable Releases:** A complete and consistent system is released to an internal or external customer. A release normally focuses on components necessary to deliver a running system. You model a release by using component diagrams which describe deployment components that constitute your system.

**To Model Physical Databases:** Component diagrams are applied to represent physical databases. A physical database is a real world realization of   a database schema relating to your system. Schemas offer API (Application Programming Interface) to the persistent information (information stored permanently for further use). If the physical database you are using is relational database, the persistent information is stored in tables. If the database is object-oriented database, the persistent information is represented as pages.

**To Model Adoptable Systems:** Systems in which components enter scene, execute and depart are called static systems. In some cases components may migrate from node to node while system is executing. Components generally migrate for the purpose of load balancing and failure recovery. You use component diagrams with some other UML facilities to model these kinds of systems.

## 19.3 Modeling Source Code

When you develop your system, you need to write code in some object-oriented programming language to implement your system. The files that contain programs in some implementation language are called source code files. When you develop software in java, your source code will be in **.java** files. If you develop your software using C++, your source code will be in **.cpp** as well as **.h** (header) files. You organize these files into larger groups as your application grows. As software development includes incremental releases of software to the user, you may have to create new versions of these source code files for each new release. So, you do configuration management of these source code components.

Your system development environment must keep track of these source code components and their relationships. This information is visible in component diagrams. These component diagrams are helpful in visualizing compilation dependencies among source code files, which are essential for building an executable system. Component diagrams helps in understanding the history of a set of source code files that are under configuration management.

### The Steps in Modeling a System's Source Code:-

❖ Apply forward or reverse engineering to identify the set of source code files. Model these source code files as components stereotyped as files indicating their relationships or inter dependencies.

❖ If the model of the source code files becomes unmanageably bigger for a larger system, use packages. Group all conceptually and semantically related components into a package.

❖ Indicate additional information about a source code component, such as its version number, its author, and the date of its last change by using tagged values. Expose this information to configuration management tools so that they automatically update this information for each new release of the software.

❖ Apply dependency relationships among source code components to model compilation dependencies among them. These dependencies help in building an executable system effectively. If possible, use automated tools to generate and manage these dependencies.

**Example:** Let us consider a part of payroll system. This system includes components to calculate monthly salary based on monthly inputs such as working days in that month and pay details and tax details for an individual. Once the monthly salary is calculated, the system generates pay slips and pay checks and prints them. This task includes source code components such as calcMonthlyPay.cpp, printMonthlyPay.cpp, monthlyInputs.h, payDetails.h, and, taxDetails.h. The inter dependencies among these source code components can be modeled as below.

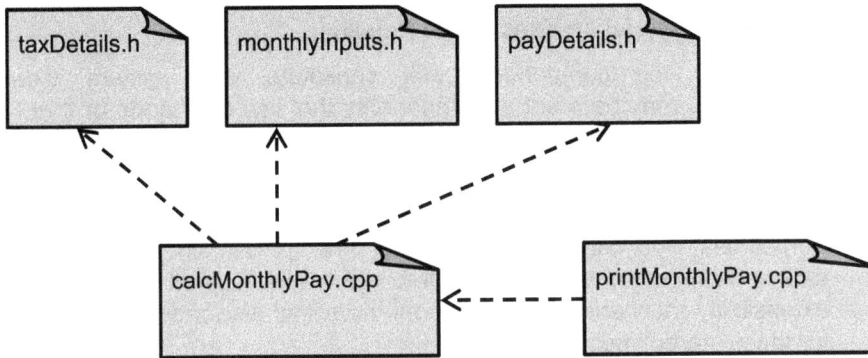

**Fig.19.3** Modeling Source Code

**Note:** Diagrams such as these can be generated by applying reverse engineering technique on the information available with configuration management tools.

## 19.4 Modeling an Executable Release

If your application is simple and monolithic, this trivial application may consist of a single executable. As there is only one component in the form a single executable file, you do not require any component diagrams. Releasing such an application is easy and strait forward.

Imagine a situation where you want to release a complex system consists of multiple number of components. Here, you need a main executable component (.exe file), with all its ancillary components, such as libraries (could be .dll files, .class, and .jar files based on your system context), databases, help files, and resource files. In case of a distributed system, you will have multiple executables with other components that spread across multiple nodes that are placed at different physical locations. All of these components may not be unique for an application. Some of these components are shareable across multiple applications. As your system evolves, you need to control the configuration of the components that constitute your system. This configuration control is an important as well as difficult task, because changes in the components of one application may affect the functioning of other applications.

Because of the above mentioned reason, component diagrams are used for configuring your deployment components and their relationships that form each release. You apply component diagrams to forward engineer a new system and to reverse engineer an existing one. Your component diagrams typically represent your system's implementation view consisting of components and their relationships. Because of this, your component diagram must address one set of components at a time.

**Steps followed to Model an Executable Release:**

❖ Identify all the components that constitute your system. These components may be a set of components that live on a node or that live across all the nodes in a system. Then, you model these components using the UML facilities.

❖ Use all standard stereotypes to represent components in an application. Sometimes, you find components that are specific and new and they cannot be modeled by standard UML definitions. Use all kinds of UML's extensibility mechanisms to represent them and also provide visual cues for these stereotypes.

❖ For each component, identify the relationships a component may have with other components in an application. These relationships expose the interfaces among components. These interfaces may be exported (realized) by some components and imported (used) by other components. You model these interfaces explicitly if you want to expose the seams in your system. If you want to build this component model at a higher level of abstraction, show only dependencies among them.

**Example**: The below diagram is a model which is a part of an   executable release of the Student Registration System for university admission.

**Explanation:** The component student.exe is an executable file for student admissions into a university. A student's security aspects are handled by a library component security.dll. Student's admission is handled by admin.dll library component. Student's course schedule is handled by schedule.dll library component. Student's information with admissions are stored in the university database. The component student.exe exports three interfaces for the purposes of carrying security check, admissions, and course schedule. It has one import interface for the purpose of interacting with the university database. The component university database contains all the persistent information pertaining to student admissions. This component has one export interface. The components admin.dll and schedule.dll have one import interface each.

The below is a component diagram, useful for configuration management during the incremental release of an application to the internal or the external user. While you are planning executable release you have to consider relevant components with their current versions. These versions or any other information can be associated with a component and can be shown in the component diagrams. So, the executable releases can be well planned based on the model of components and their relationships.

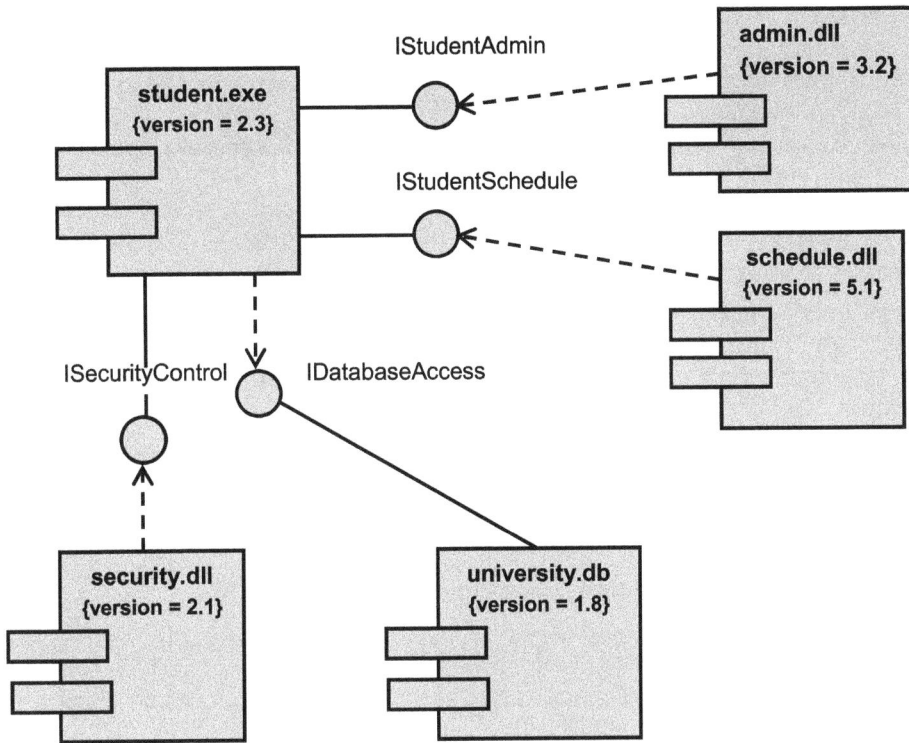

**Fig.19.4** Modeling an Executable Release

## 19.5 Modeling a Physical Database

The UML is well suited for modeling physical databases as well as logical database schemas. Generally, a logical database schema contains the persistent data (permanently stored data) and their relationships. Physically, these data is stored in a database for later retrievals and modifications. The database can be a relational database, an object-oriented database, or a hybrid (relational/object) database.

Implementing a logical database schema by an object-oriented database is simple, because not only classes but complex inheritance relationships can be implemented directly. But, mapping a logical database schema to relational database is difficult. Because, in the cases of inheritance, you need to make complex decisions about how to map classes to data tables. You apply one or more of the following strategies to implement a logical schema by relational database.

❖ Represent each class as a separate database table. This will lead to maintenance hurdles when you add new child classes or modify the existing parent classes.

❖ Make sure that all instances of any class that is participating in inheritance hierarchy has the same state. The bad impact of this approach is, you may have to store less relevant information for many instances.

❖ Represent parent and child as different and separate tables. This approach best reflects the inheritance hierarchy. But, if you want to traverse the data, it is slowed down because it requires many cross-table joins.

When you use object-oriented databases, the mapping of operations to the physical database is fairly easy and transparent. However, difficulty arises when you have to map operations to relational databases. You have certain choices to implement those operations when you are using relational database, as follows:

❖ Implement simple operations, such as create, read, update, and delete by using standard SQL or by means of ODBC calls.

❖ If the operations includes complex behavior (such as implementing business rules), implement them using triggers and stored procedures .

**The Steps followed for Modeling a Physical Database:**

❖ Identify the persistent classes in your model. These are the classes whose information is permanently stored in the database for later use and maintenance. These persistent classes represent your logical database schema.

❖ Identify a strategy of mapping these classes to database tables. If you are handling a physically distributed database, your mapping strategy will be affected based on the location on which you are placing your data.

❖ In order to describe these mappings between logical database schema to physical databases, create a component diagram. This component diagram contains stereotyped tables as its components, and their relationships.

❖ Where ever there is a chance, use automated tools to transform your logical database into a physical database.

**Example:** The following diagram shows a set of database tables drawn from a Banking System. Here, you find one database (**bank.db**, rendered as a component stereotyped as **database**) that is composed of five tables such as customer, account, loan, deposits, withdrawals.

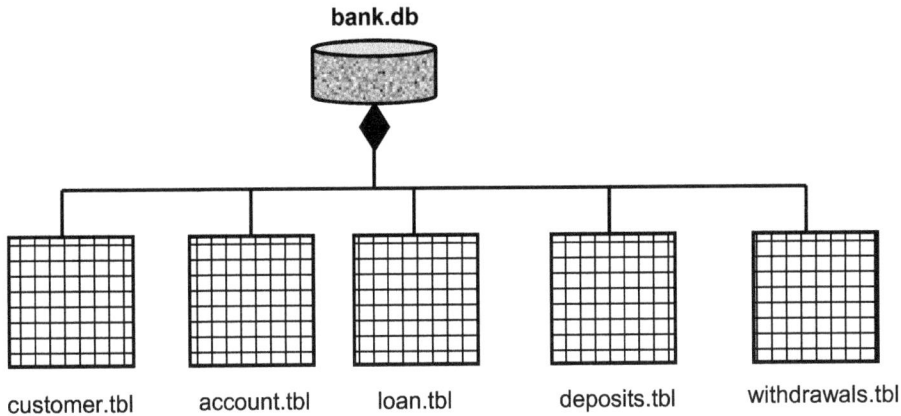

**Fig.19.5** Modeling a Physical Database

## 19.6 Modeling Adaptable Systems

Component diagrams are generally applicable to model static views of a system. It means that once the components are deployed on a node, they spend their entire life on that node. But, it may not be the same situation when you are dealing with complex and distributed systems, where you need to model dynamic views. For example, you might have a distributed system which stores multiple copies of the same database across multiple servers or nodes. This is useful when a server containing the database goes down. The system can work unstoppably. If you are modeling a globally distributed system which can work round the clock, you may encounter components that migrate from node to node to carry out certain transactions. In order to model these dynamic views, you need a combination of component diagrams, object diagrams, and interaction diagrams.

**The Steps followed to Model an Adoptable System:**

❖ Identify the components that may migrate from node to node to perform transactions. Find out the physical distribution of these components. You can specify the location of a component instance, using tagged values. Your component diagram may include component instances with their relevant physical locations.

❖ Create an interaction diagram that contains component instances. Identify the actions that cause component migrations. You can model component migrations, by drawing the same component instance more than once, but by specifying a different physical location as tagged values.

**Example:** The following diagram depicts the model of a Banking System. This is the model of the replication of the database. It shows two instances of the database component **bank.db**, which are anonymous, and both have different physical locations specified by tagged values. A note is used here to indicate which instance replicates the other.

### Forward and Reverse Engineering

Forward engineering and reverse engineering in case of component diagrams are strait forward and direct. This is because, the components are physical things and are very close to the executable system. When you forward engineer a class or a collaboration, it generates a physical component that represents the source code, libraries, or executable for that class or collaboration. Similarly, when you reverse engineer source code, libraries, or executables, it creates UML components.

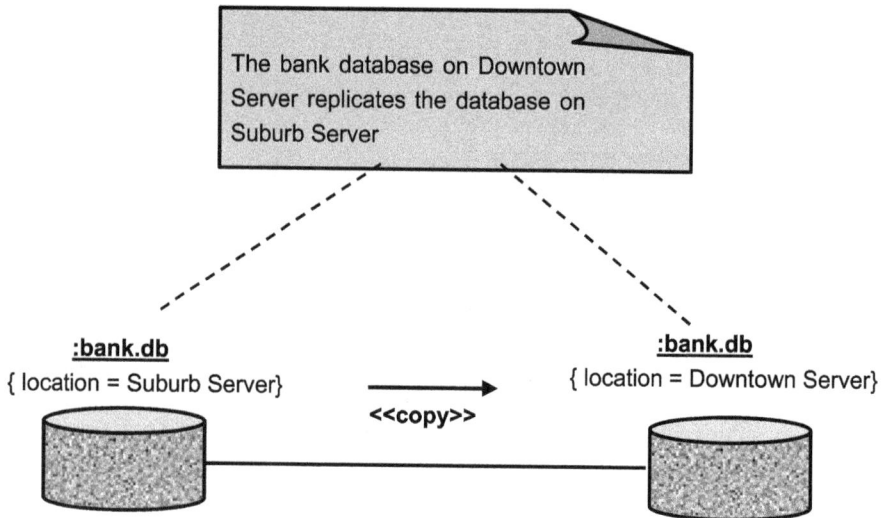

**Fig.19.6** Modeling Adaptable Systems

### The Steps followed to Forward Engineer a Component Diagram:

❖ For each component in the component diagram, identify the classes or collaborations that the component implements.
❖ Identify and choose the target for each component. This target can be a source code file (a work-product component), a binary library or an executable (a target which is part of the executable system) .
❖ Use tools to forward engineer your models.

Reverse engineering (the creation of a model from code) a component diagram may result into a loss of information. You can reverse engineer from source code back to classes without any loss of information. But, reverse engineering source code to components will uncover compilation dependencies among those files. In dealing with binary libraries, denote the library as a component and then discover its interfaces by reverse engineering. In case of handling executables, denote the executable as a component and disassemble its code.

**The Steps followed to Reverse Engineer a Component Diagram:**

❖ First identify the thing you want to reverse engineer. Source code files can be reverse engineered to components and then classes. Libraries can be reverse engineered to uncover their interfaces. Executables can be reverse engineered the least.

❖ Point your reverse engineering tools to the code and use it to generate a new model or to modify an existing model. The existing model might have been previously reverse engineered.

❖ By applying your reverse engineering tools, create a component diagram. For example, you might start with one or more components, then expand the diagram by following relationships. In order to communicate your intent better based on your context, expose or hide details of the contents of your components in the component diagram.

**Note:** Mostly the task of reverse engineering from source code happens in the context of configuration management. Each component is associated with its version by using tagged values. This way, the UML can visualize the history of a component across various releases.

## Essay Type Questions

1. Write short notes on components' concepts and contents.

2. Write short notes on common uses of component diagrams.

3. Explain briefly the below:

   (a) Modeling source code    (b) Modeling executable release.

4. Explain the following with examples:

   (a) Modeling a physical database.    (b) Modeling adaptable systems.

## Objective Type Questions

1. Component diagrams are helpful in modeling the ----------------- of a system.

   (a) static design view          (b) static process view
   (c) static implementation view  (d) static deployment view

2. ---------------- describe the organization of the components in a system

   (a) class diagram          (b) component diagram
   (c) object diagram         (d) use case diagram

3. The components include

(a) libraries                 (b) files
(c) executables            (d) All the above

4. Component diagrams commonly contain

(a) components
(b) Interfaces such as import and export interfaces
(c) both a & b
(d) none

5. Component diagrams are also helpful in

(a) improving system's performance      (b) system's maintenance
(c) None                           (d) both a & b

6. The artifacts that need to be identified before modeling a component diagram.

(a) Files used in the system
(b) Libraries and other artifacts relevant to the application
(c) Relationships among the artifacts
(d) All the above

7. The major uses of component diagrams

(a) To Model Source Code
(b) To Model Executable Releases
(c) To Model Physical Databases
(d) All the above

8. -------------------- are helpful in visualizing compilation dependencies among source code files, which are essential for building an executable system.

(a) class diagrams             (b) object diagrams
(c) component diagrams      (d) use case diagrams

9. -------------------- are used for configuring your deployment components and their relationships that form each release

(a) class diagrams             (b) object diagrams
(c) component diagrams      (d) use case diagrams

10. The data base that contain persistent data can be

(a) relational database       (b) object oriented database
(c) hybrid                   (d) All the above

11. Modeling adoptable systems include

(a) component diagrams      (b) object diagrams
(c) interaction diagrams      (d) All the above

12. Forward engineering and reverse engineering in case of component diagrams are strait forward and direct because
    (a) the components are physical things and are very close to the executable system
    (b) the components create logical databases
    (c) both a & b
    (d) none

## Answers

| | | | | | |
|---|---|---|---|---|---|
| 1. (c) | 2. (b) | 3. (d) | 4. (c) | 5. (d) | 6. (d) |
| 7. (d) | 8. (c) | 9. (c) | 10. (a) | 11. (d) | 12. (c) |

# CHAPTER 20

# Architectural Modeling Deployment Diagrams

Deployment diagrams help in modeling physical aspects of a system. Deployment diagrams represent the physical architecture of the system. They show the configuration of run time nodes and the components that live on them. They show the relationships between the software and hardware components in the system and the physical distribution of the execution.

Generally, deployment diagrams are modeled during the implementation phase of system development. They show the physical arrangement of the nodes, the artifacts that are placed on each node, and the components that the artifacts implement. Nodes are typically hardware devices such as computers, sensors, printers, and other devices that support the execution environment of a system. Deployment diagrams show connections or the communication paths between the nodes.

You apply deployment diagrams to model the static deployment view of a system. This view involves modeling hardware topology on which your system deploys and executes. Deployment diagrams are effective in modeling physical architecture of the following types of systems:

**Embedded Systems:** These systems use hardware that is controlled by external events. For example, a display that is controlled by temperature change.

**Client/Server Systems:** These systems typically differentiates between the user

**LEARNING OBJECTIVES**

*After studying the chapter, the students familiarize them-selves with the following concepts:*

- ♦ Concepts, Contents and Uses
- ♦ Modeling an Embedded System
- ♦ Modeling a Client/Server System
- ♦ Modeling a Distributed System

interface and the persistent data of the system. The required user interfaces are separately developed by using GUI (Graphical User Interface) tools, and are installed on client machines which have some processing capability. The database which is required for the system, is placed on a separate and a better processing capability machine. These machines are networked to function as a single system.

**Distributed Systems:** It is a larger system containing multiple servers which are geographically distributed at different physical locations. These servers host multiple versions of software components that form the executable environment of the system. Some of these components may even migrate from node to node to carry out transactions.

Deployment diagrams are used also for managing executable systems through forward and reverse engineering. You know that deployment diagrams focus on the configuration of the runtime processing nodes and their components. Because of this, deployment diagrams are highly effective in assessing the implications of distribution and resource allocations.

Though the UML is primarily focused to model software aspects of a system, you can use it effectively to model hardware requirements of your system. These hardware requirements are modeled by using deployment diagrams. So, your deployment diagrams specify the required hardware platform on which your software system can be deployed and can be executed.

**Note:** Deployment diagrams are different from component diagrams. A component diagram defines software components and how they are related to establish an executable system. Whereas deployment diagram defines the hardware topology of processors and devices on which your software executes.

**Example:**

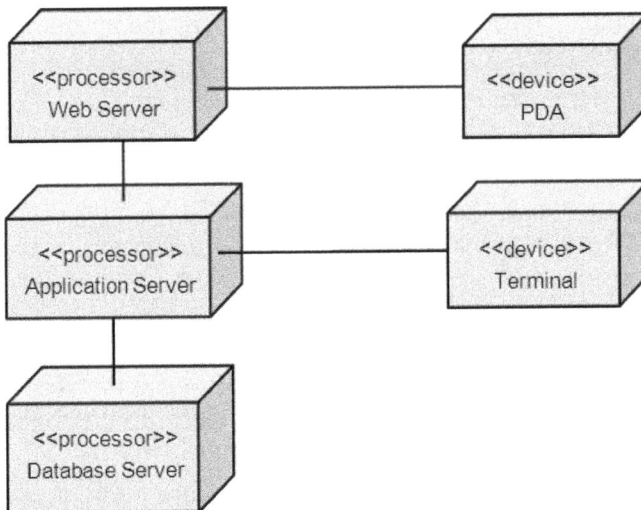

**Fig.20.1** A Deployment Diagram

## 20.1 Concepts and Contents

A deployment diagram is a diagram that shows the configuration of run time processing nodes and the components that live on them. A node in the UML is represented as a cube. A node is a physical thing that exists at run time and has some memory and some processing capability. A deployment diagram not only specifies the nodes but also specifies their relationships.

**A Deployment Diagram commonly contain:**

**Nodes:** These are model elements that represent the computational resources of a system, such as personal computers, sensors, printing devices, or servers. Nodes can be interconnected, by using communication paths.

**Node Instances:** These are model elements that represent actual occurrences of nodes.

**Components:** These are model elements that represent the physical entities in a software system. They represent physical implementation units, such as executable files, libraries, software components, documents, and databases.

**Component Instances:** These are model elements that represent actual occurrences of components.

**Devices:** These are types of nodes that represent physical computational resources in a system.

**Execution Environment:** An execution environment is a type of node that represents a particular execution platform, such as an operating system or a database management system.

**Dependency and Association Relationships:** These represent the connections among model elements, in this case, the model elements are nodes or components.

**Notes and Constraints:** These are used to specify additional information and various constraints pertaining to the model elements or the entire system.

**Note**: You can group semantically and conceptually related model elements into larger chunks, such as packages or subsystems. So, your deployment diagram may also contain packages and subsystems.

## 20.2 Common Uses of Deployment Diagrams

The major purpose of deployment diagrams is to model the static deployment view of a system. This view addresses issues, such as distribution, delivery, and installation of the parts that make up the physical system.

If you have a system that lives on one machine and uses standard devices as interfaces, you do not require any deployment diagrams for such a system.

Examples are, games on a PC. If your software interacts with devices that are not directly manageable by the host operating system, or if it physically distributes across multiple processors, then you definitely require a deployment diagram.

**The Uses of Deployment Diagrams:**

**To model embedded systems:** Embedded systems involve software that controls devices based on external events such as sensor input, object movement, and temperature changes. You can use deployment diagrams to model the devices and processors that comprise an embedded system.

**To model client/server systems:** It is a common architecture where there is a clear separation between the system's user interface (which lives on the client machine) and the system's data (which lives on the server machine). In order to model client/server architecture you need to understand how your system's software components are distributed across nodes. You can model the topology of such systems by using deployment diagrams.

**To model distributed systems:** Distributed systems are those that are widely or globally spread. They typically comprise multiple levels of servers which often host to multiple versions of software components. Sometimes components may migrate from node to node to accomplish certain transactions. As components migrate from node to node, your system's topology changes continuously. You apply deployment diagrams to visualize the system's current topology and the affect of changes on that topology as components migrate.

## 20.3 Modeling an Embedded System

When you are developing embedded systems, you need to manage the physical world in which there are moving parts, noisy signals, and non linear behavior. When you are modeling an embedded system, you should take into account its interface with the real world, unusual devices, and nodes. Deployment diagrams in an embedded system are useful to establish communication between hardware engineers and software developers. You can also use deployment diagrams make hardware/software trade-offs. Deployment diagrams specify fully your system engineering decisions.

**The Steps followed in Modeling an Embedded System:**

❖ Start with identifying the various devices and nodes that constitute your system.

❖ Apply UML's extensibility mechanisms to specify uncommon nodes. Use system specific stereotypes with appropriate icons to define unusual devices. You distinguish between processors (which contain software components) and devices (which do not directly contain software).

❖ Model the relationships among these processors and devices using a deployment diagram. Specify the relationships between the components in your system's  implementation view. Specify the relationships between the nodes in your system's deployment view.

❖ As needed, expand on any intelligent device by modeling their structure by using more detailed deployment diagram.

**Example:** The following diagram shows the hardware for a simple autonomous robot. You have one node named Pentium Motherboard stereotyped as a **processor**. There are eight devices surrounding this node each stereotyped as a **device**.

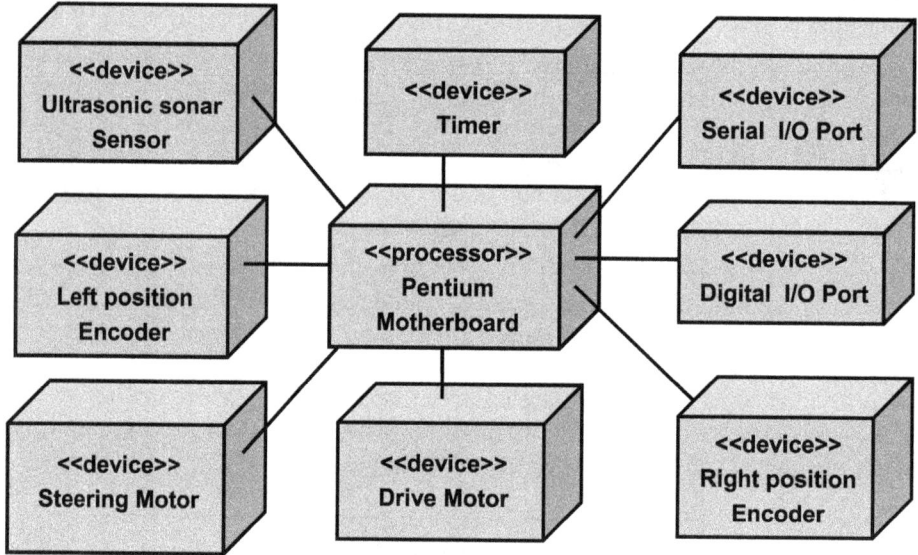

**Fig.20.2** Modeling an Embedded System

## 20.4 Modeling a Client/Server System

Client/Server system is a system where there is clear separation between the system's user interface (managed by the client) and its data (managed by the server). We need to go for these kinds of systems' architectures when you develop a system whose software no longer resides on a single machine or a processor. When you are devising physical architecture for such kinds of systems, you may have to make certain decisions such as:

❖ How do you best distribute your software components across the nodes for the efficient execution of your system.

❖ How these various components (software and hardware) communicate.

❖ How you deal with failure and noise.

While you are modelling a client/server architecture for a system, you may have to make certain considerations, such as whether to go for thin or thick clients. A thin client has limited amount of computational capacity and may manage the user interface and information visualization. Thin clients are designed not to host many components but to load components from the server. Where as a thick client has better computational capacity and carries out system's logic and business rules apart from information visualization. You may have to consider a number of technical, economic, and political factors to make an architectural decision of choosing a thin or thick client for your application.

When you are modeling client/server architecture for a system, you need to consider where to place which software component and a balanced distribution of responsibilities among those components. Most of the information management systems are three-tier architectures. In three-tier architecture, the system's GUI, business logic, and database are physically distributed.

The UML's deployment diagram is used to indicate the topology of your client/server system, and how its software components are distributed across the client and server. Generally, you create one deployment diagram for the whole system.

**The Steps followed to Model a Client/Server System:**

❖ Study the hardware implementation of your system. Identify all the nodes that comprise your system. Establish what nodes represent your clients and what nodes represent servers.

❖ Indicate those devices such as credit card readers, badge readers, and display devices etc. which are part of your system's functionality in the architecture. These are the special devices modeled by using UML's extensibility mechanisms.

❖ Model all these processors and devices using stereotypes . If needed, provide visual cues.

❖ Use a deployment diagram to model the topology of these nodes. Specify the relationships between your components in your system's implementation view. Specify the relationships between your nodes in your system's deployment view.

**Explanation:** The below diagram represents physical architecture of Banking System. This system has five client machines on which client software components are placed. These clients act as user interfaces for the banking operations. All these clients are connected to application server which implements business logic of your application. The application server is connected to the printer and to another server which is database server. This database server stores data using database management system, it handles all data processing tasks associated with your application. The above model depicts three-tier client/server architecture used as a hardware platform for a banking application.

**Example**:

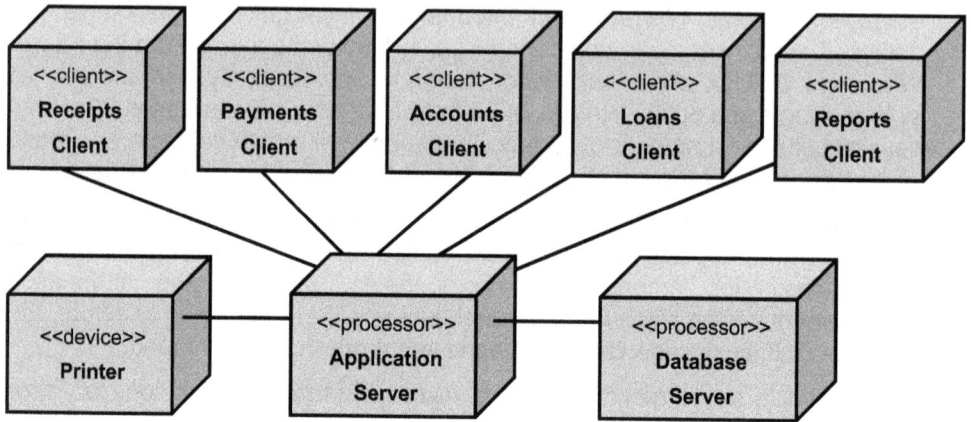

**Fig.20.3** Modeling a Client/Server System

## 20.5 Modeling a Distributed System

Distributed systems consist of multiple processors that span across many geographically distributed nodes. These systems are mostly dynamic, meaning the topology of these systems as well as the distribution of components change continuously as they perform transactions. The following things may happen, making a distribution system a non-static system.

❖ Nodes are added and removed as network traffic changes and processors fail.
❖ New and faster communication paths may be formed continuously and eventually decommissioning slower channels.
❖ Database tables may be replicated across servers. The database tables may move from node to node as traffic dictates.

**Note**: You apply deployment diagrams to visualize, specify, and document the topology of fully distributed systems.

### The Steps followed for Modeling a Distributed System:

❖ Identify the nodes for your systems. Establish what are the devices and processors that your system includes. The processors and devices are identified in a similar fashion as we do in case of client/server systems.
❖ Model the communication paths by specifying the connections among the nodes. These will help us to reason about the system's network performance as well as the impact of changes to the network.
❖ Identify the nodes that are logically connected. These nodes may be grouped into packages as they are conceptually and semantically related.

❖ Model the devices and processors you have identified as deployment diagrams. Use tools to discover your system's topology while you walk through system's network.

❖ If your intension is to model the dynamics of your system, apply use case diagrams to specify your intent. You can expand these use cases with interaction diagrams.

**Note**: When you are modeling a fully distributed system, you may consider network as a node. If your model includes internet, then it is represented as a node. You can model LAN (Local Area Network) and WAN (Wide Area Network) in a similar fashion. You can capture the properties about a network that connect nodes, by using the nodes' attributes and operations.

**Example:**

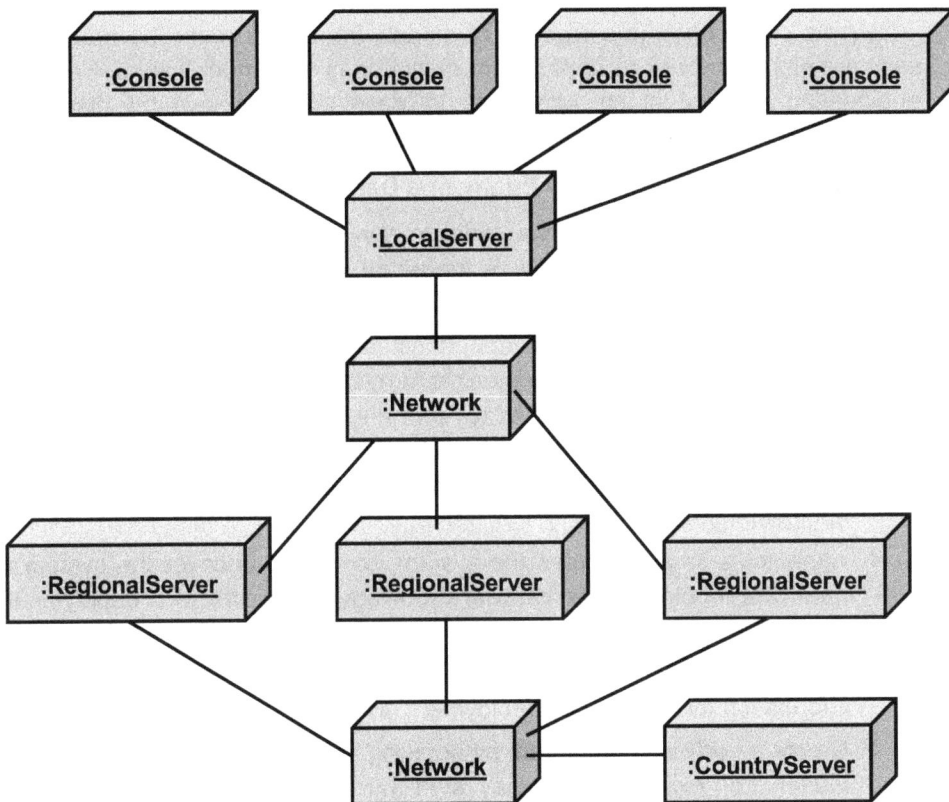

**Fig.20.4** Modeling a Fully Distributed System

**Explanation:** The Fig.20.4 shows the topology of a fully distributed system. You can consider this particular deployment diagram as an object diagram, because it contains node instances. There are four instances of the console node, one instance of the local server, in fact there are many local servers connected in the system but are not shown in the diagram. All these local servers connect to a regional server through the network. All these regional servers connect to a country server. All the country servers may connect to a global server, not shown in the figure.

## 20.6 Forward and Reverse Engineering

You can do very little forward engineering (the creation of code from models) with deployment diagrams. After you know the physical distribution of components across nodes through a deployment diagram, use tools to push these components into the real world. Forward engineering of deployment diagrams is very much useful for system administrators.

Reverse engineering (the creation of models from code) from the real world software elements back to deployment diagrams is very much useful. Reverse engineering is very much applicable in developing deployment diagrams belonging to a distributed system which is under constant change.

**The Steps followed to Reverse Engineer a Deployment Diagram:**

❖ Identify the target which you want to reverse engineer. Sometimes the entire network is considered as the target and sometimes only a portion of the system is considered.

❖ Identify the scope of your reverse engineering task. Sometimes it may be sufficient if you reverse engineer to a system's processors. Sometimes you need to expand scope of reverse engineering task where you may have to include even system's networking peripherals. All these are included in the generated deployment diagram by means of reverse engineering task.

❖ Apply tools to walk across the system, so has to uncover the system's hardware topology. This hardware topology forms part of a deployment diagram of a system.

❖ Apply tools again to discover components that live on each node. This information forms part of a deployment diagram.

❖ Create a deployment diagram by applying modeling tools by querying the model. For example, you may start with client/server topology, then, expand this diagram by populating nodes with the components that live on them. In order to communicate your intent better, you expose or hide details of the deployment diagram based on the context.

## Essay Type Questions

1. Describe briefly the concepts and contents of deployment diagram.
2. Explain the common uses of deployment diagrams.
3. Briefly explain the modeling of an embedded system with an example.
4. Describe how to model a Client/Server system using component diagrams.
5. Depict how to model a fully distributed system.

## Objective Type Questions

1. ----------------- diagrams represent the physical architecture of the system

   (a) component diagrams      (b) deployment diagram
   (c) object diagrams      (d) All the above

2. ----------------- show connections or the communication paths between the nodes

   (a) component diagrams      (b) deployment diagrams
   (c) object diagrams      (d) All the above

3. The hardware devices such as computers, sensors, printers, and other devices that support the execution environment are represented by

   (a) nodes      (b) components
   (c) classes      (d) objects

4. The static deployment view of a system is modeled by

   (a) component diagrams      (b) deployment diagrams
   (c) state chart      (d) object diagram

5. Deployment diagrams are effective in modeling physical architecture of the -------------- types of systems

   (a) Embedded Systems      (b) Client/Server Systems
   (c) Distributed Systems      (d) All the above

6. -------------- specify the required hardware platform on which your software system can be deployed and can be executed.

   (a) component diagrams      (b) use case diagrams
   (c) deployment diagrams      (d) object diagrams

7. A Deployment Diagram commonly contain

   (a) node & node instances
   (b) component & component instances
   (c) devices
   (d) all the above

8. ---------------- consist of multiple processors that span across many geographically distributed nodes

   (a) stand alone system         (b) distributed system
   (c) both a & b                  (d) none

## Answers

1. (b)     2. (b)     3. (a)     4. (b)     5. (d)     6. (c)
7. (d)     8. (b)

# Case Studies
# The Unified Library Application

## 21.1 Objective

The purpose is to design and develop an automated library system, where much of the manual activities are computerized. The major emphasis is to use the UML facilities to carry on system analysis and design of the system. Automation incredibly reduces the time of library management actives. Automation reduces the margin of errors and improves considerably the efficiency of system functionality. This case study provides you the feel of how UML is used in the real life scenarios.

## 21.2 Problem Statement

A library lends books to the members, who are registered or authorized in the system. It handles the task of purchasing new books for the library from time to time. Popular books are bought in multiple copies. Old books are removed when they are out of date or in poor condition. There are two kinds of employees who are supported by the system. A librarian is a major authority who maintains various activities of the library. A Library Clerk is a person who issues books and collects returned books and collects penalty for late returns.

A registered member can borrow a book, if it is currently available. Otherwise he can reserve a book, so that he can be notified when it is returned or a new copy is purchased by the library. The reservation is canceled when the member checks out the book or through an explicit canceling procedure. The library can create, update, or delete information about books, and about registered members. The library can generate various reports containing information about available books, about issues and also about reservations.

The system should also handle the message that is sent to the member when a reserved book becomes available or has become overdue. Notifications are sent either by e-mail or SMS according to the member preferences. Available reservations are automatically cancelled if reader doesn't come to take the book on issue for a period of time defined in system settings.

Library Clerk registers the issue of the book and sets the due return date. Library Clerk also registers the return of the issued book. If a member has kept the issued book after the due date, he is given a penalty. Librarian is responsible for managing inventory data about books. Librarian is also responsible for managing the Unified Library members and configuring system settings like default issue period, available reservation timeout, max reservations per member, etc.

The system should run on all popular technical environments, such as UNIX, Windows, and OS/2, and has a modern GUI (Graphical User Interface). The system should be easily extendable with new or modified functionality.

# 21.3 System Analysis

We figure out how the system will be used and who will be using it. The use cases specify how to use the system, where as actors are the users of the system. The functionality of this library system is modeled as use case diagrams when we apply the UML. A use case analysis includes reading and analyzing the specifications.

The actors in the library system are identified as the Librarian, Library Clerk and Members. The Librarian looks after the overall system maintenance. The Members are the registered users of the system, who can check out and reserve books. The functions of the member, such as book issue, book return, and penalty for late return are done by the Library Clerk on behalf of members.

The Identified Actors in the System are:

❖ The librarian.
❖ Library Clerk.
❖ Members.

**Note:** The actor Member can be a Student or Staff, the Librarian or the Library Clerks.

**The Identified Use cases in the System are:**

❖ Login.
❖ Browse Book.
❖ Reserve Book.
❖ Check Status.
❖ Issue Book.
❖ Return Book.
❖ Renew Book.
❖ Replace Book.
❖ Calculate Penalty.
❖ Pay Penalty.

- ❖ Inform about Reservation.
- ❖ Cancel Reservation.
- ❖ Maintain Member.
- ❖ Maintain Title.
- ❖ Maintain Book.
- ❖ Generate Report.
- ❖ Specify System Settings.

**Note:** Because a library often has several copies of a popular title, the system must separate the concept of the title from the concept of the book.

Use cases and their associated tasks:

| S.No | Use Case | Task Carried |
|------|----------|--------------|
| 1. | Login | Accepts member name and password and checks whether you are a valid member or not, you can use the system if you are a valid member. |
| 2. | Browse Book | Member makes a query in the system for his required book by supplying certain search criteria. |
| 3. | Reserve Book | If the member wants a book which is on issue, he can reserve that book. When the book will return, he will be informed. If he wants, the reserved book can be issued to him. |
| 4. | Check Status | It will verify whether a book can be issued or not, checking against system settings. During book return by the member, it will verify whether it is overdue. It will verify the book's condition, such as damaged or not. |
| 5. | Issue Book | The book can be issued to the required member after verifying the details such as Check Status and system settings. This book issue is recorded with issue and return dates into the system. This operation is carried by the actor Library Clerk. |
| 6. | Return Book | The Library Clerk receives the book and checks against late return or damage. If the book is late returned, fine is calculated, and is collected from the member. If damaged, either fine is collected or the member may be asked to replace the damaged book. If the book is returned properly, the relevant information is recorded in the system. |
| 7. | Renew Book | If the member wants to borrow the book again after he/she returns it. The Library Clerk checks whether the book is reserved or not. If the book is not reserved, then only the book can be renewed otherwise not. The relevant information is recorded in the system. |

*Table contd…*

| S.No | Use Case | Task Carried |
|---|---|---|
| 8. | Replace Book | While a member returns a book which is in very damaged condition. The Library Clerk asks the member to replace the book. If the member does not replace the book, he will be asked to pay the penalty, and the penalty is collected by the Library Clerk, and he replaces the copy of the book. This entire information is recorded in the system. |
| 9. | Calculate Penalty | While a member returns a book to the Library Clerk, and if the book is over due, or in damaged shape, the library clerk calculates penalty based on system settings and informs to the member. |
| 10. | Pay Penalty | After receiving penalty information from the Library Clerk, the member pays the penalty. The relevant information is recorded in the system by the Library Clerk. |
| 11. | Inform about Reservation | While a member returns a book, Library Clerk checks whether this book is reserved or not. If the book is reserved, he informs to the corresponding member about the availability of the book. |
| 12. | Cancel Reservation | If a member reserves a book, and the book is available, if there is no response from the member, the reservation is automatically canceled. Some times, reservation can be explicitly canceled by the Library Clerk. The relevant information is entered in the system. |
| 13. | Maintain Member | The Librarian maintains information about the authorized members of the system. The Librarian can add new members, modify the existing member information, and may remove members when they are no longer authorized to use the library. |
| 14. | Maintain Title | Based on the requirement there can be many copies of the same book. The book information is stored separately as titles. The Librarian maintains this information. He/she can add new titles as new books are purchased with different titles. He can modify existing title information, and he can remove the title of out dated or disposed books. The entire available titles in the library are stored in the system. |
| 15. | Maintain Book | For each title, there can be many books in the library. This information is maintained by the Librarian, where he can add a new book, modify the existing book information, and also he can remove a book which is out dated and disposed. |

*Table contd...*

| S.No | Use Case | Task Carried |
|------|----------|--------------|
| 16. | Generate Report | The Librarian can generate various reports based on the stock of books in the library. He can generate reports specifying current available stock, books over due, books damaged, books reserved, books on issue, books returned, books renewed and system settings etc. |
| 17. | Specify System Settings | The Librarian can set these settings. These settings include the information about rules and regulations followed in the library. It may store details, such as, how many books can be issued to a member, the amount of penalty for overdue or    damaged books ,the default issue period, available reservation timeout, max reservations per member, etc. |

Actors and their associated Use cases:

**Member:** Any person who wants to use the library facilities, approaches the librarian. The librarian verifies whether he is a valid student or staff. After the librarian verifying the identity of the user, the user might be asked to pay the fee for using library facilities. After fee payment, the Librarian may create an account for a user. Every member, who can use library facilities is given a user ID and password. All other relevant information about the member is also recorded into the system. The member can use his user ID and password to login to the library system, to avail the facilities offered by the library. The member can Login, Browse Book, Reserve Book, Pay Penalty, and get information about reservation through Inform about Reservation, and may involve in Issue Book, Return Book, Renew Book, and Replace Book use cases.

**Library Clerk:** He is the person who sits in front of the library counter. He receives member requests and issues books to them. He collects returned books. He checks for books' overdue or damage, based on which he calculates the penalty. He collects this penalty from the members. If the book is returned, and it is reserved, he sends information to the relevant member about the availability of the book. If the book is not reserved and the member wants to renew it, he/she renews it. He can cancel reservations under certain circumstances. So, the Library Clerk may involve in Login, Issue Book, Return Book, Renew Book, Inform about Reservation, Cancel Reservation, Replace Book, Calculate Penalty, and Pay Penalty use cases. The Library Clerk records all the relevant information about whatever task he does, in the system.

**The Librarian:** He is the major authority in the library. He can authorize who can use the library facilities. He can place sales orders for purchasing new books. Once the books arrive he will arrange them in proper order in the library. He will also enter the information about the books and titles in the system. He can dispose out dated and damaged books from the library and the relevant information can be entered into the system. He can de authorize certain members to use the library, if they do not pay library fee or the penalties. He can also de authorize members, who no longer wants to use the library. He can generate all the relevant information about the library system. He is the authority in specifying system settings, such as how many books can be issued to a member, the amount of penalty for overdue or damaged books ,the default issue period, available reservation timeout, max reservations per member, etc. He is involved in, Login, Maintain Member, Maintain Title, Maintain Book, Generate Report, and Specify System Settings use cases.

**Note:** The actors are the associated users of the system. During system analysis, we identify who uses the system, and what they expect from the system. The system's functions   are specified in the form of use cases. The users of the system are actors. A use case diagram indicates actors involved in a system, and the functions of the system in the form of use cases. So, a use case diagram is a pictorial representation of system's requirements.

The library system analysis is documented in a UML use case diagram as shown in the figure.

## 21.4 System Design

System design is the process of obtaining a solution to the given problem statement. Our approach to solution is being object oriented, we start with identifying classes in the vocabulary of the system. Before identifying classes, responsibilities for each class are identified. These responsibilities are evenly distributed across the classes so that we may not end up with small (trivial) classes, which make system management a tough task. If you have classes of larger size, implementation of changes in the system becomes cumbersome. Because of this we need to identify classes carefully, so that they may have optimal size. After the classes are identified, identify attributes and operations of each class based on responsibilities.

   Once the classes are identified, you need to identify interfaces so that class instances can communicate with the external word during the system's execution. An interface contains operations without their implementation. These operations of an interface are realized by an associated class. These interfaces help in establishing interaction among instances of various elements for the functionality of the system. After the interfaces, you identify objects (class instances), that communicate with each other to accomplish the purpose of your system. Once the interaction among the objects is established, we go for objects' behavior based on external and internal events. Once this logical design is complete, you should consider physical design, which comprise physical components and nodes. Model static implementation view using component diagrams. Then, model static deployment view using deployment diagrams.

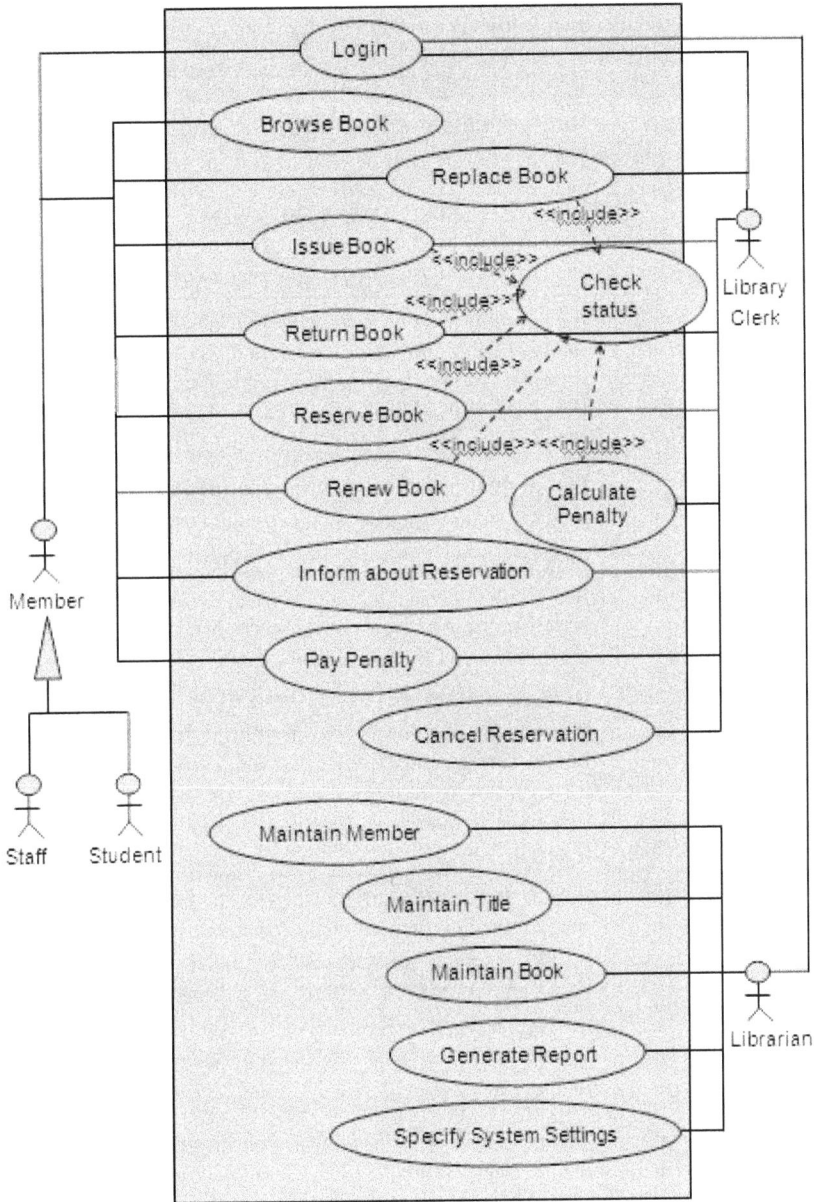

**Fig.21.1** Use Case Diagram for Unified Library

## 21.5 Classes and Interfaces

The classes which you can think of for the Unified Library System are Member, Title, Book, LIBCard, and SystemSpecs. All these classes are persistent, in the sense that the classes' information is stored in the database permanently. The class CheckStatus is a non persistent class. The following table discusses the purposes of these classes.

**Table 21.1** Classes and Purposes

| S.No. | Class | The Major Purpose |
|-------|-------|-------------------|
| 1. | Member | It is a persistent class, which provides facilities to add, modify, and remove member information. Here, the member can be a student or staff. This class is also used for verifying member login. |
| 2. | Title | It is a persistent class, which provides facilities for adding, modifying and removing titles' information. |
| 3. | Book | It is a persistent class, which provides facilities for adding, modifying, and removing books' information. |
| 4. | LIBCard | It is a persistent class, where all details of book issue, book return and book reservation are maintained. This is generally used by the Library Clerk. |
| 5. | SystemSpecs | It is a persistent class, where all library rules and regulations are specified. These may include, how many books can be issued to a member, the amount of penalty for overdue or damaged books, the default issue period, available reservation timeout, max reservations per member, etc. |
| 6. | CheckStatus | It is a non persistent class, during the book issue, the details are checked whether a desired book can be issued to the member or not. During book return, things are checked whether the book is overdue, or the book is damaged or lost. The relevant penalty is calculated and the member has to pay required penalty. |

The interfaces you can think of for the Unified Library System are ILogin, IBrowseBook, IReserveBook, ICancelReservation, IIssueBook, IReturnBook, IRenewBook  IReplaceBook, IMaintainMember, IMaintainTitle, IMaintainBook, IGenerateReport and ISystemSpec.

The following table gives the details of the purposes of these interfaces.

**Table 21.2** Interfaces and their Purposes.

| S.No. | Interface | The Major Purpose |
|---|---|---|
| 1. | ILogin | This provides the facility to accept the user ID and password and checks against Member. If the user is valid, he can work with the system. This interface is realized by the class named Member. |
| 2. | IBrowseBook | This provides the facility of querying book information, based on certain search criteria. The available book can be borrowed. If the book is on issue, it can be reserved. This interface is realized by the classes named, Title, Book, and LIBCard. |
| 3. | IReserveBook | This provides the facility of reserving a book which is on circulation. This interface is realized by the class LIBCard. |
| 4. | ICancelReservation | This provides the facility of explicitly canceling the reservation by the Library Clerk, due to certain reasons. This interface is realized by the class LIBCard. |
| 5. | IIssueBook | This provides the facility of issuing a book to the member. Before issuing, CheckStatus is used whether the book can be issued or not. Once the book is issued, this information is recorded in LIBCard. This interface is realized by the classes, CheckStatus, and LIBCard. |
| 6. | IReturnBook | This provides the facility to take back the book given to a Member. During return, the Library Clerk checks whether the book is over due/damaged against CheckStatus. In any of these cases, the penalty is calculated and collected. The return is recorded. This interface is realized by the classes, CheckStatus, and LIBCard. |
| 7. | IRenewBook | This provides the facility to renew the book which is not reserved by any other members. This interface is realized by the classes, CheckStatus, and LIBCard. |
| 8. | IReplaceBook | This provides the facility of replacing the book by the member, if the book is badly damaged during return. This interface is realized by the classes, CheckStatus, and LIBCard. |

*Table 21.2 contd...*

| S.No. | Interface | The Major Purpose |
|-------|-----------|-------------------|
| 9. | IMaintainMember | This provides the facility of maintaining the authorized members of the system. The Librarian can authorize members to use the library facilities. A new member can be added, an existing member can be modified, and a member can be removed, where he cannot continue using library facilities. This interface is realized by the class named Member. |
| 10. | IMaintainTitle | This provides the facility for maintaining titles. There can be many number of copies for each title, depending on the demand. The Librarian maintains the titles. A new title can be added, an existing title can be modified, and an outdated title can be removed. This interface is realized by the class Title. |
| 11. | IMaintainBook | This provides the facility of maintaining copies of titles or books. A new book details can be entered, an existing book information can be modified, and an out dated or damaged book can be removed. These tasks are carried by the Librarian. This interface is realized by the class named Book. |
| 12. | IGenerateReport | This provides the facility for the Librarian to generate various reports based on the search criteria. This interface is realized by the whole system. |
| 13. | ISystemSpec | This interface provides the facility for the Librarian for specifying the library rules and regulations in the form of system specifications. This interface is realized by the class SystemSpecs . The Librarian can add new specs, can modify the existing specs, and also can remove specs which are outdated or no longer used. |

Now we develop a class diagram for the unified library system. A class diagram generally contain classes and their relationships as well as interfaces. In this system, all the classes are persistent (which are stored in the database permanently for further use) except the class CheckStatus. This class, during book issue, checks whether a book can be issued to the user or not. But in case of book return, it is used to find whether the book is overdue, or damaged. In both the cases the corresponding fine is calculated.

Class Diagram for the Unified Library Application:

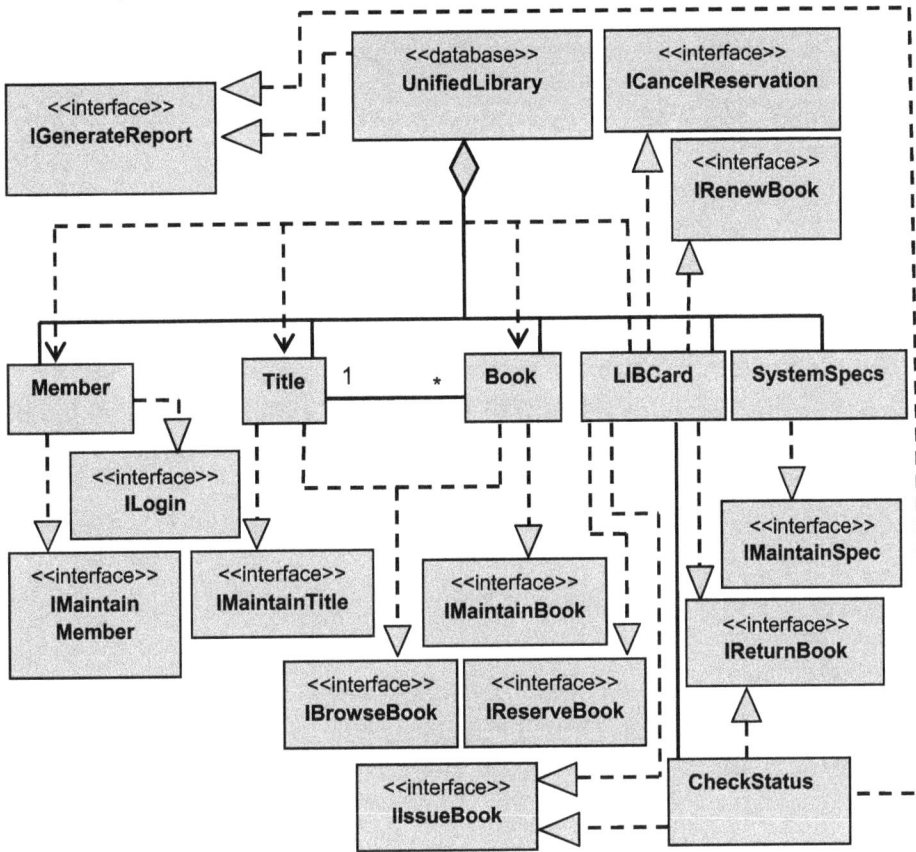

**Fig.21.2** A Class Diagram for Unified Library

**Explanation:** The interfaces and classes and their relationships are explained as follows:

1. There is one to many association between the classes Title and Book. The interfaces IMaintainTitle and IBrowseBook are realized by the class Title. The interfaces IMaintainBook and IBrowseBook are realized by the class Book. The interface IBrowseBook is used by Member, where as the interfaces IMaintainTitle and IMaintainBook are used by the Librarian.

2. The interface ILogin is realized by the class Member. A Member can be a Student, Staff, Library Clerk, or the Librarian. The interface IMaintainMember is realized by the class Member and used by the Librarian.

3. The interface IReserveBook is realized by the class LIBCard and used by a Member. The class LIBCard uses information from classes, such as Member, Title, and Book. The LIBCard class is in association with the

class named CheckStatus. The class CheckStatus is used while issuing a Book, returning a Book, renewing as well as replacing a Book.

4. The interfaces IIssueBook and IReturnBook are realized by the classes, LIBCard and CheckStatus.

5. The interfaces IRenewBook and ICancelReservation are realized by the class named LIBCard.

6. The interface IGenerateReport is realized by the whole class, which is nothing but the entire Unified Library database and another class named CheckStatus and used by the Librarian.

7. The interface IMaintainSpec is realized by the class named SystemSpecs and used by the Librarian.

8. The entire UnifiedLibrary database is in whole-and-part (aggregation) relationship with classes, such as Member, Title, Book, LIBCard, and SystemSpecs.

**The expanded forms of classes and interfaces:**

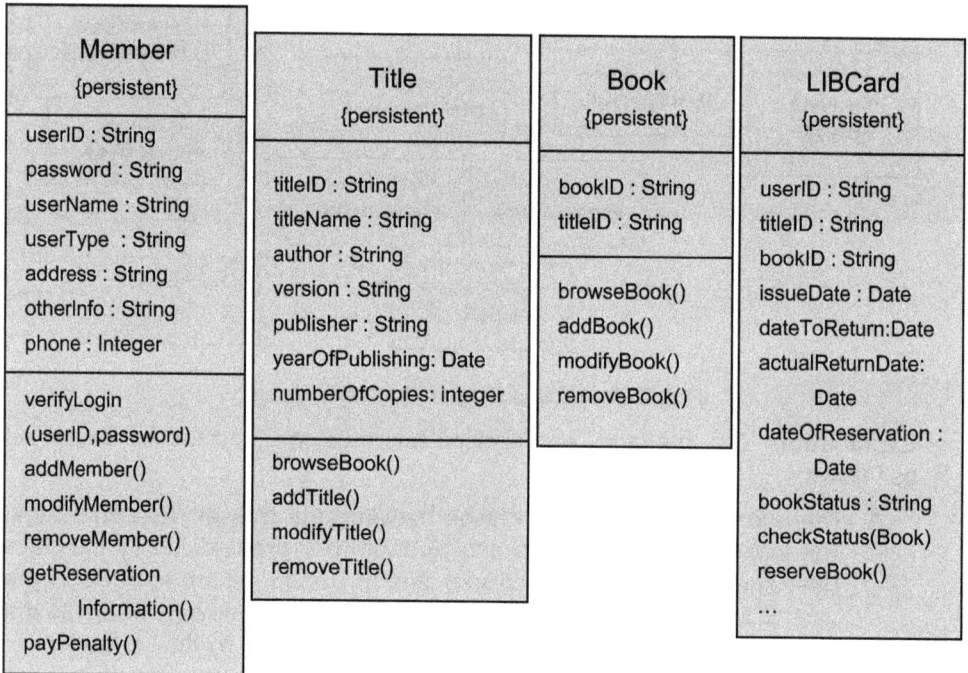

| Member {persistent} | Title {persistent} | Book {persistent} | LIBCard {persistent} |
|---|---|---|---|
| userID : String password : String userName : String userType : String address : String otherInfo : String phone : Integer | titleID : String titleName : String author : String version : String publisher : String yearOfPublishing: Date numberOfCopies: integer | bookID : String titleID : String | userID : String titleID : String bookID : String issueDate : Date dateToReturn:Date actualReturnDate: Date dateOfReservation : Date bookStatus : String checkStatus(Book) reserveBook() ... |
| verifyLogin (userID,password) addMember() modifyMember() removeMember() getReservation Information() payPenalty() | browseBook() addTitle() modifyTitle() removeTitle() | browseBook() addBook() modifyBook() removeBook() | |

| SystemSpecs |
| --- |
| {persistent} |
| specID : String |
| specDetails : String |
| defaultIssuePeriod : Integer |
| numberOfReservations : Integer |
| numberOfBooksIssued : Integer |
| lateFineperDay : Float |
| finePerDamage : Float |
| numberOfBookRenewals : Integer |
| addSpecs() |
| modifySpecs() |
| removeSpecs() |
| getSpecs() |

| CheckStatus |
| --- |
| bookID : String |
| bookReturnStatus : String |
| bookIssueStatus : String |
| bookReserveStatus : String |
| setBookReturnStatus() |
| getBookReturnStatus() |
| setBookIssueStatus() |
| getBookIssueStatus() |
| setBookReserveStatus() |
| getBookReserveStatus() |
| informAboutReservation() |

| ... LIB Card |
| --- |
| checkStatus(Book) |
| reserveBook() |
| issueBook() |
| returnBook() |
| calculatePenalty() |
| cancelReservation () |
| renewBook() |
| replaceBook() |

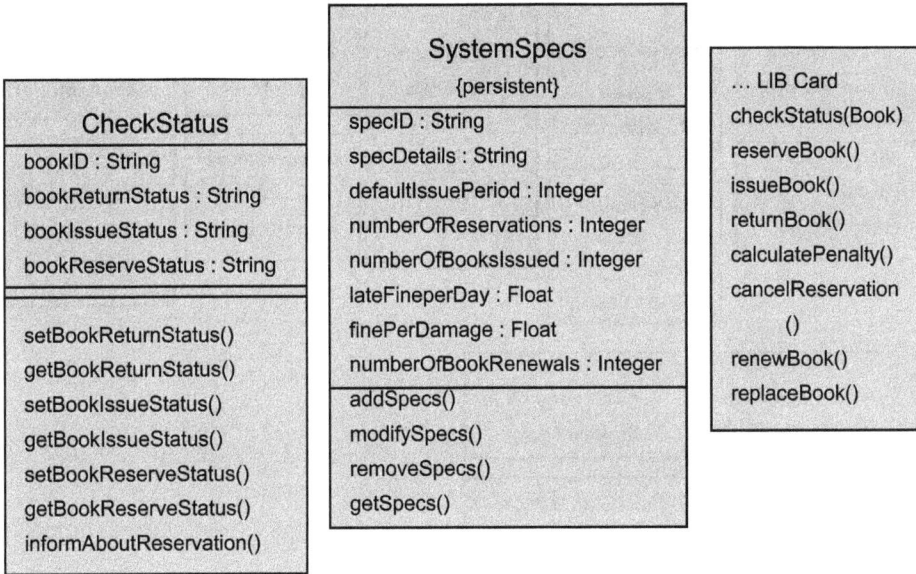

**Fig.21.3** Expanded classes

**Note:** The attribute bookStatus in LIBCard can take values available/reserved/issued/renewed. The attribute bookReturnStatus of CheckStatus can take values overdue/damaged. In this case fine is calculated. The attribute bookIssueStatus in CheckStatus class will take values eligible/ not eligible. If not eligible, the book is not issued, the member would have exhausted his limit of books.

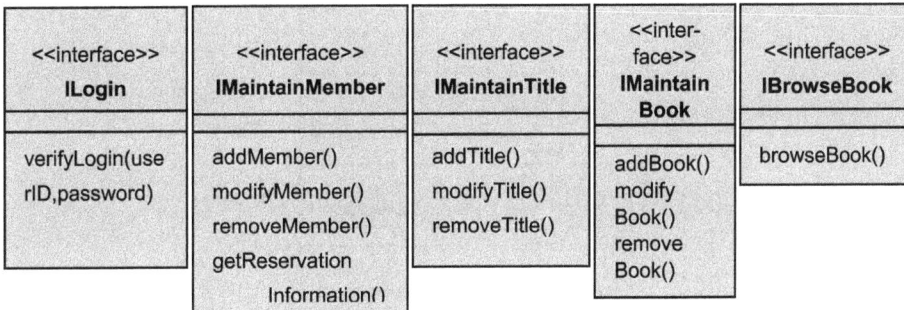

| <<interface>> **ILogin** | <<interface>> **IMaintainMember** | <<interface>> **IMaintainTitle** | <<interface>> **IMaintain Book** | <<interface>> **IBrowseBook** |
| --- | --- | --- | --- | --- |
| verifyLogin(userID,password) | addMember() modifyMember() removeMember() getReservation Information() | addTitle() modifyTitle() removeTitle() | addBook() modify Book() remove Book() | browseBook() |

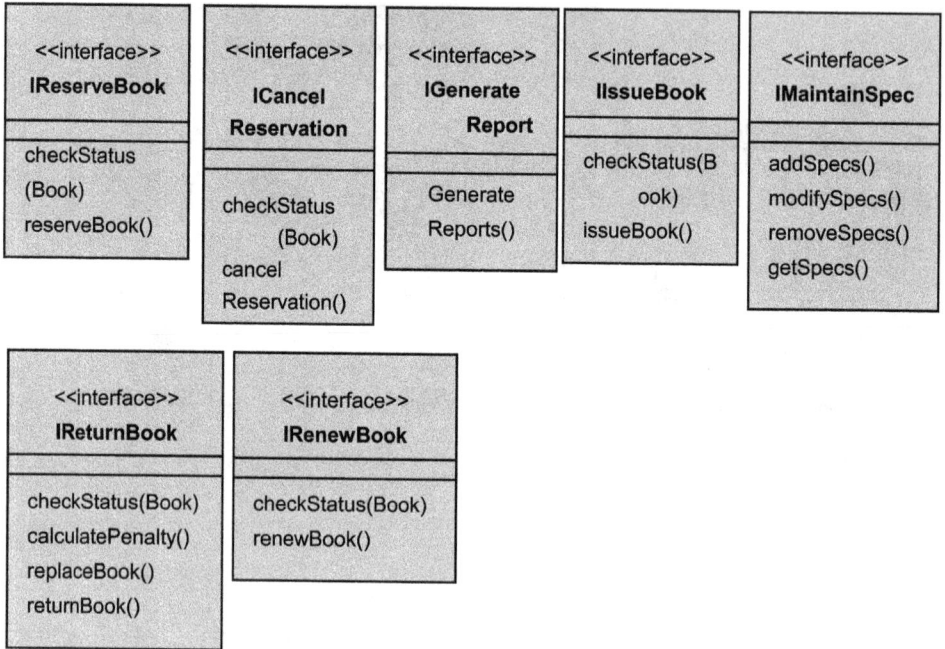

**Fig.21.4** Expanded Interfaces

The Actors and the Interfaces used by them:

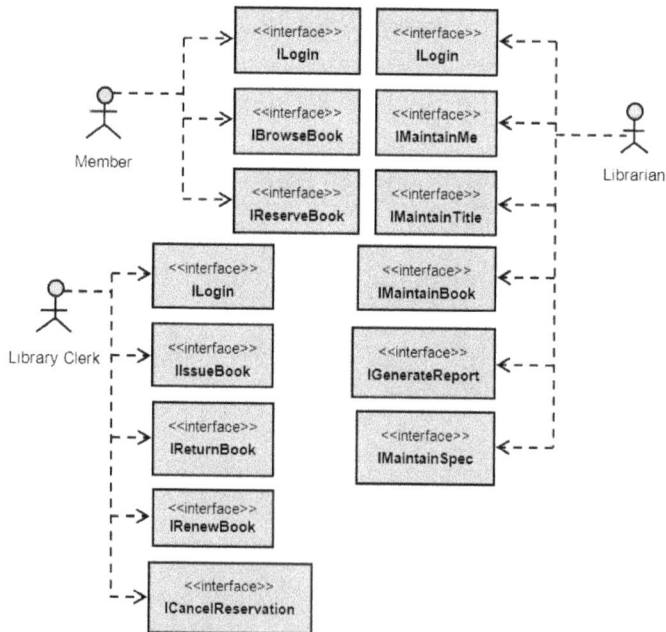

**Fig.21.5** Actors and Interfaces

## 21.6 Interaction Diagrams

There are two types of interaction diagrams, sequence diagram and collaboration diagram. Both are isomorphic, means we can generate another if you have one of them, without loosing information. Sequence diagram specifies interactions among objects with the time ordering of messages. Collaboration diagram specifies interaction among objects with the structure of messages preceded by the order of their occurrence among objects.

In the following diagram we use the instance ULSystem (Unified Library System) for interaction purposes. The actor interacts with the system through GUI screens, not shown in the following diagrams. If the actor is interacting with the instance: ULSystem, it means that he is interacting with the system through user interface screens.

<u>Sequence diagram for Login use case:</u>

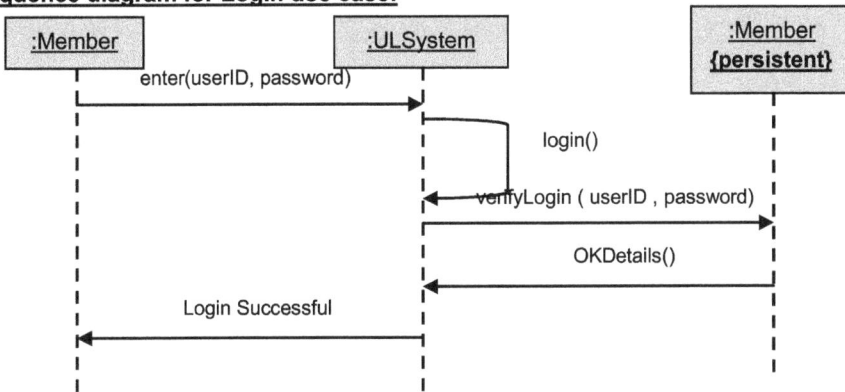

<u>Collaboration Diagram for Login use case:</u>

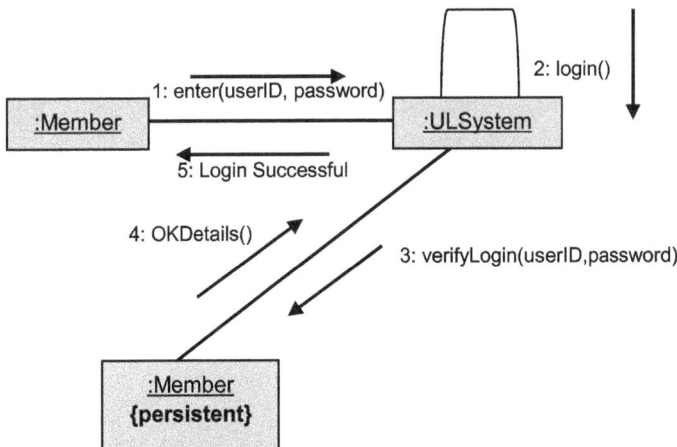

**Fig.21.6** Interaction Diagrams for Login use Case

## Sequence Diagram for Browse Book Use case:

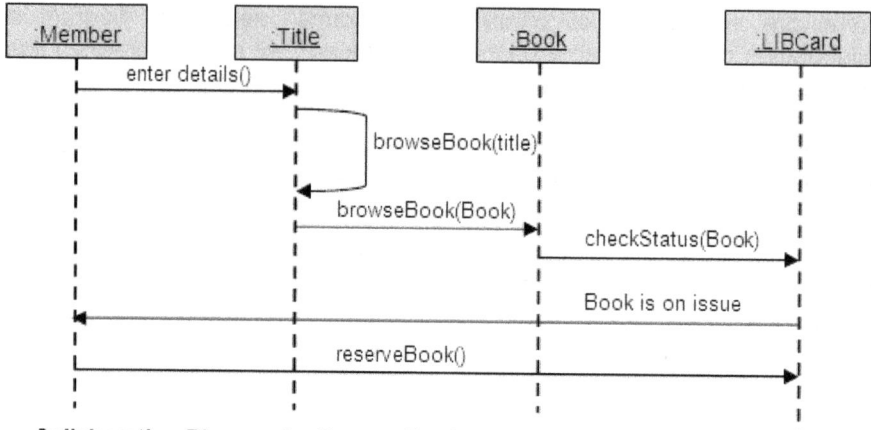

## Collaboration Diagram for Browse Book Use case:

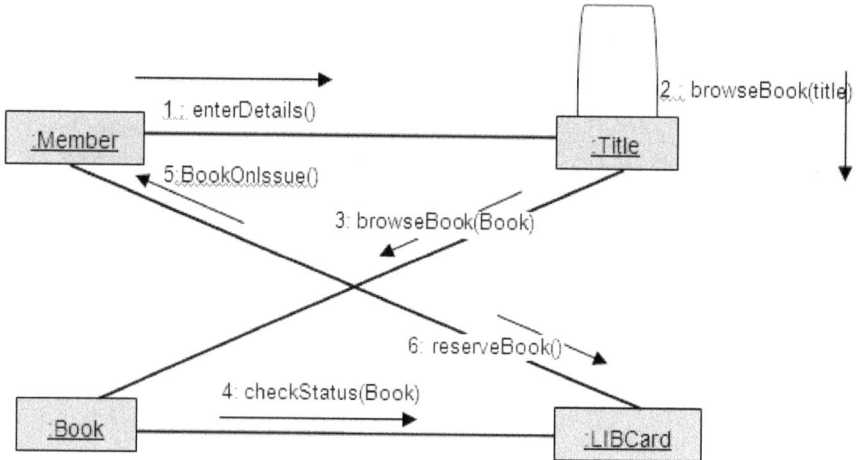

**Fig.21.7** Interaction Diagrams for Browse Book use Case

## Sequence Diagram for Maintain Member use case:

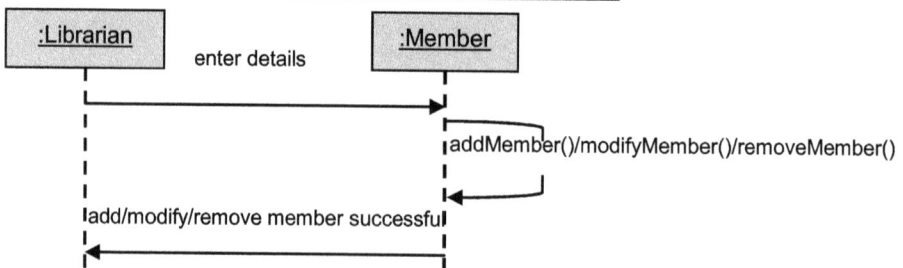

## Collaboration Diagram for Maintain Member use case:

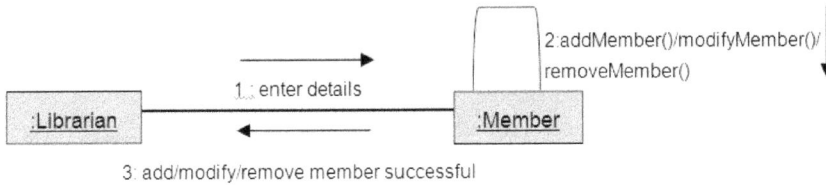

**Fig.21.8** Interaction Diagrams for Maintain Member use Case

## Sequence Diagram for Maintain Title use case:

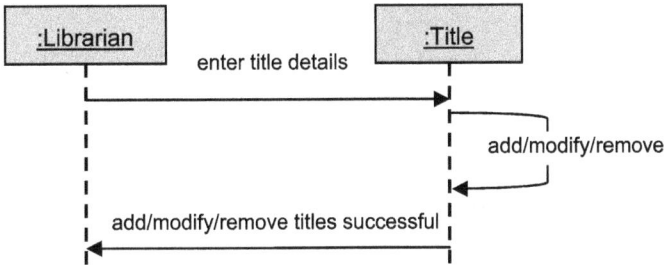

## Collaboration Diagram for Maintain Title use case:

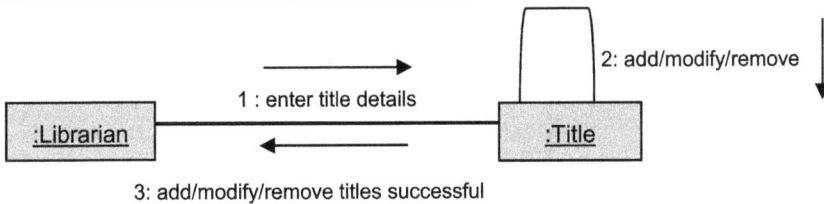

**Fig.21.9** Interaction Diagrams for Maintain Title use Case

## Sequence Diagram for Maintain Book use case:

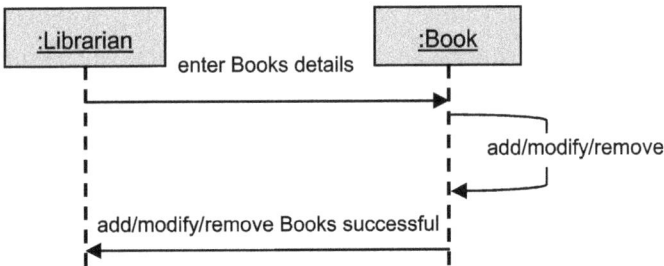

## Collaboration Diagram for Maintain Book use case:

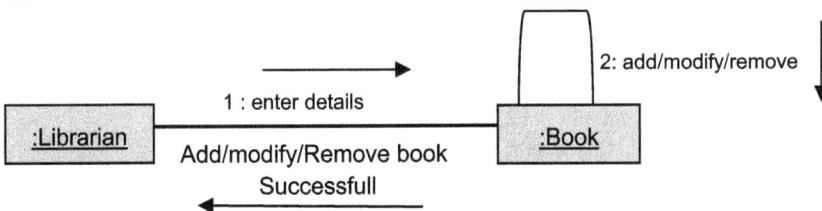

**Sequence Diagram for Cancel Reservation use case:**

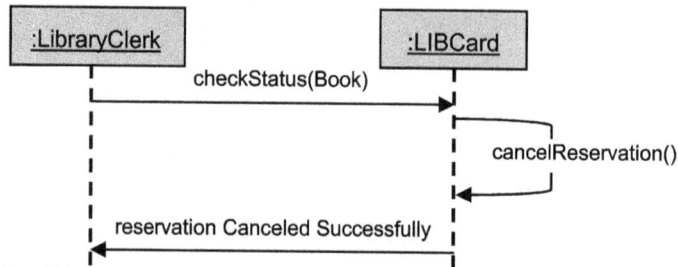

**Collaboration Diagram for Cancel Reservation use case:**

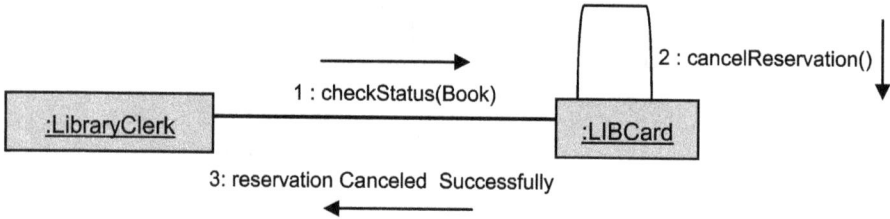

**Fig.21.10**  Interaction Diagrams for Cancel Reservation use Case

**Sequence Diagram for Issue Book use case:**

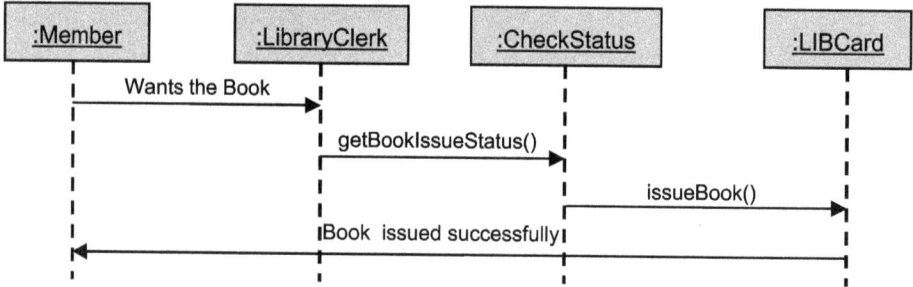

**Collaboration Diagram for Issue Book use case:**

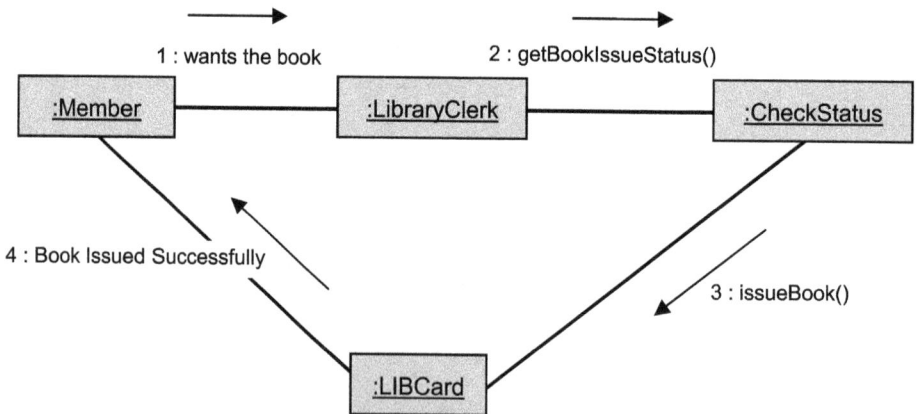

**Fig.21.11**  Interaction Diagrams for Issue Book use Case

## Sequence Diagram for Return Book use case (Overdue or Damaged):

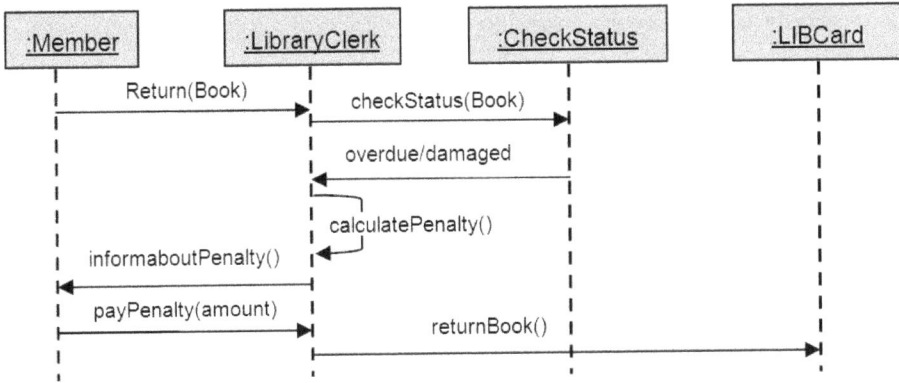

## Collaboration Diagram for Return Book use case (Overdue or Damaged):

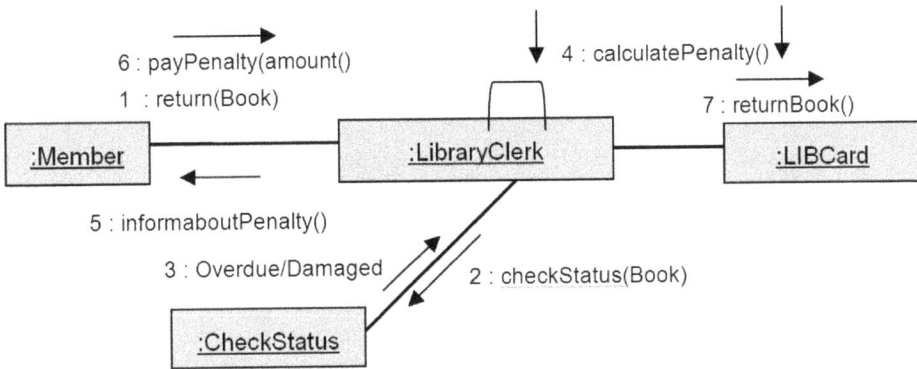

**Fig.21.12**  Interaction Diagrams for Return Book use Case

## Sequence Diagram for Return Book/Renew Book use case:

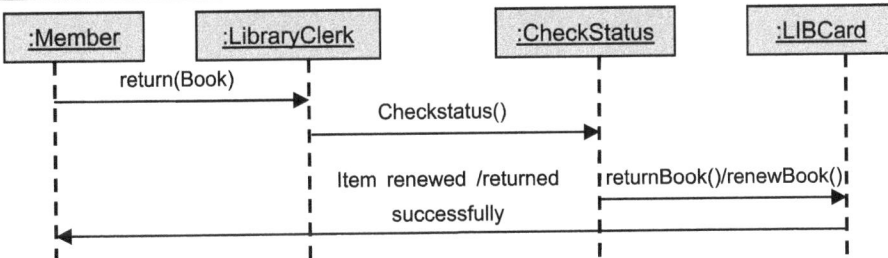

**Fig.21.13**  Sequence Diagram for Return/Renew Book use Case

## 21.7 Activity Diagram

The activity diagram corresponding to the unified library system can be as follows:

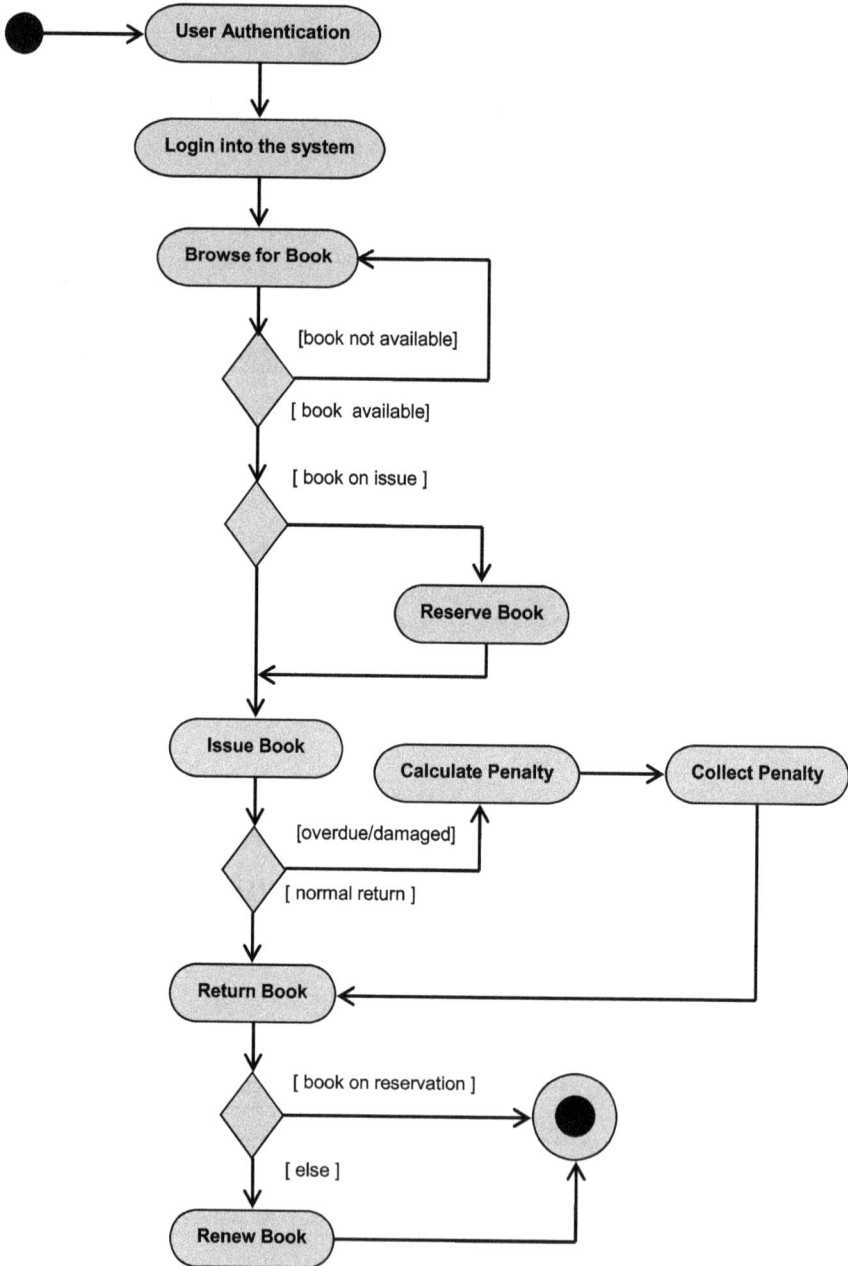

**Fig.21.14** Activity Diagram for Unified Library Application

## 21.8 State Chart Diagram for a Book

State chart diagram describes the sequence of states an object goes through during its life time, because of certain events happening. The object which you can think of in unified library is an instance of a book. This book object can go through the states, such as Available, Issued, Reserved, Overdue, Damaged, Replaced, Returned, Renewed and Disposed. The following diagram represents the state chart for the object Book.

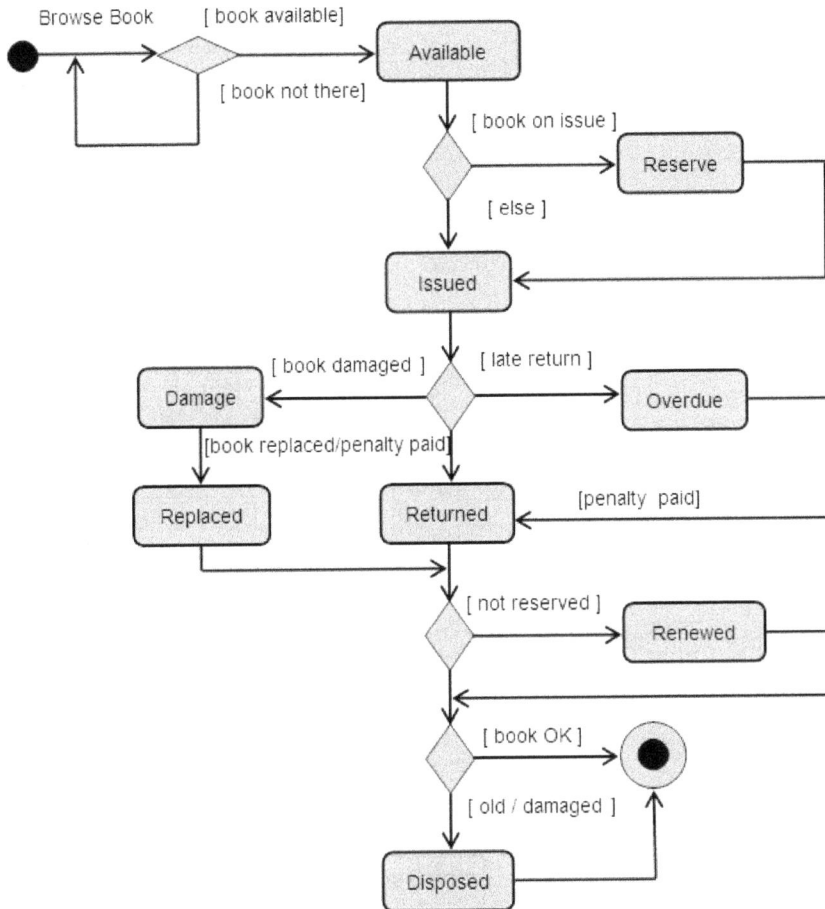

**Fig.21.15** State Chart Diagram for a Book Instance

## 21.9 Component Diagram

The component diagram contains the physical replaceable parts of the system. These components can be executables, library components, source code components and various documents. The Unified Library Application component diagram can be defined as follows:

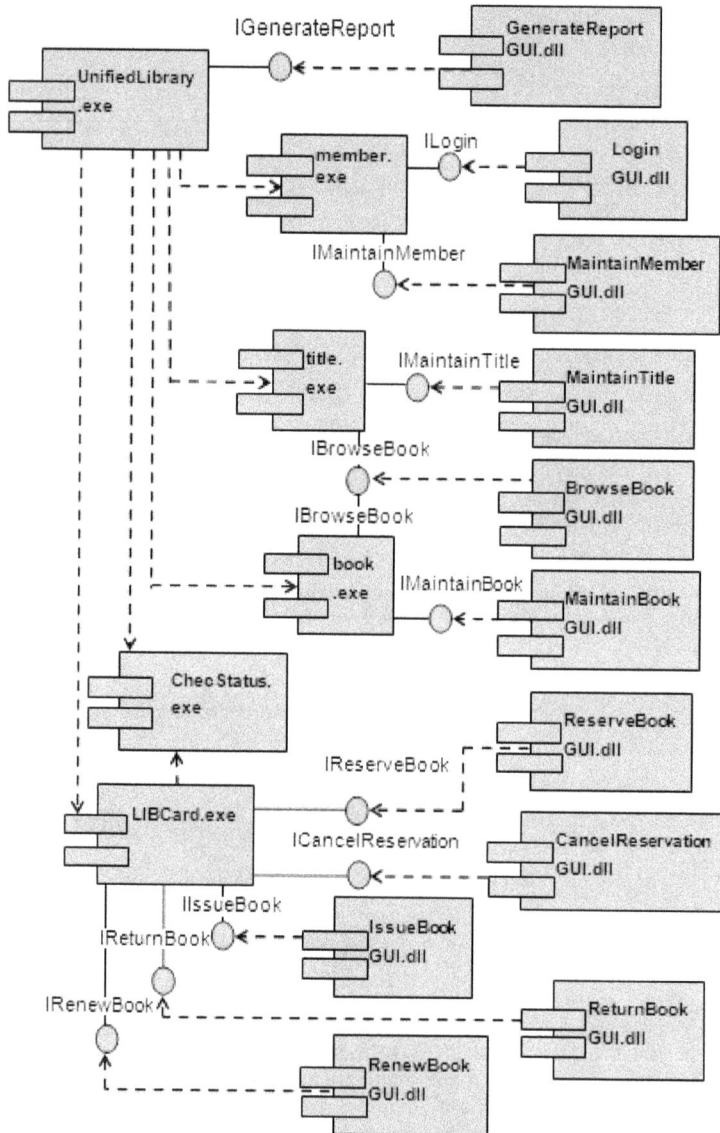

**Fig.21.16** Component Diagram for Unified Library

## 21.10 Deployment Diagram

This diagram contains the various nodes that constitute your system with their connections. The components that are deployed on each node are indicated. You are implementing your Unified Library Application using three-tier architecture, where there are two server machines, an Application Server and a Database Server. There are three client machines, User Client, Library Clerk Client, and Librarian Client, used by users, library clerks and librarian. There can be many User Clients spreading across multiple departments.

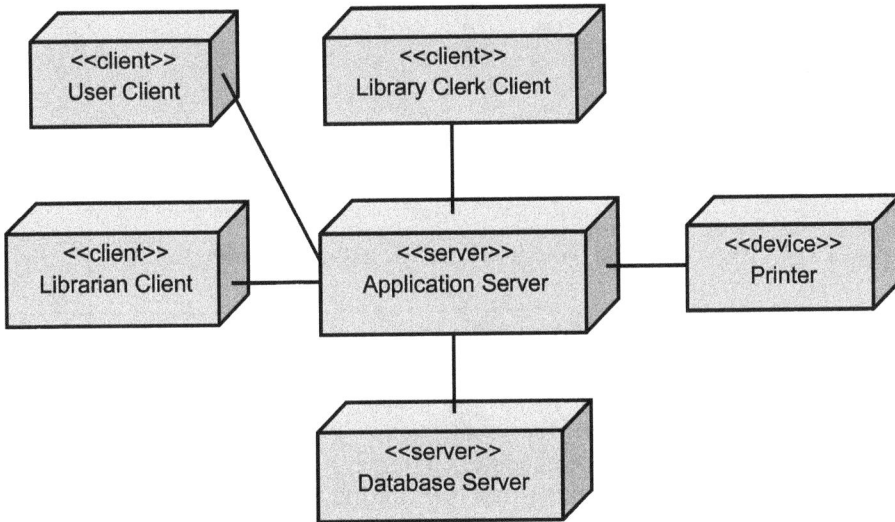

**Fig.21.17** Deployment Diagram

**Nodes with Deployed Components:**

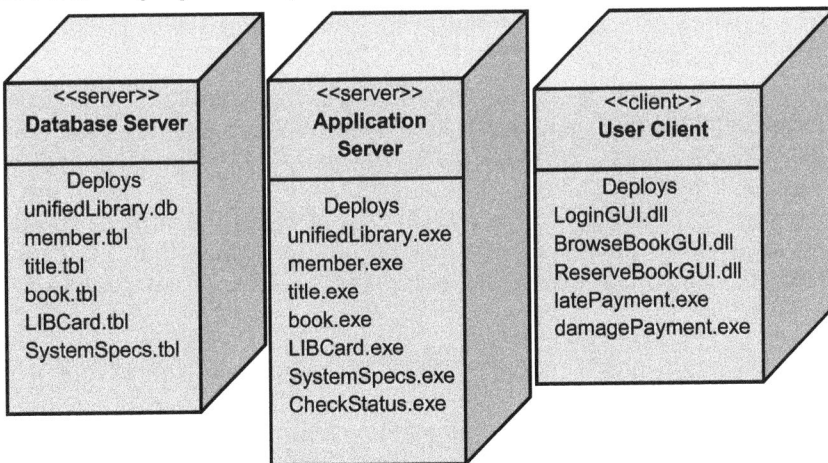

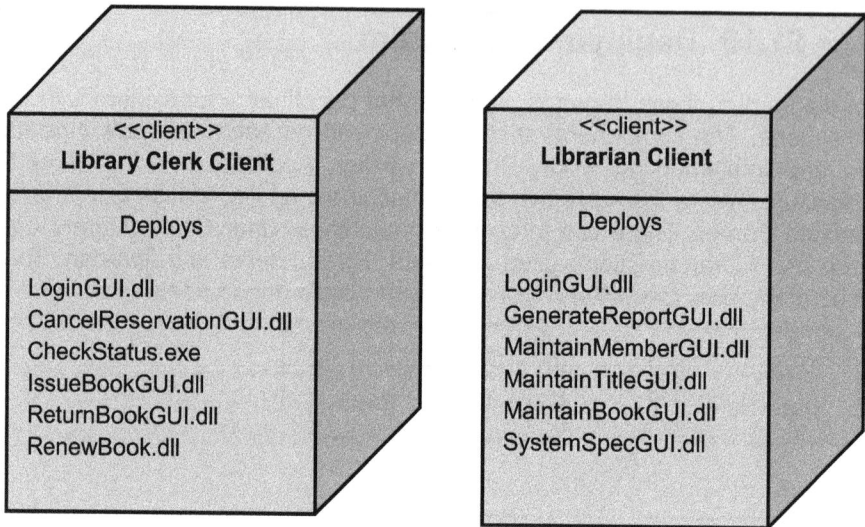

**Fig.21.18** Nodes with Deployed Components

## 21.11 Architecture Design

This is the high-level design where the packages (subsystems) are defined. This design includes the dependencies and primary communication mechanisms between the packages. Generally, we go for an architecture design, where the dependencies are few and bidirectional dependencies are avoided.

A well designed architecture promotes an extensible and changeable system. It is necessary to separate the application logic from the technical logic, so that changes in either do not impact the other. The major goals to be considered while formulating architectural design are as follows:-

❖ Set up rules for dependencies between the packages (representing subsystems) in such a way that no bidirectional dependencies are created between packages. This makes subsystems more independent and lightly integrated with each other.

❖ Identify the need for standard libraries. Libraries available nowadays address technical areas such as, the user interface, the database, or communication. But also, more application specific libraries are expected to emerge.

The packages, or subsystems in the case study, the Unified Library can be described as follows:

**User-Interface Package:** This package contains classes forming standard library components, especially useful for developing or writing user interface applications. For example, the Login.dll is a library component for login user interface, where, the user enters his user ID and password and logs into the system. This GUI (Graphical User Interface) component uses the interface named ILogin, which is realized by the component or the class named Member. This package may also include standard libraries supported by an implementation language for writing user interface applications. This package cooperates with the Business-Objects package, which contains the classes where the data is actually stored. The User Interface package calls operations on the business objects to retrieve and insert data into them.

**Business-Objects Package:** This package includes the classes from the analysis model such as, Member, Title, Book, LIBCard and so on. The design fully defines the operations for these classes and adds support for persistence. The Business-Object package cooperates with the database package, in that all Business-Object classes must inherit from the persistent classes in the database package.

**Database Package:** This package includes the database components where the information is permanently stored in the database for later use. This package supplies services to other classes in the Business-Object package, so that all the data related operations such as querying, adding, updating, and deleting can be performed.

**Utility Package:** The Utility package contains services that are used in other packages in the system.

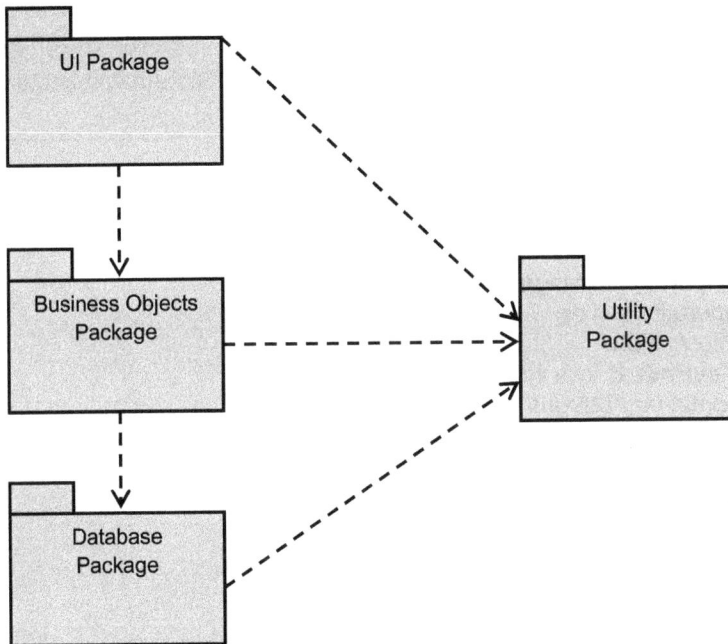

**Fig.21.19** Architectural Overview of Library Application

# CHAPTER 22

# Case Study ATM System

ATM (Automatic Teller Machine) is a computerized environment where the customer can carry on banking transactions anywhere at any time. ATM can also be called as anytime money. Customer is a person who has a bank account and contains an ATM card. Customer can approach any ATM machine which is nearby and by using his ATM card he can perform banking transactions. The customer can perform the following types of transactions such as, Balance Enquiry, Cash Withdrawal, Cash Deposit and Cash Transfer.

ATM machine contains the following Components.

❖ **CardReader:** It is the component where ATM Card is striped for performing any banking transactions.

❖ **Monitor:** It is a screen which displays messages for erroneous operations as well as status information.

❖ **KeyPad:** It is a numeric pad which contains buttons for all digits between 0 to 9 and buttons for Cancel, Esc, etc.

❖ **CashDispencer:** This component counts the required money for withdrawal by the user and places currency in the slot so that user can collect the money withdrawn from his bank in which he has account.

❖ **CashContainer:** This component contains the cash in ATM in the denominations of Rs.100, Rs.500 and Rs.2000.It supplies the required currency to the CashDispencer to dispence to the user. It is generally filled with currency by Bank Operator at the time of ATM machine maintenance.

❖ **ReceiptPrinter:** This component prints the receipt about the bank transaction performed. The printer paper and printing ink are supplied by the Bank Operator during ATM's maintenance time.

❖ **DepositBox:** This component takes the deposit amount and counts them in the order of denominations.

❖ **BankNetwork:** This component connects your ATM with the Banking Network which is a distributed system connecting all the banks in the Bank Consortium. Based on the ATM card details the required bank is identified with the associated branch of the bank. Here, ATM can interact with the account the user has in this bank's branch to perform banking transactions.

**The following gives operators who can work with ATM:**

❖ **User/Customer:** He is the person containing ATM card. He uses his ATM card to perform bank transactions through the ATM. He stripes his ATM card with Card Reader of the ATM.

❖ **BankOperator:** He is a bank employee connected with the ATM. He operates ATM. He shutdown ATM and removes the network connection with the bank. He replenishes the required cash into the Cash Container of ATM based on the available cash in the Cash Container. He performs the other maintenance activities including repair of the system. When everything is all right, The ATM machine will be started up and connection with the bank network is established. Now, the ATM waits for the user indefinitely.

❖ **BankNetwork**: It acts as an actor to connect your ATM with the required branch of the bank which is part of the Bank Consortium.

**The following mentions the functions an ATM can offer for the customer:**

ATM can be shutdown to replenish cash into it. Once the ATM is ready, it is started up and bank network connection is established. By then, ATM will be waiting for customer's striping of ATM card to perform banking transactions. Here the Bank Operator performs startup and shutdown of ATM for the purpose of its maintenance. He replenishes cash into ATM and establishes connection with the bank network.

Here, the actor Bank Operator does the following functions of ATM:

❖ SystemStartup.
❖ SystemShutdown
❖ CashReplenishment
❖ Maintenance
❖ Repair.
❖ Establish Network Connection.

Now, the customer wants to perform banking transactions, stripes the ATM card with the Card Reader of ATM. Then, ATM asks the Customer to enter

PIN (Personal Identification Number). The ATM card details with the PIN is sent to the corresponding bank through the Bank Network for the purpose of validation. If the validation is successful, the bank authorizes the Customer for performing bank transactions. If either the ATM Card details or PIN invalid, then display message to the Customer that he is not authenticated to do banking activities through Monitor of ATM. Then, ATM goes to the state of indefinitely waiting for customer's interaction. If the Customer enters wrong PIN for three consecutive times, then the ATM card is not accepted for the whole day.

If the ATM card with PIN are valid, a message is sent to the ATM authorizing the Customer to perform bank transactions by the Bank through Bank Network. If the Customer is authenticated, he can perform the following banking activities such as, Balance Enquiry, Cash Withdrawal, Cash Deposit, and Cash Transfer.

If the Customer chooses the Balance Enquiry Transaction, a message is sent to the Bank Network and Customer's Bank Account is accessed. Bank Network sends back the Account Balance retrieving it from the customer's account to the ATM. The ATM displays the account balance as message using the monitor. If the Customer wants the printed slip, he can ask for the same by entering response through Key Pad. Customer can collect the printed slip from the ATM once it is printed. The ATM asks for the customer whether to perform another transaction or not. If the Customer does not choose any transaction, the transaction is complete and ATM goes into the state, where it indefinitely waits for the Customer's interaction. If the Customer chooses to perform another transaction, the Customer can choose any of the transaction types displayed for him, by using Key Pad.

If the Customer chooses the Cash Withdrawal Transaction, the ATM displays message to the Customer through Monitor to enter cash amount to be withdrawn from the Bank. If the customer chooses further action after entering cash amount, this amount is checked against the maximum amount that can be withdrawn (typically Rs.10,000). If this customer entered amount is more than the maximum amount allowed, the ATM displays that message on the monitor and waits for the user to enter different amount **for 20 seconds**. If nothing happens for **twenty seconds** the ATM cancels the transaction and goes into the state of waiting indefinitely for Customer interaction. If the amount entered is less than the maximum allowed, then this amount is checked against available currency in the ATM Cash Container. If the entered amount is larger than the available currency in the Cash Container of ATM, this transaction cannot be approved and the corresponding message is displayed on the Monitor to the Customer. After this, ATM waits for the entry of new amount by the customer **for 20 seconds**. If nothing happens for 20 seconds, the ATM terminates the Transaction and goes into the state of waiting indefinitely for Customer interaction.

If the ATM contains the required cash, a message is sent to the bank through the Bank Network to access Customer's Account. If the amount entered is greater than the available account balance, then this transaction is not allowed and the corresponding message is sent to the ATM through Bank Network. The ATM displays this message to the Customer on Monitor and waits for the new amount to be entered for **20 seconds**. If the Customer does not respond for 20 seconds, then the Transaction is cancelled and the ATM goes in to the state of waiting indefinitely for Customer's interaction.

If the Customer entered amount is less than the account balance, then this transaction is legitimate and the account is debited with the amount. A positive message is sent to the ATM from Bank Network, then the ATM counts the required currency from the Cash Container and gives out for Customer's collection through Cash Dispenser. A corresponding message for the Customer is displayed on to the monitor to collect the cash dispensed. If nothing happens **for 20 seconds**, the dispensed cash is taken back by the ATM and the corresponding bank transaction is cancelled. Before dispensing cash, the ATM may ask for choosing a printed slip of bank transaction. If the Customer chooses for the printed slip, after cash dispensed, a slip containing the transaction details is printed for customer collection.

If Customer chooses Cash Deposit Transaction, ATM asks for the amount to be deposited into the bank. The ATM waits for currency submission by opening Deposit Box **for 20 seconds**. If nothing happens **in 20 seconds**, the Deposit Box will be closed and transaction is cancelled and the ATM displays the corresponding message to the customer on the monitor. Then ATM goes into the state of waiting indefinitely for Customer's interaction. If the currency is deposited, it is counted by ATM and compares with the amount entered. If they do not mach, the relevant message is displayed on to the monitor to the Customer and the ATM waits **for 20 seconds** for response. If nothing happens the currency submitted by the Customer is given back and the current bank transaction is cancelled and ATM goes into the state of waiting indefinitely for Customer's interaction.

If the amount entered matches with the currency submitted through Deposit Box, a message is sent into the Bank Network with the amount. Then the Bank Account is credited with this amount. If the customer wants printed slip, he can ask it by using Key Pad. Then the current transaction details with the available balance in the bank account are printed on the slip. Then, ATM asks for another transaction if the customer wants to continue working with the ATM. Otherwise, the current transaction is successfully completed and the relevant message is displayed for the Customer and the ATM goes into a state of waiting indefinitely for Customer's interaction.

If the Customer chooses Cash Transfer Transaction, the ATM asks for the Customer to enter amount for Cash Transfer and the person's ATM card number. The amount of money entered by the Customer is checked against his account balance, so as to decide whether the transaction is legal. If the transfer amount entered by the customer is larger than his account balance, a relevant message is displayed to the Customer on the monitor and the ATM waits for reentry of different amount. If the Customer does not respond for

**about 20 seconds**, ATM cancels the current bank transaction and goes into the state of waiting indefinitely for Customer's interaction.

If the transfer amount entered is less than the account balance of the Customer, then the Cash Transfer Transaction is legal. The account balance of the Customer is debited and the account balance of the cash receiver is credited with this amount through Bank Network. If the Customer wants a printed slip containing the details of the current transaction, he can do it so by choosing that option on the Key Pad. After the Cash Transfer, a slip is printed and the customer can collect the same. The ATM after this transaction may ask for another transaction from the customer. If the customer chooses no , then the current transaction is successfully completed and the ATM goes into the state of waiting indefinitely for Customer's interaction by displaying welcome message on to the monitor.

The functions of ATM with respect to the customer can be specified as follows:

❖ When Customer stripes the ATM card with the Card Reader of ATM, ATM asks for PIN, both of these details are sent to the bank for customer authentication through Bank Network.

❖ Customer can choose a Bank Transaction which can be any of the following types such as Balance Enquiry, Cash Withdrawal, Cash Deposit and Cash Transfer.

❖ During performance of a transaction, the Customer's Bank account is accessed and required modifications are made to it through Bank Network.

## 22.1  System Analysis

The following use cases can be identified for the ATM system based on its functions that it offers:

The Bank Operator performs ATM system shutdown for the purpose of maintenance, cash replenishment, and repair. He can disconnect the bank network while ATM is shutdown. When ATM is ready for operation, he can re establish Bank Network connection after system startup. The ATM displays welcome message on to the monitor and goes into the state of waiting indefinitely for customer's interaction. The following are the use cases identified:

❖ System Shutdown use case which includes use cases such as Maintenance, Repair. Maintenance use case include Cash Replenishment, Disconnect Bank Network and Diagnostics. Repair use case include Diagnostics.

❖ System Startup use case which includes use cases Connect Bank Network, make ATM system ready by waiting for User Response.

❖ The Customer stripes his card resulting into use cases Read Card and Accept PIN which includes Customer Authentication use case.

❖ The Customer can choose Bank Transaction use case which is of the following types such as Balance Inquiry, Cash Withdrawal, Cash Deposit and Cash Transfer. Here, the Bank Transaction use case includes Accept Details from the user pertaining to the transaction and Customer Authentication use case. A Bank Transaction use case may include Print Slip use case.

❖ For each Bank Transaction the customer selects , the details entered are validated against the customer's bank account. That is, each Bank Transaction use case includes Validate Details use case.

❖ If the transaction is valid, that is if there is enough of money in the account as deposit, and Cash container contains enough of currency, then the required cash is dispensed to be collected by the Customer.

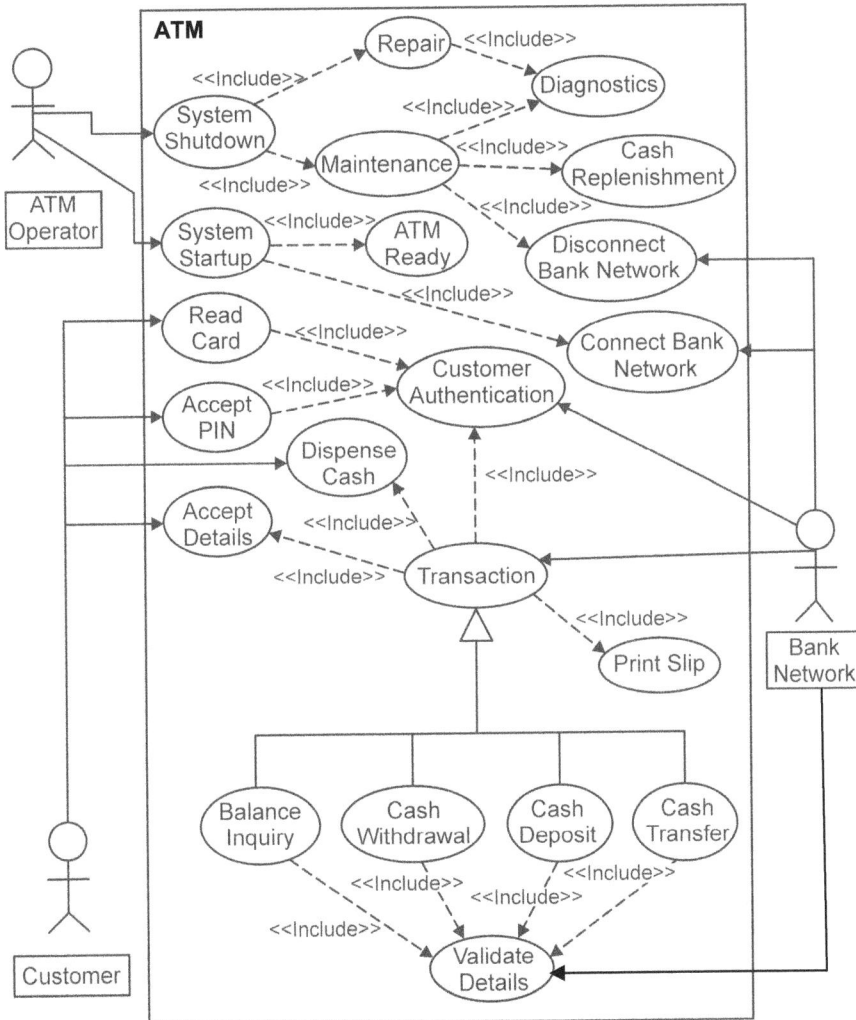

**Fig.22.1** Use Case Diagram for ATM System

## 22.2 System Design

The following diagram gives the details of class diagram where different classes are identified by going through the system specifications which are short nouns and noun phrases.

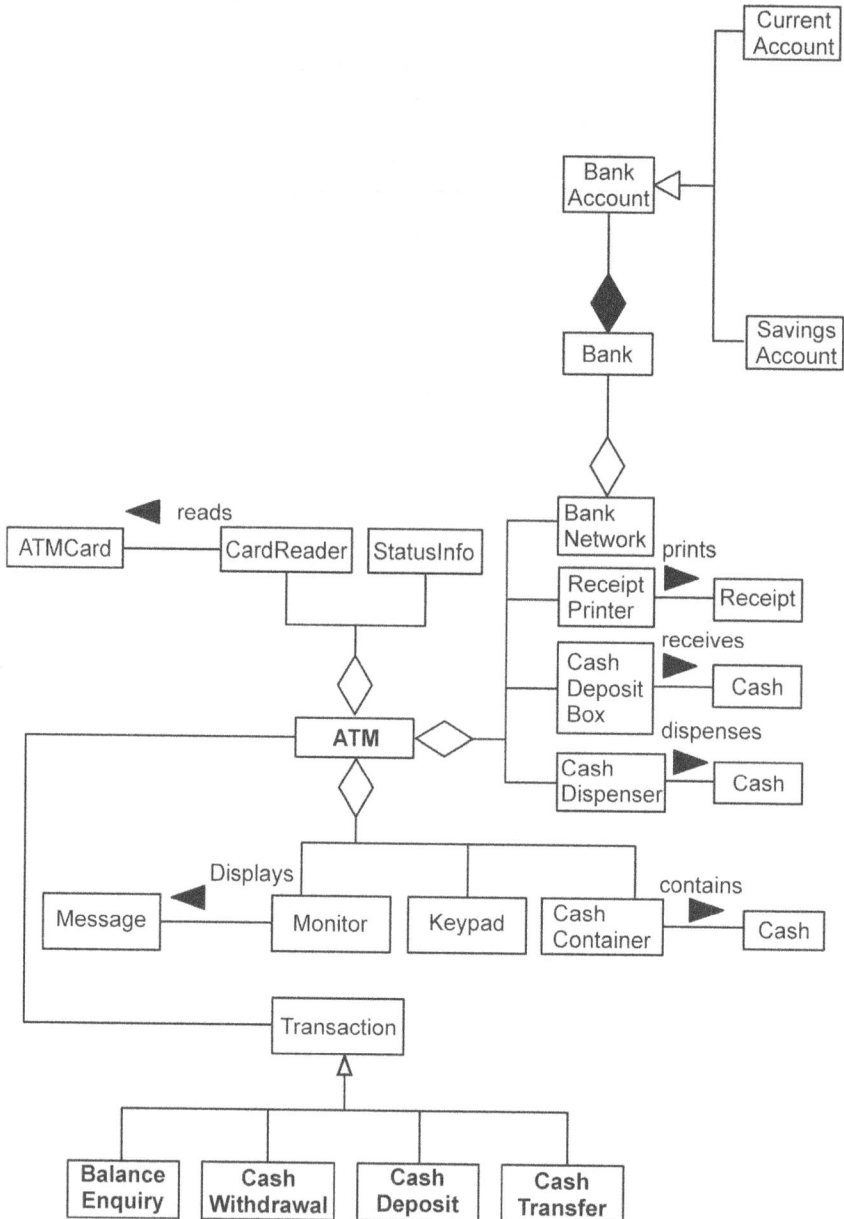

**Fig.22.2** Class Diagram for ATM System

When ATM Card is swiped by the Customer using Card Reader, the ATM Card details are read and send to the ATM. The ATM displays message to enter PIN through monitor .The PIN is keyed in by the customer using Key Pad. The ATM sends ATM Card details with PIN to the Bank Network which accesses Bank Account and determines whether the ATM customer is authenticated to perform bank transactions or not. If either the bank details or PIN are invalid, the current transaction under progress will get canceled and ATM becomes ready for next ATM Card swipe.

If the Customer is authenticated by the Bank, ATM displays prompt to choose account type. The ATM gets customer's account type and prompts for transaction type, which can be Balance Inquiry, Cash Withdrawal, Cash Deposit, and Cash Transfer. The current transaction can be canceled at any time and at any level by choosing Cancel operation on the Key Pad.

If the transaction is Balance Inquiry, the ATM displays balance amount on to the monitor and prints the receipt if printing of receipt is selected. If you choose next transaction, then a new transaction starts, otherwise the current transaction is successfully completed. Then the ATM goes into a state of waiting for customer's ATM Card by displaying welcome message on to the monitor.

If the transaction selected is Cash Withdrawal, the ATM prompts the Customer to enter amount of money to be withdrawn. This amount is checked against the availability of sufficient cash in the Cash Container of ATM. If there is no sufficient cash, the transaction is canceled by displaying corresponding message. If the ATM's Cash Container contains sufficient currency, these Customer entered details with ATM card details are sent to the Bank Network to accept customer's account to check whether he has sufficient balance or not. If there is no sufficient balance, the current transaction is canceled and relevant message is displayed to the Customer. If the customer has sufficient balance in his account, the required cash from the Cash Container is collected by the Cash Dispenser and is dispensed to the customer for his collection by displaying the relevant message. At the same time, the withdrawal amount is debited to the customer's account and equivalent currency from the Cash Container is removed.

If the transaction selected is Cash Deposit, the ATM prompts the customer to enter the amount to be deposited. After deposit amount entry the Cash Deposit Box opens to collect currency envelop. If the Customer does not respond for 20 seconds, the transaction is canceled and the Cash Deposit Box closes. If the user entered money matches with the money deposited in the Cash Deposit Box, the relevant details are sent to the customer's account through Bank Network and the bank balance is credited with the deposited amount. The ATM displays relevant messages and successfully completes the transaction.

If the transaction selected is Cash Transfer, the ATM prompts the customer to enter the amount to be transferred and the destination bank account number and the destination ATM Card number. After receiving customer's input, the details are sent to the customer's account in order to determine whether he has sufficient balance to perform cash transfer to the destination account. If there is no sufficient balance, the transaction is canceled and the ATM displays the corresponding message. If the account balance is sufficient, the source account is debited and the destination account is credited with the transfer amount. The relevant message is displayed and the current transaction is successfully completed.

The ATM asks the Customer to continue with another transaction or not. If he wants to continue, then transaction types are displayed so as to choose the relevant transaction type. The moment new transaction type is chosen a new transaction begins. If the customer does not want to continue the transaction or cancels the transaction the entire transaction is canceled and the ATM displays appropriate message and goes into a state of waiting for ATM Card swiping.

The classes which are identified are given with their full details as follows:

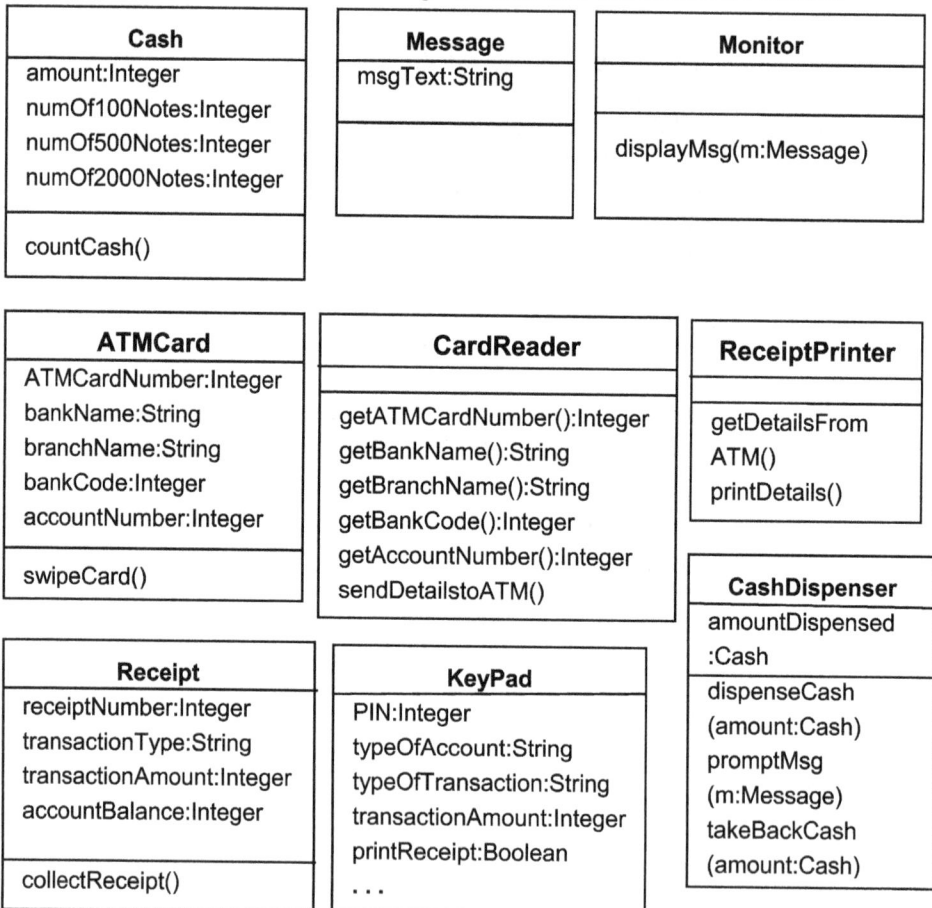

**Cash**
amount:Integer
numOf100Notes:Integer
numOf500Notes:Integer
numOf2000Notes:Integer

countCash()

**Message**
msgText:String

**Monitor**

displayMsg(m:Message)

**ATMCard**
ATMCardNumber:Integer
bankName:String
branchName:String
bankCode:Integer
accountNumber:Integer

swipeCard()

**CardReader**

getATMCardNumber():Integer
getBankName():String
getBranchName():String
getBankCode():Integer
getAccountNumber():Integer
sendDetailstoATM()

**ReceiptPrinter**

getDetailsFrom ATM()
printDetails()

**CashDispenser**
amountDispensed :Cash

dispenseCash (amount:Cash)
promptMsg (m:Message)
takeBackCash (amount:Cash)

**Receipt**
receiptNumber:Integer
transactionType:String
transactionAmount:Integer
accountBalance:Integer

collectReceipt()

**KeyPad**
PIN:Integer
typeOfAccount:String
typeOfTransaction:String
transactionAmount:Integer
printReceipt:Boolean
...

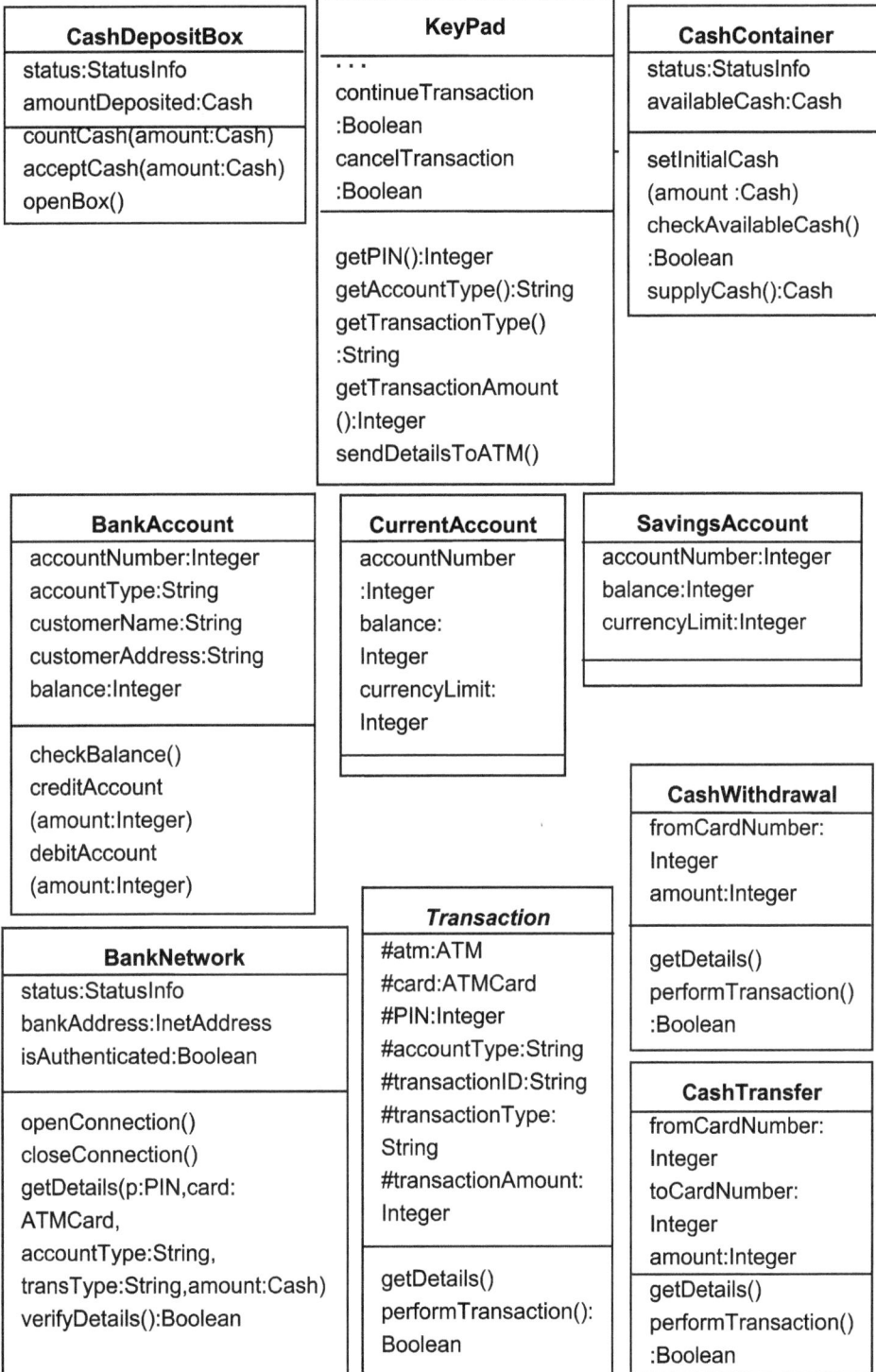

| CashDepositBox |
| --- |
| status:StatusInfo<br>amountDeposited:Cash |
| countCash(amount:Cash)<br>acceptCash(amount:Cash)<br>openBox() |

| KeyPad |
| --- |
| . . .<br>continueTransaction<br>:Boolean<br>cancelTransaction<br>:Boolean |
| getPIN():Integer<br>getAccountType():String<br>getTransactionType()<br>:String<br>getTransactionAmount<br>():Integer<br>sendDetailsToATM() |

| CashContainer |
| --- |
| status:StatusInfo<br>availableCash:Cash |
| setInitialCash<br>(amount :Cash)<br>checkAvailableCash()<br>:Boolean<br>supplyCash():Cash |

| BankAccount |
| --- |
| accountNumber:Integer<br>accountType:String<br>customerName:String<br>customerAddress:String<br>balance:Integer |
| checkBalance()<br>creditAccount<br>(amount:Integer)<br>debitAccount<br>(amount:Integer) |

| CurrentAccount |
| --- |
| accountNumber<br>:Integer<br>balance:<br>Integer<br>currencyLimit:<br>Integer |

| SavingsAccount |
| --- |
| accountNumber:Integer<br>balance:Integer<br>currencyLimit:Integer |

| CashWithdrawal |
| --- |
| fromCardNumber:<br>Integer<br>amount:Integer |
| getDetails()<br>performTransaction()<br>:Boolean |

| BankNetwork |
| --- |
| status:StatusInfo<br>bankAddress:InetAddress<br>isAuthenticated:Boolean |
| openConnection()<br>closeConnection()<br>getDetails(p:PIN,card:<br>ATMCard,<br>accountType:String,<br>transType:String,amount:Cash)<br>verifyDetails():Boolean |

| *Transaction* |
| --- |
| #atm:ATM<br>#card:ATMCard<br>#PIN:Integer<br>#accountType:String<br>#transactionID:String<br>#transactionType:<br>String<br>#transactionAmount:<br>Integer |
| getDetails()<br>performTransaction():<br>Boolean |

| CashTransfer |
| --- |
| fromCardNumber:<br>Integer<br>toCardNumber:<br>Integer<br>amount:Integer |
| getDetails()<br>performTransaction()<br>:Boolean |

| Balance Inquiry | CashDeposit | ATM |
|---|---|---|
| fromCardNumber: Integer<br>balance:Integer | intoCardNumber: Integer<br>amount:Integer | Id:Integer<br>location:String<br>bankName:String<br>bankAddress:InetAddress<br>cardReader:CardReader<br>cashDispenser:<br>CashDispenser<br>cashContainer:<br>CashContainer<br>cashDepositBox:<br>CashDepositBox<br>status:StatusInfo<br>bankNetwork:<br>BankNetwork<br>monitor:Monitor<br>keypad:KeyPad<br>receiptPrinter:<br>ReceiptPrinter<br>transaction:<br>Transaction |
| getDetails()<br>performTransaction():<br>Boolean | getDetails()<br>performTransaction ():<br>Boolean | |

| StatusInfo | Date | Time |
|---|---|---|
| transactionID:String<br>transactionDate: Date<br>transactionTime: Time<br>transactionType:String<br>accountType:String<br>ATMCardNumber: Integer<br>transactionAmount: Integer | day: Integer<br>month: Integer<br>year: Integer | seconds: Integer<br>minutes: Integer<br>hours: Integer |
| | setDate()<br>getDate() | setTime()<br>getTime() |
| maintainStatusInfo() | | |

getDetails()
sendDetails()
performTransaction()
systemOn()
systemOff()

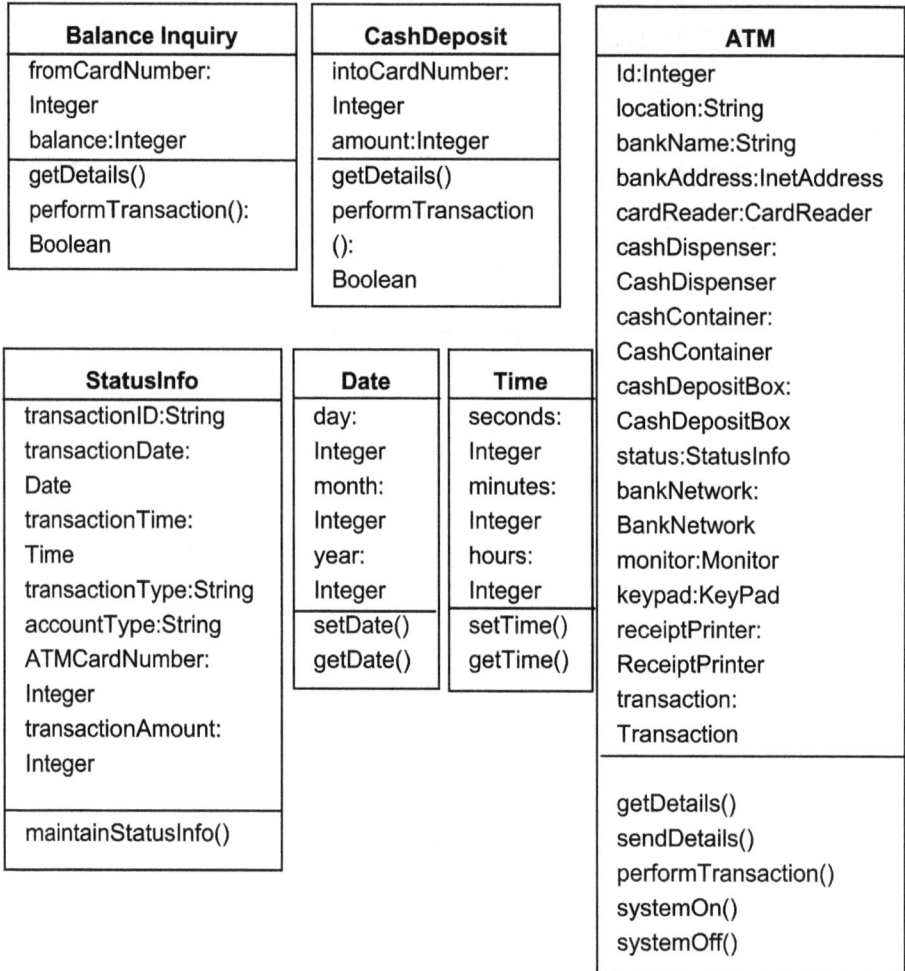

**Fig.22.3** Detailed Classes

In the following section we discuss the properties and services each class is intended for.

**Cash:** This class maintains the cash amount in various denominations. The ATM maintains the cash in multiples of 2000 notes,500 notes and 100 notes. Cash is counted when it is dispensed through CashDispenser and when it is deposited through CashDepositBox.

**Message**: This class maintains the message text to be displayed on to the Monitor.

**Monitor**: This class displays the message text which is part of Message.

**ATMCard**: This class maintains the details of the customer's card such as card number, bank name, bank code, branch name and account Number. These details are read by the CardReader when it is swiped.

**CardReader:** This class reads the details of ATMCard and sends them to the ATM.

**ReceiptPrinter:** This class gets details from ATM and prints them on a slip of paper which can be collected by the customer.

**Receipt**: This maintains the information about receipt number ,transaction type, transaction amount and the available account balance. Receipt printer prints this ,that can be collected by the customer.

**KeyPad:** This accepts PIN, type of account, type of transaction, transaction amount. The customer can choose whether to continue with next transaction, whether to print receipt for the current transaction and can cancel the current transaction. All these details are collected and sent to ATM.

**CashDispenser:** This gives out cash to the customer to collect. It displays the message for the customer to collect the cash. If the cash is not collected **within 20 seconds**, it is taken back by the ATM.

**CashDepositBox:** This provides the facility to deposit cash in multiples of 100s into the customer's account. This accepts deposited amount as entered by the customer, then the CashDepositBox opens up to collect Cash. When Cash is placed into the CashDepositBox, it is counted, if it matches the deposit amount entered, the Cash is accepted. The corresponding account balance is credited through BankNetwork.

**CashContainer:** This contains Cash in multiples of 100 ,500 and 2000 notes. Whenever CashWithdrawal transaction happens, the CashContainer is checked with the available currency. If cash is sufficiently available, the withdrawal will be successful, otherwise the transaction will be canceled. This supplies cash to the CashDispenser which dispenses cash to the Customer.

**BankAccount:** This maintains details about account number, account type, account balance, customer's name, and customer's address. The transaction amount is verified with the available balance based on the type of transaction. Whenever a transaction happens the bank account can be credited or debited based on the type of transaction. This contains two types of accounts such as CurrentAccount or SavingsAccount.

**CurrentAccount:** This maintains the account number, account balance, and currency limit that can be drawn through ATM.

**SavingsAccount:** This maintains the account number, account balance, and currency limit that can be drawn through ATM.

OBJECT-ORIENTED ANALYSIS AND DESIGN USING UML

**BankNetwork:** This maintains the information about bank consortium forming the network. It is used to authenticate the customer based on details of ATMCard and PIN entered. For each type of bank transaction, the corresponding account of the customer is accessed to see the account balance for carrying out transaction successfully. This network is used to debit or credit the bank accounts based on the type of transaction.

**Transaction:** This is an abstract class, that is, it cannot have instances. But its children can have instances. It maintains information regarding ATM, ATMCard , PIN , transactionID, account type, transaction type and transaction amount.

**CashWithdrawal:** This maintains information about ATMCard number and withdrawal amount. This class collects all details regarding ATMCard, PIN and withdrawal  amount and sends these details as part of performTransaction() which returns true if the withdrawal is successful otherwise it returns false canceling the transaction. If the withdrawal is successful ATM debits the customer's account with the withdrawal amount through BankNetwork. Status information regarding withdrawals is maintained by the ATM by using StatusInfo.

**BalanceInquiry:** This class helps in knowing customer's current account balance. This maintains information about ATMcard number and account balance. The details regarding ATMCard, PIN are combined, and based on the type of transaction, the balance can be copied from the customer's account. This is done through performTransaction() operation which returns a Boolean value indicating success or failure of transaction. . Status information regarding withdrawals is maintained by the ATM by using StatusInfo.

**CashDeposit:** This class helps in depositing amount into the customer's account. This class gets all the details such as ATMCard PIN, and account deposited. These details are sent to BankNetwork to make a successful transaction through performTransaction() operation. This operation returns true if the cash deposit is successful otherwise it returns false. If the cash deposit transaction is successful, the customer's account balance is incremented by the deposited amount. Status information regarding withdrawals is maintained by the ATM by using StatusInfo.

**CashTransfer:** This helps in transferring transaction amount from customer's account to some other account. It maintains information about customer's ATMCard number, the destination's ATMCard number, and transfer amount. These details with ATMCard details are sent to the BankNetwork by performing performTransaction() operation which returns a Boolean value. If the operation returns true, customer's account is debited and destination's account is credited with transaction amount. Status information regarding withdrawals is maintained by the ATM by using StatusInfo.

**StatusInfo:** This class records the status of each transaction by maintaining details such as transactionID, Date of transaction, time of transaction ,transaction type, transaction amount, account type, and ATMCard Number. It has only one operation named maintainStatusInfo() which maintains the values of the above attributes and prints status information regarding each transaction.

**Date:** This class maintains the current system date in terms of day, month and year. We can set date and get date by using setDate() and getDate() operations.

**Time:** This class maintains information regarding current system time in terms of hours, minutes, and seconds. You can set time and get time by using setTime() and getTime() operations.

**ATM:** This maintains details about all of its components. It collects details from various its components and sends them for verification by using getDetails() and sendDetails() operations. The transaction is performed by using performTransaction() operation.

**In the following section, we discuss interaction diagrams for each use case:**

**1). Sequence Diagram for System Startup use case:**

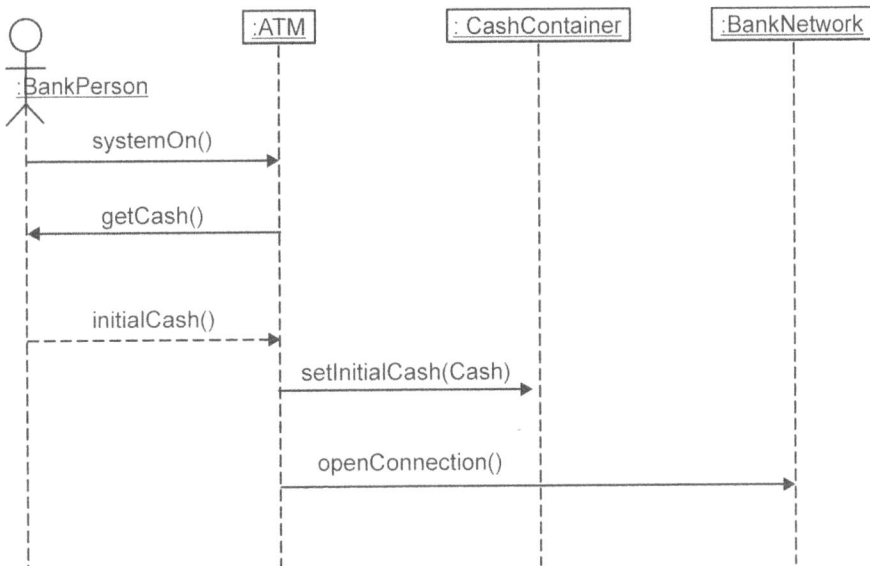

**2).The corresponding Collaboration Diagram is:**

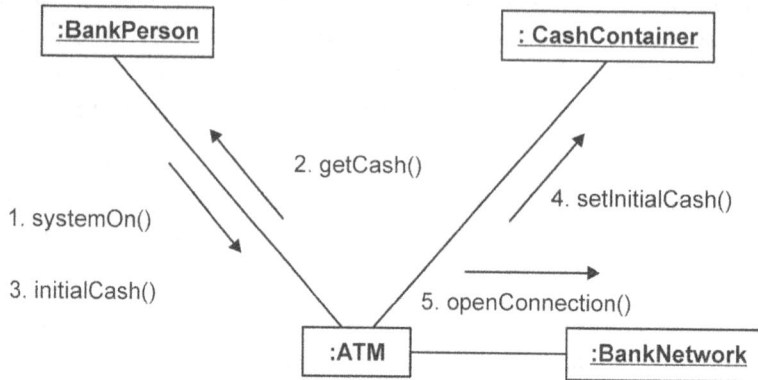

**3). Sequence Diagram for system shutdown use case:**

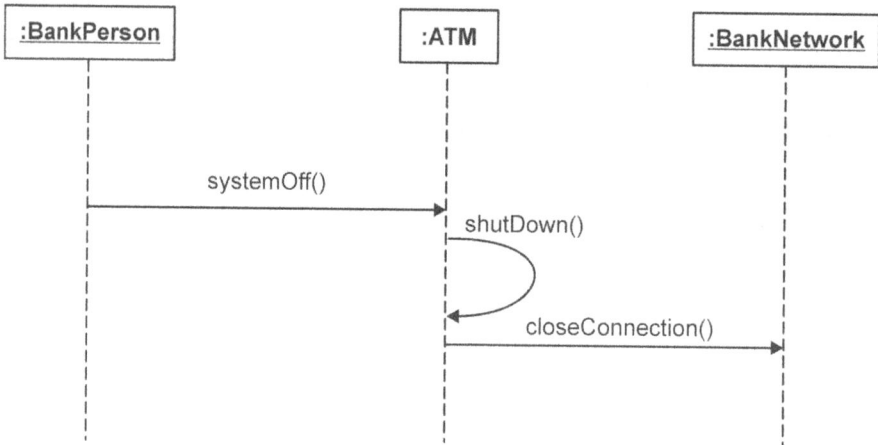

**4). Corresponding Collaboration Diagram:**

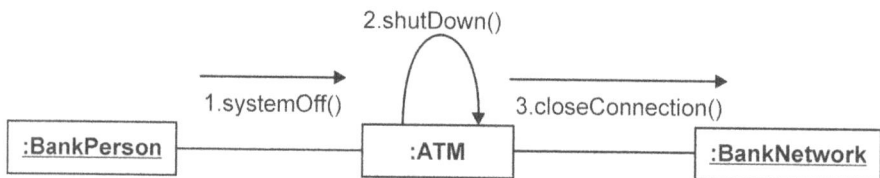

**5).Sequence Diagram for Customer Authentication use case:**

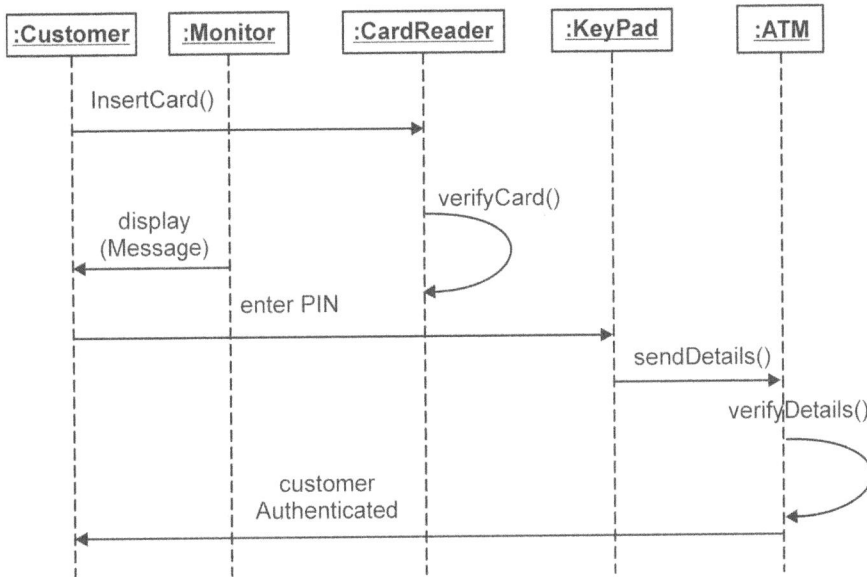

**6). Collaboration Diagram for Customer Authentication use case:**

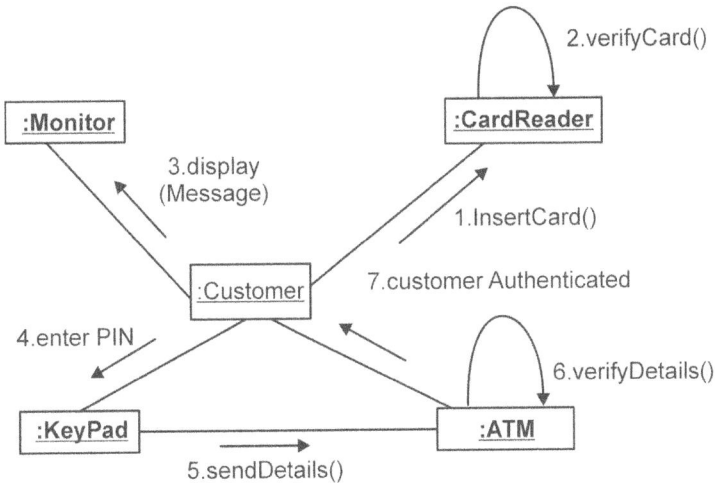

### 7). Collaboration Diagram for Balance inquiry Transaction:

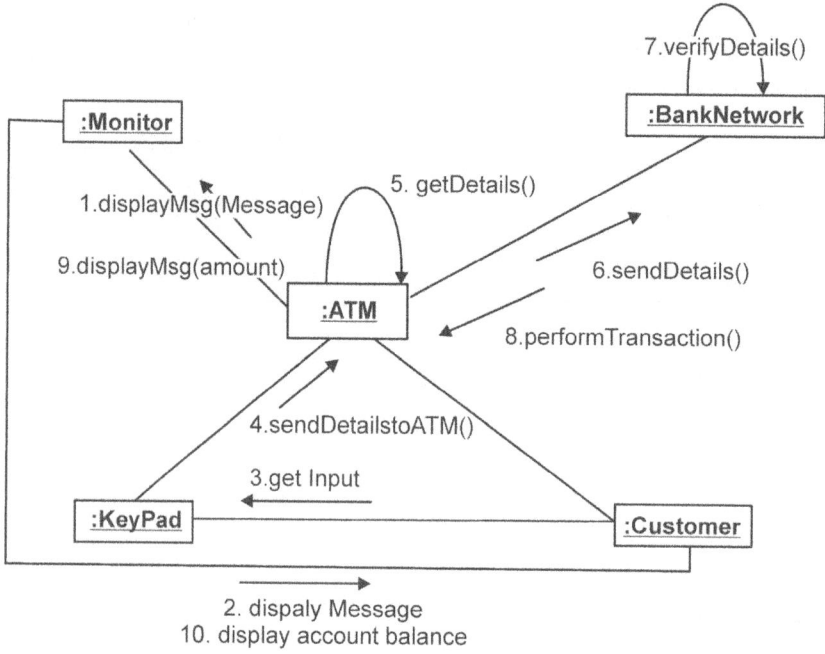

### 8). Sequence Diagram for Balance Inquiry transaction:

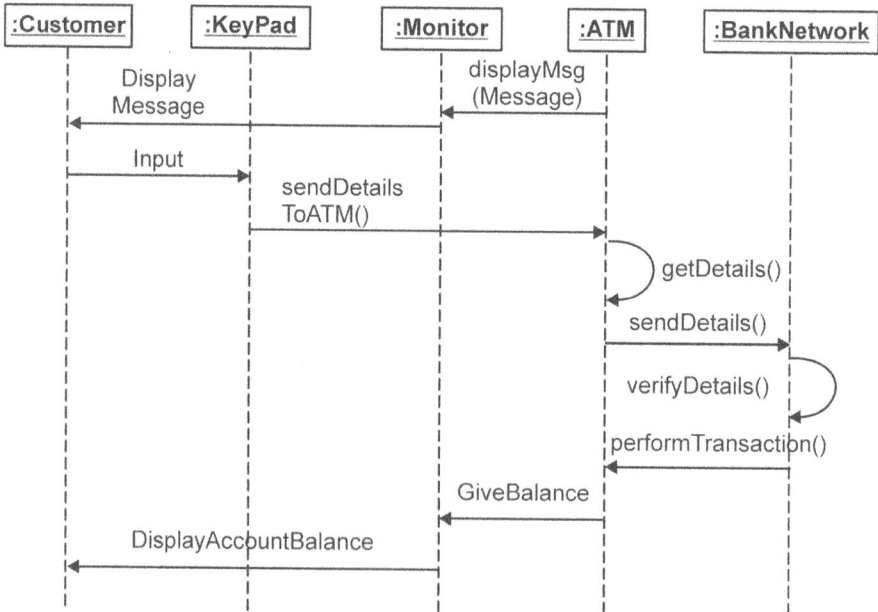

## 9).Sequence Diagram for Cash Withdrawal use case:-

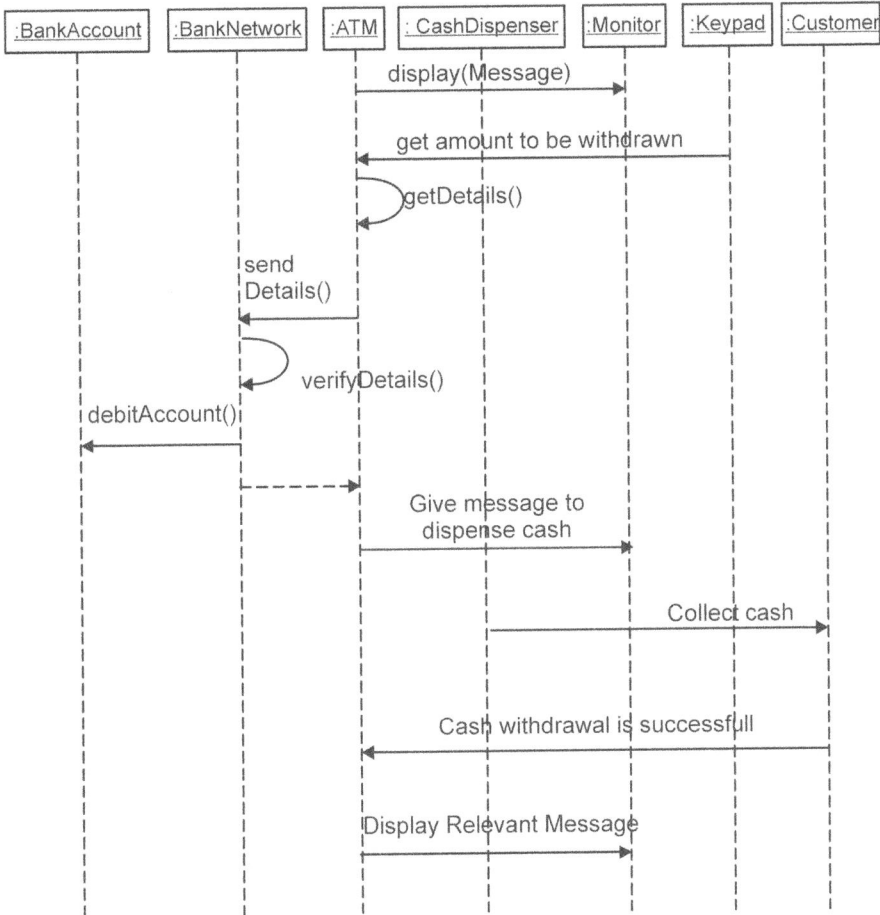

**10). Sequence diagram for cash deposit use case:**

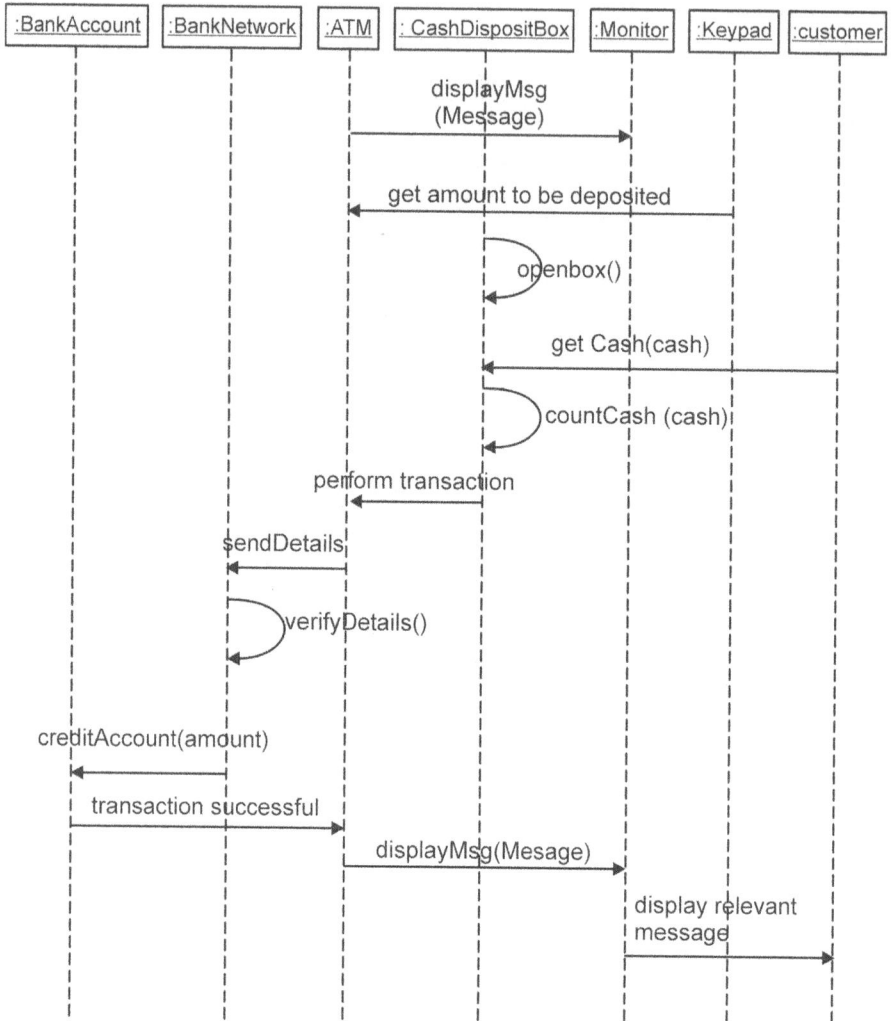

**Collaboration Diagram for Cash Deposit use case:**

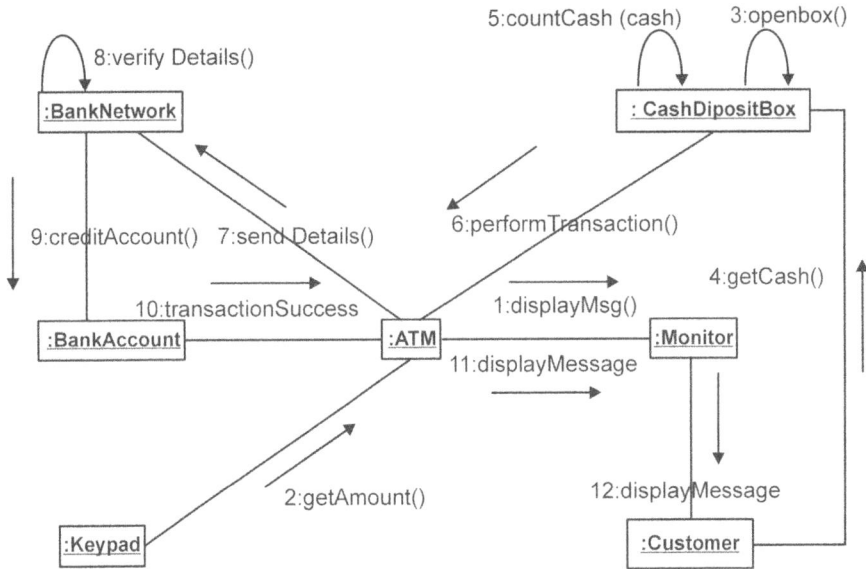

**11) Sequence Diagram for Cash Transfer use case:**

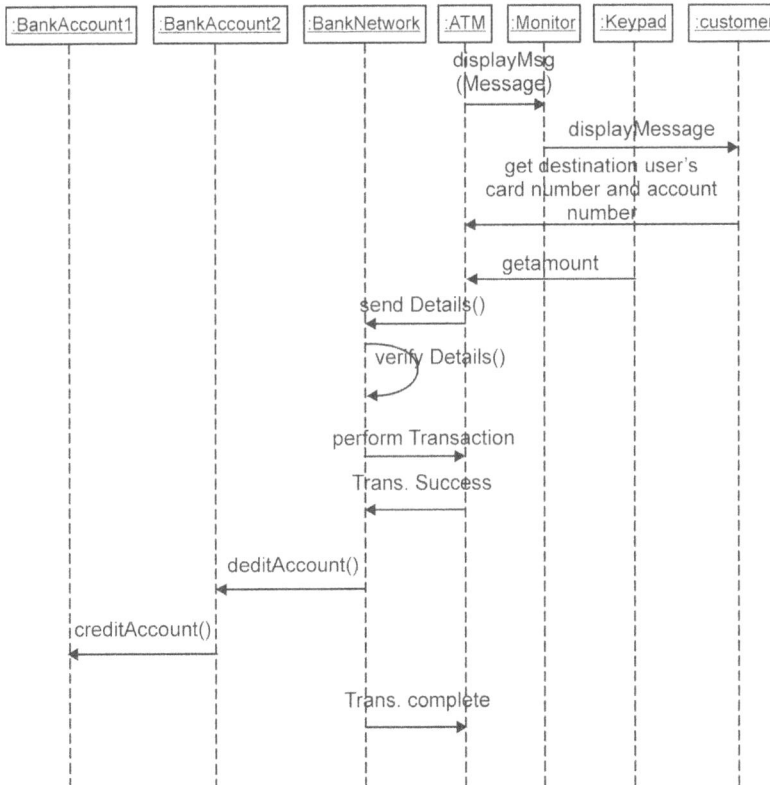

**Note:** BankAccount1 is the destination account into which amount is transferred from BankAccount2 which is the source account. Amount is debited for source bank account and the same amount is credited in destinations bank account.

**Activity Diagram for Cash Withdrawal:**

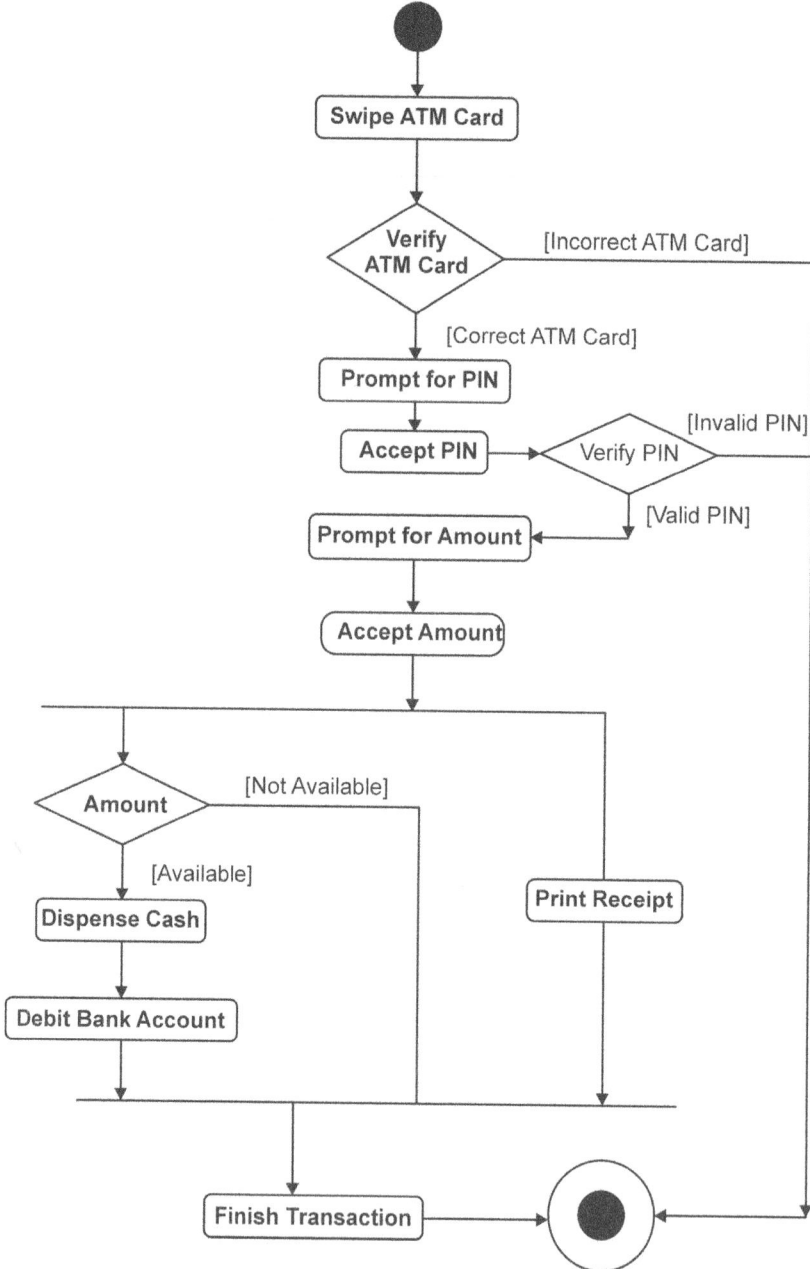

**Activity Diagram for Balance Inquiry using swim lanes:**

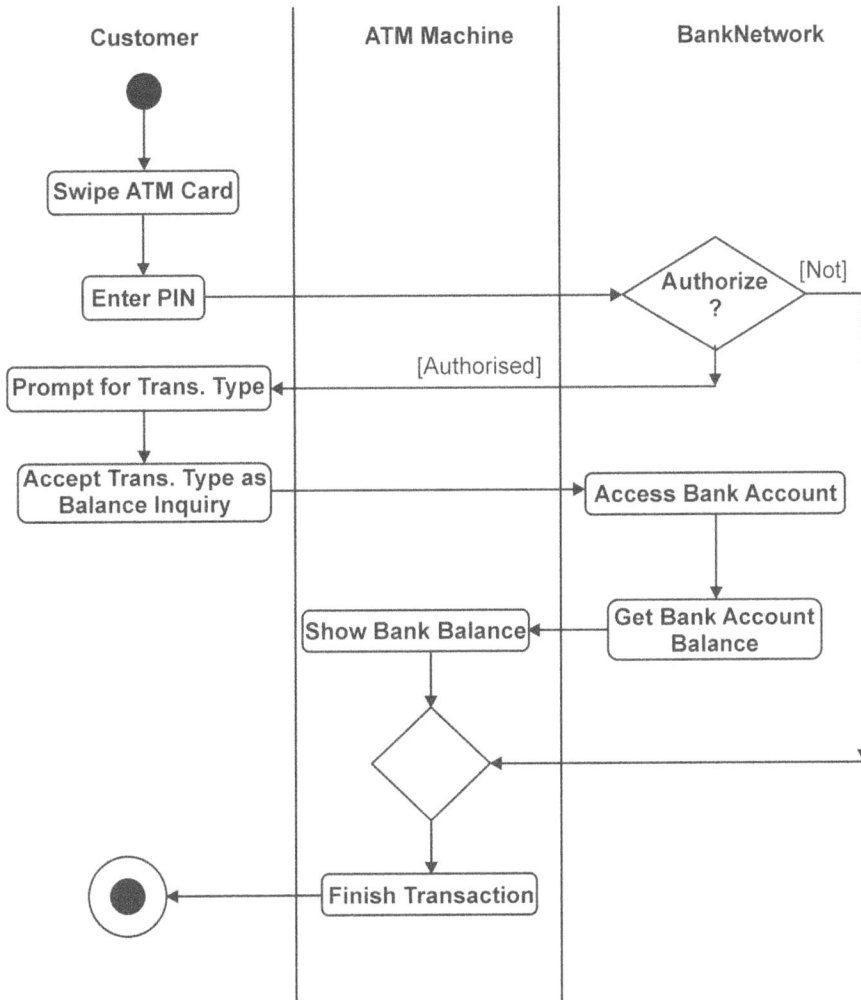

**Activity Diagram for Cash Deposit:**

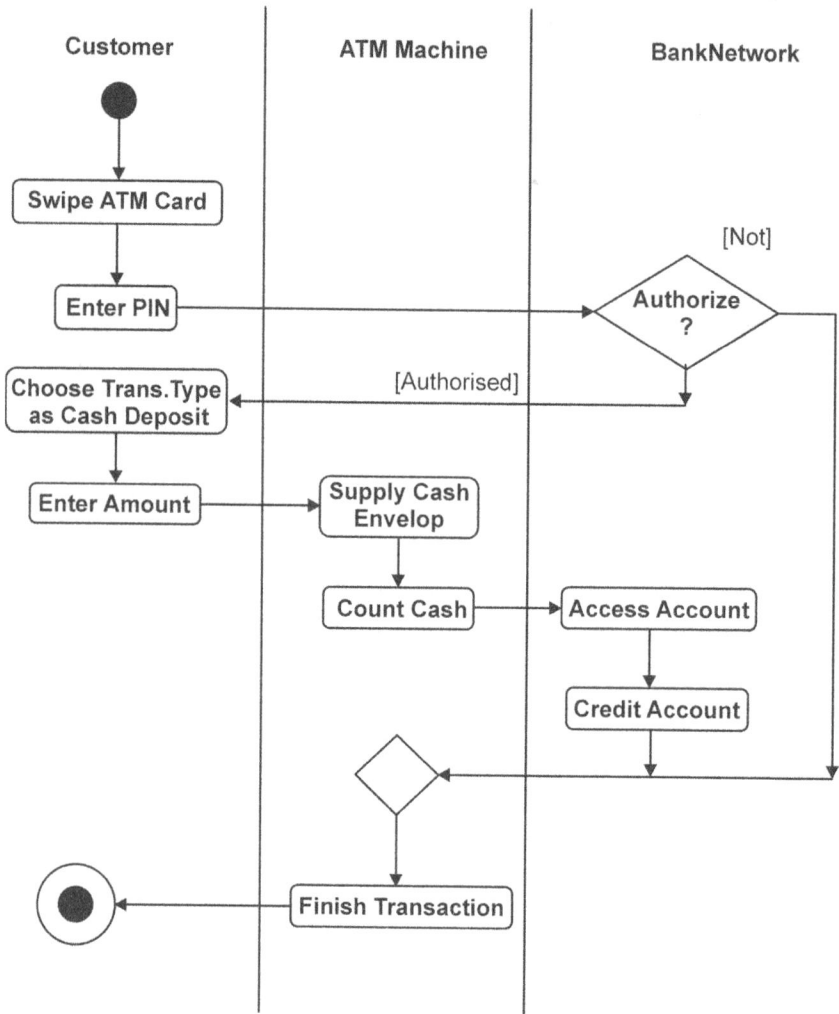

**State Chart Diagram for ATM system:**

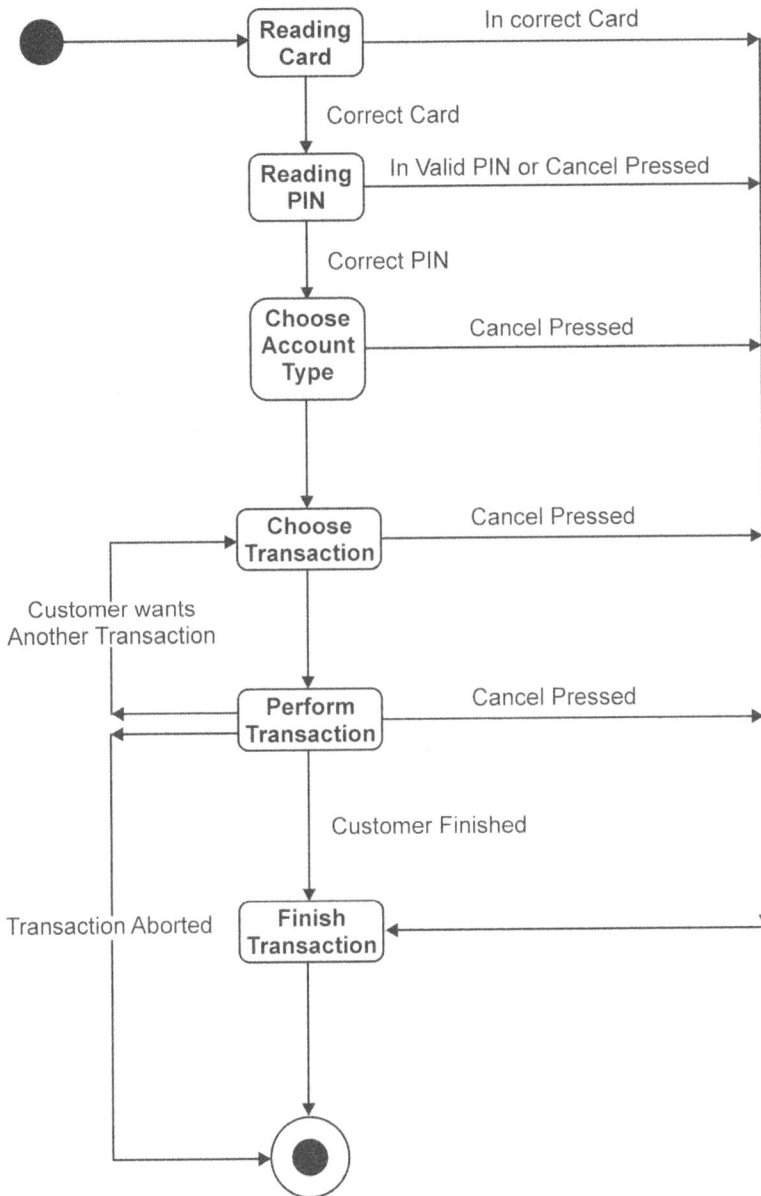

**Component Diagram for ATM System:**

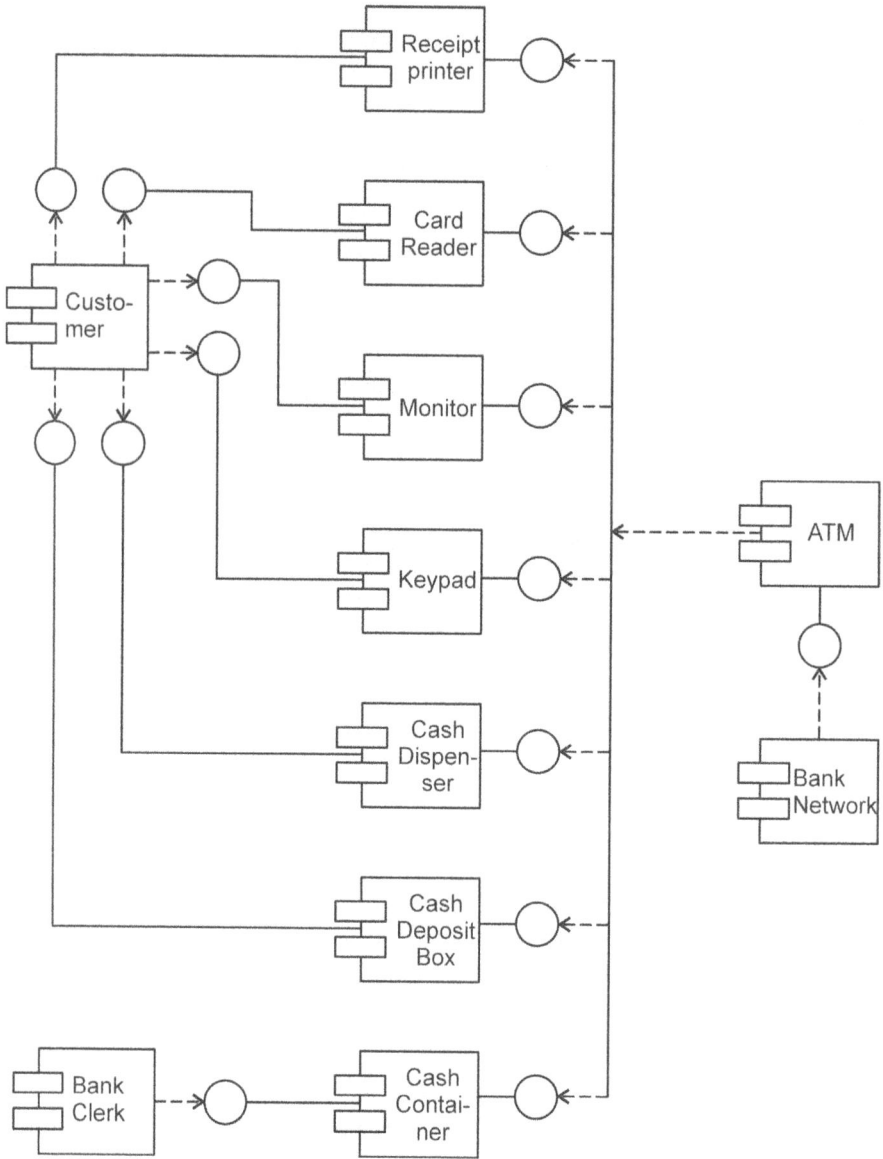

**Deployment Diagram for ATM System:**

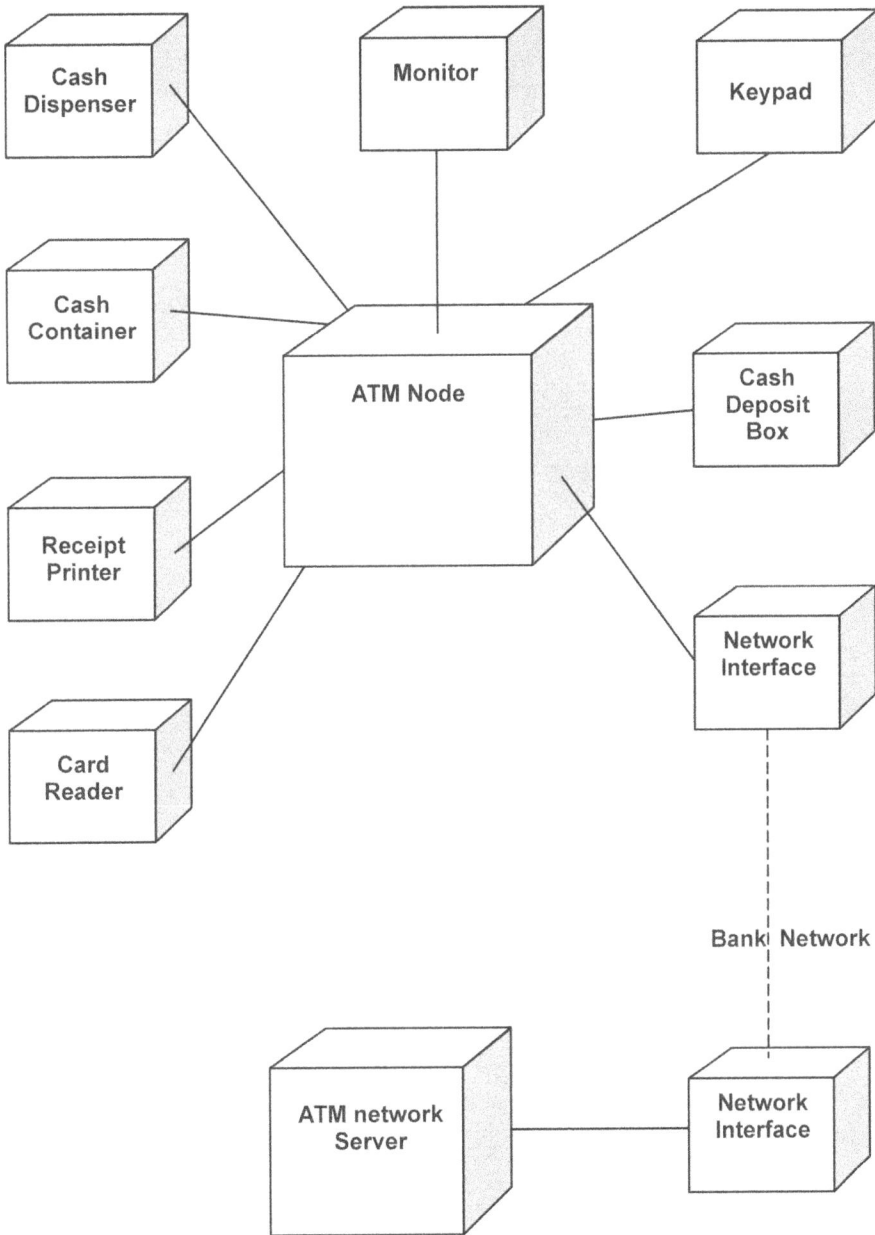

# GLOSSARY

**abstract class** A class that cannot have direct instances.

**abstraction** is the process where it is used to hide certain details and only show the essential features of an entity. In other words, it deals with the outside view of an entity.

**access** This stereotype specifies that the source package is granted the right to refer the elements of the target package. This dependency means that objects from client package can access objects (public one) from supplier package

**action state** Action states are typically executable atomic computations of the system, each representing the execution of an action.

**active class** Active class is a class whose objects contain processes or threads and which can initiate control activity.

**active object** It is an object which contain processes or threads and which can initiate control activity.

**activity** Ongoing non atomic execution within a state machine.

**activity diagram** A diagram which shows the control flow from activity to activity. Activity diagram address the dynamic view or behavioral aspect of a system.

**actor** He is a human user or some other system which interact with our system.

**addonly** If this property is specified for an attribute which has multiplicity greater than one, you can add new values, but once added, the value cannot be removed or altered.

**address space** It is the amount of memory allocated for all possible **address**es for a computational entity, such as a device, a file, a server, or a networked computer. **Address space** may refer to a range of either physical or virtual **addresses** accessible to a processor or reserved for a process.

**adornments** These are textual or graphical items, which can be added to the basic notation of a UML building block in order to visualize some details from its specification.

**advanced class** A class notation in UML provides a number of advanced features. These features help us to visualize, specify, construct and document a class to any level of detail which helps us in carrying forward and reverse engineering.

**aggregation** An aggregation relationship is an extension of association relationship, where you have a whole class and its children classes which are parts of its parent. An aggregation is basically a whole and part relationship.

**algorithmic approach** . In algorithmic approach, the basic building blocks of software are procedures or functions. A procedure or a function contains a set of instructions to accomplish a task or a purpose. In this approach, larger algorithms are decomposed into smaller ones and developed independently and later integrated. The systems built with this approach have problems in maintaining the software as requirements change or when the system grows.

**analysis** It is the task of understanding the requirements and functions of a system.

**annotational things** These are the explanatory part of the UML model; adds information/meaning to the model elements. There is only one kind of annotational thing, named Note

**anonymous instance** It is an un named instance.

**architectural description** An architectural description (AD) is a set of artifacts that documents an architecture in a way its stakeholders can understand and demonstrates that the architecture has met their concerns.

**architectural design** This is the high-level design where the packages (subsystems) are defined. This design includes the dependencies and primary communication mechanisms between the packages. Generally, we go for an architecture design, where the dependencies are few and bidirectional dependencies are avoided.

**artifact** An **artifact** is one of many kinds of tangible by-product produced during the **development** of **software**. Some **artifacts** (e.g., use cases, class diagrams, and other UML models, requirements and design documents) help describe the function, architecture, and design of **software**.

**association class** It is a class resulted from association of two other classes.

**association visibility** You can specify three levels of visibility for the elements participating in an association. You can adorn visibility by appending a visibility symbol to a role name in an association. By default the visibility of a role is public, meaning this element is also available outside the association. Private visibility means that the objects at that end are not available out side the association. Similarly, protected visibility indicates that the objects at that end are not available outside the association, except for the children of the other end.

**association** A structural relationship between two classifiers.

**attribute multiplicity** Attribute's, multiplicity constraints the number of values an attribute can have. This lets you specify attributes that can be modeled as arrays.

**attributes** The named properties of an abstraction (class). These determine the state of a class.

**background processing** A **background process** is a computer **process** that runs behind the scenes (i.e., in the **background**) and without user intervention. Typical **tasks** for these **processes** include logging, system monitoring, scheduling, and user notification.

**base class** It is a class which does not have parents but have children.

**become** This stereotype specifies that the target is the same object as the source but at a later point in time and with possibly different values of attributes, state, or roles. The source object is transformed into the target object maintaining the same identity.

**behavioral diagrams** Behavioral diagrams express the dynamic aspects of a system. Behavior diagrams emphasize what must happen in the system being modeled. Since behavior diagrams illustrate the behavior of a system, they are used extensively to describe the functionality of software systems.

**behavioral things** These are the the verbs of UML models; usually the dynamic parts of the system in question. They represent the behavior of the system over time and space. There are two kinds of behavioral things: **interaction** and **state machine.**

**binary association** It is the association between two classifiers.

**binary component** . A binary component is an executable one which is compiled , not source code. A binary component is a component which is ready to run with no assembly required.

**bind** This stereotype specifies that the source class instantiates the target class which is a template class by binding actual parameters with the formal template parameters. The purpose of this dependency with bind stereotype is to create model elements from templates.

**blue print** A design plan or other technical drawing.

**branching** When you are modeling a flow of control using activity diagrams, simple and sequential transitions are common. But some times you may include a branch which specifies alternate paths taken based on some Boolean expression. You represent a branch as a diamond.

**broad casting** In **computer networking**, **broadcasting** refers to transmitting a packet that will be received by every device on the **network**. In practice, the scope of the **broadcast** is limited to a **broadcast** domain.

**business community** The body of individuals who manage **businesses**.

**business needs** Requirements that a private or public organization must follow, such as proper recording of its material activities and transactions, proper maintenance and auditing of these records, and proper access to them by the authorized parties.

**call event** A call event represents the execution of an operation that could trigger state transition in a state machine. A call event is a synchronous event, where the sender waits for the response from the receiver.

**change event** Change event is an event that represents a change in state or the satisfaction of some condition. In the UML, change events can be modeled by using the keyword **when** followed by some Boolean expression.

**changeable** If this property is specified for an attribute, it means that the attribute value can be changed.

**child class child class** is a modular, derivative **class** that inherits one or more language entities from one or more other **classes** (called superclass, base **classes**, or parent **classes**).

**child is substitutable** Child class can be used wherever a parent class is referenced.

**class diagram** A class diagram depicts a set of classes, interfaces, and collaborations and their relationships. You build class diagram to understand the static design view of a system. A class diagram with active classes represent the static process view of a system. A class diagram may contain objects and packages and their interrelationships. Class diagrams also display relationships such as containment, inheritance, associations and others.

**class multiplicity** The number of instances a class can have.

**class name** Every class must have a name that uniquely identifies it. A class name is a textual string .

**class path** A class name can be a simple name, or a path name where the class name is prefixed with the name of the package to which the class belongs.

**class scope** . If the scope of the feature is classifier  , then there is only one value of the  feature for all instances of the classifier. Classifier scope is indicated by underlining the feature definition.

**class visibility** The visibility of an attribute or an operation of a classifier specifies whether it can be used by other classifiers. The default visibility is public visibility. The visibility can be classified into three types:- **public, private and protected.**

**class** A class is a set of objects that share similar properties, operations , responsibilities and semantics.

**classifier** A classifier can be defined as a mechanism that describes behavioral and structural features. A classifier can be a class, an interface, a data type, a signal, a component, a node, a use case, and a subsystem. All these classifiers have many advanced features rather than simply attributes and operations.

**client node** It is a system which contains system interfaces. Generally GUI components are placed on them.

**client** A **client** is a piece of **computer** hardware or software that accesses a service made available by a server.

**client/server** The **client–server** model is a distributed application structure that partitions tasks or workloads between the providers of a resource or service, called servers, and service requesters, called **clients**.

**collaboration diagram** A **collaboration diagram** demonstrates the structural organization of the objects that interact by sending and receiving messages.

**common divisions** These are used to distinguish between two things that might appear to be quite similar, or closely related to one another. There exist two main common divisions  :**Abstraction verses Manifestation** and **Interface verses Implementation**.

**communication diagram** It is a kind of UML interaction **diagram** which shows interactions between objects

**complete** If this constraint is associated with a generalization relationship, it implies that all the required children belonging to the parent are specified. The generalization is complete in the model, and no other additional children are permitted.

**component** the physical replaceable parts of the system. These components can be, executables, library components, source code components and various documents.

**component diagram** Component diagrams represent various components that are installed on the nodes and indicate inter relationships among them.

**component instance** These are model elements that represent actual occurrences of components.

**composite state** A state that has sub states(nested states) is called a composite state. A composite state may contain either concurrent or sequential sub states. You can have nesting of states to any level.

**concrete class** A class that can have instances is called concrete class.

**concrete instance** A concrete instance is the thing that exists in the real world. The task of modeling concrete instances make us to visualize real life things. For example, you cannot see physically the Customer class which is a conceptual one, but an instance of a Customer can be seen or can be felt or understood as a representation of that instance in your system.

**concurrent flows of control** When you are modeling work flows of business processes using activity diagrams, you might encounter work flows that are parallel. These are called concurrent flows of control.

**concurrent sub states** These are state machines of sub states that execute simultaneously.

**concurrent system** It is the system which supports concurrent computing. **Concurrent** computing is a form of computing in which several computations are executed during overlapping time periods—**concurrently**—instead of sequentially (one completing before the next starts).

**configuration management** It is a systems engineering process for establishing and maintaining consistency of a product's performance, functional, and physical attributes with its requirements, design, and operational information throughout its life.

**constraints** Constraints are properties for specifying semantics and/or conditions that must be held true at all times for the elements of a model. They allow you to extend the semantics of a UML building block by adding new rules, or modifying existing ones

**construction** It is a **software engineering** discipline. It is the detailed creation of working meaningful **software** through a combination of coding, verification, unit testing, integration testing, and debugging.

**control activity** Control activities are the policies and procedures that help ensure that actions identified as necessary to manage risks are carried out properly and in a timely manner.

**copy** This stereotype in dependency relationship specifies that the target is an exact, but an independent copy of the source. In this stereotyped dependency, source and target are different instances, but with the same values, same state and same role but with a distinct identity.

**cross table join** The SQL CROSS TABLE JOIN produces a result set which is the number of rows in the first **table** multiplied by the number of rows in the second **table** if no WHERE clause is used along with **CROSS TABLE JOIN**.

**data base schema** A **database schema** is the skeleton structure that represents the logical view of the entire **database**. It defines how the data is organized and how the relations among them are associated.

**data model** define how **data** is connected to each other and how they are processed and stored inside the system.

**deep history** remembers an innermost nested state to any depth, and is indicated by the symbol H*.

**deferred event** The event that is not handled in the current state of the object but handled later in another state.

**dependency** A dependency is a using relationship that states that a change in specification of one thing may affect another thing that uses it, but not necessarily the reverse.

**deployment component** This component forms the executable system. It can be a dynamic link library or an executable.

**deployment diagram** A deployment diagram is a diagram that shows the configuration of run time processing nodes and the components that live on them.

**deployment view** This view addresses issues, such as distribution, delivery, and installation of the parts that make up the physical system.

**derive** This stereotype in dependency relation specifies that the source element may be computed from the target.

**derived class** It is the class which inherits from the parent class in generalization relationship.

**design view** the design view of a system includes classes, interfaces and collaborations and their relationships.

**destroy** It is action which destroys an object during object interaction.

**developer** **Software** **developers** are the creative minds behind computer**programs**.

**disjoint** If this constraint is associated with a generalization relationship, it means that, the objects of the parent have no more than one of the children as type.

**distributed system** A **distributed system** is a model in which components located on networked computers communicate and coordinate their actions by passing messages. The components interact with each other in order to achieve a common goal.

**do action** It happens in advanced state chart. It is an action to be performed while an element is in that state.

**domain expert** He is a person who is an authority in a particular area or topic.

**domain use case** It specifies the interaction between a user and the business.

**dynamic aspect** It is the behavioral aspect of the system.

**dynamic semantics** of your system illustrate how classes collaborate with one another through interaction diagrams mainly involving active objects.

**embedded system** An **embedded system** is a computer **system** with a dedicated function within a larger mechanical or electrical **system**, often with real-time computing constraints.

**end user** He is the person who uses or interacts with the system to get its services.

**entry action**  The action performed when an element enters the state.

**enumeration** It is a data type modeled for primitive types.

**event**  An **event** in  the **Unified  Modeling  Language** (**UML**)  is  a  notable occurrence  at  a  particular  point  in  time. **Events**  can,  but  do  not  necessarily, cause state transitions from one state to another in state machines represented by state machine diagrams.

**event trigger**  It is the event, which is received by an object that results in state transition.

**execution component** These are the components that are created as a result of an executing system. It can be **.exe** file or a **DLL** component.

**execution time**  The **execution time** or CPU **time** of a given task is defined as the **time** spent  by  the  system  **executing** that  task,  including  the  **time** spent **executing** run-**time** or system services on its behalf.

**exit action** Action performed on exiting the state.

**exit condition**  Exit  conditions  reflect  the  impact  of  the  use  case  on  the environment through its execution.

**explicit binding**  A  template  may  be  instantiated  by  using  a  realization relationship stereotyped with «**bind**»—this is known as **explicit binding**.

**export interface**  It  is  an  interface  that  a  component  realizes.  This  is  an interface  that  the  component  provides  as  a  service  to  other  components.  A component may provide many export interfaces.

**extend relationship** An extend relationship is a type of dependency. It has the same graphical notation as dependency with the addition of the stereotype on the relationship. This relationship  means  that  the  base  use  case  depends  on the addition use case

**extensibility mechanisms**  Extensibility  mechanisms  in  UML,  permit  you  to extend  the  language  in  controlled  ways.  By  using  these  extensibility mechanisms,  you  can  tailor  UML  to  the  specific  needs  of  your  application domain.  These  mechanisms  include  stereotypes,  tagged  values,  and constraints.

**façade** Specifies a package that is only a view on some other package.

**final state**  which  indicates  that  the  execution  of  the  state  machine  has  been completed. A final state is represented as a filled black circle surrounded by an unfilled circle. These states are actually pseudo states

**flow of control** shows the **Control Flow**  from one action to the next and. Object **flow** is a path along which objects or data can pass.

**focus of control**  **Focus of control** (FOC) is  used  in  sequence  diagrams  to show the period of time during which an object performs an action. FOC is rendered as a thin, rectangular object that sits on top of object lifelines.

**foreground processing** In multiprocessing systems, the process that is currently accepting input from the keyboard or other input device is sometimes called the **foreground process**.

**foreign key** In the context of relational databases, a **foreign key** is a field (or collection of fields) in one table that uniquely identifies a row of another table or the same table. In simpler words, the **foreign key** is defined in a second table, but it refers to the primary **key** in the first table.

**Forking** A Fork notation in a **UML** Activity Diagram is a control node that splits a flow into multiple concurrent flows. This will have one incoming edge and multiple outgoing edges.

**forward engineering** It is the process of creating code in an implementation language from UML models.

**framework** Specifies a package consisting mainly of patterns.

**friend** This stereotype in dependency specifies that the source is given special visibility into the target. The source classifier has access to the elements of the target classifier. A friend relationship grants the source access to the target regardless of the declared visibility.

**frozen** This constraint specifies that a link once added, cannot be removed or cannot be modified.

**functional requirements** In Software engineering and systems engineering, a **functional requirement** defines a function of a system or its component. ... **Functional requirements** may be calculations, technical details, data manipulation and processing and other specific functionality that define what a system is supposed to accomplish.

**generalization** It is the relationship between general class and specific classes. Here the child class(specific class) inherits the properties and behavior of the parent class(general class).

**grouping things** These are the organizational parts of the UML models. They provide higher level of abstraction. These are the containers into which a model can be placed. There is only one kind of grouping thing, named package.

**guard condition** It is a Boolean expression that is evaluated when the transition is triggered by the reception of the event trigger. The transition fires when the guard condition evaluates to true otherwise not.

**GUI** A **graphical user interface (GUI)** is a human-computer interface (i.e., a way for humans to interact with computers) that uses windows, icons and menus and which can be manipulated by a mouse (and often to a limited extent by a keyboard as well). ... Icons are used both on the desktop and within application

**hard real time** Hard real time systems expect the required behavior within nanoseconds or milliseconds.

**hardware topology** This hardware topology describes the configuration of runtime processing nodes and the artifacts that are deployed on them. It is a platform on which your system is installed and executes.

**hide event** The Hide event makes the User Interface invisible to the user.

**history state** The history state remembers the sub state that was active before the enclosing state was exited.

**implementation view** It represents the organization and relationships of the components at a particular moment. A single component diagram cannot represent the entire system but a collection of diagrams are used to represent the whole.

**implicit binding** It is shown while you are associating a class with the template. It is similar to the C++ syntax for templates in which you define a class named with the template arguments.

**import** This stereotype in dependency relationship specifies that the public contents of the target package are added to the namespace of the source package. Here the source package can refer the public contents of the target package without qualifying them with the target package.

**import interface** It is the interface any other component uses. This is the interface that a component confirms to and so build on. A component may confirm to many import interfaces.

**incomplete** If it is associated with generalization, it means that not all children of a parent specified. Additional children are allowed.

**inception** This is the first phase in the software development process. It involves the basic idea of what to implement. The end of this phase begins the next phase, that is Elaboration.

**include**    An include relationship is a type of dependency. It has the same graphical notation as the dependency with the addition of the stereotype on the relationship. This relationship means that the base use case depends on the included use case.

**inheritance** In this relationship, child inherits the properties, services, and responsibilities of the parent, and apart from this, it can contain its own attributes and operations facilitating reusability of existing elements.

**initial state** This is the state which indicates the default starting place for the state machine. Initial state is represented as a filled black circle.

**inout** It happens when you are passing parameters to the operation. It represents both input and output parameter which can be input and modified.

**instanceof** This stereotype in dependency relationship specifies that the source is the instance of the destination.

**instance scope** instance scope meaning the named element appears in every instance of the class with different values.

**intantiate** This stereotype in dependency relation specifies that the source creates the instances of the target.

**Integrity** It is the maintenance of, and the assurance of the accuracy and **consistency** of, data over its entire life-cycle, and is a critical aspect to the design, implementation and usage of any system which stores, processes, or retrieves data.

**inter process communication Interprocess communication** (IPC) is a set of programming interfaces that allow a programmer to coordinate activities among different program**process**es that can run concurrently in an operating system. This allows a program to handle many user requests at the same time.

**interaction diagrams** These are the diagrams which capture the behavioral or dynamic aspects of the system.

**interface** An **interface** is a collection of operations that are used to specify a service of a class or a component.

**internal transition** It is transition where the source and target are the same state.

**is-a-kind of relationship** This is nothing but generalization relationship where child class(specific class) inherits the state and behavior of parent class(general class).

**isomorphic** The sequence and collaboration diagrams are isomorphic, because one can be derived from the other without loss of any information.

**isquery** If the operation is associated with this property, it means that execution of this operation will not have side effects, meaning the state of the system is unchanged.

**joining** A **join** node is a control node that synchronizes multiple flows. This will have multiple incoming edges and one outgoing edge.

**leaf class** It is a class which has one or more parents but does not have children.

**level of abstraction** A different view point of the model.

**life line** This is part of sequence diagram, life line emanating from an object indicates life span of the object in an interaction.

**links** They specify the structural connection between objects which interact by exchanging messages.

**loosely coupled** In computing and systems design a **loosely coupled** system is one in which each of its components has, or makes use of, little or no knowledge of the definitions of other separate components. Subareas include the **coupling** of classes, interfaces, data, and services. **Loose coupling** is the opposite of tight **coupling**.

**mailbox semantics** One active object might asynchronously send a signal or call an operation of another object. That kind of communication has *mailbox semantics*, which means that the caller sends the signal or calls the operation and then continues on its independent way.

**mapping language** It is the underlying language in which the code is generated from UML models during forward engineering task.

**mealy machine** A state machine whose actions are attached to transitions.

**meta class**  A **metaclass** is a class whose instances are classes. Just as an ordinary class defines the behavior of certain objects, a metaclass defines the behavior of certain classes and their instances.

**model** A model is the simplification of reality. It is the blue print which pictorially describes the system.

**more machine** It is a state machine whose actions are associated with states.

**multi object** It is used to model set of objects.

**multi casting** : If one object sends a Signal to a set of objects, it is called Multicasting.

**multiplicity** When you are modeling, you may specify the number of objects at both ends of association, indicating how many objects are involved in an instance of an association relationship. This is called multiplicity,

**mutual exclusion** It is the type of problem that arises when there is more than one flow of control in an object at the same time. This creates the risk of corrupting the state.

**named instance** It is an instance which has a name associated with it.

**n-ary association** It is the association involving more than two classifiers.

**navigation** In any association, such as College and Student, you can navigate from objects of one kind to the objects of the other kind. In any plain association, the navigation is bidirectional. When you are creating models, you may come across associations in which the navigation is unidirectional.

**near real time**   Near real time systems expect the predictable behavior in seconds or longer.

**nested state** It is a state which enclose sub states.

**network**  A **network** is a set of **computers** connected together for the purpose of sharing resources. The most common resource shared today is connection to the Internet. Other shared resources can include a printer or a file server.

**node** A **node** In the **Unified Modeling Language** (**UML**) is a computational resource upon which **UML** artifacts may be deployed for execution. There are two types of **nodes**: device **nodes** and execution environments.

**node instance** A node instance can be shown on a diagram. An instance can be distinguished from a node by the fact that its name is underlined and has a colon before its base node type. An instance may or may not have a name before the colon.

**note** A **UML note** is a modeling construct for adding textual information - such as a comment, constraint definition, or method body to **UML** diagrams. **Notes** are depicted as a rectangle with the top-right corner folded over.

**object** An instance of a class.

**object diagram** An object diagram is a graph of instances, including objects and data values. A static object diagram is an instance of a **class diagram**; it shows a snapshot of the detailed state of a system at a point in time.

**object flow** In **UML** Activity Diagrams. Control **Flow** shows the **flow** of control from one action to the next. and. **Object flow** is a path along which **objects** or data can pass.

**object oriented approach** is a popular technical **approach** for analyzing, designing an application, system, or business by applying the **object-oriented** paradigm and visual modeling throughout the development life cycles to foster better stakeholder communication and product quality.

**object oriented data base** It is a **database** management system in which information is represented in the form of **objects** as used in **object-oriented** programming.

**object state** It is the state the object currently in.

**object structures** They show how the various objects are connected that exchange messages.

**OCL** It is Object Constraint Language used for modeling new semantics more formally.

**OMG** Object Management Group which has adopted UML as de facto standard in 1997.

**operations Operation** is a behavioral feature that may be owned by an interface, data type, or class.

**ordered** It is a constraint in association relationship. There is a way to specify that the objects at one end of the association (the end where multiplicity is greater than one) are ordered or unordered. If you associate the constraint {ordered} with the association, the end where there is a set of objects are in an explicit order.

**orphan instance** It is an instance whose class is unknown.

**out** This comes into existence when you specify parameter types for an operation. If the direction is **out,** it specifies an output parameter, it may be modified to communicate with caller.

**over lapping** If this constraint is associated with generalization, it means that objects of the parent may have more than one of the children as a type. It means that the sub groups are not cleanly partitioned and they might overlap causing an object of the parent may belong to more than one sub type.

**overflow exception** The **exception** that is thrown when an arithmetic, casting, or conversion operation in a checked context results in an **overflow.**

**override** It is available with inheritance relationship. Here, child may override properties as well as operations. If operations are overridden, it is called polymorphism.

**package** In the UML, a package is a general purpose mechanism for organizing modeling elements into groups. You use packages to group semantically related elements so as to handle them as larger chunks. Packages help us to view or model the system at a higher level of abstraction (without much interior details).

**package elements** These are the elements which are grouped into a package.

**parallel activity** Parallel activities are the activities which are executed concurrently.

**parameter stereotype** They allow designers to extend the vocabulary of **UML** in order to create new model elements, derived from existing ones, but that have specific properties that are suitable for a particular domain or otherwise specialized usage

**parent class** It happens in inheritance relationship. The class from which inheritance happens is called parent class.

**passive class** A **passive class** has behaviour that is defined by its operations. This behaviour only starts when one of the operation is called on an instance of that **class**. The behaviour terminates once the operation returns. The great majority of **classes** that you will design are **passive**.

**patterns** A **pattern** is a commonly occurring reusable piece in software system that provides a certain set of functionality. The identification of a **pattern** is also based on the context in which it is used. ... The class diagram in **UML** can be used to capture the **patterns** identified in a system.

**permission dependency** A permission is a type of dependency relationship with **permit** stereotype. The permission relationship conveys that one element is granted rights to view the other element in some way. There are no standard stereotypes defined for permission dependency relationship.

**persistent object** These are the objects that they can be stored in a database for later retrieval and use. These persistent objects can be stored by using relational database, an object oriented database or a combination of relational/object oriented databases.

**physical architecture** The physical architecture, describes in more detail how the software and systems are designed, including specifics about how the architecture must fit into different technologies that exist within the organization and how the software integrates with itself and with other systems. We use several modeling elements and techniques to describe the physical architecture.

**plain class** A plain class cannot independently initiate control activity. Plain classes are considered passive because they rely on an external event to initiate control activity

**polymorphism** If the parent and child has the same operation, the child's operation overrides the operation of the parent; this is known as polymorphism, one of the major applications of object-oriented systems.

**post condition** OCL provides special syntax for specifying pre- and post conditions on operations in a UML model. Pre- and post conditions are constraints that define a contract that an implementation of the operation has to fulfill. A precondition must hold when an operation is called, a post condition must be true when the operation returns.

**power type** This stereotype in dependency relationship specifies that the target is a power type of the source. A power type is a classifier whose objects are all the children of a given parent.

**pre condition** OCL provides special syntax for specifying pre- and post conditions on operations in a UML model. Pre- and post conditions are constraints that define a contract that an implementation of the operation has to fulfill. A precondition must hold when an operation is called, a post condition must be true when the operation returns

**primary key** A **primary key** is a field in a table which uniquely identifies each row/record in a database table. **Primary keys** must contain unique values. A **primary key** column cannot have NULL values. A table can have only one **primary key**, which may consist of single or multiple fields.

**primary scenario** A **use case scenario** is a single path through the **use case**. A primary scenario when the user uses the system based on one of the use cases.

**primitive types** These are the basic data types supported by the system, such as integers, characters, strings and enumerated data types.

**private** It is a visibility constraint. This visibility is specified by a '**-**' sign preceding an attribute or an operation. Only the classifier in which it is defined, can access this feature.

**process view** Any system's process view contain processes and threads. UML provides a distinct graphical representation to model active classes. An active class is a class whose objects or instances contain a thread or a process. Graphically, an active object is represented as any ordinary object, but with thick border.

**process**   The basic building block of a **process** description in **UML** is the activity. An activity is a behavior consisting of a coordinated sequencing of actions. It is represented by an activity diagram. Activity diagrams visualize sequences of actions to be performed including control flow and data flow.

**protected**   Any attribute or an operation defined with protected visibility is available only to the current class and its inherited classes.

**prototype** A **prototype** is an early sample, model, or release of a product built to test a concept or process or to act as a thing to be replicated or learned from. It is a term used in a variety of contexts, including semantics, **design**, electronics, and software programming.

**prototypical instance** While you model dynamic interactions among objects, you might not use concrete instances that exist in the real world. Rather, you use conceptual objects to model these interactions , which are essentially proxies for real life objects. These objects are called prototypical objects and these are roles to which concrete instances confirm.

**public** Any attribute or an operation defined with public visibility is available for every one.

**qualification**   A qualified association has a qualifier that is used to select an object (or objects) from a larger set of related objects, based upon the qualifier key.

**reactive object** A reactive object sits idle waiting for an event. When it receives an event, it responses, then again it sits idle for the next event to happen. When you develop a model for a reactive object, it focuses, on the states of the object, the events that trigger state transitions, and the actions that occur on each state change.

**real-time system** A real-time system is a type of hardware or software that operates with a time constraint.

**realization**   In UML modeling, a realization relationship is a relationship between two model elements, in which one model element, implements or executes the behavior that the other model element, specifies. This relationship is available between interfaces and the classes or the components that realize them and also between use cases and the collaborations that realize them.

**refine** It is a standard abstraction stereotype which is used to specify a **refinement**relationship between model elements at different semantic levels, such as analysis, design, and implementation. It can be used to model transformations from analysis to design, design to implementation, etc.

**relationships** In **UML** modeling, a **relationship** is a connection between two or more **UML** model elements that adds semantic information to a model. In the product, you can use several **UML relationships** to define the structure between model elements.

**resource migration** It happens in network oriented or distributed systems. System resources migrate from one physical location to another across the network.

**responsibilities** A responsibility is a contract or obligation of a class to perform a particular service.

**reusability** It is one of the major application of the generalization relationship. In this relationship, child inherits the properties, services, and responsibilities of the parent, and apart from this, it can contain its own attributes and operations facilitating reusability of existing elements.

**reverse engineering** This is the process of building UML model from the source code in underlying implementation language.

**role** A role name explains how an object participates in the relationship.

**root class** It is a class which has no parents but has one or more children.

**round trip engineering** Round trip engineering is a functioning mode that combines code generation and reverse engineering.

**scalability** the ability of a computing process to be used or produced in a range of capabilities.

**scope** It is the context that gives specific meaning to the element named. For example, the scope could be instance scope meaning the named element appears in every instance of the class with different values. If the scope is classifier scope, the element will have only one value across the class, i.e for all instances.

**seams** Identifying the **seams** in a system involves identifying clear lines of demarcation in your architecture. You can then document your understanding by modeling that **seam** in the system using interfaces in the **UML** so that, later, you and others can approach that component more easily. APIs represent the programmatic **seams** in your system, which you can model using interfaces

**self association** There can be associations among objects of the same class. This relationship circles back to the same class indicating self association.

**send stereotype** This stereotype specifies that the source operation sends a target event. Generally a send dependency is indicated between a source which is an operation and a target which is a signal. This dependency stereotyped with send specifies that the source sends the target signal.

**sequence diagram** This is a behavioral diagram which specifies the time ordering of messages which are exchanged between objects.

**server node** This represents a node which acts as a server in an execution environment.

**shallow history** remembers only the outermost nested state, and is indicated by the symbol H.

**side effects** It means the state of the system being changed.

**signal event** A signal represents a named object that is dispatched asynchronously by one object and then received by another.

**single inheritance** It happens in generalization relationship, where a derived class has only one parent.

**singleton class** It is a class which has only one instance.

**software development life cycle** It is a process for planning, creating, testing, and deploying an information system.

**source state** : It is the state that the object is currently in. A transition to another state may occur due to an event or when a guard condition is met.

**specification** an act of identifying something precisely or of stating a precise requirement.

**stake holder** A **stakeholder** a person, group, or organization that is actively involved in a project, is affected by its outcome, or can influence its outcome. The term **stakeholder** is used to refer to any person or group who will be affected by the system, directly or indirectly.

**standard constraint** An application specific constraint which is already available.

**standard stereotype** An application specific stereotype which is already available.

**state chart diagram** It is a graphical representation consisting of sates, transitions, events and activities.

**state machine** A state machine displays the sequences of states that an object goes through during its life time in response to received external or internal events , together with its responses and actions.

**state transition** When an action or activity of a state completes, flow of control passes immediately to the next action or activity state. This is called state transition.

**static deployment view** A deployment diagram shows the configuration of nodes (processing elements) and the components that live on them. It gives the static deployment view of the system's architecture.

**static design view** It is represented by class diagrams as well as object diagrams.

**static implementation view** This is addressed by component diagrams.

**static process view** It is represented by class diagrams as well as object diagrams containing active classes and active objects.

**static semantics** These are the semantics captured by class diagrams.

**static type** It means the type of an object is bound at the time the object is created (an instance of a class is created).

**static use case view** It is depicted by use case diagrams.

**stereotype** They extend the vocabulary of the UML by creating new model elements derived from existing ones but that have specific properties suitable for your domain/problem. Each stereotype defines a set of properties that are received by elements of that stereotype.

**stereotyped object** It is created when stereotype is applied to an instance.

**stored procedures** A **stored procedure** is a set of Structured Query Language (SQL) statements with an assigned name, which are **stored** in a relational database management system as a group, so it can be reused and shared by multiple programs.

**structural diagrams** The UML's structural diagrams are used to visualize, specify , construct , and document the static aspects of a system. These diagrams include the elements such as , classes , interfaces, collaborations, components, and nodes.

**structural model** These are models that make people visualize and specify parts of systems and how they relate to one another.

**structural organization Collaboration diagrams** demonstrate the structural organization of the objects that interact, it shows how objects are statically connected.

**structural relationship** An association represents a structural relationship that connects two classifiers., such as classes or use cases, that describes the reasons for the relationship and the rules that govern the relationship.

**structural things** Structural things are nouns of the UML models. These are mostly static parts of the model, representing elements which are conceptual or physical.

**sub class** It is the class which inherits from the parent class. Sub class can also be called derived class.

**sub state** A sub state is a state that is nested inside another state.

**sub system** In **UML** models, **subsystems** are a type of stereotyped component that represent independent, behavioral units in a system. ... Typically, a **subsystem** has a name that describes its contents and role in the system.

**super class** A super class is a class with no parents and with one or more child classes.

**swim lane** When you are modeling work flows of business processes, the activity states in an activity diagram can be partitioned into groups. Each group represents either an actor or a business organization responsible for those activities. Each group is called a swimlane because these groups are divided from their neighbors by a vertical solid line.

**synchronization property** A problem with synchronization arises when there is more than one flow of control in an object at the same time. This creates the risk of corrupting the state of the object

**synchronous event** In case of synchronous events, the sender waits until the receiver reacted on the event.

**system thrashing thrashing** is a condition in which excessive paging operations are taking place. A **system** that is **thrashing** can be perceived as either a very slow **system** or one that has come to a halt.

**system view** Each particular **UML** diagram corresponds to one **view** of a model of a **system**. ... Even computer-aided software engineering ( CASE ) tools treat **UML** diagrams as **views**. They use a database in which the information about the model is stored.

**system's throughput** In Operating system , number of processes completed per unit time.

**tagged values** Tagged values are properties for specifying keyword-value pairs of model elements, where the keywords are attributes. They allow you to extend the properties of a UML building block so that you create new information in the specification of that element.

**target state :** It is the state reached by an object after the state transition.

**template class** In various object oriented programming languages you can write template classes, each of which defines a family of classes. The definition of template includes slots for classes, objects and values. These slots serve as template's parameters, which will be replaced by actual values when the template is bind.

**template parameter** A template class definition includes slots for classes, objects, and values. These slots serve as template's parameters.

**test cases** A **test case** is a set of conditions or variables under which a **tester** will determine whether a system under **test** satisfies requirements or works correctly.

**test procedure** A **test procedure** is a formal specification of **test** cases to be applied to one or more target program modules. **Test procedures** are executable.

**thread** A **thread** of execution is the smallest sequence of programmed instructions that can be managed independently by a scheduler, which is typically a part of the operating system.

**tightly coupled Tight coupling** is when a group of classes are highly dependent on one another. This scenario arises when a class assumes too many responsibilities, or when one concern is spread over many classes rather than having its own class.

**time event** occurs when there is passage of a designated time period. Example : after (10 minutes).

**time expressions** Time expression is an expression that evaluates to an absolute or relative value of time.

**timing constraints** Timing constraint expresses a constraint based on the absolute or relative value of time. It is a semantic statement about the relative or absolute value of time. A timing constraint is rendered similar to any constraint.

**timing marks** Time expression is an expression that evaluates to an absolute or relative value of time.

**transient** Specifies that an instance of the role is created during execution of the interaction but is destroyed before completion of the interaction

**transition** A transition from one state to other because of events happening on objects.

**triggers** A **trigger** is a special kind of stored procedure that automatically executes when an event occurs in the database **server**. DML **triggers** execute when a user tries to modify data through a data manipulation language (DML) event. DML events are INSERT, UPDATE, or DELETE statements on a table or view.

**underflow exception** is a condition in a computer program where the result of a calculation is a number of smaller absolute value than the computer can actually store in memory.

**usage dependency** This stereotype in dependency specifies that the semantics of the source element depends on the semantics of the public part of the target. This dependency is also called usage dependency, it is one in which the source classifier requires the presence of the target classifier for its correct implementation.

**use case**   It specifies the behavior of a system as a whole or a part of it in the form of set of functions. It is realized by a collaboration.

**use case diagram** It is a graphical representation consisting of use cases and actors and how they are related. Use case diagrams address the dynamic part of the system. They are helpful in modeling the behavior of the system.

**use case driven** The desired behavior of the system is established by use cases. Use cases are used as primary source for verifying, and validating the system's architecture. Use cases are used as the major resources for establishing testing, and communication among various stake holders of the system.

**use case view**  It is depicted by use case diagrams which help in modeling behavioral aspect of the system.

**user interface** It is the means by which the user and a computer system interact, in particular the use of input devices and software.

**using relationship**   A dependency is a using relationship that states that a change in specification of one thing may affect another thing that uses it, but not necessarily the reverse.

**utility class** If you specify zero instances for a class, it means that the multiplicity is zero, then such a class is called utility class that exposes only class scoped attributes and operations.

**visibility**   visibility allows to constrain the usage of a **named element**, either in **namespaces** or in access to the element. It is used with **classes, packages, generalizations, element import, package import.**

**visual model** It is the use of semantically rich, graphical and textual design notations to capture software designs. A notation, such as **UML**, allows the level of abstraction to be raised, while maintaining rigorous syntax and semantics.

**volatile data** volatile memory is computer storage that only maintains its **data** while the device is powered. Most RAM (random access memory) used for primary storage in personal computers is **volatile** memory.

**whole and part relationship** in which one class is larger called whole, and the other are smaller which may become the parts of the larger class. This kind of relationship, which is a variant  of association, is called aggregation.

**work flow** Activity diagrams are graphical representations of **workflows** of stepwise activities and actions with support for choice, iteration and concurrency. In the Unified Modeling Language, activity diagrams are intended to model both computational and organizational processes (i.e. **workflows**).

www.ingramcontent.com/pod-product-compliance
Lightning Source LLC
Chambersburg PA
CBHW061924190326
41458CB00009B/2648